RHS
WISLEY EXPERTS

GARDENERS'
ADVICE

RHS WISLEY EXPERTS

GARDENERS' ADVICE

ALAN TOOGOOD   EDITOR-IN-CHIEF

LONDON, NEW YORK, MUNICH,
MELBOURNE AND DELHI

PROJECT EDITOR Helen Fewster
PROJECT ART EDITOR Murdo Culver
MANAGING EDITOR Linda Martin
MANAGING ART EDITOR Lee Griffiths
DTP DESIGNER Louise Waller
MEDIA RESOURCES Richard Dabb
Lucy Claxton
Neale Chamberlain
PICTURE RESEARCH Anna Bedewell
PRODUCTION CONTROLLER Mandy Inness

Designed and edited in association with
Focus Publishing, Sevenoaks, Kent

First published in Great Britain in 2004
by Dorling Kindersley Limited,
80 Strand, London, WC2R ORL,
in association with the Royal
Horticultural Society

A Penguin Company

4 6 8 10 9 7 5

A CIP catalogue record for this book is
available from the British Library

ISBN 1 4053 0338 7

Colour reproduction by
Colourscan, Singapore
Printed and bound in Italy by Graphicom

Discover more at
www.dk.com

CONTENTS

General advice

Trees and shrubs

Climbers

Perennials

Bulbs

Attracting wildlife

Soils, composts and fertilizers

Water gardening

INTRODUCTION

THE ROYAL HORTICULTURAL SOCIETY'S Advisory Service, a team of scientists and horticultural advisors based at its Wisley Garden, answers more than 46,000 enquiries a year from RHS members. Around a further 16,000 enquiries a year are dealt with at RHS shows.

How to control slugs and snails is the most common enquiry, but the team also receives many enquiries about vine weevil, glasshouse red spider mite, rabbits and the dreaded plant disease, honey fungus.

However, the Advisory Service offers advice not only on problems, but also on plant identification, selecting the best plants for sites and situations, composting, and soil care. It also provides information on gardening products, suppliers, and how to find reliable contractors and other gardening professionals.

Jim England of Wisley offers vegetable advice at an RHS Show

This book, one of the titles published to mark the bicentenary of the Society in 2004, contains a selection of replies to the most frequently asked questions. It provides the best advice available on many aspects of gardening and includes information that is either unavailable elsewhere, or which is scattered throughout countless publications.

Assembled into twelve chapters, under the categories Planting Ideas, Techniques, Practical Advice and Plant Problems, this collection of over 300 topics will solve your gardening problems, help you to choose and grow the best plants, and generally enable you to achieve excellent results from your garden.

KEY TO SYMBOLS IN PLANT LISTS

Symbols used in the plant lists are intended only as a guide to the size and needs of each plant. Hardiness symbols indicate the minimum temperature at which they survive outdoors without protection. The RHS Award of Garden Merit is given to plants of outstanding excellence; they will need no specialist care if suitable growing conditions are provided.

♇ Plant has received the Royal Horticultural Society's Award of Garden Merit

↕ Typical height

↔ Typical spread

↕↔ Typical height and spread (if the same)

E Evergreen foliage

▦ Prefers full sun

▨ Prefers partial shade

▧ Tolerates full shade

◊ Prefers well-drained soil

◖ Prefers moist soil

◗ Prefers wet soil

pH Acid soil needed

❄❄❄ Fully hardy: plant can withstand temperatures down to –15°C (5°F)

❄❄ Frost hardy: plant can withstand temperatures down to –5°C (23°F)

❄ Half hardy: plant can withstand temperatures down to 0°C (32°F)

☁ Frost tender: plant may be damaged by temperatures below 5°C (41°F)

GENERAL ADVICE

BUYING PLANTS

Buying plants

Avoid buying plants before the weather is suitable for planting, unless you are able to provide suitable storage conditions; old plants in big pots can sometimes be a real bargain

It is damaging to plant into wet, sticky or frozen soil. Better to buy later, or keep plants in a sheltered site until soil conditions improve. Also, some plants on sale will have been kept in plastic tunnels and may have their growth arrested or 'checked' if they are put out too early. If foliage looks soft and vulnerable, cover plants with a double layer of horticultural fleece for a week, followed by a week under a single layer of fleece to acclimatise them to the rigours of outdoor life. Perennials, trees, shrubs, climbers and roses will appreciate early planting, so that they have a good chance of rooting into the soil before summer dry spells.

Tender plants

Hold off buying tender plants until the beginning of late spring, and remember that stock and choice are likely to be good around this time. If you want to snap up particular plants early – perhaps to secure a vital colour for your design – keep them in a cool, well-ventilated cold frame or greenhouse. They will perform much better if you remove flower buds and feed them every week with a general-purpose liquid fertiliser until they are planted out in their final positions.

Selecting healthy plants
Inspect pots carefully before you buy plants from nurseries and garden centres. Do not invest in elderly plants with roots emerging from the bottom of the pot (*above left*) or in those with sparse or spindly stems (*above*); neither will perform well. Instead, look for plants which have vigorous, well balanced top-growth with healthy-looking foliage (*left*).

Warning signs
Avoid weed-infested pots and always bin the top inch of compost in case this contains weed seeds. Once weeds like bittercress (*Cardamine hirsuta*) become established, they are difficult to erradicate.

Hardy perennials

Herbaceous perennials are a safer buy in early spring. They transplant much better then than if bought in flower during summer. Inexpensive plants in 1 litre or 10cm (4in) pots soon catch up with bigger, more costly, plants in 2 litre or 12cm (5in) pots. However, old, crowded plants that are free of pests, diseases and weeds, in big pots can be a real bargain, as they can be split to make several plants. You may need a sharp knife to divide them. Avoid plants prone to persistent diseases, such as phlox (eelworm, *see p.115*) or asters (tarsonemid mites). Vine weevil in particular is hard to spot before planting out – return infested plants (*see p.48*).

Trees, shrubs and climbers

Old stock of trees, shrubs and climbers, with pots full of roots, are easily detected by the roots coming out of the base of the pot. Avoid purchasing these as they seldom make really satisfactory plants. On the other hand, you should also be wary of choosing small plants that are offered for sale in big pots of loose compost, because this may indicate that they have only recently been potted. The small plants inside all that compost will need a great deal of additional care if they are to survive in the garden.

BUYING ROSES

With roses it is normal and acceptable practice for the growers to lift plants grown in the field and to pot them immediately before sale. When you get them home, remove them from the pot, shake off the soil and plant. The roses will successfully establish, provided they are still dormant.

Finding contractors

Some landscaping, maintenance and tree surgery may be too big or too dangerous to tackle without professional help

Private gardeners are often concerned about the reliability, skill and professionalism of people they employ. There are certain professional bodies to which contractors can belong. These have lists of approved contractors and consultants and provide some degree of assurance that their members are up to scratch, and can often help if a dispute arises.

Belonging to organisations can be expensive and there are often satisfactory local contractors who do not belong. Local contractors can offer good value as they are familiar with the area, may be recommended by word-of-mouth and there are few travelling costs. However, get references from at least two satisfied customers, ask to inspect examples of previous work and check that they have satisfactory insurance cover. Local head gardeners, horticultural colleges, council officials and garden centres or nurseries can often suggest suitable people.

Initially decide what jobs need doing, how much input you intend to have over the contractors work and how much you are willing to pay. This helps you to pick a contractor with expertise and willingness to meet these needs. Check if there is a charge for preliminary visits and whether this is refundable if the contractor undertakes the work. Find out how long they have been in business and what

Assessing the work to be done
To get a general idea of costs, ask several different contractors for estimates before making your decision. Make sure that you are both in agreement on what the job entails, and what exactly needs to be done.

qualifications they have, and check certificates of competence. Discuss the work with more than one contractor to get a general idea of costs, and then get estimates for each part of the work involved. Consider having the work done in stages, paying as you go, if firm quotes cannot be provided. Also consider keeping back about 15 per cent, to be paid later after any faults have become apparent and been rectified.

Tidying up
Ownership of surplus materials and disposal of rubbish are common causes of dispute. Make sure that follow-up advice and help are specified in the contract.

THINGS TO CHECK

- Check on the professionalism of people you are proposing to employ, and get references
- Try to inspect examples of other work that they have carried out
- Obtain estimates from several companies or individuals
- Ensure you have a clear idea of the work to be done

See also Tree safety p.56

Maintaining hand tools

Keep tools sharp and clean and you and your plants will benefit

Hand tools with sharp edges make cleaner cuts and are less effort to use. If you use your secateurs a lot they will need frequent sharpening and cleaning. Dismantle and remove all traces of plant sap with metal polish and a nylon scourer, then sharpen the blade by pushing it across a sharpening surface, such as an oilstone, in a smooth circular motion.

Replace blades when they become worn or badly notched. During work, secateurs can be resharpened without dismantling, by using a diamond sharpener. Sharpen knives in the same way as secateur blades.

After use, remove soil, then wipe all the metal parts of hand tools with an oily rag to prevent them from rusting during storage.

Sharpening secateurs
Hold the blade at the same angle as the bevel but never grind the flat edge of the secateurs, because the 'bite' of the blade will be ruined. Remove any burrs by gently rubbing the opposite side.

Choosing winter-flowering plants

Gardens should not be dull and lifeless in winter: a large selection of shrubs, hardy perennials and bulbs flower at that time of year, including many shrubs with fragrant flowers

PLANTS FOR WINTER CHEER

The dark gloomy days of winter can be brightened by winter-flowering plants, planted where they can be seen from the house. Those with fragrance are most appreciated when they are planted by doorways that are in regular use, or alongside paths. Remember, however, that most winter-flowering plants are not particularly attractive during the summer, but it may be possible to conceal or partially hide them at that time with other plants.

Shrubs with fragrant flowers

Abeliophyllum distichum ↕↔ 1.5m (5ft), white, ☐ ◊ ✳✳✳ ⬚1⬚

Chimonanthus praecox ↕ 4m (12ft) ↔ 3m (10ft), yellow, ☐ ◊ ✳✳✳

Daphne mezereum ↕ 1.2m (4ft) ↔ 90cm (36in), purple-red, ☐–▨ ◊ ✳✳✳ ⬚2⬚

Daphne odora ↕↔ 1.5m (5ft), pale purple, E ☐–▨ ◊ ✳✳

Hamamelis x intermedia cultivars ↕↔ 4m (12ft), yellow, orange, ☐–▨ ◊ ☙ ✳✳✳

Hamamelis mollis ♀ ↕↔ 4m (12ft), yellow, ☐–▨ ◊ ☙ ✳✳✳

Lonicera fragrantissima ↕ 1.8m (6ft) ↔ 3m (10ft), white, ☐–▨ ◊ ✳✳✳ ⬚3⬚

Lonicera x purpusii 'Winter Beauty' ♀ ↕ 1.8m (6ft) ↔ 2.4m (8ft), white, ☐–▨ ◊ ✳✳✳

Mahonia japonica ♀ ↕ 1.8m (6ft) ↔ 3m (10ft), yellow, E ☐–▨ ◊ ✳✳✳

Sarcococca confusa ♀ ↕ 1.8m (6ft) ↔ 90cm (36in) white, E ▨–▨ ◊ ✳✳✳ ⬚4⬚

Viburnum x bodnantense ↕ 3m (10ft) ↔ 1.8m (6ft), pink, ☐–▨ ◊ ✳✳✳

Viburnum farreri ♀ ↕ 3m (10ft) ↔ 2.4m (8ft), white, ☐–▨ ◊ ✳✳✳ ⬚5⬚

Other shrubs

Camellia japonica ↕↔ 1.8–4m (6–12ft) white, pink, red E ▨ ◊ ☙ ✳✳✳

Camellia x williamsii ↕↔ 1.8–4m (6–12ft), white, pink, red E ▨ ◊ ☙ ✳✳✳ 'Joan Trehane' ♀ ⬚6⬚

Cornus mas ↕↔ 5m (15ft), yellow, ☐–▨ ◊ ✳✳✳

Erica carnea ↕ 20–25cm (8–10in) ↔ 55cm (22in), white, pink, E ☐ ◊ ✳✳✳

Erica x darleyensis ↕ 60cm (24in) ↔ 75cm (30in), white, pink, purple, E ☐ ◊ ✳✳✳

Garrya elliptica ↕↔ 4m (12ft), grey-green, E ☐–▨ ◊ ✳✳

Jasminum nudiflorum ♀ ↕↔ 3m (10ft), yellow, ☐–▨ ◊ ✳✳✳

Rhododendron 'Praecox' ♀ ↕↔ 1.2m (4ft), rosy purple, E ☐–▨ ◊ ☙ ✳✳✳

Ribes laurifolium ↕ 90cm (36in) ↔ 1.5m (5ft), green-yellow, E ☐–▨ ◊ ✳✳✳

Salix aegyptiaca ↕ 4m (12ft) ↔ 5m (15ft), grey, ☐ ◊ ✳✳✳

Stachyurus praecox ♀ ↕ 1–4m (3–12ft) ↔ 3m (10ft), pale yellow-green, ☐–▨ ◊ ☙ ✳✳✳ ⬚7⬚

Viburnum tinus ↕↔ 3m (10ft), white, E ☐–▨ ◊ ✳✳✳

Hardy perennials

Adonis amurensis ↕ 20–40cm (8–16in) ↔ 30cm (12in), yellow, ▨ ◊ ☙ ✳✳✳ ⬚8⬚

Bergenia cordifolia ↕ 60cm (24in) ↔ 75cm (30in), pale rose red, E ☐–▨ ◊ ✳✳✳

Helleborus x hybridus ↕↔ 45cm (18in), white to purple, E ▨ ◊ ✳✳✳ 'Pluto' ⬚9⬚

Eranthis hyemalis

Helleborus niger ♀ ↕ 30cm (12in) ↔ 45cm (18in), white, E ▨ ◊ ✳✳✳

Iris unguicularis ♀ ↕ 30cm (12in) ↔ 60cm (24in), pale lavender to violet, E ☐ ◊ ✳✳✳

Bulbs

Anemone blanda ♀ ↕↔ 15cm (6in), blue, pink or white, ▨ ◊ ✳✳✳ 'White Splendour' ♀ ⬚10⬚

Crocus laevigatus ♀ ↕ 4–8cm (1½–3in) ↔ 4 cm (1½in), white to lilac, ☐ ◊ ✳✳✳

Crocus tommasinianus ♀ ↕ 8–10cm (3–4in) ↔ 2.5cm (1in), silvery lilac to red-purple, ☐ ◊ ✳✳✳ f. *albus* ⬚11⬚

Eranthis hyemalis ♀ ↕ 5–8cm (2–3in) ↔ 5cm (2in), yellow, ☐–▨ ◊ ✳✳✳

Galanthus nivalis ♀ ↕↔ 10cm (4in), white, ▨ ◊ ✳✳✳

Iris reticulata ♀ ↕ 10–15cm (4–6in) ↔ 8cm (3in), violet-blue to red-purple, ☐ ◊ ✳✳✳

Narcissus asturiensis ♀ ↕↔ 8cm (3in), pale yellow, ☐ ◊ ☙ ✳✳✳

Narcissus cantabricus ↕ 15–20cm (6–8in) ↔ 8cm (3in), white, ☐–▨ ◊ ✳✳✳ ⬚12⬚

Narcissus cyclamineus ♀ ↕ 15–20cm (6–8in) ↔ 8cm (3in), yellow, ☐–▨ ◊ ☙ ✳✳✳

Scilla mischtschenkoana 'Tubergeniana' ♀ ↕ 10–15cm (4–6in) ↔ 5cm (2in), blue, ☐–▨ ◊ ✳✳✳

Rhododendron 'Praecox'

See also Ornamental bark, p.63; Shrubs for year-round interest, pp.76–77; Evergreen shrubs, p.78; Window box and hanging

basket plants, pp.170–171

WATERING THE GARDEN

Watering the garden

During dry weather or periods of drought, aim to use water in moderation in the garden; accurately timing the use of garden sprinklers helps to avoid wastage

You will find it useful to know that 2.5cm (1in) of rain is the equivalent of about 25 litres of water per 1sq m (4½ gallons per 1sq yd). Through a sprinkler, the average hosepipe delivers up to 900 litres (200 gallons) per hour. Assuming that a sprinkler covers 9sq m (10sq yd), in one hour it will deliver about 100 litres to each square metre (20 gallons per 1sq yd). Even in early or mid-summer, 1sq m (1sq yd) of continuous vegetation cover needs only 25 litres (4½ gallons) of water every 7–10 days. In the absence of rain or watering this causes a 'soil moisture deficit' (SMD) of 2.5cm (1in). Providing 2.5cm (1in) of water restores the soil to its full moisture-holding capacity; any more would be a waste because it will drain away out of reach of plant roots.

To check delivery, buy a simple rain gauge and measure how much water is delivered in a given period. Then calculate the time required to deliver 2.5cm (1in) of water. When using watering cans or seep- or drip-hoses, use a trowel to fine-tune your estimate of water needed by examining the soil's water status before and after watering, ensuring that the rooting zone is wetted, and no more.

Check the output of sprinklers by using the rain gauge to assess how much water is applied in a given time, remembering that the spread of sprinklers is not even. Take readings at various points across the wetted area. The edges of the pattern are typically under-watered. When moving the sprinkler, let the pattern overlap the previous area wetted to ensure as even coverage as possible, by wetting the areas that get least water twice.

Lawns

Over-frequent watering is wasteful and encourages shallow rooting, making the grass more susceptible to drought. It can also encourage annual meadowgrass, a troublesome weed grass in many lawns.

Allow an estimated 2.5cm (1in) SMD to build up before watering lawns, then apply 2.5cm (1in) of water. In early and midsummer, a 2.5cm (1in) SMD occurs after a week of drought. In a long period of drought, therefore, water lawns once a week. In mid-spring and early autumn, when it takes two weeks for the same SMD to accrue, water would be needed at 14-day intervals in drought conditions.

Fruits and vegetables
When it comes to deciding what to water, fruits and vegetables take priority. Fruiting vegetables such as marrows (*right*) need watering more often when in flower and when the fruits are developing. Watering raspberries (*far right*) is beneficial as the fruits start to ripen, provided there is a water deficiency.

A well-watered lawn
Only you can decide whether or not you want the lawn to stay green during drought or dry periods. To keep it green throughout summer you will need to water when there is a water deficit, applying enough each time to penetrate to the depth of the roots.

Vegetables

Water root and tuber vegetables at 14-day intervals and leafy vegetables weekly. Seedlings and transplants may need more frequent attention. Sweetcorn and all legumes (peas and beans) need adequate water at and just after flowering to ensure good yields. Fruiting vegetables like courgettes, marrows and tomatoes need more frequent watering during and following flowering.

Ornamental plants

For established trees and shrubs allow a 7.5cm (3in) SMD before watering, and a 5cm (2in) SMD for young trees and shrubs. You can allow a 5cm (2in) SMD for herbaceous perennials before they need watering, and a 2.5cm (1in) SMD for newly or recently planted perennials and bedding plants.

Fruit trees and bushes

For established trees allow a 7.5cm (3in) SMD, and a 5cm (2in) SMD for young trees, before watering. If established trees are watered before midsummer,

See also Drought-resistant gardening, pp.16–17; Lawn care in dry weather, p.182; Watering vegetables, p.203

LAYING A SEEP HOSE

A convenient and efficient method of applying water to plants is to lay a seep hose among them. This is especially useful for permanent plants such as shrubs, hardy perennials and fruits, and also along rows of vegetables. Water slowly seeps from pores in the hose, ensuring that it reaches the roots of the plants and penetrates deeply into the soil. **1** Lay the hose evenly among the plants. **2** Conceal the hose with a mulching material such as chipped bark. Connect one end to the mains supply and when water is needed simply turn on the tap.

Using a sprinkler in dry weather
A permanent sprinkler system connected to the mains water supply is ideal for plants such as fruit trees and bushes that need to be watered during dry spells.

---

continue to water as necessary to avoid the production of small fruits. At first watering apply 5cm (2in); subsequently apply at least 2.5cm (1in), and preferably 5cm (2in) of water every 14 days from midsummer to early autumn.

Black, red and white currants benefit from watering between late spring and late summer. With raspberries watering is usually required when the first berries begin to colour, if rain is scarce. Watering can increase the yield at that period. Another application of 5cm (2in) after harvesting will improve new stem growth. Water also benefits strawberries when the fruits are ripening but avoid

Puddling in a new plant
Water in newly planted subjects if the ground is dry. Apply a canful of water immediately around the plant so that it penetrates deeply and reaches all the roots. Thereafter water new plants whenever the soil starts to dry out.

watering during the flowering period because of the risk of grey mould (*Botrytis*). When necessary, apply water in early autumn to increase future yields and during mid- and late summer to improve runner production.

Domestic waste water

During periods of drought, when there are bans preventing you from watering the garden, it is often suggested that domestic waste water should be utilised to avoid plant losses.

The most suitable waste water is free from additives and bleaching agents, such as water that has been used for washing and preparing vegetables. While moderate use of domestic waste water is unlikely to have a serious detrimental effect on soil structure, soil organisms or plant life, frequent and prolonged use of water containing detergents may raise chalk and phosphate levels, and also the soil's salt content, which could cause some harm.

It is possible that some soils may be more at risk of accumulating harmful effects than others, but it would certainly be advisable when planning to use bath water or other domestic waste water in the garden to cut out the use of additives such as bath salts or bath oils and to

avoid excessive use of water containing detergents, particularly if you are growing lime-hating plants.

Rather than watering 'little and often', less frequent but more thorough watering is a better policy. Prioritise vegetable crops, and recently planted trees and shrubs with roots that have not established sufficiently to cope in periods of drought.

COLLECTING GREY WATER

You can divert domestic waste water into water butts by tapping into downpipes. For safety reasons, you should ensure that the container has a lid, and avoid storing grey water for more than a few hours.

DROUGHT-RESISTANT GARDENING

Drought-resistant gardening

To save on garden watering, try growing drought-tolerant trees, shrubs, conifers and hardy perennials, which can be grouped together in their own special beds or borders

Many drought-tolerant plants come from the Mediterranean or similar regions where hot, dry summers and cool winters with little or no frost are the norm. For wintering outdoors take care to choose plants that are fully or frost hardy. Slightly tender plants can often be grown outside all year in mild coastal gardens, close to or trained against warm, sunny, south- or west-facing walls, or in sheltered borders.

Drought-tolerant plants are often characterized by their leaves, which may be silver or grey, covered in hairs, very small, shiny, or with a waxy covering. Some have fleshy leaves and stems that hold water, and roots may be long, growing deeply into the soil.

Water all new plants as necessary during their first year to get them established. Thereafter they should be able to cope with drought.

TREES AND CONIFERS

Trees

Ailanthus altissima ‡ 25m (80ft) ↔ 15m (50ft)
□–◙ ◊ ✱✱✱ 1

Arbutus x andrachnoides ♀ ‡↔ 8m (25ft)
E □ ◊ ✱✱✱

Betula pendula ♀ ‡ 25m (80ft) ↔ 10m (30ft)
□–◙ ◊ ✱✱✱ ‘Youngii’ 2

Celtis australis ‡↔ 20m (70ft) □ ◊ ✱✱✱

Cercis siliquastrum ♀ ‡↔ 10m (30ft) □ ◊ ✱✱✱

Cordyline australis ♀ ‡ 3–10m (10–30ft)
↔ 1–4m (3–12ft) E □–◙ ◊ ✱ ‘Variegata’ 3

Eucalyptus pauciflora subsp. *niphophila* ♀
‡ 8m (25ft) ↔ 4m (12ft) E □ ◊ ✱✱✱

Genista aetnensis ♀ ‡↔ 8m (25ft) □ ◊ ✱✱

Gleditsia triacanthos ‘Sunburst’ ♀ ‡ 12m
(40ft) ↔ 10m (30ft) □ ◊ ✱✱✱

Koelreuteria paniculata ♀ ‡↔ 10m (30ft) □ ◊
✱✱✱

Quercus ilex ♀ ‡ 25m (80ft) ↔ 20m (70ft)
E □ ◊ ✱✱

Robinia pseudoacacia ‘Frisia’ ♀ ‡ 15m (50ft)
↔ 8m (25ft) □ ◊ ✱✱✱ 4

Trachycarpus fortunei ♀ ‡ 20m (70ft) ↔ 2.4m
(8ft) E □–◙ ◊ ✱✱

Conifers

Cupressus sempervirens ‡ 20m (70ft) ↔ 1–6m
(3–20ft) E □ ◊ ✱✱✱

Juniperus horizontalis ‡ 30cm (12in) ↔ 1.8m
(6ft) □–◙ ◊ ✱✱✱

Juniperus virginiana ‡ 15–30m (50–100ft)
↔ 5–8m (15–25ft) E □–◙ ◊ ✱✱✱

Pinus mugo ‡ 3m (10ft) ↔ 5m (15ft) E □ ◊ ✱✱✱
‘Mops’ ♀ 5

Taxus baccata ♀ ‡ 10–20m (30–70ft) ↔ 8–10m
(25–30ft) E □ ◙ ◊ ✱✱✱

SHRUBS AND PERENNIALS

Shrubs (small to medium)

Brachyglottis (Dunedin Group) 'Sunshine' ♀
‡ 1.5m (5ft) ↔ 2m (6ft) E ▣ ◊ ✳✳✳

Cistus x *purpureus* ♀ ‡↔ 90cm (36in)
E ▣ ◊ ✳✳

Convolvulus cneorum ♀ ‡ 60cm (24in)
↔ 90cm (36in) E ▣ ◊ ✳✳ ⬛6

Coronilla valentina subsp. *glauca* ♀ ‡↔ 80cm
(32in) E ▣ ◊ ✳✳

Genista hispanica ‡ 75cm (30in) ↔ 1.5m (5ft)
▣ ◊ ✳✳✳

Halimium ocymoides ♀ ‡ 60cm (24in) ↔ 90cm
(36in) E ▣ ◊ ✳✳

Helichrysum italicum ♀ ‡ 60cm (24in) ↔ 90cm
(36in) E ▣ ◊ ✳✳

Ozothamnus ledifolius ♀ ‡↔ 90cm (36in) E ▣
◊ ✳✳

Perovskia 'Blue Spire' ♀ ‡ 1.2m (4ft) ↔ 90cm
(36in) ▣ ◊ ✳✳✳

Phlomis fruticosa ♀ ‡ 90cm (36in) ↔ 1.5m (5ft)
E ▣ ◊ ✳✳✳ ⬛7

Potentilla fruticosa 'Beesii' ‡ 60cm (24in)
↔ 1.2m (4ft) ▣ ◊ ✳✳✳

Rosmarinus officinalis Prostratus Group
‡ 15cm (6in) ↔ 1.2m (4ft) E ▣ ◊ ✳✳

Ruta graveolens 'Jackman's Blue' ‡ 60cm
(24in) ↔ 75cm (30in) E ▣ ▣ ◊ ✳✳✳ ⬛8

Santolina chamaecyparissus ♀ ‡ 50cm (20in)
↔ 90cm (36in) E ▣ ◊ ✳✳

Teucrium fruticans ‡ 60–90cm (24–36in) ↔ 4m
(12ft) E ▣ ◊ ✳✳

Yucca filamentosa ♀ ‡ 75cm (30in) ↔ 1.5m
(5ft) E ▣ ◊ ✳✳✳

Shrubs (medium to large)

Atriplex halimus ‡ 1.8m (6ft) ↔ 2.4m (8ft)
E ▣ ◊ ✳✳

Buddleja globosa ♀ ‡↔ 5m (15ft) ◊ ✳✳ ⬛9

Colutea arborescens ‡↔ 3m (10ft) ▣ ◊ ✳✳✳

Cytisus scoparius ‡↔ 1.5m (5ft) ▣ ◊ ✳✳✳

Genista tenera 'Golden Shower' ‡ 3m (10ft)
↔ 5m (15ft) ▣ ◊ ✳✳

Hippophae rhamnoides ♀ ‡↔ 6m (20ft) ▣ ◊
✳✳✳

Poncirus trifoliata ‡↔ 5m (15ft) ▣ ◊ ✳✳✳

Rosa rugosa ‡↔ 1.8–2.4m (6–8ft) ▣ ◊ ✳✳✳

Spartium junceum ♀ ‡↔ 3m (10ft) ▣ ◊ ✳✳

Tamarix ramosissima ‡↔ 5m (15ft) ▣ ◊ ✳✳✳

Ulex europaeus 'Flore Pleno' ♀ ‡ 2.4m (8ft)
↔ 1.8m (6ft) E ▣ ◊ ℮ ✳✳✳

Vitex agnus-castus ‡↔ 1.8–8m (6–25ft) ▣ ◊ ✳✳

Hardy perennials

Baptisia autralis ♀ ‡ 1.5m (5ft) ↔ 60cm (24in)
▣ ◊ ✳✳✳

Carlina acaulis ‡ 10cm (4in) ↔ 25cm (10in)
▣ ◊ ✳✳✳ ⬛10

Centranthus ruber ‡↔ 90cm (36in) ▣ ◊ ✳✳✳

Crambe cordifolia ♀ ‡ 2.8m (8ft) ↔ 1.5m (5ft)
▣ ◊ ✳✳✳

Echinops ritro ♀ ‡ 60cm (24in) ↔ 45cm (18in),
▣ ◊ ✳✳✳

Eryngium x *tripartitum* ♀ ‡ 60–90cm
(24–36in) ↔ 50cm (20in) ◊ ✳✳✳

Lespedeza thunbergii ♀ ‡ 1.8m (6ft) ↔ 3m
(10ft) ▣ ◊ ✳✳✳ ⬛11

Sedum spectabile ♀ ‡↔ 45cm (18in) ▣ ◊ ✳✳✳

Verbascum chaixii 'Album' ♀ ‡ 90cm (36in)
↔ 45cm (18in) ▣ ◊ ✳✳✳ ⬛12

Planning small gardens

A small space does not mean a boring garden

Divide narrow gardens to give the illusion of greater space, and keep the overall design simple.

Consider what you want to use your space for: play, entertaining, gardening or relaxing. Draw a plan showing features such as services, boundaries, trees, changes in level or views. Make a special note of the aspect, as well as which parts receive the most sun at different times of the day or year, whether part of the garden is exposed to wind or if it remains frosty in winter.

Do not plant large trees or tall hedges as they may overwhelm both the garden and your neighbours rather than provide privacy, and they cast too much shade.

Use climbers on trellis to soften boundaries and provide year-round interest. Use large shrubs, or a feature such as an arbour, to provide focal points and privacy. Choose feature plants with more than one season of interest and aim for successive planting, such as spring bulbs under summer-flowering shrubs, to give a long period of interest.

Draw a plan of the garden to scale

See also Finding contractors, p.11

Roof gardens and balconies

Don't let the prospect of strong winds and too much sunshine deter you from growing plants on your roof or balcony

The main problems with roof gardens and balconies are strong winds and excessive sunshine. Take advantage of existing protection such as walls or fences. Balconies often have the additional problem of an overhang, which prevents rain from reaching potted plants.

Before designing a roof garden consult an architect or structural engineer to find out how much weight the roof can take, and whether it is adequately waterproof.

Wind-tolerant plants
Grassy phormiums, such as 'Sundowner' (*above left*), help to filter the wind, and the evergreen shrub *Viburnum tinus* 'Variegatum' (*above right*) is excellent for creating shelter.

Containers and compost
Place containers near load-bearing walls or over a beam or joist.

Containers will dry out rapidly in the excess heat and wind, so use deep pots or tubs. If using small containers choose non-porous materials such as plastic, metal or fibreglass to reduce moisture loss. Ensure containers are light in weight and well drained. Peat or peat-substitute composts are lighter than soil-based types and can be lightened further still by adding perlite. Bear in mind, however, that adding additional drainage materials will increase water demands.

Watering and care
Potted plants need watering all year round, except in freezing conditions. In summer you may need to water twice a day, if not more. An automated watering system saves labour, but may only be cost effective for larger areas.

Check containers periodically to ensure that plant roots remain contained. Standing pots on pot 'feet' deters root escape.

Deep containers
Use deep pots as they dry out less rapidly than more shallow containers. For the same reason, choose pots made from non-porous materials such as plastic.

Plants
Windbreak plants such as *Pinus mugo* (dwarf mountain pine) and phormiums tolerate sun and wind and can act as a shield for less robust plants. Dense evergreens, including *Viburnum tinus* and junipers, create shelter. Low-growing plants avoid the worst of the winds, or are sturdy enough to withstand them. Dwarf spring-flowering bulbs can also withstand exposure. Make sure large plants are well anchored to stop them from blowing over.

See also Planting in containers, p.161; Plants for patios, p.164; Care of container plants, p.172

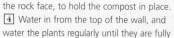

Rock garden plants

You can grow a wide range of plants in a rock garden, especially if it has been built to provide a variety of different conditions, from dry and sunny to moist and shady – and anything in between

Where possible make a large part of a rock garden south-facing as many plants will thrive in these conditions, such as penstemons, *Leontopodium alpinum* (edelweiss), most bulbs, teucriums, aethionemas and *Anacyclus pyrethrum* var. *depressus*.

Create some north-facing terraces to provide suitable sites for plants that prefer shade, such as ferns, mossy saxifrages and ramondas. Others prefer the partial shade of west- and east-facing slopes.

Many plants such as thymes, *Phlox douglasii*, *P. subulata*, helianthemums and *Pulsatilla vulgaris* (pasque flower) are adaptable to different aspects.

Crevices and walls

Plants that grow in vertical rock crevices in the wild can be planted in a similar way on a rock garden by wedging them into small gaps between rocks. This is most easily done during construction. On north-facing rocks lewisias, ramondas and haberleas thrive. For other aspects use androsaces, encrusted saxifrages, campanulas, erodiums and alyssums.

High, exposed terraces are likely to be especially well drained, so reserve these for plants that prefer such conditions, like sedums, *Acantholimon*, *Edraianthus*, helichrysums and tulips. In the lower, moist areas, and especially beside water, plant small moisture lovers such as *Primula rosea*, *P. frondosa*, *Trollius pumilus*, *Saxifraga fortunei*, *Mimulus cupreus* 'Whitecroft Scarlet' and dodecatheons.

Scree

The particularly good drainage associated with this feature suits plants from dry climates, as well as those adapted to scree conditions in the wild, further increasing the range of plants that can be grown. Suitable candidates

PLANTING IN CREVICES

Select plants to suit the conditions that the wall provides. [1] Fill the crevice with gritty compost. [2] Ease in the plant's roots (here *Campanula*). Do not try to cram them into too small a space because this can damage the plant. Cover the roots with compost, firming it with a widger.

[3] Wedge in a small stone, sloping it down the rock face, to hold the compost in place. [4] Water in from the top of the wall, and water the plants regularly until they are fully established. Check them every so often, and firm in any plants that start to work loose.

include many saxifrages, androsaces, drabas, daphnes, cyclamen, sempervivums, *Phlox nana*, Juno irises and *Ranunculus* species.

Planting

Make up a compost mix for rock gardens according to the needs and lime-tolerance of plants. A neutral mix will grow the widest range of plants. Most plants get away to a good start if they are planted in spring. Plant bulbs while they are dormant, except for snowdrops (*Galanthus*) which are best planted after flowering when in full leaf (*see p.144*).

Choose plants that will suit the size of the rock garden, and group plants of an appropriate size together. Do not allow your plants to hide the rocks too much. Use shrubs as dot plants, but if you choose dwarf conifers, double-check to ensure that they are the really dwarf kinds. Position trailing plants to spill over large rocks.

Plant spring bulbs among summer-flowering herbaceous alpines to give successional interest, but make sure the bulbs' leaves do not swamp the other plants. Go for a balanced selection of shrubs, herbaceous plants and bulbs.

Sun-loving plants
The south-facing aspect of a rock garden makes an ideal home for sun-loving plants like *Teucrium polium* (*far left*) and the edelweiss, *Leontopodium alpinum* (*left*). Plant miniature spring-flowering bulbs among these low-growing plants to create a long period of colour.

See also Trough and sink gardening, pp.22–23

Raising plants from seed

You can raise many annuals, tender perennials and vegetables from seed in containers on a windowsill or in a greenhouse; use the right compost, sowing technique and temperature to ensure success

You can give seedlings an early start on windowsills, rather than heating a greenhouse, provided you are aware of the limitations.

Make sure there is sufficient space on the windowsill to cope with the seedlings after pricking out and as they grow bigger.

Heat and moisture

To ensure seed germination, you must provide adequate heating, which means a minimum temperature of 18°C (64°F). However, temperatures that are high enough for quick germination are likely to lead to drawn seedlings. Warm conditions combined with low light levels are particularly damaging. Windowsill temperatures can fluctuate in changeable weather, and between night and day. Fluctuating conditions weaken seedlings, so where variations are likely bring them into the room at night or grow them in a room in which the radiators are turned off.

An electric windowsill propagator can be used to hasten germination, but move seedlings to cooler conditions as soon as this has occured. Wipe plastic lids regularly; the condensation that often occurs on the inside of the lid cuts out appreciable light.

When to sow

Most tender plants can be sown on windowsills in early or mid-spring. However, they grow faster in conditions provided by longer days and higher light levels, and suffer little reduction in their flowering season if you sow towards the end of this period. For example, outdoor tomatoes can be perfectly satisfactory when sowing is delayed until mid-spring. Other plants you can sow between early and mid-spring include ageratums, dahlias, impatiens, nicotianas, petunias and zinnias, but you should wait until late spring to sow cosmos, nasturtiums and 10-week stocks

Hardy plants such as sweet peas and onions can be sown early in the year as the young plants come to little harm when moved to an unheated greenhouse, cold frame or cloches.

Pricking out seedlings
Transplant seedlings using a dibber as soon as they are large enough to handle. Plastic module trays ensure ideal spacing and sufficient room for development.

Pricking out seedlings

As soon as seedlings are large enough to be easily handled, but before they become overcrowded, transplant them into other containers to give them space to grow. This is known as "pricking out". You could use ordinary seed trays for this purpose, but you may have better results using 24-cell module trays (*see above*), which allow the subsequent young plants to be potted-on or planted out with minimum root disturbance. Fill the module tray with potting compost and firm it lightly.

When pricking out, lift a few seedlings at a time with a table fork. For each seedling, use a dibber to make a hole in a cell that is deep enough to allow the roots to dangle straight down and the seed leaves (the first leaves) to remain just above compost level. Handle the seedlings by the seed leaves, not by the stems, which are easily damaged. Hold a seedling in the hole, gently push the compost around it, and firm lightly. Then water, using a can fitted with a fine rose.

Safety in numbers
Humidity can be low in centrally heated rooms, especially on windowsills above radiators. Seedlings are likely to do best where a windowsill is filled with plants. Both plants and their compost release moisture, and if enough of them are grown together they create their own area of slightly more humid conditions.

See also Sowing hardy annuals, p.158; Sowing and training sweet peas, p.171; Creating a lawn from seed, pp.177–178

SOWING SEEDS IN CONTAINERS

[1] Use seed compost for sowing in containers as its finer texture allows better seed-to-compost contact and its low fertility is designed to prevent seedling damage from excess foods. When filling the container, whether a seed tray or half pot, gently push the compost down with your fingers to make sure there are no 'soft spots'. Tap the container on the bench twice to settle the compost, then scrape off the surplus with a straight piece of wood. Make sure the compost surface is level and even.

[2] Use a presser board, or the base of a similar-sized pot or tray, to firm the surface of the compost. When pressing, leave a gap deep enough to sow and cover the seed while leaving plenty of space below the rim to allow watering.

[3] With the seed in the palm of your hand, tap your hand with the other one, or take pinches of seed from the palm, and work your way down the length of the container so that seeds fall in ones and twos on to the compost. Ensure all parts of the tray are covered, including the corners. Position large seeds individually. If you are sowing very fine seed, mix it with a carrier such as fine, dry silver sand, then sow either as described above, or use an old pepper pot as a seed dispenser.

[4] Thinly cover the seeds with fine vermiculite, which provides an ideal light, moist covering for seedlings to push their way through. Alternatively, use sieved, moist compost or perlite. Water thoroughly from the base by

placing the container in a tray of water. To prevent damping-off disease in these early sowings, mix a copper-based fungicide into the water. Place the tray in a warm propagation area, such as a heated propagating case. A well-lit windowsill is a good alternative to a greenhouse.

[5] When they are well established, move hardy plants, such as onions, lettuces, annuals and herbaceous perennials to a cold frame or place them under cloches to begin the hardening process. This frees up space indoors for the next batch of seedlings. Sheets of corrugated plastic make sturdy shelters, which snugly fit over seed trays. On frosty nights provide temporary protection with fleece or newspaper.

1

2

3

4

5

LATE DEVELOPERS

Slow-growing plants that are sown in mid- or late winter, such as begonias, pelargoniums and gazanias, might be better bought as pots of seedlings or as plugs in mid-spring. These can be pricked out or potted up and placed in an unheated greenhouse or cold frame. When frost is expected, cover the young plants with sheets of newspaper or insulate the frame.

SILVER FOIL TO AID SUNLIGHT

Windowsills are less well lit than you might think. Poor light results in elongated or leggy growth, but placing a reflective surface such as silver foil behind seedlings increases light levels. However, bright sunshine can scorch seedlings, so take care with south-facing windows.

Simple and electric propagating aids

Various items will ensure that your seeds germinate readily, and when you are no longer sowing seeds they can be used for other forms of propagation, such as rooting cuttings. Covering a single pot with a clear plastic bag is the simplest way of preventing the compost from drying out, which would

inhibit the process of seed germination. A simple electric windowsill propagator provides bottom heat and humid air, both of which encourage germination. Alternatively, an unheated propagating case, or pots, can be placed on an electric propagating blanket on the greenhouse bench, which provides bottom heat.

Plastic bag propagation

Use sticks to support plastic bag

Module tray

Thermostat can be set to required temperature

Plastic sheet protects blanket

Electric blanket

Capillary matting

Polystyrene insulation

A simple windowsill propagator

More advanced propagating blanket

Trough and sink gardening

Stone or imitation stone troughs and sinks are ideal for creating miniature landscapes with year-round interest for patios, courtyards and in the garden, and they provide a home for many small alpine or rock plants

Most alpine plants need sun and good drainage, so place the trough or sink in a sunny, open spot. Mount it on supports that are not obviously visible and ensure these are not too high. A height of 45–50cm (18–20in) from the ground to the top of the trough gives the right sort of scale, except on a paved area where a height of just a few inches will give a better effect.

Make sure the trough is level, place a layer of broken clay pots over the drainage hole, followed by a large handful of pebbles, to prevent blockage when compost is added. Fill the bottom one-third with coarse gravel and cover with a shallow layer of coarse coir, half-rotted leafmould, up-turned turf or horticultural textile to prevent the finer compost from being washed down. A proprietary soil-based potting compost with 25 per cent extra

The attractions of a trough
Troughs and sinks, whether made of natural or imitation stone, make attractive plant containers in their own right. Most gardeners plant them with rock garden plants or alpines, as shown here, and stand them on a sunny patio, but there is no reason why they should not make an ideal home for various other dwarf plants that enjoy good drainage, such as culinary herbs, especially thymes, sages and oregano.

sharp grit added will suit most alpine plants (lime haters need acid compost). Firm the compost as you fill the trough. Arrange a few 'architectural' rocks to suit the scale and eye.

Planting

You can plant a mixture of alpine plants that flower, or have attractive foliage, at different times of the year, or you could plant one type of plant, such as autumn-flowering gentians in an acid compost, or ramondas in a shady spot. A trough full of silver-leaved saxifrages will remain attractive all year round.

Choose plants carefully to avoid rampant growers that will smother the rocks and slower-growing neighbours. Leave the plants a little high when planting, to allow for a 2cm (¾in) deep layer of sharp grit – for aesthetic reasons match this with the trough and rock

Finish off your 'landscape' with sharp grit

colouring. Grit helps to conserve moisture, prevents heavy rain splashing soil on to flowers, keeps moisture away from stems to prevent rot and gives a natural finish to the garden.

Use a watering can fitted with a rose to give a really good soaking after planting, until water is seen running out of the drainage hole. Do not allow troughs to dry out. During the plants' resting time in winter no additional watering is necessary in normal conditions, but watch out for the drying action of frost, especially as some alpines start root growth in very early spring.

Maintain herbaceous plants with occasional deadheading and cutting back, and give them an annual feed of slow-release fertilizer in early spring.

Using glazed sinks

Glazed sinks can be made to look like stone versions if you cover them with a hypertufa coating.

Wait for cool but not frosty weather to carry out this treatment, as the coating mixture will remain workable for longer than in warm, dry conditions. The coating takes about three weeks to dry, after which the sink will be ready for planting up.

Mount a heavy sink on stones or old bricks, about 15–22cm (6–9in) high, and prepare it *in situ*.

See also Rock garden plants, p.19; Plants for gravel gardens, pp.122–23; Care of container plants, p.172

MAKING A HYPERTUFA TROUGH

Troughs can be made entirely from hypertufa. Make up a slightly stiffer mixture than used for coating: 1–2 parts sphagnum peat, 3 parts sharp sand, and 1 part cement (parts by bulk).

Use two wooden or rigid cardboard boxes that fit inside each other, with a 5–7cm (2–3in) cavity between them. Stand the larger box on blocks so you can easily lift it when finished. [1] Place a layer of the hypertufa mix in the base of the larger box and cover it with a piece of strong, rigid wire mesh. [2] Press thick wooden dowels or pegs through the hypertufa to make drainage holes. [3] Add another layer of the hypertufa mix. [4] Firm it down, then fit the smaller box inside the larger one, with wire mesh between the two. [5] Fill the spaces with hypertufa mix. [6] Tamp it down to remove air pockets. Cover the trough with a sheet of plastic for at least a week while the hypertufa sets and, if necessary, protect it from frost. [7] Remove the boxes when the mixture has set hard. If wooden boxes do not slide off, ease them off carefully with a hammer and chisel. [8] Roughen the trough surface using a wire brush. [9] Remove the dowels from the drainage holes, and apply a coat of liquid manure to encourage algae, to take off that 'new' look.

First remove any metal fittings, then clean and wash the sink thoroughly and allow to it dry. Where possible, chip away some of the glaze to achieve better adhesion; this can be done using an electric drill and masonry bit.

Apply a coating of PVA glue, which is obtainable from most builders' merchants or ironmongers, over about 60 x 60cm (2 x 2ft) of the surface glaze. Allow this to become tacky while mixing hypertufa.
- TRADITIONAL MIX (parts by bulk):
  1–2 parts sphagnum peat
  1 part sharp sand
  1 part cement
- LIGHTWEIGHT MIX (parts by bulk):
  1 part sphagnum peat
  ½ part sharp sand
  1 part cement
  ½ part micafil (used for insulation and available from builders' merchants)

The sphagnum peat provides the stone colouring; variations in the quantity give corresponding variations in colour of the finished product, but too much peat will make a less durable finish.

Avoid making the mixture too wet. A 9-litre (2-gallon) bucket of the mixture is roughly enough to coat the average-sized sink, so start by making half a bucketful and treat a section at a time.

Apply the mixture to the tacky PVA glue, and extend the coating over the rim, 5–8cm (2–3in) down the inside, and 8–10cm (3–4in) under the base, so that none of the original glaze shows. Apply two or three coats for greater durability and resistance to frost. To simulate stonework, mark or jab the surface with a brush or chisel as the coats dry. To create the appearance of age, apply a mixture of milk, manure water and neat seaweed liquid fertilizer with a paintbrush to encourage algae and mosses to grow.

PLANTS TO TRY

The ideal plants for troughs and sinks are rock-garden plants or alpines, as they like the good drainage that these containers provide.

Aethionema ▢
Erodium ▢
Gentiana (autumn flowering) ▢ ⬙
Hypericum olympicum ♀ ▢
Phlox douglasii and cultivars ▢
Ramonda ◉
Raoulia australis ▢
Saxifraga (including silver-leaved cultivars) ▢
Sedum spathulifolium cultivars ▢
Sempervivum ▢

Lavender planted in hypertufa trough

What to plant in a seaside garden

With good protection from wind and salt spray a very wide range of trees, shrubs, hardy perennials and rock-garden plants can be grown in gardens by the sea

Before planting a seaside garden you must establish a windbreak to protect plants against salt-laden winds. If there is no hedge or natural windbreak, wattle hurdles, or chestnut paling fences thatched with brushwood, are good temporary substitutes.

Solid structures such as stone walls are useful but it is better to plant a wind-filtering barrier of trees or shrubs of some depth – that is, two or more staggered rows. A screen of polypropylene webbing can be used until a natural barrier is established.

Several species of *Pinus* (pine) are among the trees most tolerant of direct exposure and so can be used to create natural windbreaks. One of the hardiest is *Pinus nigra* subsp. *nigra* which, as an outer barrier, can be planted about 1.8m (6ft) apart in staggered rows. It is dense-branching and although with age the lower branches will naturally begin to shed, by this time inner screening should be well established, so that there is no risk of wind funnelling under this outer belt of pines. Shrubby *P. mugo* is also effective in fully exposed situations. It only grows to 3.5m (11ft) so is useful for an inner screen.

Deciduous trees tolerant of direct exposure to sea winds and therefore suitable for use as windbreaks include *Alnus glutinosa* (alder), *Crataegus monogyna* (hawthorn), *Carpinus betulus* (hornbeam), *Acer pseudoplatanus* (sycamore), *Populus alba* (white poplar), *Quercus ilex* (holm oak), *Salix caprea* (goat willow), *Salix alba* (white willow) and *Sorbus aria* (whitebeam). Keep poplars and willows well away from buildings (*see pp.52–53*).

When a barrier of hardy wind- and salt-spray-tolerant trees and shrubs has been established, you may, depending on the severity of the climate, be able grow a wide range of coastal-tolerant plants within its shelter.

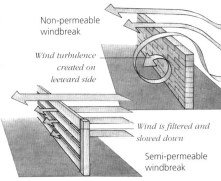

Non-permeable windbreak

Wind turbulence created on leeward side

Wind is filtered and slowed down

Semi-permeable windbreak

Reducing the effect of wind
A non-permeable windbreak such as a wall is better than nothing but it has a problem – it causes wind turbulence. Much better is a semi-permeable windbreak that filters the wind, such as plastic windbreak materials or living screens.

TREES AND SHRUBS FOR EXPOSED COASTAL SITES

Coastal-tolerant trees

Acer platanoides ♀ ‡ 25m (80ft) ↔ 15m (50ft) □–▨ ◊–◊ ✲✲✲

Betula pendula ♀ ‡ 25m (80ft) ↔ 10m (30ft) □–▨ ◊–◊ ✲✲✲

Crataegus laevigata ↔ 8m (25ft) □–▨ ◊ ✲✲✲ 'Rosea' [1]

x *Cupressocyparis leylandii* ♀ ‡ 35m (120ft) ↔ 5m (15ft) E □–▨ ◊ ✲✲✲

Picea omorika ♀ ‡ 20m (70ft) ↔ 1.8–3m (6–10ft) E □ ◊ ✲✲✲

Sorbus aucuparia ‡ 15m (50ft) ↔ 7m (22ft) □–▨ ◊–◊ ✲✲✲

Leaf and catkins of *Betula Pendula*

Salt-spray-tolerant shrubs

Atriplex halimus ‡ 1.8m (6ft) ↔ 2.4m (8ft), good for hedges, E □ ◊ ✲✲

Bupleurum fruticosum ‡ 1.8m (6ft) ↔ 2.4m (8ft) E □ ◊ ✲✲

Cistus laurifolius ♀ ‡↔ 1.8m (6ft) E □ ◊ ✲✲

Elaeagnus angustifolia ‡↔ 6m (20ft) □ ◊ ✲✲✲ [2]

Escallonia rubra var. *macrantha* ‡↔ 3m (10ft) E □ ◊ ✲✲✲

Griselinia littoralis ♀ ‡ 8m (25ft) ↔ 5m (15ft), good for hedges, E □ ◊ ✲✲

Hebe salicifolia ‡↔ 2.4m (8ft) E □–▨ ◊ ✲✲✲

Hippophae rhamnoides ♀ ‡↔ 6m (20ft) □ ◊ ✲✲✲ [3]

Olearia macrodonta ♀ ‡ 6m (20ft) ↔ 5m (15ft) E □ ◊ ✲✲

Spartium junceum ♀ ‡↔ 3m (10ft) □ ◊ ✲✲

Tamarix tetrandra ♀ ‡↔ 3m (10ft) □ ◊ ✲✲✲

Ulex europaeus 'Flore Pleno' ♀ ‡ 2.4m (8ft) ↔ 1.8m (6ft), good for hedges, E □ ◊ ⌖ ✲✲✲

Coastal-tolerant shrubs

Brachyglottis (Dunedin Group) 'Sunshine' ♀ ‡ 1.5m (5ft) ↔ 1.8m (6ft) E □ ◊ ✲✲✲

Ceanothus x *delileanus* 'Gloire de Versailles' ♀ ‡↔ 1.8m (6ft) □ ◊ ✲✲✲

Cistus x *purpureus* ♀ ‡↔ 90cm (36in) E □ ◊ ✲✲

Colutea arborescens ‡↔ 3m (10ft) □ ◊ ✲✲✲

Cytisus scoparius ‡↔ 1.5m (5ft) □ ◊ ✲✲✲

Escallonia rubra 'Crimson Spire' ♀ ‡↔ 5m (15ft), good for hedges, E □ ◊ ✲✲✲

Euphorbia characias ‡↔ 1.2m (4ft) E □ ◊ ✲✲

Fuchsia 'Riccartonii' ♀ ‡ 1.8–3m (6–10ft) ↔ 1–1.8m (3–6ft), good for hedges, □–▨ ◊ ✲✲ [4]

Hippocrepis emerus ‡↔ 1.8m (6ft) □ ◊ ✲✲✲

Hydrangea macrophylla ‡ 1–1.8m (3–6ft) ↔ 1.5–2.4m (5–8ft) □–▨ ◊ ✲✲✲

Olearia x *scilloniensis* ♀ ‡↔ 1.8m (6ft) E □ ◊ ✲✲

Pittosporum tenuifolium ♀ ‡ 4–10m (12–30ft) ↔ 1.8–5m (6–15ft), good for hedges, E □–▨ ◊ ✲✲

Rhamnus alaternus 'Argenteovariegata' ♀ ‡ 5m (15ft) ↔ 4m (12ft) E □ ◊ ✲✲

Rosmarinus officinalis ‡↔ 1.5m (5ft), good for hedges, E □ ◊ ✲✲

Santolina chamaecyparissus ♀ ‡ 50cm (20in) ↔ 90cm (36in) E □ ◊ ✲✲ [5]

Spartium junceum ♀ ‡↔ 3m (10ft) □ ◊ ✲✲

See also Rock garden plants, p.19; Preventing wind scorch, p.71; Hedging plants, p.85

ROCK PLANTS AND PERENNIALS FOR SEASIDE GARDENS

Rock-garden plants

Aethionema grandiflorum ♀ ↕↔ 20–30cm (8–12in) E ▣ ◊ ❋❋❋

Armeria maritima ↕ 20cm (8in) ↔ 30cm (12in) E ▣ ◊ ❋❋❋

Aubrieta hybrids ↕ 5cm (2in) ↔ 60cm (24in) E ▣ ◊ ❋❋❋

Aurinia saxatilis ♀ ↕ 20cm (8in) ↔ 30cm (12in) E ▣ ◊ ❋❋❋

Dianthus alpinus ♀ ↕ 8cm (3in) ↔ 10cm (4in) E ▣ ◊ ❋❋❋

Euryops acraeus ♀ ↕↔ 30cm (12in) E ▣ ◊ ❋❋

Hypericum olympicum ♀ ↕ 25cm (10in) ↔ 30cm (12in) ▣ ◊ ❋❋❋

Iris pumila ↕ 10–15cm (4–6in) ↔ 30cm (12in) ▣ ◊ ❋❋❋

Phlox subulata ↕ 5–15cm (2–6in) ↔ 50cm (20in) E ▣–▣ ◊ ❋❋❋ 'Marjorie' [6]

Pulsatilla vulgaris ♀ ↕ 10–20cm (4–8in) ↔ 20cm (8in) ▣ ◊ ❋❋❋

Silene schafta ♀ ↕ 25cm (10in) ↔ 30cm (12in) E ▣– ▣ ◊ ❋❋❋

Zauschneria californica ↕ 30cm (12in) ↔ 50cm (20in) E ▣ ◊ ❋❋

Hardy perennials

Achillea ptarmica ↕ 30–90cm (12–36in) ↔ 60cm (24in) ▣ ◊ ❋❋❋

Agapanthus campanulatus ↕ 60–120cm (24–48in) ↔ 60cm (24in) ▣ ◊ ❋❋❋

Alcea rosea ↕ 1.5–2.4m (5–8ft) ↔ 60cm (24in) ▣ ◊ ❋❋❋

Catananche caerulea ↕ 50–90cm (20–36in) ↔ 30cm (12in) ▣ ◊ ❋❋❋

Centranthus ruber ↕↔ 90cm (36in) ▣ ◊ ❋❋❋

Cortaderia selloana ↕ 2.4–3m (8–10ft) ↔ 1.8m (6ft) E ▣ ◊ ❋❋❋

Crambe cordifolia ♀ ↕ 2.4m (8ft) ↔ 1.5m (5ft) ▣ ◊ ❋❋❋

Crocosmia x *crocosmiiflora* ↕ 60cm (24in) ↔ 8cm (3in) ▣–▣ ◊ ❋❋❋

Dianthus 'Doris' ♀ ↕ 30–45cm (12–18in) ↔ 23–30cm (9–12in) E ▣ ◊ ❋❋❋

Echinops bannaticus ↕ 0.5–1.2m (1½–4ft) ↔ 60cm (24in) ▣ ◊ ❋❋❋

Erigeron karvinskianus ♀ ↕ 15–30cm (6–12in) ↔ 90cm (36in) ▣ ◊ ❋❋❋

Eryngium agavifolium ↕ 1–1.5m (3–5ft) ↔ 60cm (24in) ▣ ◊ ❋❋

Euphorbia griffithii 'Dixter' ♀ ↕ 75cm (30in) ↔ 90cm (36in) ▧ ◊ ❋❋❋

Eupatorium cannabinum ↕ 1.5m (5ft) ↔ 1.2m (4ft) ▣–▣ ◊ ❋❋❋

Hemerocallis lilioasphodelus ♀ ↕↔ 90cm (36in) E ▣ ◊ ❋❋❋

Iris germanica ♀ ↕ 60–120cm (24–48in) ↔ 60–90cm (24–36in) E ▣ ◊ ❋❋❋

Kniphofia caulescens ♀ ↕ 1.2m (4ft) ↔ 60cm (24in) E ▣–▣ ◊ ❋❋❋

Limonium platyphyllum ↕ 60cm (24in) ↔ 45cm (18in) ▣ ◊ ❋❋❋ [7]

Lychnis coronaria ♀ ↕ 80cm (32in) ↔ 45cm (18in) ▣–▣ ◊ ❋❋❋

Osteospermum jucundum ↕ 10–50cm (4–20in) ↔ 50–90cm (20–36in) E ▣ ◊ ❋❋❋ [8]

Phormium tenax ♀ ↕ 4m (12ft) ↔ 1.8m (6ft) E ▣ ◊ ❋❋

Salvia x *superba* ♀ ↕ 60–90cm (24–36in) ↔ 45–60cm (18–24in) ▣–▣ ◊ ❋❋❋

Sedum spectabile ♀ ↕↔ 45cm (18in) ▣ ◊ ❋❋❋

Stachys byzantina ↕ 45cm (18in) ↔ 60cm (24in) ▣–▣ ❋❋❋

1

2

3

4

5

6

7

8

CHOOSING PLANTS FOR GROUND COVER

Choosing plants for ground cover

Low-growing shrubs and perennials with spreading habits can quickly cover bare soil, creating a dense, attractive carpet with an impact of its own – it also helps to cut out weeding

There are plenty of plants with a low-growing and spreading habit and all may be termed "ground cover". But the prime requisite of a good ground-cover plant is that it can provide rapid cover, often with evergreen foliage or densely twiggy growth, that suppresses the germination and development of weeds, and reduces the need for weeding. Many also tolerate full or partial shade, making them a good low-maintenance solution for difficult sites. Whatever ground-cover plants you choose, some weeding will be necessary until the young plants have established and formed a good cover.

PLANTS FOR GOUND COVER

Planting distances are given, but position plants closer together on poor soils and in difficult situations. In good conditions effective cover should be achieved after two growing seasons.

Alchemilla mollis ♀ ‡ 60cm (24in), planting distance 30cm (12in) ▢–▨ ◊–◊ ❋❋❋

Berberis candidula ‡ 60cm (24in), planting distance 90cm (36in) E ▢–▨ ◊ ❋❋❋

Brachyglottis monroi ♀ ‡ 90cm (36in), planting distance 90cm (36in) E ▢ ◊ ❋❋❋

Calluna vulgaris ‡ 10–60cm (4–24in), planting distance 45–60cm (18–24in) E ▢ ◊ ❀ ❋❋❋

Cotoneaster conspicuus 'Decorus' ♀ ‡ 1.5m (5ft), planting distance 60cm (24in) E ▢–▨ ❋❋❋

Cotoneaster dammeri ♀ ‡ 20cm (8in), planting distance 60cm (24in) E ▢–▨ ◊ ❋❋❋

Cotoneaster horizontalis ♀ ‡ 90cm (36in), planting distance 60cm (24in) ▢–▨ ◊ ❋❋❋ ▢1

Cotoneaster x suecicus 'Skogholm' ‡ 60cm (24in), planting distance 90–120cm (3–4ft) E ▢–▨ ◊ ❋❋❋

Epimedium perralderianum ‡ 30cm (12in), planting distance 30cm (12in) E ▨ ◊ ❋❋❋

Erica carnea ‡ 20–25cm (8–10in), planting distance 45–60cm (18–24in) E ▢ ◊ ❋❋❋

Erica vagans ‡ 15–45cm (6–18in), planting distance 60cm (24in) E ▢ ◊ ❀ ❋❋❋ 'Lyonesse' ♀ ▢2

Euonymus fortunei 'Silver Queen' ‡ 60cm (24in), planting distance 90cm (36in) E ▢ ◊ ❋❋❋

Gaultheria procumbens ♀ ‡ 15cm (6in), planting distance 60cm (24in) E ▨ ◊ ❀ ❋❋❋

Genista hispanica ‡ 75cm (30in), planting distance 60cm (24in) ▢ ◊ ❋❋ ▢3

Geranium macrorrhizum 'Ingwersen's Variety' ♀ ‡ 50cm (20in), planting distance 45cm (18in), ▢–▨ ◊ ❋❋❋

Hebe pinguifolia 'Pagei' ♀ ‡ 30cm (12in), planting distance 45cm (18in) E ▢–▨ ◊ ❋❋❋

Hedera colchica 'Dentata Variegata' ♀ ‡ 15cm (6in), planting distance 90cm (36in) E ▨ ◊ ❋❋❋

Hypericum calycinum ‡ 60cm (24in), planting distance 45–60cm (18–24in) E ▢–▨ ◊ ❋❋❋

Juniperus rigida subsp. *conferta* ‡ 30cm (12in), planting distance 90cm (36in) E ▢–▨ ◊ ❋❋❋

Juniperus sabina 'Tamariscifolia' ‡ 1–2m (3–6ft), planting distance 1.2m (4ft) E ▢–▨ ◊ ❋❋❋

Lamium galeobdolon ‡ 60cm (24in), planting distance 60–90cm (24–36in) E ▨–▨ ◊ ❋❋❋

Lonicera pileata ‡ 60cm (24in), planting distance 60–90cm (24–36in) E ▢–▨ ◊ ❋❋❋

Mahonia aquifolium ‡ 90cm (36in), planting distance 45–60cm (18–24in) E ▨–▨ ◊ ❋❋❋

Pachysandra terminalis ♀ ‡ 20cm (8in), planting distance 30cm (12in) E ▨–▨ ◊–◊ ❋❋❋

Persicaria affinis 'Darjeeling Red' ♀ ‡ 25cm (10in), planting distance 30cm (12in) E ▨–▨ ◊ ❋❋❋

Potentilla fruticosa 'Manchu' ‡ 30cm (12in), planting distance 90cm (36in) ▢ ◊ ❋❋❋

Prunus laurocerasus 'Otto Luyken' ♀ ‡ 90cm (36in), planting distance 1–1.2m (3–4ft) E ▢–▨ ◊ ❋❋❋

Stachys byzantina 'Silver Carpet' ‡ 10cm (4in), planting distance 30cm (12in) E ▢ ◊ ❋❋❋

Stephanandra incisa 'Crispa' ‡ 60cm (24in), planting distance 90cm (36in) ▢–▨ ◊ ❋❋❋

Symphytum ibericum ‡ 40cm (16in), planting distance 30cm (12in) ▢–▨ ◊ ❋❋❋

Taxus baccata 'Repandens' ♀ ‡ 60cm (24in), planting distance 1.5m (5ft) E ▢–▨ ◊ ❋❋❋

Vinca minor ‡ 10–20cm (4–8in), planting distance 60cm (24in) E ▢–▨ ◊–◊ ❋❋❋

Waldsteinia ternata ‡ 10cm (4in), planting distance 30cm (12in) E ▨–▨ ◊–◊ ❋❋❋

Vinca minor

See also What to plant under trees, p.64; Choosing shrubs for growing in shade, pp.83–84; Best plants for shade, p.140

Raised beds

Building a raised bed in the garden allows you to grow a greater variety of plants, but it can also be a feature in its own right

Raised beds have several benefits. As well as adding interest to a garden they permit a wider range of plants to be grown on difficult soils, or soils with an inappropriate pH. Improved drainage conditions mean that the soil warms up more rapidly in spring, allowing an earlier start to the vegetable-growing season. Raised beds can reduce or even eliminate the need to bend down, so they are ideal for less agile gardeners.

Materials vary in cost and ease of construction. Brick and stone are the most expensive but offer a permanent structure if bonded with mortar. Both need concrete foundations if over four courses high. Make them up to 15cm (6in) deep and 30cm (12in) wide.

For less-ornate areas, gravel boards are a cheap, easy-to-use alternative. Simply screw them on to corner posts. Railway sleepers make good beds, and can be fixed into place by hammering metal rods into holes drilled vertically in each corner, or by using heavy-duty staples and wire.

BUILDING A BRICK BED

Think about the design before you start: a sequence of smaller linked beds, or perhaps a circular bed, may look more imaginative and interesting than the traditional rectangle. Ideally, construct the bed using frost-proof bricks. After preparing the concrete footing, lay the first course of bricks below soil level. Stagger the courses to strengthen the walls.

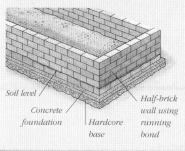

Soil level

Concrete foundation

Hardcore base

Half-brick wall using running bond

Run long vegetable beds north to south for even sunlight. Make them 1.2m (4ft) wide with a 45cm (18in) wide path in between. Cover paths in old carpet or similar material as they can become too compacted to hoe.

Line beds for lime-hating plants with plastic sheeting to separate lime mortar and garden soil from the roots.

On poorly-drained soils place drainage material in the base of permanent structures and cover with a membrane before filling with soil.

The type of soil or compost to use will be governed by the plants you intend to grow, but organic matter and grit are always useful additions. When you have filled a bed, allow the soil to settle for two weeks before planting. For vegetable beds, simply fork over the base before filling, adding organic matter to the depth of the spade blade.

Vegetable beds

If you are building beds for vegetables, make them about 1.2m (4ft) wide, and leave space for a path in between to ensure that the centre of each bed is easily accessible for sowing and cultivation.

PLANTS FOR SLOPES

On very steep slopes coarse coconut matting or a similar biodegradable material can be pegged down to prevent soil erosion until the ground cover establishes. Plant through the matting. Planting distance: 90–120cm (3–4ft).

Ceanothus thyrsiflorus var. *repens* ♀
↕ 90cm (36in) E ▣ ◊ ✳✳✳

Euonymus fortunei 'Dart's Blanket'
↕ 60cm (24in) E ▣–▣ ◊ ✳✳✳

Gaultheria shallon ↕ 1.2m (4ft) E ▣ ◊ ♨
✳✳✳ 4

Jasminum nudiflorum ♀ ↕ 15cm (6in) ▣–▣
◊ ✳✳✳

Lonicera japonica 'Halliana' ♀ ↕ 15cm
(6in) E ▣–▣ ◊ ✳✳✳

Mahonia repens ↕ 30cm (12in) E ▣–▣ ◊
✳✳✳

Parthenocissus quinquefolia ♀ ↕ 15cm
(6in) ▣–▣ ◊ ✳✳✳

Rubus tricolor ↕ 30cm (12in) E ▣–▣ ◊ ✳✳✳

Stephanandra incisa 'Crispa' ↕ 60cm (24in)
▣–▣ ◊ ✳✳✳

Symphoricarpos x *chenaultii* 'Hancock'
↕ 60–90cm (24–36in) ▣–▣ ◊ ✳✳✳

Trachelospermum jasminoides ♀ ↕ 30cm
(12in) E ▣–▣ ◊ ✳✳ 5

See also Planning small gardens, p.18; Gardening on wet soils, p.260

Making pergolas and arbours

Planned and planted with care, these supporting structures covered with climbing plants will provide an attractive garden feature that can last a lifetime

Pergolas and arbours are used as design features and also add height to a garden. At its most elaborate, a pergola is an ornate structure that leads the eye along a vista, to a focal point like a statue or sculpture. Pergolas can also be used to mark a change in path direction. In smaller gardens a pergola can be a simple timber structure over a path, used as a decorative support for climbing plants to create a floral tunnel.

Small arbours can provide intimate, enclosed seating spaces, perhaps clothed with sweetly scented climbers and offering seclusion and privacy.

Designs

There are many designs of pergola and arbour from which to choose, from the preformed, jointed and flat-packed to a bespoke made-to-measure leviathan that will take a team of skilled craftsmen a few days to erect. Between these extremes there is the self-designed pergola or arbour, made to your specifications by a local sawmill or timber merchant. Regardless, there are a few rules to observe. If building more than one in a garden, stick to the same overall style. Keep the scale and size in proportion with the house and garden. Use materials that are in harmony with the local environment.

A rustic pergola
Design your pergola to complement the style of the garden. The rustic timber pergola shown here is ideally suited to this country garden, providing sturdy supports for climbing and rambler roses.

Construction

The actual erection and construction is a relatively straightforward operation, as long as the ground is well pegged and marked out using sand, string and stakes. Constantly check measurements, and lay out the components to ensure that nothing has been forgotten. You will need at least two pairs of hands, not only for construction, but also to spread the load of the groundwork and digging.

Make pathways at least 90cm (36in) wide although wider is preferable, about 1.2m (4ft). A narrow paved path can be edged with pea shingle or ornamental gravel bounded by 15 x 2.5cm (6 x 1in) pressure-treated boards or brick edging if you have to compromise.

Provide substantial foundations for the uprights. These can be of the 'metal spike' variety or made from hardcore and concrete. As a guide, you should ensure that 20–25 per cent of the total length of the uprights is embedded in the ground. You will need a hole about 60cm (24in) deep for a 15 x 15cm (6 x 6in) timber pergola upright of 2.7m (9ft) length, giving 2.1m (7ft) clearance above the ground. Less substantial timbers of 10 x 10cm (4 x 4in) may also be used. Keep the hole no wider than a spade's width and place half a brick or large stone at the bottom. Half fill the hole around the upright with tightly packed hardcore, continuously checking

GETTING IT ALL SQUARED UP

Make sure you provide substantial foundations for the uprights of a pergola or arbour. For large-scale construction, foundations of hardcore and concrete are recommended. For smaller structures suitable for the average garden, metal post supports, like those shown here, are easy to use.

Simply hammer them into the ground with a sledgehammer. Use a spirit level to check that the post support is being driven in vertically. Hold the spirit level against all four sides in turn. Check the uprights in a similar way if bedding them in concrete. In this instance they will need temporary support to keep them vertical while the concrete sets.

See also How to plant climbers, p.95; Ways of using clematis, pp.99–100; Choosing climbing roses, pp.104–105

the vertical aspect with a long spirit level, and top up with concrete. To prevent any subsequent movement from the vertical, prop up the posts using temporary supports while you wait for the concrete to set.

When all the uprights are secure in set concrete, the various crossbars, support trusses and trellis panels can be attached. Do not attempt to take any short cuts, because these can jeopardise the stability and longevity of your feature. A nail is no substitute for the right size brass wood-screw. Although preformed brass or steel brackets can save large amounts of joinery work or angled pre-drilling, they can be unsightly when used on visible surfaces.

Planting

Try to select a good mixture of evergreen and deciduous climbers to ensure that there is plenty of colour and interest provided throughout the year. Many plants peak in spring and summer, including climbing roses, *Humulus lupulus* 'Aureus' (golden hop), *Clematis* and *Lonicera* (honeysuckle), while in autumn the intense scarlet leaves of *Vitis coignetiae* are particularly welcome.

A wide variety of clematis can be grown, but if you are partnering one with a climbing rose it is advisable to select from the Viticella or Texensis Groups, such as *C.* 'Alba Luxurians' or *C.* 'Gravetye Beauty'. These clematis will tolerate being pruned back hard annually during winter or early spring, which allows you to gain access to other shrubs or climbers for pruning and training. Annuals, such as *Tropaeolum majus* (nasturtium) and *Lathyrus odoratus* (sweet pea) cultivars, or frost-tender perennials including *Eccremocarpus scaber* and *Ipomoea* (morning glory) can serve the same purpose.

With larger pergolas a common practice is to plant two climbers near the base of each pillar – for example, a strong-growing climbing rose with a less-vigorous *Clematis* or *Lonicera* (honeysuckle), the rose providing the support for the other climber. Strong-growing climbers such as *Clematis montana* 'Rubens' or wisterias are too large and vigorous for small pergolas.

Some climbing roses may be less vigorous on a pergola than when trained against a wall. Vigorous rambling roses with long, flexible, easily trained stems are suitable for pergolas but most ramblers or strong-growing climbing roses might be considered. However, do avoid excessively tall and rampant roses such as 'Rambling Rector'.

Do not ignore valuable space along paths and at the base of columns. These can be effectively planted with shade-tolerant plants such as *Brunnera macrophylla*, or in sunny areas edged with *Lavandula* (lavender) or *Rosmarinus officinalis* (rosemary) Ground-covering plants such as *Geranium* 'Johnson's Blue' and diascias can be used to spill over paths and soften hard edges, while *Mentha requienii* (Corsican mint) will thrive in unmortared cracks in the paving.

Planting arbours, especially smaller ones, can be a problem due to the twin demands for seating space and overall visual impact. Therefore in this situation, choose more compact climbers such as the thornless climbing rose 'Zéphirine Drouhin', or plants that will recover well from hard pruning.

Ideal companions

For some interesting effects, try growing two climbers together up each of the pergola's uprights. A popular combination consists of climbing roses and clematis. Choose a clematis that can be pruned back hard each winter or early spring. Here red rose hips and the silvery seed heads of clematis provide a pleasing effect in autumn (*top left*). Two different roses could be grown together such as the pink climber 'Bantry Bay' and the white rambler 'Albéric Barbier' (*top right*). *Eccremocarpus scaber* and *Thunbergia alata* 'African Sunset' (*left*), both grown as annuals, also make exciting companions.

Cut flowers

With careful selection it is possible to have flowers for cutting all year round, whether annuals, biennials, perennials, or bulbous plants, and some can be dried for winter use

THE PICK OF THE BUNCH

Early to late winter

Galanthus Bulbous, flowers to early spring ▨ ◊ ✳✳✳

Helleborus Perennial, flowers to early spring ▨ ◊ ✳✳✳

Iris unguicularis Perennial, flowers to early spring; fragrant ▢ ◊ ✳✳✳

Narcissus (including daffodils) Bulbous, flowers to late spring; fragrant ▢–▨ ◊ ✳✳✳

Early spring

Anemone coronaria Bulbous, flowers to mid-spring ▢ ◊ ✳✳✳

Hyacinthus orientalis Bulbous, flowers to mid-spring; fragrant ▢–▨ ◊ ✳✳✳

Mid-spring

Convallaria majalis ♥ Perennial, flowers to late spring; fragrant ▢–▨ ◊ ✳✳✳

Erysimum cheiri (wallflower) Biennial, flowers to early summer; fragrant ▢ ◊ ✳✳✳

Tulipa Bulbous, flowers to late spring ▢ ◊ ✳✳✳

Late spring

Aquilegia Perennial, flowers to early summer ▢–▨ ◊ ✳✳✳

Calendula officinalis (pot marigold) Hardy annual, flowers to mid-autumn ▢ ◊ ✳✳✳

Iris Perennial, flowers to early summer ▢ ◊ ✳✳✳

Paeonia Perennial, flowers to early summer ▢–▨ ◊ ✳✳✳

Papaver orientale Perennial, flowers to early summer ▢ ◊ ✳✳✳

Early summer

Alchemilla mollis ♥ Perennial, flowers to early autumn ▢–▨ ◊ ✳✳✳

Alstroemeria Bulbous, flowers to early autumn ▢–▨ ◊ ✳✳

Centaurea cyanus (cornflower) Hardy annual, flowers to early autumn ▢ ◊ ✳✳✳

Consolida ajacis Hardy annual, flowers to early autumn; can be dried ▢ ◊ ✳✳✳

Delphinium Perennial, flowers to mid-summer; can be dried ▢ ◊ ✳✳✳

Digitalis Biennial, flowers to mid-summer ▨ ◊–◊ ✳✳✳

Gypsophila paniculata Perennial, flowers to late summer; can be dried ▢ ◊ ✳✳✳

Lathyrus odoratus (sweet pea) Hardy annual, flowers to early autumn; fragrant ▢ ◊ ✳✳✳

Limonium sinuatum Hardy annual, flowers to early autumn, can be dried ▢ ◊ ✳✳

Scabiosa atropurpurea Hardy annual, flowers to early autumn ▢ ◊ ✳✳✳

Tanacetum coccineum Perennial ▢ ◊ ✳✳✳

Midsummer

Achillea filipendulina Perennial, flowers to early autumn; can be dried ▢ ◊ ✳✳✳

Agapanthus Perennial, flowers to early autumn ▢ ◊ ✳✳✳–✳

Antirrhinum majus Half-hardy annual, flowers to mid-autumn; fragrant ▢ ◊ ✳

Echinops Perennial, flowers to late summer; can be dried ▢ ◊ ✳✳✳–✳✳

Gladiolus Bulbous, flowers to early autumn ▢ ◊ ✳

Heliopsis helianthoides Perennial, flowers to early autumn ▢ ◊ ✳✳✳

Phlox paniculata Perennial, flowers to early autumn; fragrant ▢–▨ ◊ ✳✳✳

Rudbeckia fulgida Perennial, flowers to early autumn ▢–▨ ◊ ✳✳✳

Zinnia Tender annual, flowers to late summer ▢ ◊ ☁

Late summer

Anaphalis triplinervis ♥ Perennial, can be dried ▢ ◊ ✳✳✳

Aster amellus Perennial, flowers to early autumn ▢ ◊ ✳✳✳

Cosmos bipinnatus Half-hardy annual, flowers to early autumn ▢ ◊ ✳

Dahlia Bulbous, to mid-autumn ▢ ◊ ✳

Rudbeckia hirta Hardy annual, flowers to mid-autumn ▢–▨ ◊ ✳✳✳

Solidago Perennial, flowers to early autumn; can be dried ▢ ◊ ✳✳✳

Early to late autumn

Physalis alkekengi var. *franchetii* Perennial, can be dried ▢–▨ ◊ ✳✳✳

Schizostylis Perennial, flowers to late autumn ▢ ◊ ✳✳

Sedum spectabile ♥ Perennial, flowers to mid-autumn ▢ ◊ ✳✳✳

Popular cut flowers

Left to right: Galanthus, Narcissus, Hyacinthus orientalis, Calendula officinalis, Alchemilla mollis, Digitalis, Antirrhinum majus, Cosmos bipinnatus, Sedum spectabile

Weeds and weed control

The best long-term solution to weed control is to mulch your beds and borders of permanent plants, but to eradicate persistent perennial weeds you may have to resort to weedkillers

In spring, mulch shrub and herbaceous borders with a thick layer of organic matter, such as spent mushroom compost (not for use around acid-loving plants), well-rotted manure, wood or bark chippings, spent hops, garden compost, coir, or a sawdust and manure mixture (from stables) to drastically reduce the number of weed seedlings that appear during the growing season.

In areas to be replanted with permanent plants, prepare and level the soil, then cover the bed with a planting membrane to prevent weed growth. To plant, cut a cross-shaped slit in the membrane, fold back the flaps and dig the planting hole. Replace the flaps after planting. Mulch the membrane with a thin layer of organic material or pea shingle.

Annual weeds

Many annual weed seedlings can appear during spring in unmulched borders. If you do not eliminate them, the weeds will smother your plants, robbing them of moisture and foods, and then go on to spread numerous seeds, continuing the cycle.

Shallow cultivation with a Dutch hoe can kill weeds, especially on fine, breezy days. Going deeper brings up seeds to germinate. In rainy spells, when hoeing is less effective, consider using a contact weedkiller containing

Mulching borders
In spring, spread a thick mulch of organic matter in borders with permanent plants, like shrubs and perennials, to suppress weeds (*left*). When making new, long-term plantings, use a membrane to cover the soil to prevent weed growth and plant through it (*above left*). Conceal the membrane with a thin layer of pea shingle (*above right*) or organic matter.

paraquat and diquat. This will kill any weeds it touches, even in poor weather. Since this type of weedkiller is not absorbed by brown bark it can be used right up to the base of woody plants.

Perennial weeds in borders

Perennial weeds such as *Aegopodium podagraria* (ground elder, *see p.32*), *Elymus repens* (couch grass), *Convolvulus arvensis* (field bindweed, *see p.32*) and *Ranunculus repens* (creeping buttercup) are difficult to eliminate from among valued plants.

When they have taken hold in borders the best remedy is to fork over the infested area in mid-spring and remove as much weed as possible. Spray any regrowth with weedkiller containing glyphosate as soon as the weed is noticed or spot-treat small patches with a gel formulation of glyphosate.

Hand weeding and 'winkling out' roots with a trowel weakens weeds, and a thick organic mulch helps to suppress further regrowth. However, such weeds are unlikely to be totally eliminated without the use of weedkillers.

Weedkillers containing glyphosate

Kill annual weeds by shallow hoeing

kill all plants so be careful how you use them. To kill weeds with spot applications you may need to give several treatments. Another tactic is to cover your valuable plants with plastic bags and then spray the remaining unwanted vegetation with weedkiller.

PERENNIAL WEEDS

When perennial weeds take over borders fork out as much as possible in spring. Spray any regrowth with glyphosate weedkiller, taking care to protect any valued plants. Alternatively spot treat small patches of weeds with a gel formulation of this weedkiller, reducing the risk of getting it on the leaves of garden plants.

See also Weedkiller damage, p.36; The benefits of mulching, pp.269–270

PLANT PROBLEMS

Brambles and nettles

You may need weedkillers to eradicate these perennials

Brambles (*Rubus fruticosus*), stinging nettle (*Urtica dioica*) and creeping thistle (*Cirsium arvense*) are all nuisance perennial weeds that can quickly colonise neglected ground.

Control

You may be able to fork out small patches of perennial weeds, but when large clumps have formed you may find that chemical control is the most efficient way to eradicate them.

CHEMICAL CONTROL

Contact weedkillers simply scorch the foliage, allowing new top growth to regenerate from the perennial root system. **1** Systemic weedkillers that are sprayed on to the foliage provide the best means of control. **2** The chemicals travel down to the roots and kill the plants. The most effective currently available preparations contain glyphosate, ammonium sulphamate, or 2,4-D plus dicamba plus mecoprop-P.

Each active ingredient has its own properties – for example, some are non-selective or persist in the soil for up to six to eight weeks. Before use, always check manufacturer's recommendations.

See also Weed control, p.31

PLANT PROBLEMS

Eradicating bindweed

These ubiquitous climbing weeds are very deep rooting

Field bindweed (*Convolvulus arvensis, above*) is a weak-stemmed plant with small white or pink trumpet-shaped flowers. *Calystegia sepium* (bellbind, or great bindweed) has heart-shaped leaves and large white or pink trumpet flowers.

Control

Both types of bindweed are difficult to eradicate as roots can penetrate the soil as deeply as 1.8m (6ft), and the underground stems may extend 1.8m (6ft) or more in one season.

Digging out or repeated hoeing can achieve good results if carried out regularly for one or two years. Alternatively spray with glyphosate between mid- and late summer. However, as bindweed frequently twines around cultivated plants, this weedkiller will also kill the host plant. In this case unwind the weed from the host, lay it on the ground and then spray it. Protect cultivated plants from spray drift. For more accurate treatment, apply a gel formulation of glyphosate with a brush.

For dense infestations you may need to move cultivated plants temporarily to a clean area during the winter, and carry out weedkiller treatment the following summer.

See also Weed control, p.31

PLANT PROBLEMS

Dealing with ground elder

Control this nightmare weed by manual or chemical means

Ground elder or bishop's weed (*Aegopodium podagraria*) is a widespread, invasive weed. It is usually introduced into gardens as pieces of whitish, fleshy, underground stems (rhizomes) that are hidden in the soil around roots of acquired plants or in composts.

Ground elder quickly spreads by its underground stems, and can easily choke all but the most vigorous garden plants. It is even able to push its way through tarmac.

Control

You can remove the network of underground stems by forking them out, but even the smallest remaining piece can start a new colony.

When ground elder is growing among the roots of garden plants, the most practical method of control is to dig out the cultivated plants, carefully remove the weed roots and transfer the plants to weed-free soil until the infected areas have been cleared.

Glyphosate weedkiller is the most reliable and rapid means of control where there are no valuable garden plants. Apply it to the foliage when the weed is growing vigorously.

Ground elder (*Aegopodium podagraria*)

See also Weed control, p.31

Ivy as a weed

Left unchecked, ivy climbs up buildings and trees and spreads through borders, hiding faults and smothering other plants

Common ivy (*Hedera helix*) is an evergreen, self-clinging climber that can be grown to mask unsightly concrete or brickwork. However, it may also hide structural faults or prevent the maintenance of buildings, so there may be times when you need to remove it.

Ivy is often a problem in borders, extending from the base of hedges, and rooting from each leaf joint as it spreads.

Control

When ivy is well established in borders, digging it out can be very disruptive and damaging to the roots of other plants, although it is one possible option. Where you can, control it with glyphosate weedkiller. The best period for application is during winter when ivy is relatively dormant, but avoid areas underplanted with bulbs because they can be in active growth at that time and may be damaged or killed.

If ivy is growing up trees, it can be killed by cutting through the stems close to ground level. Usually there is little or no regrowth but to guarantee this, remove a 10cm (4in) section of each stem, then apply a chemical stump killer. These include formulations of ammonium sulphamate. They can be applied as crystals to the surface of the freshly cut stump, or as a solution to thoroughly wet the stump to ground level.

Hidden flaws
Although ivy can effectively conceal eyesores, it also covers up structural problems that can develop over time.

Ivy quickly covers walls
Contrary to popular belief, ivy will not damage walls, provided they are sound. However, if the walls contain cracks, ivy may find its way in and make them worse.

Take care to prevent excessive run-off into the soil, particularly if there are garden plants growing near the base of the ivy.

Ivy is easily removed from walls and other hard surfaces simply by ripping off the stems. However, the aerial roots with which the ivy supports itself will be left behind and can look unsightly. Remove them with a wire brush or, to make life easier, fit a wire-brush attachment to an electric drill.

IVY ON TREES

Ivy seldom harms trees, merely using them for support. It gets its needs from its own leaves and roots. Usually only trees already in decline, with a thin leaf canopy, carry heavy ivy growth. Although trees with dense ivy should be inspected for safety, spare them if possible as ivy provides valuable food and shelter for wildlife.

See also Weed control, p.31; Ivy on buildings, p.103

Eliminating horsetail

The roots of this weed are too deep to dig out

Horsetail (*Equisetum arvense*) has deep, fragile roots, which means that you will be wasting your time trying to dig it out; any small pieces of root left in the soil will simply re-grow.

Control

Repeated destruction of foliage by hoeing and shallow digging will weaken, and after a year or two eliminate, this weed from beds and borders if done thoroughly and often. Improving drainage will also help.

An alternative treatment is to spray the leaves with an approved weedkiller, such as glyphosate or glufosinate ammonium, in late summer when the weeds have maximum foliage. Bruising the plants by walking or dragging a heavy object over them will help to break down the waxy leaf coating and assist in the penetration and effectiveness of the weedkiller, but even so, to control horsetail completely, you will need to make more than one application.

Horsetail (*Equisetum arvense*)

See also Weed control, p.31

KEEPING HARD SURFACES CLEAN

Keeping hard surfaces clean

Paths and patios can become covered with slippery green moss and algae, and weeds may grow in gaps; you can scrub to keep the surfaces clean, but chemical methods may also help

Moss and algae are found in damp places as not only do they need moisture for growth, but also for reproduction. Contrary to popular belief, neither of these plants actually damage hard surfaces, and they can add interest to what could be sterile areas. Walls and hard standing areas covered in moss give a mature look to a garden and may be considered an interesting feature in the right place.

Unfortunately moss and algae growing on paths and patios can make surfaces slippery and dangerous and so you may need to take steps to ensure the safety of users. Moss and algae are most likely to be a problem on hard surfaces in perpetual shade with a tendency to remain damp.

Cultural control

As moss and algae thrive in damp, sunless places where there is little air movement, try to open up the site by cutting back overhanging trees and shrubs. This will allow the drying effects of sun and wind to penetrate the site. Improving the drainage in the surrounding area will also help to deter algae and moss.

Keep steps clean
Garden steps, especially those in shade, can become very slippery with algae and moss, making them dangerous. Do not allow steps get into that state, but keep them clean using a pressure washer or by regular brushing.

Mechanical removal

A pressure washer can remove moss and algae effectively. However use this method with care in areas with poor, unsatisfactory drainage as the extra water may serve to exacerbate damp problems. Pressure washers are expensive to buy but you may be able to hire one on a daily basis. Wear goggles when using the machine. Pressure washing is the most efficient method of removing moss and algae from wooden garden features such as seats. After washing fences, sheds and other wooden structures, treat them with appropriate wood preservatives, and use teak oil on garden furniture.

Regularly brush hard surfaces with a stiff broom because this helps to prevent moss and algae from taking hold. Rake any loose surfaces such as gravel paths to ensure these areas are kept free from moss and weeds.

Chemical control

Use a proprietary path and patio cleaner according to the maker's instructions. It will remove moss, algae and stains and can also restore the natural colour of the paving. Alternatively, you could use a proprietary outdoor disinfectant. Do not

Pressure washer
This will rapidly and efficiently remove moss and algae from hard surfaces (*right*), bringing them up like new (*above*). You can also use it to clean other garden features such as seats and statuary.

SAFETY FIRST

As with many gardening jobs, protect your eyes by wearing a pair of goggles when using a pressure washer. Like most other pieces of safety equipment, these are generally readily available from suppliers of garden tools and machinery, and from some garden centres and DIY stores.

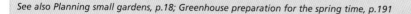

See also Planning small gardens, p.18; Greenhouse preparation for the spring time, p.191

MORTARING JOINTS

Weeds will quickly appear in gaps between bricks used for paving, as well as between paving setts and slabs. The best and most easily achieved solution is to mortar the joints after laying. **1** Brush a dry mortar mix of sand and cement into the gaps between the paving. **2** Then moisten the paved area with water and allow the mortar to set.

use lawn moss killers on paving as some of them will leave stains that are impossible to remove.

Weeds on patios

Weeds will appear in the gaps between paving slabs when they have not been mortared. Weeds are also a problem on patios created from setts where the joints are filled with sand or ground chalk instead of cement grouting. However, help is at hand, in the form of proprietary path and patio weedkillers. These contain several types of weedkiller, which both kill existing weeds and prevent weed seeds from germinating. The treatment lasts for several months. Alternatively, weeds can be winkled out from cracks using a daisy grubber. This is obviously very time consuming, although fine if there are only a few weeds to deal with.

Japanese knotweed

A relentless spreader that needs a concerted effort to kill it

Japanese knotweed (*Fallopia japonica, above*) came to Britain from Japan in 1825 as an ornamental herbaceous perennial. It is an attractive, but relentless spreader, overwhelming other garden plants. It does not produce seeds, but it can establish from very small sections of underground stem (rhizome). In Britain it is now an offence to spread Japanese knotweed in the country.

Control

Digging out roots is often difficult or impossible. A more reliable solution is to apply glyphosate weedkiller. This is most effective from mid- to late summer, but by then, with knotweed reaching 1.8m (6ft) or more in height, spraying is often impractical.

Instead, allow knotweed to reach the largest manageable size for spraying, usually no more than 1m (3ft), which will be achieved in late spring. If sprayed at this stage, there will be some regrowth in late summer or the following spring. Spray any regrowth in early autumn before the weed dies down later in the season. Check again the following spring.

See also Weeds and weed control, p.31

Invasive oxalis

Some species of oxalis are capable of spreading rapidly

Although some *Oxalis* make good ornamental plants, others are weeds, spreading rapidly by seeds or by numerous underground bulbils. The perennial bulbous species *Oxalis debilis* spreads by bulbils, while *O. corniculata* often grows as an annual, spreading by seeds.

Control

To control *O. debilis*, fork it out in spring when the tiny bulbils are firmly attached to the parent plant. If you wait until later in the season, the bulbils are more easily detached, and you may accidentally help to spread the weed.

If a border is badly infected with *O. debilis* you could grass it down permanently. It is better to sacrifice all the other plants (except perhaps bulbs) rather than risk transferring oxalis bulbils to other parts of the garden attached to the roots of shrubs or perennials.

Deep mulching can be attempted on infested shrub borders. Use at least 10cm (4in) of coarse bark or similar material.

Suppress and control *O. debilis* with glyphosate weedkiller. Apply in spring when the weed is growing strongly. You could use a gel formulation for spot treatment of small patches. Also use glyphosate against *O. corniculata*.

Oxalis bulbils are clearly visible at the base of the leaf stalks.

Oxalis species

Weedkiller damage

Signs of weedkiller damage to garden plants are striking

Two popular groups of weedkiller, hormone-based and glyphosate, often cause damage when inadvertently allowed to come into contact with ornamental plants.

Weedkiller damage

Hormone weedkillers are used for selective control of broad-leaved weeds in lawns, though some formulations are used to kill nettles, brambles and other coarse or woody weeds.

Symptoms vary according to the plant. Leaf blades may be distorted and narrow so that the veins become closely crowded and then appear to be parallel. Sometimes the foliage, leaf stalks and stems become cup shaped or twisted.

Most annual plants will not recover. Perennials and shrubs often recover within a season with no apparent long-term damage.

Glyphosate damage appears as a bleaching of the young foliage. Instead of developing normal sideshoots, stunted rosettes of short shoots emerge, bearing strap-like leaves.

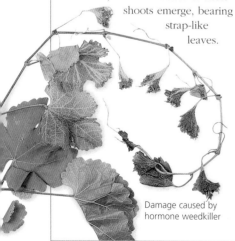

Damage caused by hormone weedkiller

See also Weeds and weed control, p.31

Avoiding pests and diseases

Chemical pesticides are not the only way of reducing the problems caused by pests and diseases

Cultural methods, which largely aim to prevent pests and diseases from occuring through good gardening practice, will not usually eliminate them altogether. However, they help to reduce the degree of damage and may sometimes make it unnecessary to resort to pesticides. Therefore even where pesticides are acceptable, cultural methods should always be considered as well. However, if you rely only on cultural controls and do not use chemical pesticides at all, you will often have to accept some damage.

Remove dead foliage to prevent disease infection

Hygiene
Remove dead and over-shaded leaves as these can easily become infected by diseases such as grey mould (*Botrytis cinerea*) which then spread to healthy leaves and flowers. They also harbour pests such as slugs and snails. Plants badly affected by pests and diseases are best removed if they are unlikely to make a quick recovery. If roots have been affected, carefully take away the whole root system and the immediately associated soil, to ensure that all traces of the pest or disease are removed.

Weeds
Remove weeds, as they compete for plant foods and water and therefore stress cultivated plants. They can also act as alternative hosts for pests, including aphids, red spider mite and whitefly, and for diseases.

Resistance
Many plants have some cultivars that are more resistant to disease or pest attack than others, especially in the case of diseases such as mildews and rusts. The resistance may be within the plant tissues or it may come as the result of a different growth pattern: for instance,

Pest-resistant day lilies
Cultivars of *Hemerocallis* that flower from mid-summer onwards, such as *H.* 'Betty Woods', *H. fulva* 'Europa' and *H.* 'Marion Vaughn' (*left to right*), all escape attacks by hemerocallis gall midge (*Contarinia quinquenotata*), which causes flower buds to become abnormally swollen and remain closed.

See also Using biological controls, pp.40–41; Growing vegetables without chemicals, pp.200–201

Luring earwigs away from plants
To trap earwigs, fill flower pots with straw, and invert them on canes among susceptible plants (particularly dahlias). Inspect traps in the morning; remove any earwigs and destroy them.

some cultivars of *Hemerocallis* (day lily) flower later in the summer, allowing them to escape attack by gall midge.

Rotation

Do not put the same types of plants in the same place year after year, since this will help soil-borne pests and diseases to build up. For example, the spores of downy mildew and leaf spot disease of pansies remain in the soil from the previous planting.

Traps

Some pests can be trapped, then removed or destroyed. For example, 'slug pubs' capture slugs or snails, and straw-filled flower pots attract earwigs.

Good cultivation

Finally, it is important to grow plants correctly with careful attention to planting, feeding, watering, deadheading, pruning, and propagation. Well-grown plants often stay healthy.

Pansy leaf spot

Systemic chemicals

Make pest and disease control easy by using systemic pesticides and fungicides; they rapidly get right to the heart of the problem

Unlike protectant or contact pesticides, which remain on the leaf surface, systemic pesticides are absorbed by the plant and then travel away from the point of application.

Systemic treatments have a number of advantages. Smaller quantities are needed for effective control, they cannot be washed off by rain, and accurate placement on the plant is less critical. They also reach sap-sucking pests within buds that are otherwise difficult to penetrate with contact insecticides. Similarly, systemic weedkillers, such as glyphosate, penetrate and kill all parts of the weed.

Since systemics cannot be washed off, great care must be taken to observe the safe 'withholding periods' before harvesting certain edible crops. As with all pesticides these are fixed so that by the end of the period the concentration of the chemical within the plant will have declined to below the maximum acceptable limit.

Chemicals initially enter plant tissues through the roots or the waxy leaf surface. Since the surface tends to be thinner on leaves' undersides, especially in broad-leaved plants, spraying the undersides enhances uptake. Once it has penetrated the leaf, movement is often only within that leaf. However, some systemics may enter the system through which liquids circulate within the plant. They may also be carried up

Tackle hollyhock rust with an approved fungicide

Use a secure, locked cupboard for storage

the plant with the 'stream' of water caused by the continual evaporation of water from leaf and stem surfaces. In this case they may move into the most actively transpiring leaves. There is little passage into old wood; movement is usually confined to recent growth.

Fungicides and insecticides

The range of systemic fungicides and insecticides has been drastically reduced in recent years but there are still several very useful products.

Examples of systemic fungicides are penconazole, myclobutanil and flutriafol. These provide rust, powdery mildew and blackspot control on ornamental plants.

The only garden systemic insecticide is imidacloprid, which controls sap-sucking pests such as aphids, whitefly, mealybug and scale insects on ornamental plants and certain ▷

See also Using fungicides, pp.38–39; Disposing of old chemicals, p.39

SYSTEMIC CHEMICALS

greenhouse vegetables. Some container composts contain imidacloprid to control pests such as vine weevil grubs, aphids and fungus gnats (*Bradysia* species). Imidacloprid can also be applied as a drench for pot plants.

Pesticide 'cocktail' products, which contain a systemic fungicide as well as an insecticide, are available to help to control diseases and pests that attack roses, including rose black spot, rose powdery mildew, rose rust and aphids.

The statutory conditions on pesticide labels now include specified uses for each product, and safety precautions that are legally enforceable.

Viburnum whitefly pupae
Whitefly, including those that attack *Viburnum tinus* (laurustinus), can be controlled with the systemic insecticide imidacloprid. This also controls other sap-sucking pests such as aphids.

USING CHEMICALS SAFELY

- Read the product label to determine precisely what the chemical is for and whether it is appropriate for the problem and the plant you have in mind
- Always apply chemicals according to the manufacturer's instructions
- Avoid contact with the eyes and skin, and do not inhale chemicals
- Wear rubber gloves when handling concentrates
- Do not mix different products together
- Keep children and animals well away, and never eat, drink or smoke when applying chemicals
- Do not use pesticides in windy weather
- Spray in the late afternoon, early evening or early morning
- Carefully consider any risk to children if using composts containing chemicals
- Ensure adequate ventilation if spraying in enclosed areas such as greenhouses or conservatories; take particular care to avoid skin contact or inhalation
- Under glass, avoid spraying in the hotter, brighter parts of the day to reduce risk of scorching

PREPARING AND APPLYING CHEMICAL SPRAYS

1 Always read the manufacturer's instructions carefully. Wear rubber gloves to prevent contact with the skin and take care not to spill any of the chemical. Accurately measure out the required amount of concentrate. Try not to make up any more of the preparation than you need, to avoid having to store or dispose of the surplus afterwards.

2 Partially fill the sprayer with water and then carefully pour the concentrate in. Rinse out the measurer with water and add this to the sprayer. Top up to the required level with water and close all containers. Return the chemical container to a secure storage place.

3 If possible, when applying the chemical mixture to plants, spray both the upper and lower surfaces of the leaves to achieve maximum uptake. This is less important with systemic pesticides than for contact types. The best time to spray is at dusk or very early in the morning to minimize risk to pollinating insects and to help prevent scorching of plants.

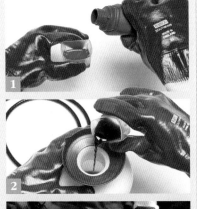
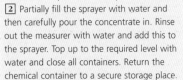

Using fungicides

Apply fungicides as a preventative measure before disease strikes

As the name suggests, fungicides are designed to kill fungi that cause plant diseases. The product label indicates which plants may be treated. It is a statutory requirement to follow these instructions, and illegal to use fungicides for purposes other than those indicated on the label, or to use an unlabelled compound for disease control.

Protectant or systemic?

Protectant fungicides include old-fashioned products such as copper, mancozeb and sulphur. They are relatively cheap, and control a wide range of fungal diseases, which are less likely to develop resistance when these chemicals are used frequently.

However, protectant fungicides only protect the plant's surface from attack and do little to check the growth of diseases inside the plant. Although systemic fungicides usually have a narrower range of activity, and fungi may develop resistance to them more easily, they are highly effective. Once systemic fungicides are taken into and moved around the plant's tissues, they offer protection against growth of a fungal disease even after an attack has occurred. If you can, alternate between protectant and systemic fungicides to minimise risk of resistance.

Fungal attack
Apple powdery mildew is a typical fungal disease. A powdery white growth appears on the upper and lower leaf surfaces, causing the foliage to wither and die.

See also Avoiding pests and diseases, pp.36–37

See also Avoiding pests and diseases, pp.36–37;

Effective spraying
For best results when using fungicides, aim to apply a closely spaced, even layer of droplets, ideally on both sides of the leaves (*above*). Use a sprayer that produces a fine, even spray (*left*). Apply in cool, dry, calm conditions to avoid accidentally spraying the foliage of neighbouring plants.

When to apply?

It is best to apply protectant fungicides before diseases develop, although protectants can sometimes also slow down the spread of diseases such as leaf blight. Re-apply them after heavy rain because protection is lost when the fungicide is washed off.

Systemics can slow down fungal growth after infection and, once they have been absorbed by the plant, are less affected by rain. However, neither protectant or systemic fungicides are particularly effective at protecting new growth, so you may need to make several applications to rapidly growing plants. Some diseases that are difficult to control, such as rose black spot, require a regular schedule of spraying.

How to apply?

Apply a closely spaced, even layer of spray droplets to the upper and lower leaf surfaces. Lower surfaces may be difficult to reach, but are important to protect. Some sprayers have poor-quality nozzles; choose one that produces a fine, even spray, without producing large drops. Aim for a dense, even coverage of droplets that remain on the plant to dry. Apply sprays in cool, dry, calm conditions. During hot weather, spray in the evening to avoid scorching foliage.

Integrated use

Fungicides are more effective when combined with cultural methods of control. Start with healthy plants. If you can, choose disease-resistant cultivars and minimize the likelihood of infection by attention to hygiene. Well-grown plants that are not subjected to stress are less likely to succumb to disease. Spray plants promptly at the first signs of disease; fungicides cannot undo damage that has already occurred.

COMPRESSION SPRAYERS

Fungicides may be easily applied with a compression sprayer. These come in various sizes, and may be used to treat small or large areas. Prime the equipment by pumping the handle up and down, then spray, using the trigger to control the flow. The spray head can be adjusted to give a fine or coarse spray, as required. After use, wash out the sprayer thoroughly with plain water and also flush through the hose. Do not use the same sprayer to apply weedkillers.

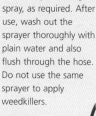

Compression sprayer

Disposing of old chemicals

Make sure you dispose of old garden pesticides with care

Concentrates can be stored for two years or more if they are kept in cool, dark conditions, but ready-to-use sprays that require no mixing, and store just as long, are usually more economical for small areas.

Never pour surplus pesticides down drains or watercourses. To dispose of them safely, dilute small amounts and spray permitted plants in accordance with the instructions on the label.

Dispose of empty containers, after they have been rinsed thoroughly, through normal household waste routes; do not recycle them. Dispose of rinsings as per surplus pesticides.

To dispose of larger quantities contact your local authority's waste disposal section to find out which refuse sites take chemicals. Ensure containers are well sealed and clearly labelled with the name and active ingredient of the product. Do not mix surplus chemicals.

If pesticides are withdrawn from the market for economic reasons, a two-year grace period usually comes into force to allow stock to be used up. If you find unlabelled containers or old pesticides contact your local authority's waste disposal section.

Do not hoard old chemicals

Growing vegetables without chemicals, pp.200–201

Using biological controls

Many of the pests that infest greenhouse plants breed rapidly during the summer and can be difficult to control with pesticides, but the major kinds can be controlled with parasites or predators

Glasshouse whitefly

Use the small chalcid wasp (*Encarsia formosa*) to control glasshouse whitefly (*Trialeurodes vaporariorum*). Female wasps lay 50–100 eggs singly in the scale stage of the whitefly's life cycle. Parasitized scales later turn black and can be readily distinguished from the whitish-green healthy scales. Parasitized whitefly die, and adult parasites emerge through circular holes cut in the surface of their scales. Adult parasites feed on the sugary excretion, known as honeydew, that whiteflies produce.

Encarsia is supplied in the form of black scales on pieces of leaf or pasted onto cards. Fix these cards or leaf portions securely in a shaded position on infested plants. Adult parasites emerge within a few days and the first blackened scales should appear on the plants after about three weeks.

Common greenhouse pests
A fine, pale mottling of the upper leaf surface is an indication that glasshouse red spider mite is present (*above*). The mottled effect is caused by its feeding; at this stage the tiny mites are found on the leaf undersides. Release a predatory mite to control it. Glasshouse whitefly breeds very rapidly (*left*); this may also be controlled biologically, using a small parasitic wasp.

Glasshouse red spider mite

Like whitefly, glasshouse red spider mite (*Tetranychus urticae*) breeds very rapidly and is difficult to control with chemicals, especially if resistant strains of the mite are present. A predatory mite (*Phytoseiulus persimilis*) is widely used in preference to chemicals. Both the adult predators and their nymphs feed on the eggs, nymphal and adult stages of red spider mite. The predators are supplied as nymphs and adults; place them in sheltered positions on infested plants.

Mealybugs

Mealybugs (*Pseudococcus* and *Planococcus* species) secrete waxy fibres over themselves and their eggs, and this protective coating, combined with their habit of infesting relatively inaccessible places on plants, reduces the effectiveness of insecticides. A ladybird predator (*Cryptolaemus montrouzieri*) can overcome these

problems. The adult beetles and their larvae feed on mealybugs and their eggs.

Adult ladybirds can lay up to 500 eggs if they have a plentiful supply of food. As with most biological controls, the mealybug predator needs warm conditions and does best when daytime temperatures are around 27°C (80°F). Release the predator on to infested plants in the evening when temperatures are cooler to reduce the risk of adult ladybirds flying up and escaping through the ventilators. The beetles generally stay

This pest secretes waxy fibres

Mealybug colony
This common greenhouse pest infests relatively inaccessible places on plants, reducing the effectiveness of insecticides. Control it with a ladybird predator.

on the plants once they have settled, although they will wander about if there is insufficient food.

Scale insects

Some greenhouse species such as soft scale (*Coccus hesperidum*) and hemispherical scale (*Saissetia coffeae*) can be kept in check by releasing a parasitic wasp called *Metaphycus helvolus*. This lays its eggs in young scale nymphs, which become darkened and are killed before reaching maturity. At 27°C (80°F) the life cycle from egg to adult parasite takes about 12 days but is slower at lower temperatures. Introduce the wasp from late spring to midsummer for the best results.

Soft scale colony
Under glass, infestations of this common pest can be treated biologically, with a parasitic wasp. The wasp lays its eggs in the young scale nymphs, which subsequently die.

See also How to control aphids, p.42; Vine weevil, p.48; Red spider mite, p.197;   *Mealybugs, scale insects, whitefly, p.198*

USING BIOLOGICAL CONTROLS

The predators, parasites and pathogenic agents that are commercially available are intended for use against specific pests. It is therefore essential that pests are accurately identified. The various biological controls are compatible with each other and are suitable for use in combination. However, they must not be used with any chemical control, or immediately afterwards, as predators and parasites are very susceptible to most insecticides. Biological controls are best regarded as alternatives to chemical methods, not as additional treatments. The instructions for use should indicate the period that must elapse between the application of chemicals and that of the biological control. Release the controls on to infested plants as soon as obtained. In the case of pathogenic nematodes, water them into the soil or potting compost as soon as you receive them.

A sticky trap
Yellow traps are used to catch winged insects under glass. They can let you know when whitefly are present, and need controlling.

Whitefly control
Encarsia formosa, which controls glasshouse whitefly, is supplied as black scales, often pasted on to cards to attach to infested plants.

Encarsia in action
Adult glasshouse whitefly and black, parasitized scales. The scales may also be supplied on pieces of leaf (*inset*).

Aphids

Control greenfly and blackfly with a small midge, *Aphidoletes aphidomyza*, whose larvae prey on aphids and can give effective control in greenhouses from mid-spring to early autumn. The adults are tiny delicate flies, which lay eggs at night on the foliage. The eggs hatch in about three days and the small orange-white larvae take 7–14 days to complete their feeding before pupating in silk cocoons in the soil. Adults emerge about three weeks later. Stand pot plants on trays of damp sand, otherwise fully fed midge larvae will drop down and fail to find anywhere to pupate on the benching or hard floor of a greenhouse.

The larvae attach themselves to an aphid's leg joint and suck out the body contents. Aphid control may be less satisfactory on plants with hairy leaves. *Aphidoletes* is supplied in the form of larvae, which you can gently transfer to an aphid-infested plant with a soft paint brush, or as pupae, to be put in a cool damp place at the base of plants.

Vine weevil

The larvae of vine weevil (*Otiorhynchus sulcatus*) feed on the roots of many plants, especially those grown in pots or other containers. Most insecticides available to amateur gardeners are not sufficiently persistent or powerful to give effective control. Control the grubs by watering into the potting compost a suspension of a pathogenic eelworm or nematode, *Steinernema kraussei*. Nematodes enter the bodies of vine weevil grubs and infect them with a fatal disease. For best results use nematodes in late summer on well-drained potting compost or light soil, which must be moist and not below temperatures of 5°C (41°F).

Effective use

There is no point in introducing biological controls before pests become active because the predators and parasites can only breed when their appropriate prey or host is present.

Beneficial insects and mites are very susceptible to bifenthrin: avoid using it for 8–10 weeks before introducing predators or parasites. The safest insecticides are insecticidal soaps and rape seed oil. Fungicides are generally safe, but keep their use to a minimum.

Predatory midge larvae at work
A larva of the midge *Aphidoletes aphidomyza* will kill and consume as many as 80 aphids, even though it is only 3mm long.

Vine weevil and nematodes
The larvae of vine weevil are controlled with nematodes, supplied in a fine carrier (*inset*) which is added to water.

How to control aphids

The most widespread plant pests, there are few plants that are not attacked by aphids. They are, however, relatively easy to control

There are over 500 species of aphid in Britain. They are commonly known as greenfly, blackfly, or plant lice and all feed by sucking sap from plants.

While many species are black or green, others may be yellow, pink or grey and some, like the woolly aphids on apple and beech, are covered with waxy filaments.

The life cycles of aphids are varied and complex. Most species winter as small, shiny black eggs, which are laid on trees and shrubs. These hatch in the spring into wingless female aphids and begin feeding on the new plant growth. As the new growth hardens off at the beginning of the summer, winged aphids develop and these fly off to the herbaceous plants, which act as their summer hosts. The colonies on the winter host die out at this time.

Symptoms

Throughout late spring and summer dense colonies can be found on young plant shoots and, in addition to weakening the plant, they cause discoloration and distortion of leaves or the formation of galls. Aphids have sucking mouthparts, which are inserted into the sap-conducting vessels of the plant, and they extract large quantities of sap. Superfluous sugars are excreted as a sweet substance called honeydew. This makes the leaves sticky and shiny, but a superficial sooty mould often develops, which makes the upper leaf surface appear to have turned black. Some aphids are also important carriers of plant viruses.

Aphid attack
Left: The head of a globe artichoke colonized by black aphids, which attack many garden plants.
Above: An adult ladybird makes short work of an aphid colony feeding on an apple shoot.

Control

Aphids have many natural enemies, including ladybirds, lacewings, hoverfly larvae and several parasitic wasps. Towards the end of the summer these beneficial insects are sufficiently numerous to cause a drastic reduction in aphid numbers. Biological controls can be bought from mid-spring to early autumn for controlling aphids in greenhouses (*see pages 40–41*).

There are several approved insecticides that you can use against aphids during spring and summer. Systemic insecticides are generally best as they are absorbed by the plant and the aphids are poisoned as they feed (*see pages 37–38*). Aphids hidden in curled leaves will therefore be affected even if they are missed by the spray.

Organic contact insecticides that are effective against aphids include pyrethrum, derris/rotenone, vegetable oils, rape seed oil, and fatty acids. These have a low toxicity to humans and are suitable for use on listed food plants. When treating vegetables or fruits, check the product packaging to ensure that it is approved for that type of food plant.

Plants affected

Aphids affect a huge range of plants, from woody plants like trees and shrubs (including top and soft fruit), to perennials, annuals, many greenhouse plants and vegetables.

APHID HUNTERS

In the garden aphids are likely to be attacked and devoured by many natural enemies, the best known of which are ladybirds. Both the adults and larvae feed voraciously on these pests. Natural predators are at their most numerous towards the end of summer and will drastically reduce aphid numbers at this time of year. However, make sure that you do not wipe out these beneficial creatures with chemical insecticides.

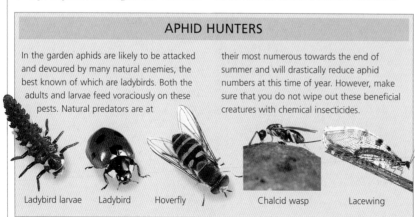

Ladybird larvae   Ladybird   Hoverfly   Chalcid wasp   Lacewing

---

See also Avoiding pests and diseases, pp.36–37; Systemic chemicals, pp37–38; Using biological controls, pp.40–41

Living with ants

Although ants disturb plants, they are not serious pests

Several species of ants occur in gardens, including the black ant (*Lasius niger*), the yellow meadow ant (*Lasius flavus*) and red ants of various *Myrmica* species. Ants often cause concern but they are nuisance insects rather than serious pests. They feed mainly on insects (including other ants) and sweet liquids, such as honeydew excreted by aphids.

Symptoms
Indirect harm to plants may occur by ants protecting aphids from ladybirds, or through their nest-building activities. Ants can loosen the soil around roots and bury low-growing plants with excavated soil.

Control
Use proprietary ant powders but limit control measures to nests that are causing particular problems. Complete eradication of ants is not possible because treated gardens soon become recolonized by queen ants flying in from elsewhere. Many young queens fall victim to predatory ants from existing nests before they can establish their own colonies.

Ants climbing a tree to reach aphids

Woodlice and millipedes

Woodlice, centipedes and millipedes are found in most gardens but only occasionally cause plant problems

Woodlice
Woodlice (*Oniscus asellus*, *Porcellio scaber* and *Armadillidium vulgare*) have a hard, segmented covering over their bodies. They abound in most gardens and are often blamed for damage caused by other pests.

Symptoms
Woodlice are mainly scavengers, feeding on rotting vegetation. Their mouthparts are poorly adapted for feeding on mature plants, but they sometimes feed on soft growth, such as seedlings or strawberry fruits. However, they may enlarge damage initiated by other pests.

Control
Since woodlice are not a significant problem there is little point in trying to control them. In greenhouses, where seedlings may be vulnerable, good hygiene reduces their numbers and removes hiding places.

Centipedes
Centipedes have long segmented bodies with many legs and are often confused with millipedes. However, it is useful to be able to distinguish between them, since while some millipedes are occasionally harmful, centipedes are never pests, and can even be beneficial as they feed on other small soil creatures.

> ### THE LEG COUNT
>
> The simplest way to distinguish centipedes from millipedes is to count the legs: centipedes have one pair per body segment whereas millipedes have two pairs. The British species of centipede are a dark or yellowish brown, and move rapidly when disturbed.
>
>
>
> *One pair of legs per segment*   *Two pairs of legs per segment*
>
> Centipede   Millipede

Millipedes
Millipedes have long, segmented, cylindrical or flat bodies. Structurally, they are more diverse than centipedes, from which they can be distinguished by the possession of two pairs of legs per body segment. The species most frequently encountered as a garden pest is the spotted snake millipede (*Blaniulus guttulatus*).

Symptoms
Millipedes feed mainly on decaying plant matter. They sometimes damage seedlings and soft growth such as strawberry fruits, as well as enlarging damage on potato tubers and bulbs started by other pests like slugs.

Control
Natural enemies include birds, frogs, toads, hedgehogs and ground beetles. Good hygiene will create less favourable conditions by removing hiding places and accumulations of decaying vegetation.

A colony of woodlice   Blackbirds are natural enemies of millipedes

See also Encouraging wildlife, pp.250–251

How to deter cats

Although you cannot prevent cats from visiting your garden, you can keep them away from particular areas using a range of ingenious methods

Much-loved pet cats can be the bane of nearby gardeners, whose plots they use as toilet areas. They scrape holes in flower beds or seed rows to receive the excrement, and sometimes it is deposited on lawns or paths. Tomcats also scent-mark their territories by spraying urine on plants, scorching the foliage. Damage caused to the bark of trees and shrubs when cats sharpen their claws is another form of scent marking. Cats also have the annoying habit of sunbathing in inconvenient places, crushing plants in the process.

How to deter cats

Cats are territorial animals and it is difficult to convince them that the garden is yours rather than theirs. They are too agile to be excluded from gardens by fencing or netting, although you may find that nets keep cats away from small areas in the garden.

Try densely planting flower beds and borders with perennial plants that cover the soil to make them less attractive as toilet areas, although herbaceous beds containing plants that die down over winter can then become vulnerable. Keep seed rows watered to speed plant growth through the vulnerable seedling stage and also to deter cats. If they have a choice, cats invariably

A territorial animal
Cats are highly territorial creatures and tomcats scent their territories with urine. It is difficult to stop unwanted cats from visiting gardens, which they use as toilet areas. They scrape holes in soil, smothering small plants and disturbing seeds.

make toilet pits in loose soil or mulch that is dry rather than wet.

Use animal repellents that keep cats away, available from garden centres. These are intended to offend the cat's sense of smell or taste without causing any harm. In practice, any protection given is short term and frequent re-applications are needed, especially after rain, to maintain the deterrent effect. Remove cat excrement before applying a repellent. There are no plants that reliably repel cats, but they will avoid direct contact with thorny plants.

Ultrasonic sound

Try an electronic cat-scaring device that produces ultrasonic sound. This is barely audible to human ears but can be a cacophonous noise to a cat. Ultrasound can he baffled by solid or semi-solid objects such as fences or shrubs, so the best results are obtained in relatively open gardens. The sound travels away from the device in the direction the speaker is facing, so place it at one end of the garden. Ultrasonic devices are mainly available from mail-order garden suppliers.

Ways to deter cats
Cat don't like water so try scaring them away by spraying them with water whenever they appear in your garden, using a hosepipe or even a hand sprayer. Even more effective is to install an electronic cat-scaring device that produces ultrasonic sounds.

WHY DO CATS EAT GRASS?

Cats consume grass as an emetic to induce vomiting and get rid of fur balls. Cats will eat ornamental as well as long lawn grasses but this causes little damage. Oats, *Avena sativa*, is sold as 'cat grass' by several seed companies.

Preventing bird damage

Most birds are welcome visitors but some are destructive pests

In winter bullfinches feed on flower buds of tree and bush fruits and ornamental trees. Sparrows are seed-feeding birds, and pigeons are mainly a winter and early summer problem.

Symptoms
As they feed, bullfinches drop the outer bud scales on the ground. Sparrows go for grass seed and also destroy lettuce, beetroot and peas. Pigeons eat a wide range of seeds and seedlings and are particularly troublesome on brassicas and peas.

Control
Protect rows of pea seedlings and other vegetables with netting or horticultural fleece. Spray animal and bird repellents on to plants and purchase grass seed that has been treated with bird repellent.

A female bullfinch

Bird proofing cherries
Netting is the only certain way of keeping birds off plants. It can be draped over plants temporarily but ideally grow fruits and vegetables in a permanent bird-proof cage. A mesh size of 2cm (¾in) will exclude all damaging garden birds.

See also Destructive bullfinches, p.72

Deer as plant vandals

Deer munch their way through ornamental and edible plants

In gardens, the most troublesome deer are usually roe deer and muntjac, but in some areas fallow deer, red deer, or sika may be the main cause for concern.

Deer-damaged bark

Symptoms
Deer feed on a wide range of plants, including some of the more attractive garden plants, as well as vegetables and fruits. They can consume enormous amounts of young foliage and shoots and they also damage the bark of young trees.

Control
Use fencing to exclude deer from gardens: 1.5m (5ft) tall for muntjac, and 1.8m (6ft) for roe and other deer. Use tree guards to protect bark of young trees: 1.2m (4ft) high for muntjac, and taller guards for larger deer. Use animal repellents to encourage deer to feed elsewhere, or an ultrasonic device to scare them off.

DEER-RESISTANT PLANTS

Bamboos	Lavandula
Berberis	Lonicera
Buddleja	Magnolia
Buxus	Mahonia
Choisya	Potentilla fruticosa
Clematis	Rhododendron
Cornus	Ribes
Daphne	Rosa rugosa
Forsythia	Spiraea
Gooseberries	Viburnum
Hydrangea	Weigela

Combating earwigs

These common pests eat both foliage and flowers

The common earwig (*Forficula auricularia*) is one of the most easily recognised garden insects because of the distinctive pincers seen on the end of its abdomen.

Symptoms
Earwigs feed on various plants, particularly the flowers and young foliage of clematis, dahlias and chrysanthemums. They make ragged holes in the petals and leaves. In some years earwigs are particularly abundant and will damage a much wider range of plants.

Earwigs hide in sheltered places during the day and only emerge after dark to commence feeding. Torchlight inspections will confirm whether damage to plants is being caused by earwigs or by other nocturnal pests.

Control
Trap earwigs by placing upturned flower pots or similar containers loosely stuffed with hay or straw on canes among any plants being attacked, and those known to be vulnerable. Every morning shake out the pots and remove the earwigs. This may not be enough to protect plants when earwigs are particularly abundant, so if extensive damage is occurring you may need to spray with an approved insecticide. Do this at dusk on mild evenings when bees are not visiting flowers.

Earwig-damaged dahlia flower

See also Avoiding pests, pp.36–37

CONTROLLING SLUGS AND SNAILS

Controlling slugs and snails

Snails and slugs attack a wide range of plants, and are the bane of every gardener's life; excercise constant vigilance to prevent them ruining your display

SNAILS

The snail most usually found in the garden is the common garden snail *Helix aspersa*, but banded snails (*Cepaea hortensis* and *C. nemoralis*) may also be numerous.

Symptoms

Look out for irregular holes rasped in foliage, stems and flowers. They feed on young, tender plant tissue and, unlike slugs, which must always be close to the soil or moist conditions, snails are able to forage further afield and can climb considerable distances to find succulent shoots.

Control

Control snails by using proprietary slug pellets during their active period in spring and summer. These will, however, be ineffective during the winter months. Alternatively use an aluminium sulphate based slug control product in the spring against newly hatched snails. This option is safer for wildlife and pets. Various proprietary traps are also available. During winter control measures are confined to turning over likely hiding places and either leaving the snails exposed to predators, such as thrushes, or removing them for destruction.

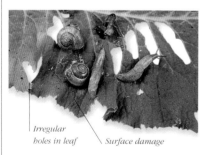

Irregular holes in leaf · *Surface damage*

Slugs and snails in feeding mode
Both slugs and snails feed mainly at night and eat irregular holes in foliage or graze away the surface tissues. Many plants are affected, especially those with soft leaves.

See also Using biological controls, pp.40–41

INGENIOUS METHODS OF CONTROL

There is no need to use slug pellets around plants to control slugs and snails as there are various non-chemical ways of combating these pests. For example, plastic bottles with the bottoms removed, like mini bell jar cloches, can be used for covering small vegetables that are prone to slug damage (*below left*). Plants in patio containers, such as vulnerable hostas (plantain lilies), can also be attacked by slugs and snails. To stop them making the 'leap' over the edge of a container, place a band of copper around it; neither pest likes contact with this metal (*below right*). Alternatively smear the pot edges with grease, which they also dislike.

Recycled plastic bottles

Copper band on hosta pot

SLUGS

Several species of slugs can be found in gardens, including grey field slug (*Deroceras reticulatus*), the large black slug (*Arion ater*), garden slug (*A. hortensis*) and keeled slugs (*Milax* species). They cause damage throughout the year but are particularly troublesome in spring. They can continue feeding whenever the temperature is above 5°C (41°F). Warmer weather, combined with damp conditions, increase their activity.

Symptoms

Slugs can damage a wide range of plants. Irregular holes are eaten in leaves, flowers and stems. The soft growth of seedlings and the emerging shoots of herbaceous plants are especially vulnerable.

Control

Scatter proprietary slug pellets thinly around vulnerable plants or use slug control products containing aluminium sulphate. There are also various proprietary traps available.

Try biological control in the form of a nematode, *Phasmarhabditis hermaphrodita*. This is watered into the soil and enters slugs' bodies where it releases bacteria that cause a fatal disease. The nematodes need moist but well-drained soil and temperatures in the range of 5–20°C (41–68°F), and therefore they are most effective when applied during spring or autumn. The nematodes are available from specialist mail-order suppliers and can be ordered from some garden centres.

Song thrush
Try to encourage birds like the song thrush, which is extremely partial to snails, into your garden. It smashes the shells against hard surfaces such as paths and stones to enable it to extract the flesh.

Slug-resistant plants

Beat slugs and snails by growing plants they dislike

PLANTS WORTH TRYING

As slugs and snails are so numerous and damage so many plants, it makes sense to grow as many ornamental plants as possible that are relatively resistant to these pests. They tend to go for herbaceous perennials in particular, as they have soft young growth, so try this selection of plants that are less likely to be eaten.

Acanthus mollis, Achillea filipendulina, Agapanthus, Alchemilla mollis ♥, Anemone hupehensis, A. x hybrida, Aquilegia, Armeria, Aster amellus, Aster x frikartii, A. novae-angliae, Astilbe x arendsii, Astrantia major, Bergenia, Centaurea dealbata, C. montana, Corydalis lutea, Cynara cardunculus ♥, Dicentra spectabilis ♥, Digitalis purpurea, Eryngium, Euphorbia, Foeniculum vulgare, Gaillardia aristata, Geranium, Geum chiloense, Hemerocallis, Liatris spicata, Lysimachia punctata, Myosotis, Nepeta x faassenii ♥, ornamental grasses and sedges, Papaver orientale, Phlox paniculata, Physostegia virginiana, Polemonium foliosissimum, Polygonum, Potentilla, Pulmonaria, Rudbeckia fulgida, Salvia x superba ♥, Saxifraga x urbium ♥, Scabiosa caucasica, Sedum spectabile ♥, Sempervivum, Sisyrinchium, Solidago, Stachys macrantha, Tanacetum coccineum, Thalictrum aquilegiifolium, Tradescantia virginiana, Tropaeolum and Verbascum

Liatris spicata

Excluding rabbits

Ideally, try to keep these pests out of the garden

Rabbits often live together in colonies and under ideal conditions are prolific breeders. They are a menace in rural and semi-rural gardens.

Symptoms

Rabbits feed on a wide range of vegetables and ornamental plants, sometimes grazing them close to the ground. They gnaw bark from young trees and shrubs.

Control

For best control, erect a rabbit-proof fence around the garden. Make it from 2.5cm (1in) mesh wire netting, 120–140cm (48–54in) in height. Bury the bottom 30cm (12in) below ground level and bend the lower 15cm (6in) outwards to prevent rabbits from tunnelling underneath.

Use proprietary animal repellents to keep rabbits away from plants.

Choose plants that are relatively resistant to rabbits. A few examples are *Alchemilla mollis, Aquilegia, Bergenia, Clematis, Dahlia, Digitalis, Euphorbia, Galanthus, Helleborus* (not *H. niger*), *Hemerocallis, Narcissus, Paeonia, Primula vulgaris,* and *Stachys byzantina.*

Young tree protected with rabbit guard

See also Deer, p.45

Problems with squirrels

The grey squirrel damages many garden plants while feeding

The grey squirrel (*Sciurus carolinensis*), introduced into Britain from North America during the late 19th century, has found this country much to its liking and while it is attractive to watch, it can be highly destructive.

Squirrels love hazelnuts

Symptoms

The most serious damage, bark stripping, occurs on many trees. Squirrels also bite off shoot tips and flower buds, and eat fruits and nuts. In spring they feed on young shoots and flower buds of oak, horse chestnut, magnolia, walnut and other trees. Squirrels are fond of crocus corms and tulip bulbs and will raid tubs and other planters to find them.

Control

Protect fruit by growing it under a fruit cage, constructed of wire netting, as squirrels will easily bite through plastic. Cover tubs of bulbs and corms with wire netting to prevent squirrels from helping themselves.

Bark stripped from shoot of tree by squirrels

See also Bird damage, p.45

VINE WEEVIL

Vine weevil

A destructive pest that attacks a wide range of plants, especially those grown in containers; the grubs devour roots, while adult beetles feed on leaves, resulting in notched margins

Adult vine weevils (*Otiorhynchus sulcatus*) are always female. They are long-lived and can lay up to 1,000 eggs between late spring and autumn. Eggs laid early will produce grubs large enough to cause noticeable damage by late summer. These grubs may become adults by autumn but most of the population winter as grubs, which pupate in spring.

Vine weevil grubs are plump and creamy white with pale brown heads, and grow up to 1cm (½in) long. The pupae are creamy white and show some adult features such as wing pads, legs and antennae.

Adult weevils are dull black with small, yellowish-brown flecks on the wing cases. They are 8–9mm (⅜in) long, and have pear-shaped bodies with antennae bent at right angles. The adults cannot fly or run, but they are persistent crawlers and have no difficulty in scaling the sides of pots or climbing walls to reach plants. They are mainly nocturnal.

Symptoms

Vine weevils attack an extremely wide range of ornamental plants in houses, greenhouses and gardens. Strawberries and some bush fruits can also be affected.

Notches made by adults

Vine weevil adult

Vine weevil damage
The creamy white grubs feast on roots and tubers while the adults attack leaves of various plants, such as the rhododendron shown above.

Plants attacked by grubs show poor growth and have a tendency to wilt. Investigation of the root system will reveal that most of the roots have been eaten and the grubs may also have gnawed away the bark from the base of the plant's stem. Vine weevil grubs will also bore into the tubers of plants such as begonias and cyclamen. Plant deaths mainly occur between autumn and spring. Adult vine weevils eat irregular notches in the leaf margins of plants throughout summer.

Control

Protect vulnerable ornamental plants in pots or other containers with the insecticide imidacloprid. For established pot plants, apply this as a drench to the compost, and it will provide protection for up to six months. Alternatively you can buy it pre-mixed in proprietary container composts. These composts give protection for up to a year, and the indoor container compost is useful for seedlings, cuttings and plug plants, and for potting begonia and cyclamen tubers.

Alternatively use a biological control in the form of a pathogenic nematode,

COMBAT TIPS

- Biological control, using a pathogenic nematode, can efficiently control grubs
- Grubs in pot plants may be controlled with a drench of imidacloprid; or use compost containing this insecticide
- In small spaces, search for adult vine weevils by torchlight from spring to autumn; each one destroyed reduces the number of eggs

Biological control drench
Watering a pathogenic nematode on to the potting compost of container plants will help to control vine weevil grubs. This will be most effective if it is applied during late summer.

Steinernema kraussei. This is watered on to the potting compost or soil and then enters the bodies of vine weevil grubs, infecting them with a fatal bacteria. To ensure maximum success, you should apply the nematode to a moist, open compost or soil in the temperature range 5–20°C (41–68°F) during the late summer months. The nematode is available by mail order from suppliers of biological controls.

Hunting adult vine weevils
You can track down adult vine weevils at night using a torch. Whenever you find them, simply knock the weevils off the leaves into a bucket, and dispose of them well away from your plants.

See also Avoiding pests and diseases, pp.36–37; Using biological controls, pp.40–41

TREES & SHRUBS

Choosing trees for small gardens

If you have space for only a single tree, look for one with several seasons of interest, such as ornamental fruits or autumn leaf colour following the flowers

FLOWERS AND COLOURED LEAVES AND BARK

Flowers

Cercis siliquastrum ♀ ↕↔ 10m (30ft), rose-purple, mid- to late spring, ◻–◙ ◊ ❋❋❋

Cornus kousa var. *chinensis* ♀ ↕ 7m (22ft) ↔ 5m (15ft), white, early summer, ◻–◙ ◊ ❋❋❋

Crataegus laevigata 'Paul's Scarlet' ♀ ↕↔ 8m (25ft), dark red, late spring or early summer, ◻–◙ ◊ ❋❋❋ ☐1

Genista aetnensis ♀ ↕↔ 8m (25ft), yellow, midsummer, ◻ ◊ ❋❋ ☐2

+ *Laburnocytisus* 'Adamii' ↕ 8m (25ft) ↔ 6m (20ft), yellow and purple, late spring, ◻ ◊ ❋❋❋

Laburnum x *watereri* 'Vossii' ♀ ↕↔ 8m (25ft), yellow, late spring, ◻ ◊ ❋❋❋

Magnolia x *loebneri* 'Leonard Messel' ♀ ↕ 8m (25ft) ↔ 6m (20ft), lilac-pink, spring, ◻–◙ ◊ ❋❋❋

Malus floribunda ♀ ↕↔ 10m (30ft), pink and white, spring, red or yellow fruits, ◻ ◊ ❋❋❋

Malus x *moerlandsii* 'Profusion' ↕↔ 12m (40ft), purple-red, mid-spring, purple fruits, ◻ ◊

Prunus 'Accolade' ♀ ↕↔ 8m (25ft), soft pink, late spring, ◻ ◊ ❋❋❋

Prunus 'Pandora' ♀ ↕ 10m (30ft) ↔ 8m (25ft), deep pink, early spring, ◻ ◊ ❋❋❋

Prunus x *subhirtella* 'Autumnalis Rosea' ♀ ↕↔ 8m (25ft), blush pink, winter, ◻ ◊ ❋❋❋

Prunus 'Ukon' ♀ ↕ 8m (25ft) ↔ 10m (30ft), white, mid-spring, ◻ ◊ ❋❋❋

Coloured spring and summer leaves

Acer negundo 'Flamingo' ↕ 15m (50ft) ↔ 10m (30ft), cream and pink with green, ◻–◙ ◊ ❋❋❋

Acer palmatum 'Atropurpureum' ↕ 8m (25ft) ↔ 10m (30ft), bronzy crimson, ◻–◙ ◊ ▥ ❋❋❋

Gleditsia triacanthos 'Sunburst' ♀ ↕ 12m (40ft) ↔ 10m (30ft), golden-yellow, ◻ ◊ ❋❋❋ ☐4

Prunus cerasifera 'Nigra' ♀ ↕↔ 10m (30ft), dark purple, ◻ ◊ ❋❋❋

Pyrus salicifolia 'Pendula' ♀ ↕ 5m (15ft) ↔ 4m (12ft), silver-grey, ◻ ◊ ❋❋❋

Robinia pseudoacacia 'Frisia' ♀ ↕ 15m (50ft) ↔ 8m (25ft), bright yellow, ◻ ◊ ❋❋❋

Coloured bark

Acer capillipes ♀ ↕↔ 10m (30ft), red twigs, green-and-white branches, ◻–◙ ◊ ▥ ❋❋❋

Acer griseum ♀ ↕↔ 10m (30ft), dark, flaking bark revealing orange beneath, ◻–◙ ◊ ▥ ❋❋❋

Acer palmatum 'Sango-kaku' ♀ ↕ 6m (20ft) ↔ 5m (15ft), coral-red shoots, ◻–◙ ◊ ▥ ❋❋❋

Betula ermanii 'Grayswood Hill' ♀ ↕ 20m (70ft) ↔ 12m (40ft), white, ◻–◙ ◊ ❋❋❋

Betula utilis var. *jacquemontii* ↕ 18m (60ft) ↔ 10m (30ft), pure white, ◻–◙ ◊ ❋❋❋

Eucalyptus pauciflora subsp. *niphophila* ♀ ↕ 6m (20ft) ↔ to 15m (50ft), grey-greens, ◻ ◊ ❋❋❋

Prunus serrula ♀ ↕↔ 10m (30ft), shiny, mahogany brown, ◻ ◊ ❋❋❋ ☐5

See also Trees and buildings, pp.52–53; Trees with colourful foliage, pp.57–58; Growing trees in containers, p.59; Autumn colour, p.62

AUTUMN COLOUR AND WINTER STRUCTURE

Autumn leaf colour and fruits

Acer japonicum 'Aconitifolium' ♀ ‡ 5m (15ft) ↔ 6m (20ft), ruby crimson leaves, ▢–▨ ◊ ♨ ❋❋❋

Acer palmatum 'Ôsakazuki' ♀ ‡↔ 6m (20ft), fiery scarlet leaves, ▢–▨ ◊ ♨ ❋❋❋

Acer tataricum subsp. *ginnala* ‡ 10m (30ft) ↔ 8m (25ft), orange and crimson leaves, ▢–▨ ◊ ❋❋❋

Amelanchier lamarckii ♀ ‡ 10m (30ft) ↔ 12m (40ft), leaves in flame shades, ▢–▨ ◊ ♨ ❋❋❋ ▢3

Crataegus x *lavalleei* 'Carrierei' ♀ ‡ 7m (22ft) ↔ 10m (30ft), long-lasting orange-red fruits and dark foliage colour, ▢–▨ ◊–◊ ❋❋❋

Malus x *robusta* 'Red Sentinel' ♀ ‡↔ 7m (22ft), long-lasting red fruits, ▢ ◊ ❋❋❋

Malus tschonoskii ♀ ‡ 12m (40ft) ↔ 7m (22ft), orange to purple leaves, yellowish fruits, ▢ ◊ ❋❋❋

Malus x *zumi* 'Golden Hornet' ♀ ‡ 10m (30ft) ↔ 8m (25ft), yellow fruits, ▢ ◊ ❋❋❋

Nyssa sinensis ♀ ‡↔ 10m (30ft), rich red leaf tints, ▢–▨ ◊ ♨ ❋❋❋

Prunus 'Pandora' ♀ ‡ 10m (30ft) ↔ 8m (25ft), rich orange-red leaf tints, ▢ ◊ ❋❋❋

Sorbus aucuparia 'Aspleniifolia' ‡ 15m (50ft) ↔ 7m (22ft), red fruits and good scarlet and orange foliage colour, ▢–▨ ◊ ❋❋❋

Sorbus hupehensis ♀ ‡↔ 8m (25ft), pink-white fruits and good red foliage colour, ▢–▨ ◊ ❋❋❋

Sorbus 'Joseph Rock' ‡ 10m (30ft) ↔ 7m (22ft), amber yellow fruits and orange to purple foliage colour, ▢–▨ ◊ ❋❋❋

Sorbus vilmorinii ♀ ‡↔ 5m (15ft), rose red fruits turning white, red and purple foliage, ▢–▨ ◊ ❋❋❋

Evergreen

Arbutus unedo ♀ ‡↔ 8m (25ft), white flowers in mid- to late autumn, red fruits, ▢ ◊ ❋❋❋

Cotoneaster frigidus 'Cornubia' ♀ ‡↔ 6m (20ft), red berries, semi-evergreen, ▢–▨ ◊ ❋❋❋

Eucalyptus pauciflora subsp. *niphophila* ♀ ‡ 6m (20ft) ↔ to 15m (50ft), grey-green leaves, patchwork bark, ▢ ◊ ❋❋❋

Ilex x *altaclerensis* 'Golden King' ♀ ‡ 6m (20ft) ↔ 4m (12ft), female form with yellow leaf margins and red berries, ▢ ◊ ❋❋❋

Ilex aquifolium 'Madame Briot' ♀ ‡ 10m (30ft) ↔ 5m (15ft), female form with yellow leaf margins and red berries, ▢ ◊ ❋❋❋

Ligustrum lucidum ♀ ‡↔ 10m (30ft), white flowers in late summer to early autumn, ▢–▨ ◊ ❋❋❋ ▢6

Photinia davidiana ‡ 8m (25ft) ↔ 6m (20ft), red berries, some leaves colour bright red in autumn, ▢–▨ ◊ ❋❋❋

Narrow (fastigiate or columnar)

Betula pendula 'Fastigiata' ‡ 20m (70ft) ↔ 6m (20ft), a stiff, erect form, ▢–▨ ◊ ❋❋❋

Fagus sylvatica 'Dawyck Gold' ♀ ‡ 18m (60ft) ↔ 7m (22ft), a tall, columnar tree broadening with age, with yellow juvenile foliage, ▨ ◊ ❋❋❋

Malus tschonoskii ♀ ‡ 12m (40ft) ↔ 7m (22ft), erect with a conical habit, orange and purple autumn leaf colour, ▢ ◊ ❋❋❋ ▢7

Prunus 'Amanogawa' ♀ ‡ 8m (25ft) ↔ 4m (12ft), columnar with erect branches ▢ ◊ ❋❋❋

Prunus 'Spire' ♀ ‡ 10m (30ft) ↔ 6m (20ft), vase-shaped, orange and red autumn tints, ▢ ◊ ❋❋❋

Sorbus aucuparia 'Fastigiata' ‡ 8m (25ft) ↔ 5m (15ft), slow growing, columnar tree with closely erect stems, ▢–▨ ◊ ❋❋❋

Weeping

Betula pendula 'Youngii' ‡↔ 8m (25ft), white bark, ▢–▨ ◊ ❋❋❋

Buddleja alternifolia ♀ ‡↔ 4m (12ft), mauve flowers in early summer, ▢ ◊ ❋❋❋ ▢8

Cotoneaster 'Hybridus Pendulus' ‡↔ 1.8m (6ft), evergreen with red fruits, ▢–▨ ◊ ❋❋❋

Laburnum alpinum 'Pendulum' ‡↔ 3m (10ft), yellow flowers in late spring, ▢ ◊ ❋❋❋

Malus x *gloriosa* 'Oekonomierat Echtermeyer' ‡↔ 5m (15ft), crimson flowers in mid-spring, purple fruits, ▢ ◊ ❋❋❋

Prunus 'Kiku-shidare-zakura' ♀ ‡↔ 3m (10ft), pink flowers in mid-spring, ▢ ◊ ❋❋❋

Prunus pendula 'Pendula Rubra' ♀ ‡↔ 8m (25ft), pink flowers in early spring, ▢ ◊ ❋❋❋

Pyrus salicifolia 'Pendula' ♀ ‡ 5m (15ft) ↔ 4m (12ft), silvery foliage, ▢ ◊ ❋❋❋

Salix purpurea 'Pendula' ♀ ‡↔ 3m (10ft), purple twigs, ▢ ◊ ❋❋❋

6

7

8

Trees and buildings

Tree roots can cause damage to drains and the fabric of buildings; some trees – especially the large, vigorous kinds – are more of a problem than others

Trees growing close to houses can contribute to structural problems in various ways. It would be very wrong, however, to automatically assume that all trees growing close to buildings are potentially hazardous. Where structural damage occurs it would be equally wrong to blame the close presence of trees without careful assessment of the site. Other factors may be responsible for damage to the structure.

Damage to drains and walls

Roots may block, crack, and burst drains. The subsequent flow of water into the soil can wash soil particles away, causing a cavity. Where there are large cavities in the soil there is no support for the foundations, which may then fail to support the building adequately at that point.

Modern drainage systems are normally well sealed and have flexible joints installed where root growth or soil movement are likely, and roots seldom penetrate and block well-maintained drains. Damaged drains are vulnerable and should be repaired. Roots can be numerous in soil around drains, often taking advantage of the moist conditions next to the pipes, where water condenses, but this rarely causes a problem.

Similarly, roots are likely to penetrate brickwork only where the brickwork is old and crumbling due to breakdown

Trees can block out light and damage foundations

of the mortar, or of poor-quality bricks. Roots, particularly those of shallow-rooting trees such as *Prunus*, may disturb paving and other hard surfaces, which is unsightly but less serious.

The spread of branches reduces light and may in time cause damage to roofs and gutters. Physical damage can also occur where a tree is growing very close to a building or boundary wall; as the root or stem increases in girth there is actual contact with, and pressure on, the structure. In these cases lightweight buildings such as garages and porches are most likely to be at risk.

Shrinkage and heave

Damage to the foundations of buildings or structures where the foundations are relatively shallow can occur as a result of the root action of nearby vigorous evergreen and deciduous trees absorbing water from the soil. Damage of this type appears to be confined to shrinkable clay soils, and also some shrinkable peat soils, and is found particularly in areas

where seasonal rainfall is low and summer temperatures are high.

During drought, a clay soil may naturally dry out considerably, to the extent that it shrinks and cracks. This results in the foundations becoming displaced due to lack of support, leading to structural cracking, particularly around windows and doorways. This shrinkage is greatly increased where a large, fast-growing tree is nearby, taking up moisture from the clay and losing it through its leaves.

If a tree causes the soil to shrink near a house this will occur at the side where the tree is growing. The weight of the building may then push the foundations on that side downwards and outwards. Where this is repeated year after year, the foundations, increasingly lacking the support of the soil on the tree-facing side, subside and collapse outwards. This will cause distortion and outward movement of the walls at that point, with structural cracking and the loss of alignment of doors and windows. Rains will swell the clay and close the soil cracks to a greater or lesser extent each winter, but the weight of the building ensures that there is a slow outward movement of the clay.

Conversely, removing large trees that have previously kept the soil around a building in a permanently drier condition may cause swelling or soil heave, the reverse of shrinkage. Soils other than shrinkable clays are seldom affected by either of these problems, as they do not swell and contract as much when they are wet or dry out.

Root spread

Soil type, situation, soil-moisture levels, and relationship to other trees nearby are all variable factors that can influence root spread and development. The habit of a tree can also vary greatly, from the extremes of tall and narrow to low and

---

TREAT WITH CAUTION

Poplars (*Populus*) account for much damage, but other fast-growing trees, such as lime (*Tilia*), willow (*Salix*), oak (*Quercus*), and elm (*Ulmus*), also cause problems. Vigorous or large trees should be planted as far from buildings as is practical; the maximum tree-to-damage distance recorded for willows is 40m (132ft).

See also Legal protection for trees, p.54; Are your trees safe?, p.56

A young, vigorous tree poses the greatest risk

weeping. In view of such variables, it is not reliable to equate the root spread of a tree with its height. Only a limited amount of information has been published on the subject, but it seems that roots can often extend for a radius wider than the height of the tree. In any case, unless the conditions around a tree are uniform (which would be unusual in a garden), the extent of the root system is likely to follow an irregular pattern and be very difficult to predict accurately.

The extent of any tree's roots is partly dependant on species, but varies greatly, extending at least as far as its height, commonly up to 2.5 times the height of the tree, and radiating irregularly, being most abundant where soil is most moist.

Assessing the risks

To assess potential risks to a property, the type, age, and construction materials of buildings must be considered. There appears to be more risk with buildings up to four storeys high constructed before the 1950s, as they will frequently have foundations only about 45cm (18in) deep, whereas the foundations of later buildings are usually 1m (3ft) or more.

The type of soil and its degree of moisture may vary considerably. Clays with a high plasticity level appear to pose the greatest risk. The nature of the surrounding area, what other trees and shrubs are planted there, and whether the soil is prone to drying out or a ground-water flow helps to keep it constantly moist, must all be considered.

The distance from tree to property is also significant. A high proportion of recorded instances of damage relate to trees positioned about 10m (33ft) or less from a property, but only a few recorded

instances result from trees standing 20m (66ft) or more from a property.

The type, age, and health of the trees also influence how likely they are to cause problems. The greatest risk is from young, vigorously growing trees. As trees reach maturity, their moisture demands decrease and, therefore, so do the risks.

Large and vigorous trees should not be planted near a house (see box). Consider trees of more moderate size and growth rate if limited space means that there is a need to plant fairly close to buildings, such as for screening.

Trees and the law

A tree, shrub, or climber normally belongs to the land on which it is growing, regardless of how it got there, and is the property and responsibility of the owner of the land. The owner may be liable should the tree cause any damage to neighbouring property.

Before taking steps to remove or reduce in size any tree thought to pose a risk to property, make sure it is not protected by a tree preservation order (see p.54). Trees that make a significant contribution to an area may be covered by such an order served by the local planning authority, whose permission must be obtained before any protected tree is pruned or felled. Similar constraints apply to trees in a conservation area.

Seeking advice

If you have any worries about trees near your property, seek professional advice. Some aspects of tree assessment such as identity, condition, age, potential size, and growth rate need the specialized knowledge of a qualified arboriculturist. A structural engineer should be able to advise on soil characteristics, building construction, and any structural damage encountered. Chartered building surveyors can advise on structural damage, potential damage, or the construction of new buildings and extensions near to existing trees.

Pressure from an expanding tree trunk can destroy a boundary wall

PRACTICAL ADVICE

Legal protection for trees

Tree preservation orders legally protect trees from damage or removal, and you could face a hefty fine if you ignore them

Tree preservation orders are a legal means of protecting and preserving trees from deliberate damage or removal. They aim to preserve trees, including those on private property, both for public enjoyment and for environmental, especially visual, purposes. Bushes, shrubs, and hedges are not covered.

Restrictions on what can be done to trees apply in conservation areas. These exist to protect the character and appearance of certain localities. Notification of intended work has to be given six weeks in advance. If the planning authorities object, they can make a tree preservation order. Local planning authorities can advise if trees are in a conservation area.

No work of any sort may be carried out on a protected tree, even one in a private garden, without prior notice. Penalties are severe if unauthorised work is carried out, with hefty fines. It may be possible to fell or undertake tree surgery on a protected tree but, again, consultation is needed, and the local authority may insist that a replacement is planted. Public notice of all applications is given and objections can be made. Whatever the action intended, details of work to be done, why it is necessary, and which tree is involved are required. The advice of a tree surgeon could be helpful.

Even if a tree on your land is covered by a tree preservation order, as the owner you remain responsible for the tree and for any damage that the tree may cause. Although removing or pruning diseased or dying trees without notice is not prohibited, you should be sure that the situation constitutes an emergency, otherwise you could be prosecuted if the local authority disagrees with your assessment of the situation. For your own protection give at least five days' notice.

Trees are preserved for public enjoyment

If your trees or those in your area need protection, contact your local planning authority stating why you feel the trees are worth preserving, and provide a detailed map so that the request can be investigated. Notice of new tree preservation orders is served on the owner or occupier. A copy has to be made available for inspection. Often a new order is also made known to neighbours. There is opportunity to comment in support of, or object to, new orders within 28 days. These influence the local authority when it decides whether or not to confirm the order, and if confirmed, whether to modify it.

OTHER LEGAL BOUNDARIES

- Leaves and fruit belong to the owner of the tree, but they do not have to clear them from a neighbour's property
- Branches that overhang a neighbour's property or roots growing into their soil may be cut back to the boundary; branches should be offered to the tree's owner

See also Trees and buildings pp.52–53; Are your trees safe?, p.56

TECHNIQUES

Moving large shrubs

Planning ahead is vital when transplanting large shrubs

Moving any established shrub is a risk, however carefully it is carried out. The plant will suffer some degree of stress when uprooted, which results in a check to growth. Avoid transplanting shrubs such as magnolias, roses, broom (*Cytisus*), elaeagnus, and cistus, because they resent root disturbance.

Move deciduous plants between mid-autumn and early spring. Transplant evergreens, such as rhododendrons, during mid-autumn when the soil is still warm, or in early to mid-spring, when the roots re-establish quickly.

Preparation

When moving moderately large shrubs, up to about 1.8m (6ft) high, prepare well beforehand. Ideally, six to twelve months before moving the plant, try to determine the extent of root spread and then dig a trench, the width of a spade blade, around the root system, cutting through the side roots. Fill the trench with sharp sand. This will encourage the shrub to produce new fibrous roots, which help it to establish quickly after transplanting. Note that the main area covered by feeding roots can extend beyond the spread of the branches. Larger specimens may have root masses of 90–120cm (3–4ft) or more in diameter and 40–45cm (16–18in) or more in depth.

Making the move

The ground must be moist when the shrub is finally undercut from all sides prior to moving. Cut cleanly through any deeply penetrating roots with a knife or secateurs. Loosely tie in spreading branches, and then lift the shrub with as large a rootball as possible. If there are few or no fibrous roots then it may not re-establish satisfactorily. Where possible, lift and

See also Successful planting, pp.60–61

Time to move: *Pyracantha atalantioides* is obscuring the view to the rest of the garden

transplant in one complete operation, otherwise cover the roots with plastic or damp sacking to prevent them from drying out.

Prepare the new site in advance. Make the planting hole 30–60cm (12–24in) greater than the root spread. Dig down to at least the depth of the rootball and then loosen soil at the bottom. Adding organic matter to planting holes is not recommended, as the sinking caused by its decay can lead to shrubs settling deeper than they should. Carefully place the plant in the hole and check that the

roots can be fully spread out. If necessary, adjust the size of the hole. Use the old soil mark on the stem as a guide to planting depth to prevent replanting too deeply, and avoid the extremes of deep and shallow planting. Large plants and those being planted in windy sites will need staking for the first season. It can be helpful to thin heavy top-growth by up to 25 per cent. Firm well to eliminate air pockets as you fill in the planting hole. Break down the sides of the hole, particularly if you have clay soil, so that the roots do not become contained. Evergreens transplanted in mid-autumn will benefit from temporary wind protection until spring to prevent drying out. Use hessian or plastic sheeting fixed to canes around the plant, leaving the top exposed for ventilation.

Storing before replanting

If plants are to be moved to another garden or cannot be re-planted for some time, first spread leafmould, well-rotted garden compost, or processed shredded bark on a piece of hessian. Set the plant on this, then work more of the material over and around the roots. Draw the hessian around the stem and tie it firmly, but not so tightly that the bark is damaged. If it cannot be re-planted for some time, place the plant in a cool situation out of direct sun or in dappled shade, pile leafmould around and over the wrapped roots, untie the branches,

and keep it well watered. In hot spells, evergreen shrubs and conifers will benefit from light overhead spraying in the evening or early morning. This treatment is particularly useful if you are planning a move in late spring and wish to take valued plants with you. They can be lifted in advance when still dormant and, with care, can remain preserved in this way until the following autumn, when weather and soil conditions are suitable for planting.

Aftercare

Water in thoroughly after planting and continue to water in dry periods. A 5cm (2in) deep mulch of organic matter, such as well-rotted garden compost or chipped bark, will help to conserve soil moisture and suppress weeds. In spring, as growth begins, apply a general-purpose or shrub fertilizer. Do this before applying a mulch. Where roots have been unavoidably damaged, foliar feeding will aid re-establishment of the plant. Spray deciduous plants occasionally if buds are slow in breaking, particularly during a period of cold, drying winds.

Evergreens need particular attention after planting to prevent them drying out. Spray them overhead with plain water during warm or dry weather until well established. They can suffer from drought, even in the winter, when newly planted.

TRANSPLANTING AN ESTABLISHED SHRUB

1 Mark out a circle around the shrub, here *Ilex aquifolium* 'Golden Milkboy', and dig a trench around it. **2** Loosen the soil inside the trench and fork it away from the rootball to reduce weight. **3** Lift and tilt the shrub, pull hessian through underneath it and tie it around the rootball to protect the roots. **4** Move the shrub to its new location, remove the hessian wrapping, and replant at the same depth.

Are your trees safe?

Many tree problems can be prevented by selecting the right tree for the site and soil, but you should inspect existing mature trees regularly for defects and potential problems

Most trees do not normally shed branches or fall over – they are able to withstand normal stresses such as wind, provided their inherent strength is not compromised by defects or decay.

Inspect a tree once a year if it appears healthy. If there is a defect that may get worse, check the tree more frequently. Keep a detailed record, which will be helpful for future reference. Pay special attention to trees near highways, buildings, or boundaries with other properties, where the risk of injury or damage is higher. As the owner of a tree, you have to think about your legal liability should an accident occur.

Keep an eye on old pruning wounds, as they are potential trouble spots. The fact that a wound has been painted or has completely healed over does not exclude the possibility of a rot – pruning paints may even increase decay by trapping moisture inside.

Tightly forked branches or competing leading shoots are structurally weak, so are more prone to failure or decay. They can be prevented through formative pruning on young trees; on older trees pruning can reduce the weight of these branches.

Signs of problems

Most problems have visible external symptoms, although some, including internal decay, may not. Look for areas of dead bark, or cracks in the bark of a tree, which can indicate structural stress, injury, or decay. Late appearance of foliage, a thin crown, early leaf fall, late flowering, poor extension growth, dieback, or movement of the root system in windy weather can all indicate that a problem may exist at or below the ground. Bear in mind, however, that late flowering or early leaf fall can also be brought on by environmental stresses such as drought.

Danger signs
The heavy branches of this ancient hornbeam (*Carpinus betulus*) are in danger of splitting away from the trunk (*top*). Bracket fungus at the base of a mature tree indicates possible decay (*bottom*).

Toadstools growing from the base of a tree or the ground at the base may also indicate root problems, but there are many fungi that are harmless or even beneficial to trees. Bracket fungi, such as *Ganoderma applanatum*, growing at the base or on the trunk are usually a sign of internal decay, although many trees survive with these for some years.

If there are signs that all is not well with your tree it does not always mean that the tree is unsafe. Because of your legal responsibility, however, you should seek the opinion of a tree expert who can carry out further assessment before deciding whether any action is necessary. A qualified arboriculturist should have the training, relevant third-party liability insurance, and experience to inspect trees and carry out appropriate work safely.

See also Trees and buildings, pp.52–53, Legal protection for trees, p.54

Trees and shrubs with colourful foliage

Plenty of green is needed in gardens to create a soothing effect, but it also makes an excellent background for trees and shrubs with golden, purple, red, silver, and variegated foliage

GOLD AND YELLOW

To create a balanced and more interesting planting scheme, try to include trees and shrubs with colourful foliage, both evergreen and deciduous, as well as those noted for their flowers, fruits, berries, autumn leaf colour, and ornamental bark. Evergreens really come into their own in winter, of course, and deciduous kinds create their display in spring and summer. There is a huge range of coloured-leaved trees and shrubs to choose from, particularly with variegated foliage – in other words, green leaves that are marbled, splashed, striped or streaked with white, silver, yellow, or gold (*further colours are covered on p.58*).

Trees

Acer cappadocicum 'Aureum' ♀ ‡ 15m (50ft) ↔ 10m (30ft), ▢–▣ ◊ ❋❋❋

Acer negundo 'Auratum' ‡↔ 8m (25ft), ▢–▣ ◊ ❋❋❋

Gleditsia triacanthos 'Sunburst' ♀ ‡ 12m (40ft) ↔ 10m (30ft), ▢ ◊ ❋❋❋

Laurus nobilis 'Aurea' ♀ ‡ 8m (25ft) ↔ 4m (12ft), E ▢–▣ ◊ ❋❋ [1]

Robinia pseudoacacia 'Frisia' ♀ ‡ 15m (50ft) ↔ 8m (25ft), ▢ ◊ ❋❋❋ [2]

Sorbus aria 'Chrysophylla' ‡ 10m (30ft) ↔ 7m (22ft), ▢–▣ ◊ ❋❋❋

Smaller shrubs

Caryopteris x *clandonensis* 'Worcester Gold' ♀ ‡ 90cm (3ft) ↔ 1.5m (5ft), ▢ ◊ ❋❋❋ [3]

Escallonia laevis 'Gold Brian' ‡↔ 90cm (36in), E ▢ ◊ ❋❋

Euonymus fortunei 'Sheridan Gold' ‡ 45cm (18in) ↔ 90cm (36in), E ▢ ◊ ❋❋❋

Ilex crenata 'Golden Gem' ♀ ‡ 1.1m (3½ft) ↔ 1.2–1.5m (4–5ft), E ▢ ◊ ❋❋❋

Salvia officinalis 'Kew Gold' ‡ 20–30cm (8–12in) ↔ 30cm (12in), ▢ ◊ ❋❋❋

Spiraea japonica 'Goldflame' ‡ 75cm (30in) ↔ 75cm (30in), ▢ ◊ ❋❋❋ [4]

Larger shrubs

Acer shirasawanum 'Aureum' ♀ ‡↔ 6m (20ft), ▢–▣ ◊ ❋❋❋ [5]

Berberis thunbergii 'Aurea' ‡ 1.5m (5ft) ↔ 1.8m (6ft), ▢–▣ ◊ ❋❋❋

Choisya ternata Sundance ('Lich') ♀ ‡↔ 2.4m (8ft), ▢ ◊ ❋❋❋

Cornus alba 'Aurea' ♀ ‡↔ 3m (10ft), ▢ ◊–◊ ❋❋❋

Corylus avellana 'Aurea' ‡↔ 5m (15ft), ▢ ◊ ❋❋❋

Lonicera nitida 'Baggesen's Gold' ♀ ‡↔ 1.5m (5ft), E ▢–▣ ◊ ❋❋❋ [6]

Rubus cockburnianus 'Goldenvale' ♀ ‡ 2.4m (8ft) ↔ 2.4m (8ft), ▢ ◊ ❋❋❋

Sambucus racemosa 'Sutherland Gold' ♀ ‡↔ 3m (10ft), ▢–▣ ◊ ❋❋❋

Weigela 'Looymansii Aurea' ‡↔ 1.5m (5ft), ▢–▣ ◊ ❋❋❋

See also Choosing trees for small gardens, pp.50–51; Tree surgery, p.68

TREES AND SHRUBS WITH COLOURFUL FOLIAGE

PURPLE AND RED

Trees

Acer palmatum 'Bloodgood' ♀ ‡↔ 5m (15ft), ▢–▢ ◊ ❄❄❄

Acer palmatum 'Burgundy Lace' ♀ ‡ 4m (12ft) ↔ 5m (15ft), ▢–▢ ◊ ❄❄❄

Acer platanoides 'Crimson King' ♀ ‡ 25m (80ft) ↔ 15m (50ft), ▢–▢ ◊ ❄❄❄

Betula pendula 'Purpurea' ‡ 10m (30ft) ↔ 3m (10ft), ▢–▢ ◊ ❄❄❄

Cercis canadensis 'Forest Pansy' ♀ ‡↔ 10m (30ft), ▢–▢ ◊ ❄❄❄

Prunus cerasifera 'Nigra' ♀ ‡↔ *10m (30ft),* ▢ ◊ ❄❄❄ 1

Smaller shrubs

Berberis thunbergii 'Golden Ring' ♀ ‡ 1.5m (5ft) ↔ 2.4m (8ft), ▢ ◊ ❄❄❄

Weigela florida 'Foliis Purpureis' ♀ ‡ 90cm (36in) ↔ 1.5m (5ft), ▢–▢ ◊ ❄❄❄

Larger shrubs

Berberis x *ottawensis* f. *purpurea* 'Superba' ♀ ‡↔ 2.4m (8ft), ▢–▢ ◊ ❄❄❄

Corylopsis sinensis var. *sinensis* 'Spring Purple' ‡↔ 4m (12ft), ▢ ◊ ❄❄❄

Corylus maxima 'Purpurea' ♀ ‡ 6m (20ft) ↔ 5m (15ft), ▢ ◊ ❄❄❄

Cotinus coggygria 'Royal Purple' ♀ ‡↔ 5m (15ft), ▢ ◊ ❄❄❄

Pittosporum tenuifolium 'Purpureum' ‡ 3m (10ft) ↔ 1.5m (5ft), E ▢ ◊ ❄❄

Sambucus nigra 'Guincho Purple' ‡↔ 6m (20ft), ▢–▢ ◊ ❄❄❄

SILVER AND GREY

Trees

Eucalyptus pauciflora subsp. *niphophila* ♀ ‡ 6m (20ft) ↔ 6–15m (20–50ft), E ▢ ◊ ❄❄❄

Pyrus salicifolia 'Pendula' ♀ ‡ 5m (15ft) ↔ 4m (12ft), ▢ ◊ ❄❄❄

Sorbus aria 'Lutescens' ‡ 10m (30ft) ↔ 8m (25ft), ▢–▢ ◊ ❄❄❄

Smaller shrubs

Convolvulus cneorum ♀ ‡ 60cm (24in) ↔ 90cm (36in), E ▢ ◊ ❄❄

Helichrysum splendidum ♀ ‡↔ 1.2m (4ft), E ▢ ◊ ❄❄❄

Perovskia 'Blue Spire' ♀ ‡ 1.2m (4ft) ↔ 90cm (36in), ▢ ◊ ❄❄❄ 2

Potentilla fruticosa 'Beesii' ‡ 60cm (24in) ↔ 1.2m (4ft), ▢ ◊ ❄❄❄

Salix repens var. *argentea* ‡ 90cm (36in) ↔ 1.8m (6ft), ▢ ◊ ❄❄❄

Santolina chamaecyparissus ♀ ‡ 50cm (24in) ↔ 90cm (3ft), E ▢ ◊ ❄❄

Larger shrubs

Atriplex halimus ‡ 1.8m (6ft) ↔ 2.4m (8ft), E ▢ ◊ ❄❄❄

Buddleja alternifolia ♀ ‡↔ 4m (12ft), ▢ ◊ ❄❄❄

Elaeagnus 'Quicksilver' ♀ ‡↔ 4m (12ft), ▢ ◊ ❄❄❄

Hippophae rhamnoides ♀ ‡↔ 6m (20ft), ▢ ◊ ❄❄❄

Olearia macrodonta ♀ ‡ 6m (20ft) ↔ 5m (15ft), E ▢ ◊ ❄❄❄

VARIEGATED FOLIAGE

Trees

Acer negundo 'Flamingo' ‡ 15m (50ft) ↔ 10m (30ft), ▢–▢ ◊ ❄❄❄

Cornus controversa 'Variegata' ♀ ‡↔ 8m (25ft), ▢–▢ ◊ 🝢 ❄❄❄

Ligustrum lucidum 'Excelsum Superbum' ♀ ‡↔ 10m (30ft), E ▢ ◊ ❄❄❄

Smaller shrubs

Abelia x *grandiflora* 'Francis Mason' ‡ 1.5m (5ft) ↔ 1.8m (6ft), E ▢ ◊ ❄❄

Euonymus fortunei 'Emerald 'n' Gold' ♀ ‡ 60cm (24in) ↔ 90cm (36in), E ▢ ◊ ❄❄❄

Yucca filamentosa 'Bright Edge' ♀ ‡ 75cm (30in) ↔ 1.5m (5ft), E ▢ ◊ ❄❄

Larger shrubs

Griselinia littoralis 'Dixon's Cream' ‡ 3m (10ft) ↔ 1.8m (6ft), E ▢ ◊ ❄❄❄

Ilex aquifolium 'Ferox Argentea' ♀ ‡ 8m (25ft) ↔ 4m (12ft), E ▢ ◊ ❄❄❄ 3

Ligustrum ovalifolium 'Argenteum' ‡↔ 4m (12ft), E ▢ ◊ ❄❄❄

Osmanthus heterophyllus 'Variegatus' ♀ ‡↔ 3m (10ft), E ▢–▢ ◊ ❄❄

Pittosporum tenuifolium 'Silver Queen' ♀ ‡ 1–4m (3–12ft) ↔ 1.8m (6ft), E ▢ ◊ ❄❄

Prunus laurocerasus 'Castlewellan' ‡↔ 5m (15ft), E ▢–▢ ◊ ❄❄❄

Rhamnus alaternus 'Argenteovariegata' ♀ ‡ 5m (15ft) ↔ 4m (12ft), E ▢ ◊ ❄❄

Weigela 'Florida Variegata' ♀ ‡ 1.8–2.4m (6–8ft) ↔ 1.8–2.4m (6–8ft), ▢–▢ ◊ ❄❄❄

1

2

3

See also Choosing trees for small gardens, pp.50–51

PLANT PROBLEMS

Dealing with green shoots

Don't let green shoots dominate variegated trees and shrubs

Pruning out non-variegated growth

Variegated trees and shrubs – those whose leaves are attractively streaked, striped, edged, or splashed with another colour, such as white or yellow – usually originate as a variegated shoot on a normal green plant. They have to be propagated from cuttings to keep the variegation.

Variegated plants are not always stable, and some shoots can revert to the original green. This often occurs, for instance, with the popular evergreen shrub *Euonymus fortunei* 'Emerald 'n' Gold' and with variegated box elders (*Acer negundo*). The green reverting shoots contain more green colouring (chlorophyll) and produce more food for growth. This makes them more vigorous than variegated ones, and so green shoots will finally overtake variegated growth in size and vigour if they are not removed.

Remove reverting shoots as soon as they are seen by cutting them back to wood with variegated foliage. This often means removing entire shoots.

Occasionally shoots will change to entirely cream or yellow leaves, but because of the lack of green colouring they often grow weakly and so are less of a problem.

PRACTICAL ADVICE

Growing trees in containers

Trees in containers are ideal for small gardens, courtyards, or patios, where they can be used to frame doorways and provide focal points

Ideal trees for containers include those suitable for topiary, such as yew (*Taxus*), holly (*Ilex*), and box (*Buxus*), as well as fruit trees on dwarfing or semi-dwarfing rootstocks. You could also grow tender trees such as citrus or olives (*Olea*), moving them to frost-free conditions for the winter.

In most cases, growing a tree in a container will restrict its growth. It is still best to avoid large, fast-growing trees, except perhaps for short-term planting, as they may quickly become too large and prone to toppling over in windy weather. But trees that can be coppiced (cut hard back annually to a low framework) are a possibility, including tulip tree (*Liriodendron tulipifera*), eucalyptus, Indian bean tree (*Catalpa bignonioides*), and willow (*Salix*).

Choosing containers

Choose terracotta pots for stability, but make sure they are frost resistant. Square, wooden, Versailles-type tubs are also recommended. Light plastic pots allow you to move plants around, but are less stable than heavy pots.

Trees will need potting on in stages, aiming for minimum final pot size of 45cm (18in) in diameter and depth if the plant is to be moved around. You can use larger pots for trees that are to remain in their position permanently.

Looking after pot-grown trees

Use soil-based potting compost, as it provides weight for greater stability. For plants that need lime-free soil use ericaceous potting compost, which is usually soilless. Place 5cm (2in) of broken clay pots or gravel over the drainage holes and raise the pots on feet to avoid waterlogging in winter.

Container-grown trees are more prone to drying out than plants in the open ground and need regular and thorough watering. Several waterings may be needed to wet the full depth of compost. Use rainwater for ericaceous plants, although tap water is better than none if you run out. Apply controlled-release fertilizer at the start of the growing season, or use a liquid feed once a fortnight in spring and summer. Refresh the compost in spring by removing the top 5cm (2in) and replacing it with fresh compost. If trees are known to be tolerant of root disturbance, repot them every few years when they are dormant. Remove the tree from its pot, tease out the roots, and remove the old compost. Trim the larger roots and then repot in fresh compost, using the same size pot.

Bay (*Laurus nobilis*) is good in containers

WHY GROW TREES IN POTS?

- Less hardy trees can be moved into protected conditions during the winter
- The size of trees will be restricted by the pot, allowing naturally large trees to be accommodated in smaller gardens
- Growing trees in containers ensures roots or suckers cannot damage house foundations and drains

See also Choosing trees for small gardens, pp.50–51; Growing fruit trees in pots, pp.234–235

Successful tree and shrub planting

Buying a top-quality plant, preparing the site well, and planting correctly should ensure success when planting trees and shrubs, particularly if you also look after the plant well in subsequent years

Planting a tree is an investment for the future, but its long-term benefits will never mature if the initial groundwork at the planting stage is overlooked.

The planting techniques for container-grown, bare-root, and root-balled plants differ slightly. Plant deciduous trees and shrubs in late autumn or winter when dormant (but not when the ground is frozen or very wet), evergreens in early to mid-autumn or in early to mid-spring, when the soil is warm. Container-grown trees can be planted at any time. Prune damaged roots, and water thoroughly before planting. Where drainage is poor, plant on a slight mound.

Some suppliers offer a one-year guarantee covering initial establishment failure; check if this is the case with your plant. Trees may die many years after planting if not enough care is taken over maintenance before the tree is fully established.

Container-grown plants

Good quality container-grown plants are easy to plant: simply dig a hole slightly larger than the rootball – about three times the diameter of the pot is ideal – in well-prepared ground, place the plant in the hole, insert a stake just beyond the root ball if needed, and then return fine soil around it, firming several times as you fill in.

If the root spread of a container-grown plant is deeper than just below the soil surface, remove a little compost and plant the tree more shallowly to bring it to the right level. If a plant is at all pot-bound, with the roots circling the pot, gently tease them out so that they will grow outward into the soil. Because this disturbs the roots, it is best done while the tree is dormant.

Bare-root trees and shrubs

The roots of bare-root plants are wrapped in hessian or plastic material to prevent them from drying out. Plant bare-root trees and shrubs as soon as possible. If you cannot avoid a delay, heel them in, digging a trench and placing the plant in it at an angle, so that the trunk or stem is supported. Cover the roots and the base of the trunk or stem with moist soil.

Before planting, inspect the roots, and if they are dry soak them in a bucket of water for a couple of hours. Trim any broken, damaged, and very long roots.

Prepare the site thoroughly before planting, and dig a planting hole sufficiently large to take the root spread. Fork over the sides and base of the hole to break up the surrounding soil, which will allow roots to spread into it more easily. This is particularly important on heavy clay soils. If you intend supporting a tree with a single stake, insert it into the hole just off centre before planting, to prevent root damage.

Check that the planting depth is correct by placing a cane across the hole alongside the stem. Add or remove soil so that the soil mark on the trunk or stem (indicating the depth the plant was growing at on the nursery) is level with the cane. Then gently spread out the roots and work fine soil between them in stages, firming every 15cm (6in) depth of soil by treading to remove air pockets. Take care not to firm too much on clay soil, as this may compact the soil and prevent drainage. Shorten top growth, if needed, to balance it with the root system. Finally, secure to the stake and, where necessary, use a tree guard to protect the trunk from rabbit or other animal damage. Water thoroughly and apply a 5–8cm (2–3in) mulch to conserve moisture.

PLANTING BARE-ROOT SHRUBS AND TREES

Remove any perennial weeds and improve the soil in advance if possible. **1** Dig a hole larger than the existing root system: aim for three times the width and twice the depth. **2** Fork the sides and bottom of the hole to make root penetration easier, and add organic matter if necessary. **3** Check that the soil mark on the stem will be level with the ground; it may be useful to fan the roots out over a cone of soil in the bottom of the hole. **4** Fill soil in around the roots, firming gently to prevent damage to roots: avoid digging your heels in or stamping.

See also Buying a new tree, pp.64–65; Support for new trees, p.65

PLANTING ROOT-BALLED TREES AND SHRUBS

Trees and shrubs that have many fibrous roots are often sold root-balled. **1** Dig a hole larger than the root ball, so that the roots will be able to spread once the wrapping is removed. **2** Place the tree in the hole and draw the wrapping out from underneath the root ball; enlist a helper if the tree is large. To avoid damaging the roots when staking, use a stake driven in at an angle with the bottom end away from the roots, rather than an upright one (see p 65)

Root-balled plants

Some trees and shrubs, particularly evergreens and conifers, are supplied with a ball of soil around the roots tightly wrapped in hessian or plastic material. Root wrappings provide protection and support to the rootball between lifting and replanting.

As hessian may take several years to rot, and plastic will not rot at all, remove the root wrap before filling the planting hole. With smaller trees, simply tilt the root ball in the planting hole and carefully draw the wrapping away. Stabilize large trees when in the planting hole with temporary staking or by partly filling the hole, and then cut away the root wrap. If removing the wrapping is not possible, cut large holes through the sides to help roots penetrate into the surrounding soil.

Removing the root wrapping will enable you see that the tree is planted at the correct depth. Always plant trees or shrubs with the root spread at the base of the stem near the soil surface.

Do not disturb the ball of soil around the roots when planting, but simply work fine soil around it, firming as you proceed, in much the same way as you would plant a pot-grown tree or shrub.

Staking newly planted trees

Large trees and shrubs need support to prevent wind-rock from disturbing newly formed roots or creating air pockets for water to collect in. Overhead guys are useful on soft ground with particularly tall trees, but otherwise do not allow sufficient movement of the stem, which aids establishment. Guying consists of three wires in a triangular formation, attached around the lower branches and

STAKING A YOUNG TREE

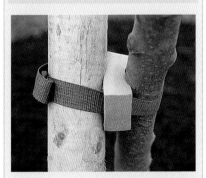

Almost all trees and some tall shrubs should be staked at first to allow the roots to establish. Always use a proper tree tie, with a buckled strap and a buffer block to prevent chafing of the bark, and loosen as the trunk thickens.

secured at the ground with short stakes. Protect tree bark by enclosing the wires with rubber or plastic hosepipe.

When using a normal tree stake, ensure it is not more than one-third the height of the tree, to allow for movement and strengthening of the stem. Regularly check ties to ensure they are secure, and loosen them as necessary. Remove the supports when the roots are well established, which is generally a year from planting.

Aftercare

Failure can occur years after planting and is often due to poor aftercare. Regularly water a wider area than the original planting hole, using enough water to completely soak the root area, to encourage young roots to spread outwards. Avoid daily watering, as this may encourage the formation of surface roots, which are more sensitive to drought or frost. Keep the area around the base of the tree clear of weeds and grass, which compete for water and plant foods. Maintain a permanent mulch to discourage weed growth, reduce water loss, and keep the soil temperature even. Apply a general-purpose fertilizer in late winter or early spring each year.

Planting large trees

Large trees provide instant impact and lend maturity to a site, but bear in mind that they can fail to establish. Skill and care in transporting and handling the plant, and good preparation, planting, and aftercare are needed to reduce transplant "shock" and prevent death. Thorough site preparation is vital; new roots will not grow out into compacted or poorly aerated soil.

Planting semi-mature trees is popular today, when an instant effect is so often desired. You need a deep pocket, though, for apart from the high cost of the actual tree, you will have to pay the supplier to have it transported and planted. There are nurseries that specialize in extra-large and semi-mature trees and shrubs.

The cream of autumn colour

Every garden should have some trees and shrubs for autumn leaf colour and colourful fruits, but choose carefully, for not all live up to expectations

Autumn is a season of great change in the garden. Although many perennials and annuals continue their summer display, it is the colourful leaves and fruits of deciduous trees and shrubs that most capture the imagination. This should be the most spectacular time of all in the garden, as beds and borders, and specimen trees, erupt in fiery orange and red shades, or more subtle yellows and golds, before the more restrained displays of winter.

Autumn colour shows up best with a solid, dark background, such as conifers and evergreen shrubs, so consider this when planning your planting. Include hardy, autumn-flowering perennials and bulbs; ornamental grasses, such as pampas grass (*Cortaderia*) also look good with shrubs sporting autumn colours.

TREES AND SHRUBS FOR AUTUMN COLOUR

Small trees with autumn leaf colour

Acer griseum ♀ ↕↔ 10m (30ft), ▢–▨ ◊ ᵞ ❋❋❋

Crataegus persimilis 'Prunifolia' ♀ ↕ 8m (25ft) ↔ 10m (30ft), ▢–▨ ◊ ❋❋❋

Malus tschonoskii ♀ ↕ 12m (40ft) ↔ 7m (22ft), ▢ ◊ ❋❋❋

Nyssa sylvatica ♀ ↕ 20m (70ft) ↔ 10m (30ft), ▢–▨ ◊ ᵞ ❋❋❋

Parrotia persica ♀ ↕ 8m (25ft) ↔ 10m (30ft), ▢–▨ ◊ ᵞ ❋❋❋

Prunus 'Hillieri' ↕↔ 10m (30ft), ▢ ◊ ❋❋❋

Prunus sargentii ♀ ↕ 20m (70ft) ↔ 15m (50ft), ▢ ◊ ❋❋❋

Shrubs with autumn leaf colour

Acer japonicum 'Aconitifolium' ♀ ↕ 5m (15ft) ↔ 6m (20ft), ▢–▨ ◊ ᵞ ❋❋❋

Amelanchier lamarckii ♀ ↕ 10m (30ft) ↔ 12m (40ft), ▢–▨ ◊ ᵞ ❋❋❋

Berberis thunbergii ♀ ↕ 1.5m (5ft) ↔ 2.4m (8ft), ▢ ◊ ❋❋❋

Cotinus 'Flame' ♀ ↕↔ 5m (15ft), ▢–▨ ◊ ❋❋❋ [1]

Euonymus alatus ♀ ↕ 1.8m (6ft) ↔ 3m (10ft), ▢–▨ ◊ ❋❋❋

Rhododendron luteum ♀ ↕↔ 4m (12ft), ▨ ◊ ᵞ ❋❋❋

Rhus typhina 'Dissecta' ♀ ↕ 1.8m (6ft) ↔ 3m (10ft), ▢ ◊ ❋❋❋

Small trees for colourful autumn fruits

Arbutus unedo ♀ ↕↔ 8m (25ft), E ▢ ◊ ❋❋❋ [2]

Ilex aquifolium 'J.C. van Tol' ♀ ↕ 6m (20ft) ↔ 4m (12ft), self-fertile female, E ▢–▨ ◊ ❋❋❋

Malus x *zumi* 'Golden Hornet' ♀ ↕ 10m (30ft) ↔ 8m (25ft), ▢ ◊ ❋❋❋

Sorbus cashmiriana ♀ ↕ 8m (25ft) ↔ 7m (22ft), ▢–▨ ◊ ❋❋❋

Sorbus vilmorinii ♀ ↕↔ 5m (15ft), ▢–▨ ◊ ❋❋❋

Shrubs with colourful autumn fruits

Berberis x *carminea* 'Pirate King' ♀ ↕ 1.5m (5ft) ↔ 2.4m (8ft), E ▢ ◊ ❋❋❋

Callicarpa bodinieri var. *giraldii* 'Profusion' ♀ ↕ 3m (10ft) ↔ 2.4m (8ft), ▢–▨ ◊ ❋❋❋

Cotoneaster frigidus 'Cornubia' ♀ ↕↔ 6m (20ft), E ▢ ◊ ❋❋❋

Cotoneaster salicifolius 'Rothschildianus' ♀ ↕↔ 5m (15ft), E ▢ ◊ ❋❋❋

Euonymus europaeus 'Red Cascade' ♀ ↕ 3m (10ft) ↔ 2.4m (8ft), ▢–▨ ◊ ❋❋❋

Hippophae rhamnoides ♀ ↕↔ 6m (20ft), male and female plants needed for berry production, ▢ ◊ ❋❋❋

Pyracantha 'Orange Glow' ♀ ↕↔ 3m (10ft), E ▢–▨ ◊ ❋❋❋ [3]

Rosa 'Geranium' ♀ ↕ 2.4m (8ft) ↔ 1.5m (5ft), ▢ ◊ ❋❋❋

Skimmia japonica 'Nymans' ♀ ↕ 90cm (36in) ↔ 1.8m (6ft), female, needs a male plant for berry production, E ▨–▨ ◊ ❋❋❋

Symphoricarpos albus var. *laevigatus* ↕↔ 1.8m (6ft), ▢–▨ ◊ ❋❋❋

Viburnum dilatatum ↕ 3m (10ft) ↔ 1.8m (6ft), ▢–▨ ◊ ❋❋❋

Viburnum opulus 'Xanthocarpum' ♀ ↕ 5m (15ft) ↔ 4m (12ft), ▢–▨ ◊ ❋❋❋

See also Choosing trees for small gardens, pp.50–51; Shrubs for year-round interest, pp.76–77; Perennials for seasonal colour, pp.110–11

PLANTING IDEAS

Choosing plants with attractive winter bark

Trees and shrubs with ornamental bark are often sadly neglected by gardeners, yet they make a great contribution to the garden in winter when their stems show to best effect

Gardeners who think that nothing happens in gardens during winter miss out on some of the most exciting plants of all. As well as plants with delicious scents and subtle or brightly coloured flowers, there are many trees and shrubs with attractive bark. They have this bark all the year round, of course, but it shows up particularly well in winter, when many plants are devoid of leaves. Be sure to place these plants, particularly those with very brightly coloured bark, such as willows (*Salix*) and dogwoods (*Cornus*), in a sunny position, so that the winter sun makes the stems really glow.

Forms of *Salix alba*, *Cornus alba*, and *C. sericea* benefit from hard pruning in the spring to encourage the production of vigorous young growths, which have the best colour. Where this type of pruning is carried out, keep the plants in good condition by applying a mulch of well-rotted garden compost or manure in spring each year. *Leycesteria formosa*, *Stephanandra tanakae*, *Salix daphnoides*, and all the *Rubus* may be treated in a similar way, but usually give better results if a form of renewal pruning is carried out. Each spring cut down to the ground about one-third to half of the shoots. These will normally be replaced by fresh growths from the base. Again, mulch in the spring.

TREES AND SHRUBS FOR ORNAMENTAL BARK

Trees

Acer capillipes ♀ ↕↔ 10m (30ft), white-striped bark, ▫–▩ ◊ ♨ ❋❋❋

Acer davidii ↕↔ 15m (50ft), white-striped bark, ▫–▩ ◊ ♨ ❋❋❋

Acer griseum ♀ ↕↔ 10m (30ft), peeling warm brown bark, ▫–▩ ◊ ♨ ❋❋❋ [1]

Acer grosseri var. *hersii* ♀ ↕↔ 15m (50ft), white-striped bark, ▫–▩ ◊ ♨ ❋❋❋

Acer palmatum 'Sango-kaku' ♀ ↕ 6m (20ft) ↔ 5m (15ft), coral-red shoots, ▫–▩ ◊ ♨ ❋❋❋

Acer pensylvanicum 'Erythrocladum' ↕ 12m (40ft) ↔ 10m (30ft), brilliant pink young shoots, ▫–▩ ◊ ♨ ❋❋❋

Arbutus x *andrachnoides* ♀ ↕↔ 8m (25ft), red-brown bark, ▫ ◊ ❋❋❋

Betula albosinensis var. *septentrionalis* ♀ ↕ 25m (80ft) ↔ 10m (30ft), orange-brown bark, ▫–▩ ◊ ❋❋❋

Betula papyrifera ↕ 20m (70ft) ↔ 10m (30ft) white bark, ▫–▩ ◊ ❋❋❋

Betula utilis var. *jacquemontii* ↕ 18m (60ft) ↔ 10m (30ft), white bark, ▫–▩ ◊ ❋❋❋ [2]

Eucalyptus pauciflora subsp. *niphophila* ♀ ↕ 6m (20ft) ↔ 6–15m (20–50ft), whitish grey bark, ▫ ◊ ❋❋❋

Prunus maackii ↕ 10m (30ft) ↔ 8m (25ft), peeling chestnut brown bark, ▫ ◊ ❋❋❋

Prunus serrula ♀ ↕↔ 10m (30ft), peeling, glossy, red-brown bark, ▫ ◊ ❋❋❋ [3]

Salix alba subsp. *vitellina* ♀ ↕ 25m (80ft) ↔ 10m (30ft), bright yellow young shoots if cut hard, ▫ ◊ ❋❋❋

Salix alba subsp. *vitellina* 'Britzensis' ♀ ↕ 25m (80ft) ↔ 10m (30ft), bright orange-red young shoots if cut hard, ▫ ◊ ❋❋❋

Salix daphnoides ↕ 8m (25ft) ↔ 6m (20ft), purple young shoots overlaid with white bloom, ▫ ◊ ❋❋❋

Shrubs

Berberis dictyophylla ♀ ↕ 1.8m (6ft) ↔ 1.5m (5ft), red-brown stems covered with white bloom, ▫ ◊ ❋❋❋

Cornus alba 'Sibirica' ♀ ↕↔ 3m (10ft), brilliant crimson young shoots if cut hard, ▫ ◊ ❋❋❋ [4]

Cornus sericea 'Flaviramea' ♀ ↕ 1.8m (6ft) ↔ 4m (12ft), bright yellow-green young shoots if cut hard, ▫ ◊ ❋❋❋

Leycesteria formosa ♀ ↕↔ 1.8m (6ft), pea-green young shoots, ▫–▩ ◊ ❋❋❋

Rosa sericea subsp. *omeiensis* f. *pteracantha* ↕ 2.4m (8ft) ↔ 2.2m (7ft), young shoots and large prickles deep red, ▫ ◊ ❋❋❋

Rubus biflorus ♀ ↕↔ 3m (10ft), white stems, ▫ ◊ ❋❋❋

Rubus cockburnianus ↕↔ 2.4m (8ft), white stems, ▫ ◊ ❋❋❋

Stephanandra tanakae ↕↔ 3m (10ft), orange-brown young shoots, ▫–▩ ◊ ❋❋❋

1

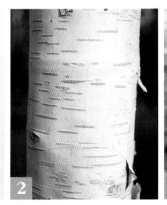

2

3

4

See also Choosing winter-flowering plants, pp.12–13; Choosing trees for small gardens, pp.50–51

WHAT TO PLANT UNDER TREES

What to plant under trees

Trees add character and structure, but the dry shade cast by their canopies can make it difficult to establish plants beneath them

Shade-loving plants
The area beneath a tree can be improved with a dense carpet of shade-loving plants (*left*). Numerous hardy ground-cover perennials that grow naturally in woodland are suitable, including epimediums (barrenworts, *below left*) and *Convallaria majalis* (lily-of-the-valley, *below right*). Improve the soil with bulky organic matter before planting to help retain moisture.

Improving the soil beneath trees prior to planting can make all the difference between success and failure. Add bulky organic matter to help provide a reservoir of moisture for developing plant roots, and a well-balanced base fertilizer to replenish impoverished soil.

After planting, water well if necessary; new plantings will be more prone to drying out than usual. Use an organic mulch, renewing it each spring, to help with moisture retention where tree roots are shallow and dense.

Woodland plants form the majority of plants suitable for growing under trees, particularly where lower branches have been removed. Many look delicate in flower, but ground-cover plants such as lily of the valley (*Convallaria majalis*), dead nettle (*Lamium maculatum*), barrenwort (*Epimedium*), and sweet

violet (*Viola odorata*), are surprisingly robust. Others good for carpeting larger areas include bergenias, *Brunnera macrophylla*, sweet woodruff (*Galium odoratum*), *Geranium macrorrhizum*, foam flower (*Tiarella cordifolia*), Persian ivy (*Hedera colchica*), and greater periwinkle (*Vinca major*). For a splash of colour, try *Liriope muscari* or *Iris foetidissima*. Plant spring bulbs and, for autumn flowers, *Cyclamen hederifolium* under deciduous trees such as beech, hornbeam, birch, or oak.

Plants tolerant of dry shade tend not to have the most flamboyant flowers, but some will make up for it either by their fragrant blooms, such as Christmas box (*Sarcoccoca*) and *Osmanthus* x *burkwoodii*, or their winter berries, including *Skimmia*, snowberry (*Symphoricarpos*), and cotoneasters.

Buying a new tree

Always check a new tree before you buy or plant it

Trees and shrubs are often supplied as container-grown plants in pots, but a wider range is available from nurseries, grown in the open ground then lifted and sold either bare-root, without any soil around the roots, or root-balled or root-wrapped, with a ball of soil around the roots.

When buying any tree or shrub, check that the plants have a well-developed root system that balances the top growth. The roots of container-grown plants should be established in the pot and hold the compost together, but should not be pot-bound. Avoid trees with signs of pest, disease, or mechanical damage.

Some trees are supplied by nurseries with the root ball wrapped in hessian. Such root wraps provide protection and support to the root ball during transport and placement in the planting hole, but it is not possible to see the roots when they are wrapped this way. When buying a tree do try to make sure that the overall root system looks in proportion to the rest of the tree. A large tree with a seemingly tiny root system is unlikely to survive. When you get the tree home you should soak the root ball, still in its root wrap, with water as it may have started to dry out while still on the nursery. Then water thoroughly again before planting.

Removing the wrapping will give you the opportunity to inspect the root ball to check that the roots are healthy and adequate for the tree size, and that they are not damaged or circling the root ball. It will also enable you see that the tree is planted at the correct depth. Where wire is used to surround the wrapping it is best cut away, at least from the top part of the root ball, to avoid subsequent damage to the roots.

See also Choosing plants for ground cover, pp.27–27; Choosing shrubs to grow in shade, p.83

See also Successful tree and shrub planting,

Support for new trees

A newly planted tree may need support until it becomes established, but don't be tempted to leave stakes in place for too long

A newly planted tree more than 1.5m (5ft) tall may need staking during its initial establishment. The purpose of the stake is to allow the tree to establish a good anchorage system and a straight, vertical stem. Very young trees less than this height, called whips, do not generally need staking.

There are two methods of staking you can choose from: an angled stake inserted at 45 degrees for container-grown or root-balled trees, and an upright stake for bare-root trees. Do not use a tall stake, as it will prevent the trunk from building up strength. A low, upright stake, about one-third of the tree's height, enables the tree to flex slightly in the wind, promoting strong stems and roots.

Use wooden tree stakes that have been treated with wood preservative. Insert the stake in the planting hole before the tree is planted: never drive the stake through the root ball. Place an upright stake on the windward side of the tree, and insert an angled stake leaning into the prevailing wind so that any tree movement is away from the

stake, thus avoiding friction. Secure the tree stem to the stake with a non-abrasive material that has some flexibility. Proprietary buckle-type tree ties hold the tree securely, but not rigidly. Always use a rubber spacer or padding to keep the stake clear of the trunk to avoid chafing the tender bark.

Check the ties each spring and loosen them as the tree girth expands, otherwise they will cut into the bark and restrict the uptake of foods and water to the crown. This damage may weaken the tree, and ties that are not regularly loosened as the tree grows can cause considerable damage.

Remove the stake as soon as the tree is securely anchored by its own roots. Establishing trees is a slow process, but if soil conditions are favourable, most trees do not need staking for more than two growing seasons, and the tree may well be sufficiently established one year from planting. If a stake is left in place too long, the tree comes to rely on it for support and may not produce an adequate root system to support itself.

Hessian wrap: supports and protects root ball

Some people plant trees with the hessian root wrap left intact in the belief that removing it may cause damage to the existing roots and that it will not hinder the development of new roots. If soil conditions are good and the soil moist on both sides of the wrapping, roots may well be able to reach out into the soil and the wrapping may decay, but establishment failures can occur where the root wrappings are left in place after planting. However, some suppliers will not guarantee to replace a tree where wrappings are removed, so do check this when buying.

POINTS TO CHECK

- Always buy from a reputable nursery to get a good plant with the correct name
- Check that the union on any grafted plants is strong and well healed (see Choosing an apple or pear tree, p.233)
- Trees below 1.2m (4ft) tall cost less and establish faster than larger trees planted at the same time

Buckle-type tie: holds tree securely but not rigidly

Angled stake: for containerized or root-balled trees

pp.60–61; Trees for small gardens, pp.50–51

See also Successful tree and shrub planting, pp.60–61

Why trees and shrubs fail

Death after planting usually comes down to poor planting

Congested roots: tease out to prevent failure

Failure with newly planted trees and shrubs may be due to one or more of the following factors:

• Planting hole was not deep enough to allow the plant to be established at its original soil level, or not wide enough to take the roots when fully spread out.

• There are air pockets around the roots. This is due to lack of firming and not working fine soil between roots when planting.

• Roots of container-grown trees were not teased out, or the root ball was not roughened to encourage outward growth of roots.

• When soil was returned around the roots, the sides of the planting hole were not broken down with a fork to encourage root spread. This is most important on clay soils to avoid creating a water-collecting sump in the hole that causes waterlogging and airless conditions.

• The soil was over-firmed around the roots, compacting it, excluding air, and preventing the roots from functioning effectively.

See also Successful planting, pp.60–61

Summer pruning of ornamental trees

Although it is not advisable to prune ornamental trees regularly, summer can be a suitable time to carry out limited tree work

Depending on the species of tree involved, problems such as competing leading shoots can be remedied during the growing season.

Why prune?

It is best to avoid pruning ornamental trees, as it can reduce the tree's growth rate and carries the risk of allowing disease to enter the plant. However, shaping of young trees is sometimes necessary when they have developed crowded branches and lack a clear main shoot or leader.

Remove shoots that compete with or prevent light from reaching the leader. This type of pruning aims to create a tree with a roughly conical shape – with sufficient branches at the top to feed the stem and leader without competing with it, and some shortened stems lower down to feed the stem.

Best time to prune

Trees have different optimum times of year for pruning. Aim to prune at a time when the tree is most likely to make a good recovery.

Autumn and early winter have long been thought of as ideal times. Yet in autumn, the tree's defences are weak and its wood is dry and oxygen rich, favouring the decay fungi whose spores are abundant at this time. In winter, trees are inactive, but fungi may continue to be active and able to invade during warm spells. In spring and early summer, renewed growth depletes the tree's resources for healing and defence, although pruning just before growth begins should avoid this.

In summer, some trees are active, rich in resources, and able to recover quickly. Ornamental and fruiting *Prunus*, such as cherries and plums, are much less susceptible to silver leaf disease when pruned in early summer.

Summer pruning is also recommended for *Cercidiphyllum*, magnolia, birches (*Betula*) and oaks (*Quercus*), late summer or early autumn being best as this avoids the risk of further shoot growth.

However, if trees have been pruned in winter, it is unlikely to do them serious damage.

SUMMER PRUNING A YOUNG TREE

Carry out shaping while the tree is young, using secateurs to ensure clean cuts. **1** This young tree lacks a leader. **2** Remove crowded branches to thin out the tree. **3** Remove shoots that compete, leaving one clear leading stem. **4** The end result is a well-balanced tree.

See also Tree surgery, p.68

PRACTICAL ADVICE

Bleeding from pruning cuts

Don't be alarmed if trees lose sap through pruning cuts

Bleeding from pruning cut: not serious

Though unsightly, bleeding from pruning cuts seldom harms trees: in fact, maple syrup is made from sap collected from *Acer saccharinum* by exploiting this phenomenon in a controlled way.

Bleeding results from the pressure of sap in the water-conductive tissues, usually in late winter to early spring. Wounds on larger deciduous trees, such as maple (*Acer*) and birch (*Betula*) can bleed heavily when pruned at this time. There may be some loss of sugars, and in severe cases it can delay wound healing. There are no practical measures to stem the flow of sap, but it subsides naturally in time.

Trees that are prone to bleeding are best pruned between midsummer and early winter. They include maple, birch, *Carpinus*, *Carya*, walnut (*Juglans*), laburnum, spring-flowering deciduous magnolias, mulberry (*Morus*), some poplars (*Populus*), *Sophora* and limes (*Tilia*). Check the pruning needs of specific trees and the best time to prune in a reference book on pruning.

See also Tree surgery, p.68

TECHNIQUES

How to remove suckers

These shoots are vigorous and can soon dominate a tree or shrub, so remove them as soon as they are noticed

Shoots arising below soil level, from the roots rather than from the stem of the plant, are known as root suckers. Stem suckers are shoots that appear just beneath the graft union on the rootstock of a grafted or budded plant. Suckers of a grafted plant may quickly become larger than the top growth or even replace it within a few years, so that the rootstock species predominates rather than the grafted cultivar.

Many trees produce suckers from their root system. In the garden these can be a considerable nuisance, appearing in borders, lawns, between paving slabs, or through bituminous paths. Some trees are naturally shallow rooting, but the roots of many other trees may develop near the soil surface if there are difficult growing conditions, such as a high water table or an impervious sub-soil that restricts drainage. Near-surface roots are the most likely to produce suckers.

Root suckers can appear after root damage resulting from digging or forking around plants, lawn spiking, damage to surface roots during lawn mowing, or where roots are accidentally or deliberately cut during excavations. If suckers are allowed to grow unnoticed they will, in time, develop into trees. Poplars (*Populus*), cherries and plums (*Prunus*), stagshorn sumach (*Rhus*), lilacs (*Syringa*) and false acacia (*Robinia pseudoacacia*) are among the most troublesome garden trees and shrubs, and *Sorbus* – especially when it is grafted onto hawthorn (*Crataegus monogyna*) – can produce shoots at the base of the trunk.

Dealing with suckers

Remove root suckers as close as possible to the point of origin on the root. It is better to tear away the shoot rather than use secateurs, so that the majority of dormant basal buds are removed, reducing the possibility of regrowth. You may have to scrape the soil away to reach the base of the suckers. In lawns where roots are surfacing, strip off the turf and raise the soil by 5–8cm (2–3in) before replacing the turf. Do this between mid-autumn and late winter.

Stem suckers arising from the rootstock of budded or grafted trees and shrubs are again best removed by pulling them off at their point of origin rather than cutting them off cleanly with secateurs. In the latter instance there is chance of regrowth, as mentioned above.

Suckers on a witch hazel (*Hamamelis*)
Witch hazel cultivars are often grafted onto *H. virginiana*, which suckers vigorously; the suckers usually hold their leaves longer than the cultivar. Ideally, rub out suckers when they are still buds; otherwise, pull them off.

See also Tree stump removal, p.73

| TECHNIQUES | PRACTICAL ADVICE | TECHNIQUES |

Pruning for winter interest

Prune hard for thickets of coloured stems in winter

Shrubby dogwoods (*Cornus*) and willows (*Salix*) with coloured stems can be hard pruned or coppiced in early spring before bud break for winter stem interest. Coppicing means cutting back all stems to within 5–8cm (2–3in) of the ground or to the previous year's stubs in the second and subsequent years after planting.

Both these genera flower on old wood, so cutting them back each year will deprive you of flowers (or catkins) and fruits. To get the best of both worlds, try cutting back only one-third of the stems each year, removing the oldest and thickest ones. Alternatively, only hard prune every two or three years. *Cornus sericea* 'Flaviramea', *C. alba* 'Sibirica', *Salix alba* subsp. *vitellina* 'Britzensis' and *S. irrorata* all respond well. Annual pruning is also not ideal for less-vigorous plants such as *Cornus sanguinea* and variegated *C. alba* 'Elegantissima', so remove one stem in three annually, or coppice every other year.

Coppicing *Cornus sericea* 'Flaviramea'

See also Attractive winter bark, p.63

Tree surgery

Whether or not to call out a tree surgeon is a difficult decision

Tree surgeons have specialist equipment

Tree surgeons' bills can be expensive and how do you go about choosing a reputable surgeon? Could you even do the work yourself? Simple tasks such as small branch removal or cutting back can be carried out by two competent gardeners, if a ladder is the only climbing equipment needed; larger jobs needing specialist climbing and cutting equipment should only be tackled by qualified tree surgeons.

Some problems, such as over-sized trees, are easily recognized. Crown lifting and thinning can improve light and reduce wind resistance, but are jobs for professionals. Lightning or storm damage often leaves visible wounds. Fungal attack can be harder to identify, so if in doubt, take advice.

In Britain owners are legally liable for any damage their trees cause. This includes roots as well as falling limbs. Qualified arboricultural consultants can assess the risk from roots, and investigate any risks from falling trees or branches. They should be able to recommend qualified tree surgeons to carry out any work needed.

See also Are your trees safe?, p.56

Creating mop-headed trees

Pollarding produces interesting architectural effects

Pollarding involves regularly cutting the branches of a tree right back to the trunk to encourage the growth of young shoots. This process produces "mop-headed" trees that have vigorous annual growth from the top of a short stem for interesting architectural effects. The shape is distinctive, with numerous branches arising from the same point

Variegated *Acer negundo*: amenable to pollarding

on the tree. These shoots emerge from dormant buds under the bark, and there is often a thickened base where the shoot meets the trunk. Over the years a noticeably swollen "pollard head" or "boll" forms where new shoots spring up each year.

Good shrubs and trees for pollarding have showy foliage, stems, or buds, flower on the current season's growth, and break freely from dormant buds. Common lime (*Tilia* x *europaea*) and London plane (*Platanus* x *hispanica*)

See also Trees and shrubs with colourful

are well known as pollarded street trees. Species of maple (*Acer*), alder (*Alnus*), tree of heaven (*Ailanthus*), eucalyptus, bean trees (*Catalpa*), ash (*Fraxinus*), *Hydrangea paniculata*, oak (*Quercus*), tulip tree (*Liriodendron*), *Paulownia*, mulberry (*Morus*), and willow (*Salix*) are also suitable.

Maintaining a pollard

Having a large tree pollarded regularly by an arboriculturist is expensive, but left unpruned the tree may need more extensive surgery to remove larger parts at a greater height. You should be able to safely tackle smaller garden trees using hand tools. Cut branches above the previous pollarding cuts to avoid exposing older wood, which may increase risk of decay.

The best time to pollard many trees is in late winter or early spring, when they have a good reserve of food and are not under water stress; do not prune maples in spring, as at this time they are prone to bleeding (*see p.67*). After the spring flush of growth, food reserves are depleted, so this is not a good time to pollard. Summer, when food reserves

Creating a mop-headed tree
This Indian bean tree (*Catalpa bignonioides*) was not growing well. After pollarding, it made vigorous new growth (*left*). This tree produces particularly large leaves when pollarded (*right*).

have been replenished, can be suitable, but in dry weather the tree will be under drought stress.

Pollarding is best started on young trees, as the wood recovers rapidly after wounding, reducing the risk of decay. Initially grow the tree to the desired height and branch framework. Once started, continue with regular pruning, or the weight and angle of the branches can lead to weakness, particularly where branches are crowded together.

Initially cut back single-stemmed young plants in spring to a height of about 60–90cm (2–3ft) and allow side shoots to grow. Cut back these strong shoots close to their point of origin to encourage the development of yet more shoots, or thin them out if too crowded.

The following spring, remove all the annual growth, leaving just one or two single or paired dormant buds at the base of each shoot. Feed plants well to support the large amount of growth.

THINNING NEW GROWTH

After cutting back, plants produce many new shoots. Use secateurs to thin these (here on *Salix alba* subsp. *vitellina* 'Britzensis'), taking care not to damage the enlarged head.

WHY POLLARD?

Pollarding has practical advantages, as well as producing an attractive, rounded tree shape or coloured shoots. Pollarding a tree restricts its size, confining it to its allotted space. It will also reduce the shade cast by the tree, and prevent overgrown branches from damaging overhead cables or gutters.

foliage, pp.57–58; Choosing plants with attractive winter bark, p.63; Bleeding from pruning cuts, p.67

How to deal with overgrown conifers

If replacing an unruly conifer is not an option, try to contain it by reducing the height, judicious pruning, or tying in branches

Conifers such as *Chamaecyparis lawsoniana* (Lawson cypress) and x *Cupressocyparis leylandii* (Leyland cypress) often grow too large for the size of the garden. In the long run it may be best to replace them with trees of a more appropriate mature height, because heavy pruning will spoil their natural shape. As with many conifers, neither of these will regrow from cuts made into the bare wood.

One alternative is to reduce their height, removing no more than one-third of the tree in mid-spring as new growth is about to begin. This will check their growth, leaving a flat-topped tree. However, vigorous individuals will thicken up at the top to modify this stark appearance. Tall trees are best pruned by a qualified arboriculturist. Side branches at the base of older trees should be removed entirely, as little new growth is likely. Younger trees may respond to

trimming, but take care not to cut back too severely. Foliage may not extend far into the tree at the base, and cuts beyond green leaves will not regrow.

By contrast, *Taxus baccata* (yew) responds well to pruning, producing new growth from old wood. Be careful not to spoil the natural shape of a mature yew tree, and spread pruning over several years, cutting back to different points within the tree to remove branches selectively. Where large trees are involved, pruning is best carried out by an arboriculturist.

Fastigiate conifers have a strongly erect, narrow crown and virtually upright branches that are almost parallel with the main stem. If they start to open up or become unruly, you can tie them in with strands of galvanised or plastic-coated wire to maintain a tight columnar shape. Although wires are visible initially they are quickly covered by new growth.

TYING IN A CONIFER

Fastigiate conifers have a strong natural shape that needs very little maintenance. **1** Specimens that threaten to get out of hand can be tied in to preserve their shape. **2** The wires will soon be concealed by new foliage.

See also Trees and buildings, pp.52–53; Are your trees safe?, p.56

Avoiding frost damage

Plants can be damaged by sudden early autumn or late spring frosts

Hardy woody plants adapt well to winter cold, becoming 'hardened' in autumn by increasingly cold days.

Deciduous trees and shrubs shed their vulnerable leaves, but leave resilient buds containing new leaves and flowers to overwinter. Ice crystals that form within plant tissues will fatally rupture cells but plant tissues also accumulate soluble materials that act as antifreeze, protecting them down to about -1 or -2°C (30–28°F). Further protection from temperatures as low as -40°C (-40°F) can be achieved because hardy plants allow their liquid content to cool to below 0°C (32°F) without actually freezing.

Redoubtably hardy plants, such as birches (*Betula*) and willows (*Salix*) from alpine or Arctic areas, move water to areas outside their cells and allow it to freeze there, where it causes less harm. Despite becoming extremely desiccated, the cell contents remain undamaged and are able to rehydrate again in spring.

Broad-leaved evergreens are more vulnerable because the leaves they retain can be damaged by cold; garryas and camellias are among the plants commonly affected. Moisture that is lost from the leaf cannot be replenished when the soil is frozen. The damage to the plant can be severe if frozen soil coincides with windy conditions or with mild warm air, which efficiently extracts moisture from foliage.

Plants can be 'caught' by a sudden, sharp, autumn or spring frost when the hardening process is either incomplete, or when the plants are starting to lose their resistance to cold. This can severely damage plant material. Buds of walnut (*Juglans*) and chestnut (*Castanea*) are especially vulnerable in spring; the young foliage of buddlejas

Frost damage on leaves

and *Hydrangea anomala* subsp. *petiolaris* are also easily harmed by a late freeze. Repeated freezing and thawing, as chill nights alternate with sunny days, is particularly damaging.

Frost damage results in longitudinal splitting of stems and distorted leaves. It is most likely to be seen on trees and shrubs that are tender, or those that have put on late growth in the autumn. Freezing and rapid thawing will damage the new buds of plants such as hydrangeas, camellias and magnolias if they are exposed to the morning sun in an east-facing aspect.

Shrub foliage may be protected with a double layer of fleece over the leaves. Wrapping bubble plastic around containers will help to stop their contents from freezing. You can also apply organic mulches around the base of plants; this creates a protective layer over the soil surface that will help to prevent the roots from becoming frozen.

In low-lying gardens, try to avoid growing vulnerable plants in frost pockets, and on south- and east-facing aspects where injuries caused by freezing and thawing are likely to be severe. Young trees and shrubs are especially vulnerable to this kind of damage, so it is advisable to protect them with tree shelters and fleece.

If your plants have been damaged by frost or cold, prune out the dead shoots, where this is possible, to help the plants recover. Regrowth usually does occur, although it may not appear until mid-summer.

FROST DAMAGE

1 The effects of frost can be severe, damaging foliage and causing plant stems to split. **2** In spring, when all danger of frost has passed, remove any dead or damaged shoots to promote new growth. **3** Use bubble plastic or fleece to protect the foliage of young or vulnerable plants.

Preventing wind scorch

Unsightly brown patches are usually a sign of wind scorch

Gardens in exposed locations are often subjected to strong winds. This rapid air movement causes moisture to be lost from the foliage and soil, and can result in physical damage to plants, especially evergreen trees and shrubs during winter. Vulnerable plants are unable to replace the moisture that is lost from their foliage quickly enough, so their leaves become desiccated and scorched.

• Plant shrubs in the lee of deciduous garden hedges, which filter the wind. However, dense evergreen hedges, garden walls and fences may deflect the wind, causing some damaging turbulence on the leeward side.
• Mulch the soil around plants to reduce the drying effect of wind.
• Place container-grown plants against a sheltered house wall, but be careful to avoid wind tunnels.

WINDBREAKS

Erect windbreaks using netting, proprietary windbreak materials, or woven hurdles, to reduce the strength of the wind. A screen that filters wind by 50–60 per cent is ideal.

See also Seaside gardens, pp.24–25

DESTRUCTIVE BULLFINCHES

Destructive bullfinches

Cover vulnerable plants with netting to prevent damage

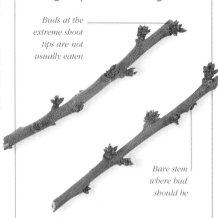

Buds at the extreme shoot tips are not usually eaten

Bare stem where bud should be

The bullfinch (*Pyrrhula pyrrhula*) occurs throughout Britain, although in many parts it has declined. For much of the year it causes no damage to garden plants as its diet consists largely of weed, grass and wild flower seeds. But in winter, when the seed supply runs out, it seeks alternative food and takes flower buds from a variety of trees and shrubs.

Fruit trees and bushes are favoured, but ornamentals such as almond, flowering cherry (*Prunus*) and forsythia can also lose a large proportion of their flower buds. Plum, cherry, pear and gooseberry buds are eaten between late autumn and early spring, but apple and blackcurrant are usually left until early to mid-spring, when the buds have begun to open.

Preventing damage is not easy on plants too large to be protected by netting. Scaring devices or repellent substances often have no more than a short-term effect. In gardens where bullfinches are a problem, cover any vulnerable plants with netting or invest in a fruit cage. A mesh size of 2cm (¾in) is suitable. Remove or lift netting during the flowering period to give bees and other pollinating insects access to the flowers.

See also Bird pests, p.45

Beating honey fungus

This lethal disease attacks many ornamental and fruiting trees and shrubs and spreads rapidly, so remove affected plants promptly

Honey-coloured toadstools

Honey fungus 'bootlaces'

Honey fungus, also known as the bootlace fungus, is potentially the most devastating disease to occur in gardens. It affects mainly trees and shrubs but also attacks some perennials. The fungus that causes the disease, usually *Armillaria mellea*, feeds off dead and dying woody tissue. It spreads through the soil and from plant to plant by means of tough, dark, leathery structures, or 'bootlaces', that grow at a rate of up to 1m (39in) per year, mostly through the upper 20cm (8in) of soil. When they reach a host plant, the tip of the 'bootlace' penetrates the bark at the base of the trunk or on the roots. The infected plant dies when the fungus invades the plant vessels, disrupting the flow of water and foods. Later, the fungus rots the wood.

COMBAT TIPS

- Try halting the spread of the 'bootlaces' by placing vertical barriers of tough plastic sheeting in the ground, extending to a depth of at least 80cm (32in)
- Regular feeding and mulching helps to keep plants healthy, and better able to withstand infection
- Remove all the root systems of affected plants promptly

Symptoms

Above ground, plants may suffer for a relatively short period of time or may appear sickly for several years before dying. Symptoms often become apparent in spring when trees fail to come into leaf or buds fail to open.

Below ground, confirmation of honey fungus infection can be obtained by examining the roots and base of the trunk at ground level. When the bark of infected areas is peeled away, it reveals a creamy-white fungal layer.

Toadstools may appear around the base of infected plants in late summer and autumn.

Control

The most effective means of controlling honey fungus is by removing its food source. When the 'bootlaces' have been severed from the stump or the dead plant they have colonised, they will starve and will no longer be infective. Therefore, promptly remove all dead or dying plants, including as much of their root systems as possible. In hedges remove the plants on either side of the affected plant as they are likely to be at an early stage of infection. Keep plants healthy by feeding and mulching, to make them less prone to infection.

See also Avoiding pests and diseases, pp.36–37

PRACTICAL ADVICE

Tree stump removal

Removing a tree leaves an area for development. For this space to be successfully planted, remove or grind down the stump

Although tree stumps can be left after felling and covered with sprawling plants, such as herbaceous clematis, this can lead to problems with suckering where new shoots arise from the trunk and roots (*see page 67*). Dead stumps do not form suckers, but they can play host to root diseases such as honey fungus (*see opposite*).

The physical removal of the stump is the best solution. It may be most convenient to pay the tree surgeon to do this when felling the tree. Otherwise it is advisable to have tree stumps removed by a specialist.

The stumps of smaller trees may be pulled out using a winch, which can be hired. If you intend to use this method, it is necessary to leave a stub on the stump for leverage, rather than cutting it off at ground level.

Grubbing out by hand or using a mini-excavator can remove most of the root system. Mini-excavators and operators can also be hired.

Alternatively, hire a contractor to remove the stump mechanically with a machine known as a stump grinder, which grinds out the main root plate leaving fine sawdust. Some roots will inevitably be left in the ground but the majority should eventually rot.

Be sure to have any diseased wood removed completely, and specify how deep you would like them to grind out the stump. Shallow grinding, 20–25cm (8–10in), is normally sufficient for laying turf, but allow for deeper grinding, to 30cm (12in) or more, if you intend replanting or landscaping.

Where stumps cannot be removed, drill holes into the outer layer of the stump, ideally just after felling the tree, and fill the holes with weedkiller. The tree roots should be killed within six weeks, but the stump may take several years to rot away. Weedkillers, such as ammonium sulphamate, or brushwood killer should be applied according to the manufacturer's instructions.

REMOVING A TREE STUMP

Although stump grinders are available for hire, they are potentially hazardous and should only be used by gardeners confident that they can use the machinery safely. **1** Stump grinders mechanically grind out the main root plate of the tree. **2** Compost the resulting sawdust and use it as a mulch around flowers or vegetables, but not woody plants.

See also Finding contractors, p.11

PLANTING IDEAS

Fragrant trees and shrubs

Flowers and foliage can provide scent in every season of the year

Fragrant flowers of *Buddleja davidii* 'Harlequin'

Fragrance is often forgotten when planting a garden, particularly when it comes to trees and shrubs. Yet among plants there are as many shades of fragrance as there are of colours: they can affect mood, take you back to your childhood, or whisk you off to a far-off land with a single sniff. The most strongly scented flowers are often white, or insignificant in appearance, but make their presence felt in other ways.

While flowers tend to have sweet, fruity perfumes, leaf scents tend to be spicy or resinous. Many plants with scented foliage need gentle stroking or pinching to release their perfume. It is likely that these plants evolved their scents to make themselves less appealing to insect pests, but gardeners find them irresistible. ▷

See also Climbers for fragrance, p.130

FRAGRANT TREES AND SHRUBS

FRAGRANT FLOWERS

Large shrubs

Buddleja davidii ↕ 3m (10ft) ↔ 5m (15ft), summer to autumn, ◻ ◊ ❋❋❋

Philadelphus 'Virginal' ↕ 3m (10ft) ↔ 2.4m (8ft), early summer, ◻–◼ ◊ ❋❋❋

Viburnum farreri ♀ ↕ 3m (10ft) ↔ 2.4m (8ft), winter to early spring, ◻–◼ ◊ ❋❋❋

Medium shrubs

Choisya ternata ♀ ↕↔ 1.8m (6ft), late spring, autumn and winter, E ◻ ◊ ❋❋❋ 1

Corylopsis pauciflora ♀ ↕ 1.5m (5ft) ↔ 2.4m (8ft), spring, ◻ ◊ ❦ ❋❋❋

Lonicera fragrantissima ↕ 1.8m (6ft) ↔ 3m (10ft), winter, ◻–◼ ◊ ❋❋❋

Philadelphus x lemoinei ↕↔ 1.5m (5ft), early summer, ◻–◼ ◊ ❋❋❋

Syringa pubescens subsp. *microphylla* 'Superba' ♀ ↕↔ 1.8m (6ft), early summer, ◻ ◊ ❋❋❋

Small shrubs

Coronilla valentina subsp. *glauca* ♀ ↕↔ 80cm (32in), spring, E ◻ ◊ ❋❋

Daphne mezereum ↕ 1.2m (4ft) ↔ 90cm (36in), late winter/early spring, ◻ ◊ ❋❋❋

Philadelphus 'Sybille' ♀ ↕ 1.2m (4ft) ↔ 1.8m (6ft), early summer, ◻–◼ ◊ ❋❋❋

Sarcococca hookeriana var. *humilis* ↕ 60cm (24in) ↔ 90cm (36in), winter E ◻–◼ ◊ ❋❋❋

FRAGRANT FOLIAGE

Trees

Eucalyptus pauciflora subsp. *niphophila* ♀ ↕ 6m (20ft) ↔ 6–15m (20–50ft) E ◻ ◊ ❋❋❋

Laurus nobilis ♀ ↕ 12m (40ft) ↔ 10m (30ft) E ◻–◼ ◊ ❋❋

Shrubs

Artemisia abrotanum ♀ ↕↔ 90cm (36in) ◻ ◊ ❋❋❋

Helichrysum italicum ♀ ↕ 60cm (24in) ↔ 90cm (36in) E ◻ ◊ ❋❋ 2

Lavandula angustifolia ↕ 90cm (36in) ↔ 1.2m (4ft) ◻ ◊ ❋❋❋

Rosa rubiginosa ↕↔ 2.4m (8ft) ◻ ◊ ❋❋❋

Rosmarinus officinalis ↕↔ 1.5m (5ft) E ◻ ◊ ❋❋

Salvia officinalis ↕ 80cm (32in) ↔ 90cm (36in) E ◻ ◊ ❋❋❋

Santolina chamaecyparissus ♀ ↕ 50cm (20in) ↔ 90cm (36in) E ◻ ◊ ❋❋

Conifers

Calocedrus decurrens ♀ ↕ 20–40m (70–130ft) ↔ 2–9m (6–28ft) E ◻–◼ ◊ ❋❋❋

Cupressus macrocarpa ↕ 30m (100ft) ↔ 4–12m (12–40ft) E ◻ ◊ ❋❋❋

Juniperus chinensis ↕ 20m (70ft) ↔ 6m (20ft) E ◻–◼ ◊ ❋❋❋

Thuja plicata ↕ 20–35m (70–120ft) ↔ 6–9m (20–30ft) E ◻ ◊ ❋❋❋

1

2

See also Choosing fragrant perennials, p.130

Hardwood cuttings

An easy way to propagate deciduous trees and shrubs

A wide range of deciduous trees, shrubs and climbers can be raised from hardwood cuttings. Take hardwood cuttings from after leaf fall in late autumn to just before bud burst in early spring. Suitable cuttings range from a few centimetres in length to 90cm (3ft) long cuttings sometimes used for willow (*Salix*), but the usual cutting is about 20cm (8in) long with a girth slightly greater than a pencil. Take cuttings from the current season's growth, with the exception of *Ficus carica* (fig) which can be up to three years old. Use secateurs for preparing all hardwood cuttings.

Rooting outdoors

For robust trees and shrubs such as willow and *Sambucus* (elder) you can plant cuttings directly outside in a prepared bed. Light, sandy, well-drained soil that warms up quickly in spring produces the best results. Improve heavier soils by incorporating sharp sand and grit. Make sure the site is sheltered from drying winds.

Insert cuttings in a groove made by inserting a spade into the soil. Run some sharp sand into the base of the groove to give the cuttings extra drainage and air at their rooting zone. Insert cuttings so that only the top third shows above ground. Space cuttings 10cm (4in) apart in the row with 30–45cm (12–18in) between rows.

The leafless cuttings can easily be inserted upside-down. To ensure they are planted the right way up, prepare them with a sloping cut above the top bud and a horizontal one at the base, just below a bud or pair of buds (node). All dormant buds are retained.

Firm the cuttings in well to ensure that they have good contact with the soil, there are no air pockets at the

See also How to propagate climbers, p.98

ROOTING CUTTINGS IN CONTAINERS

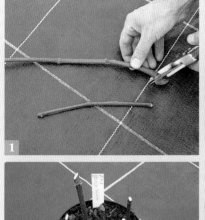

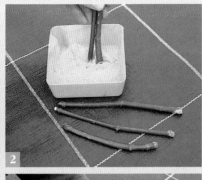

Choose firm material for cuttings and discard any weak tips. You can fit 5–10 cuttings into a 15cm (6in) diameter pot. **1** Cut the base of the cuttings below a bud and the top just above a bud. **2** Dip in hormone rooting powder. **3** Insert cuttings in a pot that takes two-thirds of the length, without it touching the base. Use compost of equal parts by volume of peat substitute and coarse sand with a pinch of controlled-release fertilizer. Coir and perlite are also suitable. **4** Water, then stand the pots on a heated bench or in an open propagating case; a soil temperature of 12–15°C (54–59°F) is ideal. Keep aerial parts cool but frost-free. Ensure good ventilation to prevent them coming into leaf early. **5** Remove cuttings from pot when root system is fully established, after several months. **6** Separate, and pot up into individual containers to grow on.

base of the cuttings which would lead to drying out, and they are sufficiently secure to prevent frost lifting them out of the ground. In spring, as the soil warms and is more likely to dry out, water the cuttings and control weeds. Even when planted in late autumn, rooting will not begin until spring, so leave the cuttings *in situ* until the following autumn, when they will be large enough to lift and plant straight into the garden.

Rooting in a cold frame

You can increase the range of plants to propagate from hardwood cuttings by providing winter protection in a cold frame. Insert cuttings in containers or push them directly into the soil in the frame. Keep the frame closed for much of the winter, but open it on sunny days to prevent overheating, and in early spring to allow the cuttings to be well aired to prevent premature growth before roots have formed. Rooting will be quicker than for unprotected cuttings, but the plants will need watering more often. Though growing strongly by early summer, cuttings will need shading with fleece or green netting to prevent young growth being scorched. Gradually 'wean' the plants by periodically removing the frame cover until it is warm enough for them to be removed completely.

Cuttings to root in containers

For small quantities, root cuttings in long pots (*see above*). Provide protection and gentle bottom heat in a cool greenhouse in winter and move them to a cold frame when they have begun to root in spring.

SUITABLE PLANTS

Cuttings to root outdoors

Buddleja, Forsythia, Ligustrum, Populus, Prunus cerasifera, Rubus, Salix, Sambucus, Sorbaria, Symphoricarpos, Weigela

Cuttings to root in a cold frame

Abutilon, Berberis, Caryopteris, Chaenomeles, Clematis, Cornus, Deutzia, Fuchsia, Hypericum, Jasminum, Kerria, Laburnum, Leycesteria, Lonicera, Perovskia, Philadelphus, Physocarpus, Platanus, Potentilla, Ribes, Rosa, Spiraea, Stephanandra, Viburnum

Cuttings to root in containers

Actinidia, Ficus carica (shown above), *Hibiscus, Metasequoia, Parthenocissus, Polygonum, Tamarix, Vitis, Wisteria*

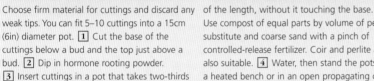

SHRUBS FOR YEAR-ROUND INTEREST

Shrubs for year-round interest

Deciduous and evergreen shrubs help to form the permanent framework in a planting scheme; a good collection will provide colour and interest in your garden for every month of the year

When choosing shrubs for the garden make your selection wide enough to ensure colour and interest all the year round. This may be mainly provided by flowers, but also consider foliage effects – particularly in autumn and winter – and autumn or winter fruits and berries. Also, aim for a good balance of deciduous and evergreen kinds – say, a third evergreen to two-thirds deciduous.

There is a huge range of shrubs available so there is no excuse for any part of the year to be devoid of their interest. Where space is limited, opt for the smaller kinds. The widest selections of shrubs will be found in the catalogues of specialist nurseries, although a good garden centre should also be able to offer you a reasonably versatile choice of plants.

SMALL SHRUBS FOR SEASONAL INTEREST

These shrubs are listed according to season of flowering or major interest. Some will provide interest, such as berries or autumn leaf colour, at other seasons and evergreen plants are attractive throughout the year.

Shrubs with variegated leaves, or coloured foliage such as red or gold, are especially worth combining with flowering shrubs, and you will find a small but choice selection of these listed under large shrubs for foliage effect.

Spring

Berberis x *stenophylla* 'Corallina Compacta' ♀ ↕↔ 30cm (12in) E ▣–▣ ◊ ✳✳✳ 1

Ceanothus thyrsiflorus var. *repens* ♀ ↕ 90cm (36in) ↔ 2.4m (8ft) E ▣ ◊ ✳✳✳

Chaenomeles x *superba* 'Knap Hill Scarlet' ♀ ↕ 1.5m (5ft) ↔ 1.8m (6ft) ▣–▣ ◊ ✳✳✳

Cytisus x *beanii* ♀ ↕ 60cm (24in) ↔ 90cm (36in) ▣ ◊ ✳✳✳

Daphne odora 'Aureomarginata' ♀ ↕↔ 1.5m (5ft) E ▣ ◊ ✳✳

Genista lydia ♀ ↕ 60cm (24in) ↔ 90cm (36in) ▣ ◊ ✳✳✳

Syringa meyeri 'Palibin' ♀ ↕↔ 1.5m (5ft) ▣ ◊ ✳✳✳

Vinca minor 'Azurea Flore Pleno' ♀ ↕ 20cm (8in) ↔ 1.8m (6ft) E ▣–▣ ◊ ✳✳✳

Summer

Artemisia 'Powis Castle' ♀ ↕ 60cm (24in) ↔ 90cm (36in) ▣ ◊ ✳✳

Brachyglottis (Dunedin Group) 'Sunshine' ♀ ↕ 1.5m (5ft) ↔ 1.8m (6ft) E ▣ ◊ ✳✳✳

Caryopteris x *clandonensis* ↕ 90cm (36in) ↔ 1.5m (5t) ▣ ◊ ✳✳✳

Chamaecytisus purpureus 'Atropurpureus' ♀ ↕ 45cm (18in) ↔ 60cm (24in) ▣ ◊ ✳✳✳

Fuchsia 'Tom Thumb' ♀ ↕↔ 30cm (12in) ▣–▣ ◊ ✳✳

Phlomis fruticosa ♀ ↕ 90cm (36in) ↔ 1.5m (5ft) E ▣ ◊ ✳✳✳ 2

Ruta graveolens 'Jackman's Blue' ↕ 60cm (24in) ↔ 75cm (30in) E ▣–▣ ◊ ✳✳✳

Santolina chamaecyparissus ♀ E ↕ 50cm (20in) ↔ 90cm (36in) ▣ ◊ ✳✳

Spiraea japonica 'Nana' ♀ ↕ 45cm (18in) ↔ 60cm (24in) ▣ ◊ ✳✳✳

Teucrium fruticans 'Azureum' ♀ ↕ 75cm (30in) ↔ 4m (12ft) E ▣ ◊ ✳✳

Autumn

Abelia schumannii ♀ ↕ 1.8m (6ft) ↔ 3m (10ft) ▣ ◊ ✳✳

Ceratostigma plumbaginoides ♀ ↕ 45cm (18in) ↔ 30cm (12in) ▣ ◊ ✳✳✳

Hydrangea macrophylla 'Pia' ↕ 60cm (24in) ↔ 90cm (36in) ▣–▣ ◊ ✳✳✳

Hypericum 'Hidcote' ♀ ↕ 1.2m (4ft) ↔ 1.5m (5ft) E ▣–▣ ◊ ✳✳✳

Potentilla fruticosa 'Vilmoriniana' ↕ 1.2m (4ft) ↔ 90cm (36in) ▣ ◊ ✳✳✳

Rosa 'Fru Dagmar Hastrup' ♀ ↕ 90cm (36in) ↔ 1.2m (4ft) ▣ ◊ ✳✳✳

Viburnum davidii ♀ ↕↔ 1.5m (5ft) E ▣–▣ ◊ ✳✳✳ 3

Winter

Cotoneaster dammeri ♀ ↕ 20cm (8in) ↔ 1.8m (6ft) E ▣ ◊ ✳✳✳

Cotoneaster microphyllus ↕ 90cm (36in) ↔ 1.5m (5ft) E ▣ ◊ ✳✳✳

Euonymus fortunei 'Emerald Gaiety' ♀ ↕ 90cm (36in) ↔ 1.5m (5ft) E ▣ ◊ ✳✳✳

Euonymus fortunei 'Emerald 'n' Gold' ♀ ↕ 60cm (24in) ↔ 90cm (36in) E ▣ ◊ ✳✳✳

Gaultheria mucronata 'Bell's Seedling' ♀ ↕↔ 90cm (36in) E ▣ ◊ ❧ ✳✳✳

Mahonia aquifolium 'Apollo' ♀ ↕ 60cm (24in) ↔ 90cm (36in) E ▣–▣ ◊ ✳✳✳

Mahonia pinnata ↕↔ 1.5m (5ft) E ▣–▣ ◊ ✳✳✳

Pachysandra terminalis; *P. terminalis* 'Variegata' ♀ ↕ 20cm (8in) ↔ 60cm (24in) E ▣–▣ ◊–◊ ✳✳✳

Ruscus aculeatus ↕ 75cm (30in) ↔ 90cm (36in) E ▣–▣ ◊–◊

Sarcococca hookeriana var. *humilis* ↕ 60cm (24in) ↔ 90cm (36in) E ▣–▣ ◊ ✳✳✳

Skimmia japonica 'Nymans' ♀ ↕ 90cm (36in) ↔ 1.8m (6ft) E ▣–▣ ◊ ✳✳✳

See also *Trees and shrubs with colourful foliage, pp.57–58; The cream of autumn colour, p.62; Choosing plants with attractive winter bark, p.63;*

LARGE SHRUBS FOR SEASONAL INTEREST

Spring

Berberis 'Goldilocks' ↕4m (12ft) ↔ 3m (10ft) E ▢–▧ ◊ ✽✽✽

Magnolia liliiflora 'Nigra' ♀ ↕3m (10ft) ↔ 2.4m (8ft) ▢–▧ ◊ ☖ ✽✽✽

Osmanthus x *burkwoodii* ♀ ↕↔3m (10ft) E ▢–▧ ◊ ✽✽✽ ▢4▢

Pieris 'Forest Flame' ♀ ↕4m (12ft) ↔ 1.8m (6ft) E ▢–▧ ◊ ☖ ✽✽

Rhododendron (many, including deciduous azaleas) ↕↔ 0.3–12m (1–12ft) E ▧ ◊ ☖ ✽✽✽

Summer

Abelia x *grandiflora* ♀ ↕3m (10ft) ↔ 4m (12ft) E ▢ ◊ ✽✽

Buddleja alternifolia ♀ ↕↔4m (12ft) ▢ ◊ ✽✽✽

Escallonia 'Peach Blossom' ♀ ↕↔ 2.4m (8ft) E ▢ ◊ ✽✽

Kolkwitzia amabilis 'Pink Cloud' ♀ ↕3m (10ft) ↔ 4m (12ft) ▢ ◊ ✽✽✽ ▢5▢

Rosa (many shrub roses) ↕↔ 1.2–2.4m (4–8ft) ▢ ◊ ✽✽✽

Weigela 'Mont Blanc' ↕1.2m ↔ 1.5m (5ft) ▢–▧ ◊ ✽✽✽

Autumn

Abelia x *grandiflora* ♀ ↕3m (10ft) ↔ 4m (12ft) E ▢ ◊ ✽✽

Cotoneaster bullatus ♀ ↕4m (12ft) ↔ 3m (10ft) E ▢ ◊ ✽✽✽

Hydrangea paniculata 'Grandiflora' ♀ ↕3m (10ft) ↔ 2.4m (8ft) ▢–▧ ◊ ✽✽✽ ▢6▢

Rosa 'Geranium' ♀ ↕2.4m (8ft) ↔ 1.5m (5ft) ▢ ◊ ✽✽✽

Rosa sericea subsp. *omeiensis* f. *pteracantha* ↕2.4m (8ft) ↔ 2.2m (7ft) ▢ ◊ ✽✽✽

Winter

Cotoneaster lacteus ♀ ↕↔4m (12ft) E ▢–▧ ◊ ✽✽✽

Hamamelis x *intermedia* 'Jelena' ♀, *H.* x *i.* 'Pallida' ♀ ↕↔4m (12ft) ▢–▧ ◊ ☖ ✽✽✽

Lonicera fragrantissima ↕1.8m (6ft) ↔ 3m (10ft) ▢–▧ ◊ ✽✽✽

Mahonia x *media* 'Charity' ↕5m (15ft) ↔ 4m (12ft) E ▢–▧ ◊ ✽✽✽

Symphoricarpos orbiculatus ↕↔ 1.8m (6ft) ▢–▧ ◊ ✽✽✽

Viburnum farreri ♀ ↕3m (10ft) ↔ 2.4m (8ft) ▢–▧ ◊ ✽✽✽

Viburnum tinus ↕↔ 3m (10ft) E ▢–▧ ◊ ✽✽✽

Foliage effect

Cornus alba 'Elegantissima' ♀; *C. alba* 'Spaethii' ♀ ↕↔3m (10ft) ▢ ◊–◊ ✽✽✽

Elaeagnus pungens 'Maculata' ↕4m (12ft) ↔ 5m (15ft) E ▢–▧ ◊ ✽✽✽

Fatsia japonica ♀ ↕↔4m (12ft) E ▢–▧ ◊ ✽✽ ▢7▢

Ilex aquifolium 'Handsworth New Silver' ♀ ↕8m (25ft) ↔ 5m (15ft) E ▢–▧ ◊ ✽✽✽

Photinia x *fraseri* 'Red Robin' ♀ ↕↔ 5m (15ft) E ▢–▧ ◊ ✽✽

Prunus lusitanica 'Variegata' ↕↔ 6m (20ft) E ▢–▧ ◊ ✽✽

Sambucus racemosa 'Sutherland Gold' ♀ ↕↔ 3m (10ft) ▢–▧ ◊ ✽✽✽

Selecting evergreen shrubs, p.78; Choosing shrub roses, pp. 88–89; Perennials for seasonal colour, pp.110–111

Selecting evergreen shrubs

When choosing shrubs for your garden make sure you include plenty of evergreens in your selection; they will reward you with colour and interest all year round

CHOOSING EVERGREEN SHRUBS

Evergreen shrubs are sometimes considered drab and sombre. This harks back to Victorian "shrubberies" which mostly contained evergreens with dark green foliage, and certainly created a heavy, sombre effect. Today there is a vast selection of bright, cheery evergreen plants; some have ornamental fruits, attractive flowers, and coloured and variegated foliage, and they have many uses in the garden. But do not be tempted to plant too many, as this can create a heavy, even claustrophobic effect. Instead mix them well with plenty of deciduous shrubs; a good balance is about one-third evergreens to two-thirds deciduous shrubs.

Ornamental berries and fruit

Cotoneaster x watereri 'John Waterer' ♀ ↕↔ 5m (15ft) ▱–▨ ◊ ✳✳✳

Gaultheria mucronata 'Bell's Seedling' ♀ ↕↔ 1.2m (4ft), need male and female plants, ▨ ◊ ▥ ✳✳✳

Pyracantha (many) ↕↔ 3–4m (10–12ft) ▱–▨ ◊ ✳✳✳–✳✳ [1]

Skimmia japonica var. *reevesiana* ↕↔ 75cm (30in) ▨–▨ ◊ ✳✳✳

Attractive flowers

Camellia x williamsii ↕ 2–5m (6–15ft) ↔ 1–3m (3–10ft), late autumn to late spring, ▨ ◊ ▥ ✳✳✳ [2]

Hypericum 'Hidcote' ♀ ↕ 1.2m (4ft) ↔ 1.5m (5ft), summer, ▱–▨ ◊ ✳✳✳

Lavandula angustifolia 'Hidcote' ♀ ↕ 60cm (24in) ↔ 75cm (30in), summer, ▱ ◊ ✳✳✳

Golden-yellow or variegated leaves

Aucuba japonica 'Picturata' ↕↔ 3m (10ft) ▱–▨ ◊ ✳✳✳

Calluna vulgaris 'Beoley Gold' ♀ ↕ 35cm (14in) ↔ 60cm (24in) ▱ ◊ ✳✳✳

Pieris japonica 'Variegata' ↕↔ 1.8m (6ft) ▱–▨ ◊ ▥ ✳✳✳

Weigela 'Florida Variegata' ♀ ↕↔ 1.8–2.4m (6–8ft) ▱–▨ ◊ ✳✳✳ [3]

Silver or grey leaves

Artemisia abrotanum ♀ ↕↔ 90cm (36in) ▱ ◊ ✳✳✳

Convolvulus cneorum ♀ ↕ 60cm (24in) ↔ 90cm (3ft) ▱ ◊ ✳✳ [4]

Hebe pimeleoides 'Quicksilver' ♀ ↕ 30cm (12in) ↔ 60cm (24in) ▱–▨ ◊ ✳✳

For dry shade

Buxus sempervirens ♀ ↕↔ 5m (15ft) ▱–▨ ◊ ✳✳✳ 'Lalifolia Maculata' ♀ [5]

Euonymus fortunei ↕ 60cm (24in) ↔ 45cm–1.5m (18in–5ft) ▱–▨ ◊ ✳✳✳

Hypericum calycinum ↕↔ 60cm (24in) ▱–▨ ◊–◊ ✳✳✳ [6]

Lonicera pileata ↕ 60cm (24in) ↔ 2.4m (8ft) ▱–▨ ◊ ✳✳✳

For moist shade

Daphne laureola ↕ 90cm (3ft) ↔ 1.5m (5ft) ▱–▨ ◊ ✳✳✳

Fatsia japonica ♀ ↕↔ 4m (12ft) ▱–▨ ◊ ✳✳

Gaultheria procumbens ♀ ↕ 15cm (6in) ↔ 90cm (36in), ▨ ◊ ▥ ✳✳✳ [7]

Leucothoe fontanesiana ♀ ↕ 1–1.8m (3–6ft) ↔ 3m (10ft) ▨–▨ ◊ ▥ ✳✳✳

Vinca minor ↕ 10–20cm (4–8in) ↔ 90cm (36in) ▱–▨ ◊ ✳✳✳

For dry soil and full sun

Berberis ↕ 30cm–3m (12in–10ft) ↔ 45cm–5m (18in–15ft) ▱–▨ ◊ ✳✳✳

Cistus x cyprius ♀ ↕↔ 1.5m (5ft) ▱–▨ ◊ ✳✳

Fremontodendron 'California Glory' ♀ ↕ 6m (20ft) ↔ 4m (12ft) ▱ ◊ ✳✳ [8]

Lavandula ↕↔ 30–90cm (12–36in) ▱ ◊ ✳✳✳

Phlomis fruticosa ♀ ↕ 90cm (36in) ↔ 1.5m (5ft) ▱ ◊ ✳✳✳

Pyracantha ↕↔ 3–4m (10–12ft) ▱–▨ ◊ ✳✳✳

Rosmarinus officinalis ↕↔ 1.5m (5ft) ▱ ◊ ✳✳

Salvia officinalis ↕ 80cm (32in) ↔ 90cm (36in) ▱ ◊ ✳✳✳

Santolina chamaecyparissus ♀ ↕ 50cm (20in) ↔ 90cm (36in) ▱ ◊ ✳✳

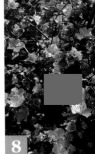

See also Successful tree and shrub planting, pp.60–61; Shrubs for year-round interest, p.76–77; Evergreens in pots, pp.168–169

Why won't shrubs produce berries?

There are several reasons why ornamental shrubs will not produce berries; perhaps male and female plants are needed, or the shrubs are suffering from lack of water or suitable plant foods

Skimmia japonica: no male plant means no berries

Female skimmias will crop heavily when pollinated by a male

When a shrub you expected to produce berries fails to perform, the problem may be one of sexual compatibility. Some plants, such as *Skimmia, Gaultheria mucronata, Viburnum davidii* and hollies, bear male and female flowers on separate plants. Only female plants produce berries and they need a male plant close by for pollination and subsequent berry production. For optimum berry numbers plant male and female plants no more than 5m (16ft) apart, ideally one male in a group of females.

Different cultivars of the plants listed above have different sexes. For example, *Skimmia japonica* 'Veitchii' is female and needs a male cultivar such as *S. japonica* 'Rubella' to pollinate it.

Plants are sometimes unable to pollinate themselves, which is described as self-incompatible. *Viburnum betulifolium*, for example, has variable self-incompatibility (it is partially or fully self-sterile) and therefore a single plant may not produce berries. To ensure good pollination, buy two plants from different sources.

Seed-raised plants can be especially variable in their berrying capacity and may even be sterile if they are hybrids. Potassium deficiency can occur on light sandy soils. This plant food encourages wood to ripen and harden, preparing it for flowering and fruiting. A deficiency can cause poor wood ripening in autumn, making the plant more prone to

Callicarpa and berry production
To ensure good crops of berries (*above*) instead of just foliage (*top*), plant *Callicarpa bodinieri* var. *giraldii* in groups, and feed in spring to ensure vigorous growth.

frost damage. Apply sulphate of potash at 15g per sq m (about ½oz per sq yd) in early spring to an area extending at least 1m (3ft) beyond the canopy of poorly fruiting shrubs.

Flowers and berries are often borne only on stronger, young growths, such as *Callicarpa* and *Euonymus*, so a plant lacking vigour may not flower and fruit well. Where growth is sparse, in early spring apply a top dressing of general-purpose fertiliser at 100–125g per sq m (3–4oz per sq yd) to the estimated area of root spread.

Many shrubs respond well to renewal pruning, where one stem in three is removed to within 5–8cm (2–3in) of the ground level each spring. Avoid this on particularly weak plants, grafted plants, or slow-growing shrubs that dislike pruning, such as *Daphne*.

Poor pollination can occur in cold, wet weather. This will be aggravated if plants are growing in an open, windy site as it deters pollinating insects. Late spring frosts can damage flowers and reduce berry production. Early-flowering plants such as *Malus* and *Prunus* are especially prone to frost damage. To avoid this, plant them in sheltered sites and avoid frost pockets.

See also How to prune shrubs, pp.80–81; Building your soil's fertility, p.259; Using fertilizers, p267

HOW TO PRUNE SHRUBS

How to prune shrubs

→ See Garde to Gardening - se

Make sure you tackle shrubs that need cutting back at the right time of year, and according to their flowering habit, to maximize the benefits of successful pruning *Pruning Hydrangeas.*

There are three basic reasons for pruning shrubs: first, to keep them healthy by removing dead, diseased or damaged growth; secondly, to maintain an attractive shape and appearance; and thirdly, to obtain the maximum decorative effect from flowers, foliage, fruits and stems.

Bear in mind, however, that not all shrubs need pruning every year. Many will grow well to maturity with no more than the occasional removal of a damaged branch or an awkwardly positioned shoot.

Pruning for health
Remove all dead, diseased or damaged wood immediately, to reduce risk of infection. Prune affected stems cleanly, back to healthy, undamaged wood.

Pruning to maintain the shape
In its simplest form this means removing any branch or shoot that grows out awkwardly, detracting from the natural symmetry and outline of the shrub. Where necessary, it also involves pruning to encourage a shrub towards balanced growth by cutting any weak stems back hard to stimulate vigorous shoot growth, and pruning strong growths very lightly, if at all, where growth is satisfactory and no stimulation is needed.

Deciduous shrubs for flowers or fruit
For shrubs that flower in spring or early summer on strong stems grown in the previous year, such as *Philadelphus* (mock orange), *Forsythia* and *Weigela*, prune immediately after flowering. Remove the shoots that have flowered, cutting back to just above developing new growth. Occasionally cut back older stems to near soil level. This pruning stimulates strong young growth from low down on the plant that will carry the following year's flowers.

PRUNING DECIDUOUS FLOWERING SHRUBS

Shrubs that flower in spring or early summer, like *Weigela*, respond well to pruning, which diverts the plant's energy away from seed production and encourages new flowering shoots. After flowering, cut back the flowered shoots and remove any dead or spindly stems. Prune out some of the older main stems occasionally, cutting them back to within 5–8cm (2–3in) of soil level (*above, left*). Also remove any weak or crossing stems to create an open-centred, well-balanced framework for the shrub. Cut dead wood back to healthy buds or sideshoots (*above, right*). Cut back or remove any over-vigorous, upright, new growth that spoils the shape.

Cut back to healthy buds or sideshoots

Remove or shorten over-vigorous new growth, if necessary

Cut old or weak stems to base

Deciduous shrubs for stems or leaves
Several shrubs, such as dogwoods (*Cornus alba* cultivars and others) and brambles like *Rubus cockburnianus*, are grown for the brilliant colour provided by their young stems, which are at their most conspicuous during the winter months. To encourage vigorous and strong new shoots, prune these shrubs severely in early or mid-spring, cutting all the stems right down, almost to ground level.

Shrubs such as *Weigela* 'Florida Variegata' and the variegated dogwoods including *Cornus alba* 'Elegantissima' are generally grown for their attractive foliage. If you prune them back hard in early spring these shrubs will respond with strong growths, and produce larger leaves than unpruned specimens.

See also Pruning for winter interest, p.68; Renovating overgrown shrubs, p.82; How to prune roses, pp.90–91

PRUNING HYDRANGEA PANICULATA

Hydrangea paniculata flowers on the current year's growth. For larger blooms on established plants, cut back all the previous year's growth to a pair of healthy buds in spring.

The aim is to create a well-balanced framework of four or five well-spaced main stems. This can be as low as 25cm (10in) or over 60cm (24in) tall at the back of borders.

Summer-flowering shrubs

Shrubs that flower on new young shoots produced in the same year benefit from pruning in spring or they become weak and flower badly. Cutting back encourages strong new shoots; although this means that the shrub flowers later, the blooms will be better. Some shrubs including *Buddleja*, *Caryopteris*, the deciduous cultivars of *Ceanothus*, *Hydrangea paniculata*, and herbs such as rue (*Ruta*), sage (*Salvia officinalis*) and *Artemisia* are best cut back to a basic framework, to ensure a shapely bush is formed when the shrub grows again. Cut back all the previous year's stems to a pair of buds. Where wind damage during winter is a problem, trim back by about one-third in early autumn to reduce the danger of branches breaking in gales.

Do not prune these shrubs heavily too early in their life. Remove any weak, straggly stems, but otherwise allow them to grow unpruned until they have become fully established with a well-formed framework before starting regular pruning.

Long-established shrubs may become congested after successive years of regular pruning. If this is the case, it is worthwhile thinning out the crowded framework, removing the older stubs, so that the remaining shoots are more evenly spaced. Alternatively, pruning stems right down to near ground level can be successful, but involves higher risk to the plant.

Shrubs such as hardy *Fuchsia*, *Ceratostigma* and *Perovskia* respond well to cutting down to ground level. The earlier in the year pruning is undertaken, the longer flowering wood has to develop. However, pruning too early in the season produces growth susceptible to late-spring frost damage; in frost pockets wait until late spring.

Evergreen shrubs

These need much less pruning and can usually be left to attain maturity with only the occasional removal of an awkwardly developing branch or shoot. Many evergreens are very hardy but others can suffer in frosty conditions and may also be subject to scorching by cold winds in late winter or early spring, particularly if the soil is dry (*see Avoiding frost damage, pp.70–71*).

Evergreens are sometimes slow to start into growth and may not do so until late spring, or even early summer. Prune where necessary, when the first signs of new growth are seen. At this stage in the year, danger of further weather damage is unlikely, so you should also cut out any weather-damaged growths. Do not prune evergreen plants in late summer or autumn as this may stimulate late, soft new growth, which is susceptible to damage by the first winter frosts.

PRUNING ESTABLISHED EVERGREENS

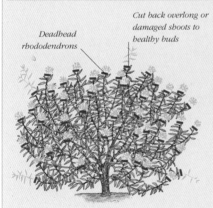

Deadhead rhododendrons

Cut back overlong or damaged shoots to healthy buds

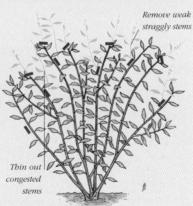

Remove weak straggly stems

Thin out congested stems

Minimal pruning
Delay pruning until all danger of frost has passed. For camellias, gaultherias and rhododendrons, trim overlong shoots and any that spoil the outline in mid-spring. Deadhead rhododendrons.

Renovating evergreens
Cut out straggly growth, diseased or damaged wood, and thin congested stems. Some evergreens, like aucubas, *Berberis darwinii*, and *Prunus laurocerasus*, tolerate hard pruning if they need to be renovated.

RENOVATING OVERGROWN SHRUBS

Renovating overgrown shrubs

Many long-lived deciduous and evergreen shrubs that have grown too large and become congested can be pruned very hard to rejuvenate them – they generally respond by producing a mass of new shoots

Shrubs are born survivors and neglected, overgrown bushes can usually be renovated as long as they are free of disease. *Syringa* (lilac), *Deutzia*, *Philadelphus* (mock orange) and *Viburnum* are all long lived and respond well to cutting back hard. Fast-growing, short-lived shrubs such as *Lavatera*, *Hebe* and *Cistus* are better replaced eventually with a new plant.

Prune deciduous shrubs when they are dormant, after leaf fall in autumn and before bud burst in spring. Remove dead and old, woody branches, then shorten healthy shoots, according to their condition and their situation in the garden. You can even cut the whole shrub down to 30cm (12in) in height.

Regrowth consists of a mass of vigorous shoots. Often these may be so numerous that the shrub becomes too twiggy. Thin them out to remedy the situation. Sometimes new shoots will continue to emerge for some time after the main burst of growth. These add to congestion, so remove them. When the shrub has reached the desired size, control it by regular removal of about one-third of its growth every winter.

Syringa (lilac) shoots regrow after hard pruning

PRUNING A NEGLECTED EVERGREEN SHRUB

[1] Old, tangled or overgrown shrubs, such as this mahonia, may be rejuvenated by pruning over a two-year period. Prune evergreens in mid-spring. [2] Cut back half of the oldest stems to within 5–8cm (2–3in) of ground level. If possible reduce the remaining stems by about half to new, vigorous replacement shoots. Apply a general fertilizer, water well, and mulch around the plant. [3] When the reduced stems regrow, shorten the remaining older stems. Thereafter, keep the shrub in check with normal annual pruning.

However, a vigorous shrub cannot be heavily restrained by pruning and still remain a floriferous, attractive plant. A reasonable strategy is to maintain the bush at about half the size it would make if left unrestricted.

Extremely aged shrubs occasionally die after drastic pruning. If this is a concern, spread the work over two or three years. This allows new shoots to form, which will maintain the plant and provide some protection before the final removal of older stems.

Tackle pruning of evergreen shrubs in mid- or late spring before new growth resumes. Evergreens that respond well to hard cutting back include *Aucuba*, *Elaeagnus*, *Prunus laurocerasus* (cherry laurel), *Taxus* (yew) and *Rhododendron*. Again, reduce main branches to about 30cm (12in), and remove spindly shoots entirely. Treat regrowing shoots as for deciduous shrubs. *Mahonia x media* cultivars such as 'Charity' often develop long, bare stems and these can be cut back hard. They will be replaced with new growth.

Evergreens often respond best to drastic pruning. Unshortened shoots tend to prevent regrowth of shortened ones. So cut back all shoots, some by a third to a half and the remainder to near the base. In future years longer shoots can be cut back in turn.

Some evergreen shrubs such as lavender, rosemary and *Santolina* are somewhat reluctant to regrow after pruning. Look near the base for signs of new growth in spring. If this is present, prune to just above it. If there are no young shoots, the plant will have to be cut back anyway.

RECOVERY TIPS

- To speed recovery of a pruned shrub, scatter a balanced fertilizer over the area previously shadowed by its branches
- Mulch with well-rotted organic matter to keep it moist
- Keep the area free from weeds, which will compete for water
- Water well in dry spells

See also How to deal with overgrown conifers, p.70; How to prune shrubs, pp.80–81

TECHNIQUES

Creating topiary shapes

Training shrubs into different shapes can be great fun

Box (*Buxus*) is a favourite plant for topiary

Choose a young, well-proportioned plant with dense growth. Box and yew (*Taxus*) can be tightly clipped for detailed work. Faster-growing plants will need more trimming.

Basic shapes

Globes, cones, pyramids and obelisks are easiest to make. Start shaping in early summer. Trimming can be done freehand, but cut too little rather than too much. To make a globe, cut a band around the centre, then trim the top and bottom. For a cone, pyramid or obelisk, cut a vertical strip up the four 'corners', then clip in between. Alternatively, place a former over the plant and start clipping once the plant has grown through it. Unlike a frame, the former can be removed when the outline of the shape has developed.

Complex shapes

Frames of sturdy wire help with more complicated shapes such as spirals, cakestands, arches and animals. Large or horizontal shapes may need more than one stem. Pinch back young shoots to encourage bushiness. With conifers allow the central leader to reach the full height before cutting.

See also Evergreens in pots, pp.168–169

PLANTING IDEAS

Choosing shrubs to grow in shade

Shade is not necessarily the problem that many people imagine, there are many shrubs that thrive in full or partial shade

Buildings, walls or fences, trees and shrubs all create shade. Conditions vary depending on the source; for instance, plants under trees may suffer growth restrictions due to dry soil around tree roots or lack of air movement caused by overhanging branches.

To grow shrubs well in shady areas you need to know the type of shade that a plant either needs or will tolerate: full shade with no sun at all, partial shade with sun for part of the day, or the dappled or broken shade cast by trees. Few shrubs will thrive where shade is very deep, particularly when coupled with dry, impoverished soil. If your soil is dry, add plenty of organic matter such as garden compost or composted bark when preparing the ground to help conserve moisture. ▷

SHRUBS FOR FULL SHADE

Aucuba japonica ↕↔ 3m (10ft) E ◊–◊ ❋❋❋

Buxus sempervirens ♥ ↕↔ 5m (15ft) E ◊ ❋❋❋

Danae racemosa ↕↔ 90cm (36in) E ◊ ❋❋

Daphne pontica ♥ ↕ 90cm (36in) ↔ 1.5m (5ft) E ◊ ❋❋❋

Euonymus fortunei 'Emerald 'n' Gold' ♥ ↕ 60cm (24in) ↔ 90cm (36in) E ◊ ❋❋❋

Hypericum androsaemum ↕ 75cm (30in) ↔ 90cm (36in) ◊ ❋❋❋

Ilex aquifolium ↕ 25m (80ft) ↔ 8m (25ft) E ◊ ❋❋

Leucothoe fontanesiana ♥ ↕ 1–2m (3–6ft) ↔ 3m (10ft) E ◊ ⌗ ❋❋❋ ☐1

Lonicera pileata ↕ 60cm (24in) ↔ 2.4m (8ft) E ◊ ❋❋❋

Mahonia aquifolium ↕ 90cm(36in) ↔ 1.5m (5ft) E ◊ ❋❋❋

Osmanthus decorus ↕ 3m (10ft) ↔ 5m (15ft) E ◊ ❋❋❋

Prunus laurocerasus 'Otto Luyken' ♥ ↕ 90cm (36in) ↔ 1.5m (5ft) E ◊ ❋❋❋ ☐2

Prunus lusitanica ♥ ↕↔ 20m (70ft) E ◊ ❋❋

Ruscus aculeatus ↕ 75cm (30in) ↔ 90cm (36in) E ◊–◊ ❋❋❋

Sarcococca confusa ♥ ↕ 1.8m (6ft) ↔ 90cm (36in) E ◊ ❋❋❋

Skimmia japonica ↕↔ 1–5m (3–16ft) E ◊ ❋❋❋

Symphoricarpos x doorenbosii 'Mother of Pearl' ↕↔ 1.8m (6ft) ◊ ❋❋❋

See also What to plant under trees, p.64; Perennials for shade, p.140

GROUND COVER SHRUBS FOR FULL SHADE, AND SHRUBS FOR PARTIAL SHADE

Ground-cover shrubs for full shade

Cotoneaster dammeri ♀ ‡ 20cm (8in) ↔ 1.8m (6ft) E ♦ ✳✳✳

Euonymus fortunei var. *radicans* ‡ 15cm (6in) ↔ 90cm (36in) E ♦ ✳✳✳

Gaultheria procumbens ♀ ‡ 15cm (6in) ↔ 90cm (36in) E ♦ ཕ ✳✳✳

Hedera hibernica ♀ ‡ 15cm (6in) ↔ 10m (30ft) E ♦ ✳✳✳ [1]

Hypericum calycinum ‡ 60cm (24in) ↔ 90cm (36in) E ♦ ✳✳✳

Sarcococca hookeriana var. *humilis* ‡ 60cm (24in) ↔ 90cm (36in) E ♦ ✳✳✳

Symphoricarpos x chenaultii 'Hancock' ‡ 90cm (36in) ↔ 1.5m (5ft) ♦ ✳✳✳

Viburnum davidii ♀ ‡↔ 1–1.5m (3–5ft) E ♦ ✳✳✳

Shrubs for partial shade

Berberis darwinii ♀ ‡↔ 3m (10ft) E ♦ ✳✳✳ [2]

Berberis x stenophylla ♀ ‡↔ 3m (10ft) E ♦ ✳✳✳

Cornus alba ‡↔ 3m (10ft) ♦ ✳✳✳

Corylopsis pauciflora ♀ ‡ 1.5m (5ft) ↔ 2.4m (8ft) ♦ ཕ ✳✳✳

Cotoneaster frigidus 'Cornubia' ♀ ‡↔ 6m (20ft) E ♦ ✳✳✳

Daphne mezereum ‡ 1.2m (4ft) ↔ 90cm (36in) ♦ ✳✳✳

Euonymus fortunei 'Emerald Gaiety' ♀ ‡ 90cm (36in) ↔ 1.5m (5ft) E ♦ ✳✳✳

Fatsia japonica ♀ ‡↔ 4m (12ft) E ♦ ✳✳

Garrya elliptica ‡↔ 4m (12ft) E ♦ ✳✳

Gaultheria mucronata ‡↔ 1.2m (4ft) E ♦ ཕ ✳✳✳

Hydrangea macrophylla ‡ 1–1.8m (3–6ft) ↔ 1.5–2.4m (5–8ft) ♦ ✳✳✳

Hydrangea quercifolia ♀ ‡ 1.8m (6ft) ↔ 2.4m (8ft) ♦ ✳✳✳

Ilex aquifolium ♀ ‡ 25m (80ft) ↔ 8m (25ft) E ♦ ✳✳✳

Itea virginica ‡ 1.5–3m (5–10ft) ↔ 1.5m (5ft) ♦ ཕ ✳✳✳

Kalmia latifolia ♀ ‡↔ 3m (10ft) E ♦ ཕ ✳✳✳ [3]

Kerria japonica 'Pleniflora' ♀ ‡↔ 3m (10ft) ♦ ✳✳✳

Leycesteria formosa ♀ ‡↔ 1.8m (6ft) ♦ ✳✳✳

Mahonia japonica ♀ ‡ 1.8m (6ft) ↔ 3m (10ft) E ♦ ✳✳✳

Nandina domestica ♀ ‡ 1.8m (6ft) ↔ 1.5m (5ft) E ♦ ✳✳ [4]

Pieris formosa var. *forrestii* 'Wakehurst' ♀ ‡ 5m (15ft) ↔ 4m (12ft) E ♦ ཕ ✳✳

Pyracantha rogersiana ♀ ‡↔ 4m (12ft) E ♦ ✳✳

Stachyurus praecox ♀ ‡ 1–4m (3–12ft) ↔ 3m (10ft) ♦ ཕ ✳✳✳

Viburnum acerifolium ‡ 1–1.8m (3–6ft) ↔ 1.2m (4ft) ♦ ✳✳✳

Viburnum cinnamomifolium ♀ ‡↔ 5m (15ft) E ♦ ✳✳

Viburnum opulus ‡ 5m (15ft) ↔ 4m (12ft) ♦ ✳✳✳

Viburnum tinus ‡↔ 3m (10ft) E ♦ ✳✳✳

Ground-cover shrubs for partial shade

Arctostaphylos uva-ursi ‡ 10cm (4in) ↔ 50cm (20in) E ♦ ཕ ✳✳✳

Cotoneaster salicifolius 'Gnom' ‡ 30cm (12in) ↔ 1.8m (6ft) E ♦ ✳✳✳

Cotoneaster x suecicus 'Skogholm' ‡ 60cm (24in) ↔ 3m (10ft) E ♦ ✳✳✳

Gaultheria mucronata 'Wintertime' (female) ‡↔ 1.2m (4ft) E ♦ ཕ ✳✳✳ [5]

Mahonia nervosa ‡ 45cm (18in) ↔ 90cm (36in) E ♦ ✳✳✳

Rubus pentalobus ‡ 10cm (4in) ↔ 90cm (36in) E ♦ ✳✳✳

Vinca major ‡ 45cm (18in) ↔ 1.2m (4ft) E ♦–♦ ✳✳✳

Vinca minor ‡ 10–20cm (4–8in) ↔ 60–90cm (24–36in) E ♦–♦ ✳✳✳

See also Choosing plants for ground cover, pp26–27; The best plants for shade, p.140

PRACTICAL ADVICE

TECHNIQUES

Plants for hedges

Buy plants that have been specifically produced for hedging

HEDGING PLANTS

Most hedges consist of plants raised by nurserymen specifically for that purpose. Unless otherwise stated, those listed here should be maintained at a height of 1–1.8m (3–6ft), or as taller hedges and screens.

Choose bushy, well-branched plants

If pot grown, ensure plant is not pot bound

For clay soils

Berberis darwinii ♀ E; *Ilex aquifolium* ♀ (common holly) E; *Potentilla fruticosa* 'Jackman's Variety' ♀ best maintained at 30–90cm (12–36in); *Prunus lusitanica* ♀ (Portugal laurel); *Ribes sanguineum* 'Pulborough Scarlet' ♀; *Viburnum farreri* ♀

For cold, exposed inland gardens

Carpinus betulus (hornbeam) ♀; *Crataegus monogyna* (hawthorn); *Fagus sylvatica* ♀ (beech); *Taxus baccata* ♀ (yew) E

For a conifer screen

Chamaecyparis lawsoniana (Lawson cypress) E; *Cupressus macrocarpa* (Monterey cypress) E; *Thuja plicata* 'Atrovirens' ♀ E

For seaside gardens

Brachyglottis monroi ♀ best maintained at 30–90cm (12–36in) E; *Elaeagnus* x *ebbingei* E; *Fuchsia* 'Riccartonii' ♀; *Griselinia littoralis* ♀ E; *Hippophae rhamnoides* ♀ (sea buckthorn)

See also How to trim hedges, p.86

How to plant a hedge

Thoroughly prepare the planting holes to give hedges a good start

Most deciduous hedging plants are supplied as bare-root specimens, which should be planted during winter while they are dormant – but do not plant them in frozen or very wet soil. Plant evergreens, including conifers, in early to mid-spring.

PLANTING A HEDGE

1 Mark out planting positions with canes and prepare holes after digging in organic matter and improving poorly drained soils by mixing in horticultural grit. **2** Water plants thoroughly to ensure the root ball is moist. **3** Remove pot, trim back damaged roots to healthy growth, and gently tease roots apart to encourage outward growth. **4** Replant at the same depth; use a cane to check against the previous soil mark on the stem – useful for bare-root plants. **5** Work fine soil between the roots, and firm plants in with your foot. **6** Water and mulch well. Planting distances vary from 30–60cm (12–24in), depending on the height and spread of the plant. For quick results or a thick hedge, plant a double, staggered row 45cm (18in) apart, with plants at twice the interval recommended for single rows.

HOW TO TRIM HEDGES

How to trim hedges

Hedges are divided into three groups for the purpose of pruning or trimming, which starts immediately after planting; formal hedges need more trimmng than those grown informally

Group 1

Upright plants including *Crataegus monogyna* (hawthorn), and *Ligustrum ovalifolium* (privet); also *Buxus sempervirens* (box), *Escallonia* and *Lonicera nitida* (honeysuckle).

• INITIAL PRUNING: on planting privet and hawthorn, cut back plants to 15cm (6in). In summer trim sideshoots lightly. In late winter or early spring of the second year, cut back growth by half. Throughout summer, trim sideshoots to maintain tapered sides, and in autumn cut leading shoots to the desired height. On planting box, *Escallonia* and honeysuckle, cut back all stems by one-third. Repeat at the same time the following year.

• SUBSEQUENT ANNUAL PRUNING: during late spring to early autumn, trim top growth and sideshoots every four to six weeks to maintain desired shape.

Group 2

Stocky deciduous shrubs, naturally bushy at the base, such as *Fagus sylvatica* (beech), *Carpinus betulus*

HEDGE SHAPE

The classic, formal A-shaped yew hedge has sloping sides to allow better light penetration, making for more even growth (*left*). Make hedges narrow at the top to deflect strong winds or snow; in areas with heavy snowfall, tapered tops, as on this hornbeam (*right*), prevent snow settling and causing damage.

(hornbeam), *Corylus avellana* (hazel) and flowering shrubs such as *Forsythia* and *Ribes sanguineum*.

• INITIAL PRUNING: For a sturdy hedge and quick establishment leave the leading shoots unpruned until the hedge is near the desired height. Trim the sides to ensure it is narrow but bushy.

• SUBSEQUENT ANNUAL PRUNING: in early summer or after flowering, and again in late summer, clip to a tapered shape.

Group 3

Conifers and most evergreens.

• INITIAL PRUNING: on planting, leave the leading shoot unpruned, but lightly cut back straggly sideshoots. In summer, trim sideshoots and tie in the leading shoot to a cane as it grows. Use secateurs for broad-leaved evergreens such as *Prunus laurocerasus* (laurel)

• SUBSEQUENT ANNUAL PRUNING: up to three times during summer, until late summer, clip to the desired shape. Stop the leading shoot at the desired height.

Flowering and fruiting hedges

Prune informal hedges selectively to allow flowering and/or fruiting. Prune plants such as fuchsias, which flower on the current season's growth, once in spring. For plants flowering on one-year-old shoots, such as pyracanthas, reduce the current season's growth by half in summer.

ACCURATE TRIMMING OF A FORMAL HEDGE

1 When trimming a formal hedge, stretch a level string between two upright posts as a guide to height. Cut the top of the hedge along this line. **2** Make a shaping frame or template from a piece of plywood. This can be an invaluable tool, especially when shaping a hedge in its early years. It provides a precise guide to cut into, which is more reliable than judging by eye. Place it over the hedge, and cut following the line of the template, moving it along the hedge as you proceed, then trim the sides. **3** Once you reach the end of the hedge, remove the template and the posts and string. Trim the ends of the hedge neatly, and then tidy up any stray or untidy bits you may have missed.

See also Plants for hedges and How to plant a hedge, p.85; Tackling a neglected hedge, p.87

PRACTICAL ADVICE

A Leyland cypress hedge

Don't let this fast-grower get out of hand

Trim Leyland hedges regularly when in growth

If a hedge of Leyland cypress (x *Cupressocyparis leylandii*) is not pruned correctly in the early stages, it can quickly get out of control.

In the first year trim back overlong sideshoots in mid-spring. Trim the sides lightly in midsummer. In the second year trim the sides again to encourage more dense growth and to maintain a neat appearance over winter. In subsequent years continue to trim the sides as required, leaving the leading shoot untouched until it has reached the desired height.

When the hedge is the required height, shorten the leading shoot to 15cm (6in) beneath this level in the following spring. New growth will make up the difference and the top of the hedge will begin to fill in.

Trim the top and sides up to three times a year in the growing season, and keep the hedge clipped into an inverted wedge shape – or flat-topped A-shape – with the widest point at the base, otherwise the lower parts of the hedge can become bare.

See also Overgrown conifers, p.70

TECHNIQUES

Tackling a neglected hedge

Country hedges can be renovated by laying, but ornamental garden hedges may need to be rejuvenated by hard pruning

Over time hedges will deteriorate, especially if they are neglected. If the hedge is in a very poor state, it may be necessary to coppice the stems or grub it out and replant it altogether.

Renovating country hedges

Where growth is good but thinning near the base, laying will rejuvenate a country hedge by encouraging new growth. *Crataegus monogyna* (hawthorn) is the best species for laying but many of the most common deciduous hedging shrubs and trees, including *Fraxinus excelsior* (ash), *Prunus spinosa* (blackthorn), *Ulmus* (elm), *Acer campestre* (field maple), and *Corylus avellana* (hazel), are also suitable for laying.

Hedge laying should be carried out in winter. Allow the hedge to grow to 2.5–5m (8–16ft) in height with main stems 5–10cm (2–4in) thick at the base. Remove stems larger than about 20cm (8in), and any that are awkwardly shaped or out of line.

Cut away side growth from the lower stems. Remove any elder (*Sambucus nigra*) and dig out the stump, because it will not lay.

Cut almost through the main upright stems (known as pleachers) near the ground on the opposite side of the face to the direction of lay and push them over at an angle of about 35 degrees in the direction of the rising slope. Drive stakes of hazel or ash into the hedge line every 40cm (16in) and weave the pleachers between them. Then twist binders or heathers of coppiced hazel, sweet chestnut or willow around the top of the stakes to secure the pleachers. Fill the gap at the end of a laid hedge with unwanted pleachers cut from the hedge.

Hedge laying is a highly skilled activity. It is also potentially dangerous, and requires the appropriate equipment and safety wear. Many agricultural colleges run courses on laying hedges, so contact your local college if you need further help and advice.

RENOVATING ORNAMENTAL HEDGES

As spring approaches and new growth is beginning to appear, tidy up or renovate ornamental garden hedges.

To restore overgrown hedges of beech (*Fagus sylvatica*) and hornbeam (*Carpinus betulus*) to a manageable shape and size, cut back hard in spring before the leaves appear. Renovate neglected hedges over several years, reducing one side and the height in the first season, and the other side when it has recovered.

The renovation of evergreen hedges such as *Prunus laurocerasus* (cherry laurel) and *Taxus baccata* (yew) is best left until the growing season is under way, during mid- or late spring, depending on the weather conditions and your locality. If drastic pruning is necessary, spread the work over several years as suggested above.

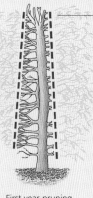

Cut back growth to near the main stems on one side of an overgrown deciduous hedge and trim the other side as usual

First year pruning

Cut back hard on the other side in the following year

Second year pruning

See also How to trim hedges, p.86

Choosing shrub roses

Many shrub roses have attractive foliage and colourful autumn fruits as well as flowers; grow them in mixed borders with other plants or use them for hedging and ground cover

Shrub roses are a good choice for gardens as they need little or no pruning, and many are relatively disease free.

Choosing roses is a personal matter regarding flower form and colour. Before buying roses, try to see them in bloom by visiting nurseries and gardens to avoid possible disappointment later.

Flowering behaviour is indicated in the list below. 'Repeat' means that several flushes of flowers are produced each flowering season. 'Perpetual' implies continuous flowering through the season. 'One flowering period' means a single flush of blooms per season. For optimum flowering and performance, plant all roses in full sun with moist but well-drained soil.

HARDY SHRUB ROSES

Attractive foliage

Rosa fedtschenkoana ↕↔ 2.2m (7ft), white flowers; Repeat

Rosa multibracteata ↕ 1.8m (6ft) ↔ 1.5m (5ft), pink flowers; one flowering period

Rosa primula ♥ ↕ 3m (10ft) ↔ 1.8m (6ft), pale yellow flowers; one flowering period [1]

Rosa virginiana ♥ ↕ 1.2m (4ft) ↔ 1.5m (5ft), fragrant pink flowers; one flowering period

Rosa xanthina f. *hugonis* ♥ ↕ 2.4m (8ft) ↔ 1.8m (6ft), fragrant yellow flowers; one flowering period

Decorative autumn fruits

Rosa 'Fru Dagmar Hastrup' ♥ ↕ 90cm (36in) ↔ 1.2m (4ft), fragrant pink flowers; Perpetual

Rosa 'Geranium' ♥ ↕ 2.4m (8ft) ↔ 1.5m (5ft), red flowers; one flowering period

Rosa glauca ♥ ↕ 1.8m (6ft) ↔ 1.5m (5ft), pink flowers; one flowering period

Rosa multibracteata ↕ 1.8m (6ft) ↔ 1.5m (5ft), pink flowers; one flowering period

Rosa rugosa ↕↔ 1–2.4m (3–8ft), fragrant cerise or white flowers; Repeat [2]

Small shrub roses

Cardinal Hume ('Harregale') ↕↔ 90cm (36in), fragrant purple flowers; Perpetual

'Mrs John Laing' ↕ 90cm (36in) ↔ 75cm (30in), fragrant pink flowers; Repeat [3]

'Paul Neyron' ↕ 90cm (36in) ↔ 60cm (24in), fragrant pink flowers; Repeat

'The Fairy' ♥ ↕↔ 60–90cm (24–36in) pink flowers; Repeat

Medium shrub roses

'Baronne Adolph de Rothschild' ↕ 1.5m (5ft) ↔ 90cm (3ft), fragrant deep rose-pink flowers; Repeat

'Königin von Dänemark' ♥ ↕ 1.5m (5ft) ↔ 1.2m (4ft), fragrant pink flowers; one flowering period

'Madame Pierre Oger' ↕ 1.5m (5ft) ↔ 1.2m (4ft), fragrant creamy-pink flowers; Perpetual

'Reine des Violettes' ↕ 1.5m (5ft) ↔ 1.2m (4ft), fragrant violet-purple flowers; Perpetual

'Tuscany Superb' ♥ ↕ 1.2m (4ft) ↔ 90cm (36in), fragrant crimson-purple flowers; one flowering period [4]

See also Planting roses, p.89; How to prune roses, pp.90–91; Choosing climbing roses, pp.104–105

Small Shrub Roses

.5m (5ft) ↔ 2.2m (7ft), fragrant
owers; Perpetual 7

‡ 1.5m (5ft) ↔ 1.2m (4ft),
t-pink flowers; Perpetual

'Haÿ' ♀ ‡ 2.1m (7ft) ↔ 1.8m
purple-red flowers; Perpetual

round cover

rimro') ♀ ‡ 60cm (24in) ↔ 3m
ant pale pink flowers; Repeat

♀ ‡ 30cm (12in) ↔ 1.2m (4ft), pale
flowers; one flowering period 8

t ('Kordapt') ‡ 50cm (20in) ↔ 3m
ep pink flowers; Repeat

ket ('Intercell') ‡ 75cm (30in)
(4ft), fragrant rosy red flowers;
al

jacksonii 'Max Graf' ‡ 60cm (24in)
n (8ft), fragrant deep pink flowers; one
ng period

Planting roses

Make sure you plant roses at the correct depth

Plant in late autumn at leaf fall, or from mid-winter to early spring before growth resumes.

To plant a rose, dig a hole roughly twice the width of the plant's roots and the depth of a spade blade. Mix organic matter into the bottom of the planting hole. Place the rose in the centre of the hole and, using a small cane to identify the top of the planting hole, ensure that the "graft union", where the cultivar joins the rootstock and the point from which the branches originate, is below soil level. Return the soil and firm well.

Ensure that the roots of bare-root plants are well spread out and set to their previous growing depth. Carefully tease out the roots of container plants, or they may be slow to establish and be more susceptible to drier conditions. Spacing depends on the type and habit of the individual rose; check the catalogue or the details on the label. If plants are unpruned, shorten back to 15cm (6in) in early spring, then apply rose fertilizer and mulch well with a layer of organic matter.

PLANTING

Ensure the planting hole is twice the width of the plant's roots, and that it is sufficiently deep. You can check that the graft union will be just below soil level by laying a small cane across the planting hole.

See also How to prune roses, pp.90–91

PLANTING ROSES

How to prune roses

The pruning technique depends on the type of rose, and some need more pruning than others; shrub roses need the least pruning so they make a good choice for the busy gardener

When and how to prune

Shorten branches of tall bush cultivars by about one-third in autumn, to prevent them being rocked by strong winds over winter. With the exception of ramblers, prune roses in early spring when growth is just beginning. That is when the uppermost buds are beginning to swell. In mild areas this is usually early spring, but in colder regions it may not be until the beginning of mid-spring. Earlier pruning risks causing damage to the uppermost growth buds if it is followed by a mild, growth-encouraging spell. A return to cold conditions brings with it the need to prune a second time, harder than before, to remove shoots that have died back.

Use sharp secateurs for pruning and make a clean cut slightly above a growth bud, but no more than 5mm (¼in) above it, and angled down, away from the bud, at an angle of about 45 degrees. Prune to outward-facing buds

to allow light and air to reach the centre of the bush.

A quicker if less attractive method of pruning hybrid tea and floribunda bush roses is to use an electric hedge trimmer. Cut all shoots in 'table top' fashion to within 45–60cm (18–24in) of the ground. The ragged cuts look unsightly but do not, as you might expect, generally become infected with diseases. After several years the growth becomes rather tangled, so tidy up with secauteurs. After this use the hedge-trimmer method again.

Distinctions between the various groups of roses, such as hybrid teas (large-flowered) and floribundas (cluster-flowered) is becoming increasingly obscure in the complexities of modern breeding. Therefore, adapt or modify pruning according to the vigour of each cultivar, regardless of type.

Pruning newly planted roses

If you are planting roses in autumn or winter, wait until early to mid-spring before pruning. When planting roses in spring, prune them at planting time.

First, remove all dead, damaged and weak growth.

• HYBRID TEA (LARGE-FLOWERED) TYPES: prune the remaining strong stems hard back to within 10–15cm (4–6in) of the ground.
• FLORIBUNDA (CLUSTER-FLOWERED) TYPES: prune the remaining strong stems moderately hard back to within about 15cm (6in) of the ground.
• RAMBLERS AND CLIMBERS: prune the remaining strong stems back to within 30–40cm (12–15in) of the ground, if this has not already been done at the nursery. Climbing versions of bush cultivars may revert if they are pruned back hard.
• SHRUB ROSES AND SPECIES: leave the remaining strong stems unpruned. English roses need no pruning in the year of planting.

PRUNING IN GENERAL

When pruning, first remove dead, diseased or damaged shoots, which may harbour infection. Reduce crossing stems to a suitable bud; if they are left to rub against each other, the bark may become damaged, putting the plant at risk from diseases. Cut out old, unproductive stems to make space for young shoots to develop.

Rosa 'American Pillar': a rampant rambler

Pruning established roses

For each type of rose, you should first remove all dead, diseased, or damaged wood, as well as any weak and spindly young shoots.

• HYBRID TEA (LARGE-FLOWERED) TYPES: shorten the strongest remaining shoots to four to six buds, 10–15cm (4–6in), from the base, the point where last year's growth began. Shorten less-vigorous shoots to about two to four buds, 5–10cm (2–4in) from the base. Aim to cut out all three-year-old wood, leaving younger, more vigorous growth, which produces better flowers.

See also Choosing shrub roses, pp.88–89; Pruning climbing roses, p.104; Renovating climbing roses, p.104

- FLORIBUNDA (CLUSTER-FLOWERED) TYPES: shorten the strongest remaining shoots only moderately, leaving 25–30cm (10–12in) of growth, but prune less-vigorous shoots severely. Occasionally prune some older stems hard back to within a few centimetres of the ground, to encourage stronger growth from the base of the plant.
- PATIO (LOW-GROWING FLORIBUNDA) TYPES: reduce the strongest remaining growths by about one-third of their height. If plants are very twiggy, carry out some thinning to prevent the bush from becoming too crowded and to improve air circulation.
- MINIATURE TYPES: limit pruning to shortening any weak growth and the occasional pruning back of older growth to near soil level.
- GROUND-COVER TYPES: hard prune any upright growth, and then reduce strongly growing shoots by approximately one-third. Shorten the sideshoots to two or three buds.
- CLIMBERS: aim to build up the basic framework from which strong sideshoots are produced. In autumn, after flowering

has finished, remove any unwanted wood, then tie or re-tie the remaining growth to supports. In early or mid-spring, shorten each stem by about one-third of the previous year's growth and reduce sideshoots from these stems to within two or three buds of the base, about 5–8cm (2–3in). Cut out old, worn-out stems as necessary to ground level, and train in young replacement shoots.
- RAMBLERS: true ramblers flower only once each season. Immediately after flowering, cut out all the old flowered stems, taking them down to ground level. Tie in new shoots if they are well developed, or progressively tie them in during late summer or autumn. Where there are too few new stems, as can happen with less-vigorous cultivars, or where a larger plant is required to make a feature or to fill more space, restrict pruning to the removal of one in three of the old flowered shoots. Shorten the sideshoots of the remaining stems by one-third and tip prune the stems, removing 5–8cm (2–3in). This will help to encourage good flowering during the following year.

- SHRUB AND SPECIES ROSES: there are many kinds of shrub and species roses, with widely differing flowering and growth habits (see pp. 88–89). Basically, the main requirement is to keep the plants free of dead, diseased and damaged wood and to remove any crossing or rubbing branches. If they become leggy and bare at the base, remove one or two stems to near ground level. This usually encourages new basal growth. To maintain a balance, reduce strong new growths by up to one-third and shorten strong sideshoots to two or three buds in early or mid-spring. Do not allow the excessive build up of older, unproductive wood; this will prevent the centre of the shrub from becoming too crowded. Remove ageing branches as necessary, either cutting them out completely, or well back to just above a strong young developing shoot.
- ENGLISH ROSES: in early or mid-spring prune back the previous season's growths by one-third to half their length. Harder pruning will give better-quality but fewer blooms.

PRUNING MODERN BUSH ROSES

Most modern bush roses flower repeatedly throughout summer if you remove dead flowerheads. The main aim of pruning is to ensure a plentiful supply of strong, new shoots. Hybrid tea roses and floribundas are best pruned hard back each year to a low, open framework of strong young stems; other types respond well to less severe pruning.

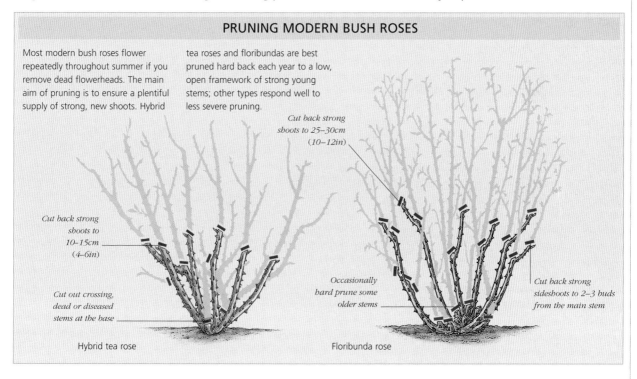

Cut back strong shoots to 25–30cm (10–12in)

Cut back strong shoots to 10–15cm (4–6in)

Cut out crossing, dead or diseased stems at the base

Hybrid tea rose

Occasionally hard prune some older stems

Cut back strong sideshoots to 2–3 buds from the main stem

Floribunda rose

Goodbye to rose diseases

You can use chemical or cultural methods to overcome the infamous three diseases – black spot, powdery mildew and rust – but you have to be persistent; choosing roses with disease resistance will also help

Black spot on leaves

Leaf yellowing

Diffuse purple-black spots

BLACK SPOT

The cause of this serious disease is the fungus *Diplocarpon rosae*, which overwinters on stem lesions, bud scales and fallen leaves. It can spread through water splash or wind-blown rain, and wet weather creates the most favourable conditions for infection.

Symptoms

Diffuse purple-black spots or blotches develop on the leaves, which then yellow and fall prematurely. The spots enlarge and may sometimes join together. Smaller spots may also develop on the stems.

Control

Promptly remove infected and fallen leaves. In spring prune out any damaged stems showing lesions. Spray with an approved fungicide immediately after pruning in spring, and repeat according to the manufacturer's instructions. Several applications may be necessary during the growing season to control this disease. Choose roses with good disease resistance (see rose growers' catalogues or a good rose encyclopedia).

ROSE POWDERY MILDEW

The fungus *Sphaerotheca pannosa* overwinters on plants as stem infections and in dormant buds. It is spread by wind. Powdery mildew is encouraged by dry conditions around the plant's roots and by moist air around the foliage.

Symptoms

Powdery, white fungal growth develops on the upper leaf surface. When young leaves are attacked by the fungus, they become severely distorted. Mildew may also develop on the stems, flower buds and thorns. Affected leaves fall prematurely.

Control

Prune out badly infected stems and spray with an approved fungicide according to the maker's instructions. Keep plants well watered during dry periods, but take care not to wet the foliage. Choose cultivars with good disease resistance (see rose-growers' catalogues or a good rose encyclopedia).

Powdery white fungal growth

Rose powdery mildew

Small orange spots

Leaves affected by rose rust

ROSE RUST

This disease is caused by the fungus *Phragmidium*, most commonly *P. tuberculatum*. Moist air is essential for the development and spread of the infection, which travels on air currents. The fungus may persist in the stems of plants and can overwinter as resting spores on fallen leaves and elsewhere.

Symptoms

Rust on roses can severely weaken plants, which causes the leaves to fall, and the stems to die back. Small orange spots appear on both sides of the leaves in spring and summer. In late summer or early autumn dark brown spots appear on the undersides of the leaves. At this time plants can suffer premature and severe defoliation.

Control

Prune out any stems showing spring infection as soon as you spot them, and prune to improve air circulation. Remove and destroy fallen leaves. Spray affected plants with an approved fungicide in spring and summer, following the manufacturer's instructions carefully.

See also Avoiding pests and diseases, pp.36–37; Using fungicides, pp.38–39

CLIMBERS

RECOMMENDED CLIMBERS AND WALL SHRUBS

Recommended climbers and wall shrubs

Whether the aspect is sunny and warm, or cool and shady, there are many suitable plants which make the most of vertical spaces, such as walls and fences, and increase the growing area of the garden

As well as true climbing plants, many shrubs are suitable for growing or training against walls and fences. By planting a selection, you can create a more interesting overall effect from the variations in shape, flowers or fruit.

To ensure optimum growth and flowering, it is important to choose plants suited to the conditions. For instance, warm, sunny walls and fences provide an ideal opportunity to grow some of the more tender kinds, especially if you live in a mild area without hard frosts. Equally there are many climbers and shrubs that will thrive in a colder, shady situation.

SUNNY WALLS AND FENCES

South- and west- facing walls or fences often receive prolonged direct sunlight and conditions can be very warm and dry. Plants may be subjected to long periods of direct and reflected heat from the backing wall or fence. Self-clinging climbers will attach themselves to the wall or fence, but twining climbers benefit from additional support and training.

Self-clinging climbers

Campsis x *tagliabuana* 'Madame Galen' ♀
‡ 10m (30ft) ◊ ✳✳

Euonymus fortunei 'Coloratus' ‡ 5m (15ft) E
◊ ✳✳✳

Parthenocissus quinquefolia ♀ ‡ 15m (50ft)
◊ ✳✳✳

Pileostegia viburnoides ♀ ‡ 6m (20ft) E
◊ ✳✳✳

Trachelospermum jasminoides ♀ ‡ 9m (28ft)
E ◊ ✳✳

Twining or scrambling

Actinidia kolomikta ♀ ‡ 5m (15ft) ◊ ✳✳✳

Clematis armandii ‡ 3–5m (10–15ft) E ◊
✳✳

Clematis cirrhosa var. *balearica* ‡ 2.5–3m
(8–10ft) E ◊ ✳✳

Eccremocarpus scaber ‡ 3–5m (10–15ft),
sheltered site, E ◊ ✳✳

Humulus lupulus 'Aureus' ♀ ‡ 6m (20ft) ◊
✳✳✳ 1

Jasminum officinale ♀ ‡ 12m (40ft) ◊ ✳✳

Lonicera periclymenum 'Graham Thomas' ♀
‡ 7m (22ft) ◊ ✳✳✳

Passiflora caerulea ♀ ‡ 10m (30ft) E ◊ ✳✳

Solanum crispum 'Glasnevin' ♀ ‡ 6m (20ft) E
◊ ✳✳

Vitis coignetiae ♀ ‡ 15m (50ft) ◊ ✳✳✳

Wisteria floribunda ‡ 9m (28ft) ◊ ✳✳✳

Wisteria sinensis ♀ ‡ 9m (28ft) ◊ ✳✳✳

SHADY WALLS AND FENCES

Conditions against north- or east-facing walls and fences can be cold and bleak, as plants often receive little direct sunlight. Self-clingers will climb unsupported, but twining plants will need a little more support and encouragement. Alternatively, try training shrubs up cool walls.

Self-clinging climbers

Hedera colchica 'Dentata Variegata' ♀ ‡ 5m
(15ft) E ◊ ✳✳✳

Hydrangea anomala subsp. *petiolaris* ♀
‡ 15m (50ft) ◊ ✳✳✳

Parthenocissus tricuspidata ♀ ‡ 20m (70ft)
◊ ✳✳✳

Schizophragma integrifolium ♀ ‡ 12m (40ft)
◊ ✳✳

Twining climbers

Akebia quinata ‡ 10m (30ft) ◊ ✳✳✳

Berberidopsis corallina ‡ 5m (15ft) E ◊ ✳✳

Celastrus scandens ‡ 10m (30ft), male and
female plants needed to produce fruit, ◊ ✳✳✳

Clematis alpina ♀ ‡ 1.8–3m (6–10ft) ◊ ✳✳✳ 2

Lonicera japonica 'Halliana' ♀ ‡ 10m (30ft) E
◊ ✳✳✳

Shrubs for training to walls

Chaenomeles speciosa 'Moerloosei' ♀ ‡ 2.4m
(8ft) ↔ 5m (15ft) ◊ ✳✳✳

Cotoneaster henryanus ‡ 4m (12ft) ↔ 3.6m
(12ft) E ◊ ✳✳✳

Cotoneaster horizontalis ♀ ‡ 90cm (36in)
↔ 1.5m (5ft) ◊ ✳✳✳

Forsythia suspensa ‡ 3m (10ft) ↔ 3m (10ft)
◊ ✳✳✳

Garrya elliptica 'James Roof' ♀ ‡ 4m (12ft)
↔ 4m (12ft), sheltered site, E ◊ ✳✳

Pyracantha 'Orange Glow' ♀ ‡ 3m (10ft)
↔ 3m (10ft) E ◊ ✳✳✳

See also Making pergolas and arbours, pp.28–29; Climbers for fragrance, p.99

How to plant climbers

Due to their unique growth habits, climbers have the means to raise themselves above other plants; however, they need careful planting and some method of support to make maximum impact

Planting technique

Soil at the base of walls is frequently poor and dry, so to improve the growing conditions add generous quantities of organic matter.

Plant tender, herbaceous and evergreen climbers any time from early spring onwards when ground conditions are suitable. Deciduous woody climbers can be planted in early spring or mid- to late autumn.

Dig a hole twice the diameter of the roots and the same depth as the rootball. Clematis need deeper

planting. Plant climbers 30–45cm (12–18in) from the walls of the house to avoid the rainshadow effect of the eaves. Place a cane at the base of the plant, angled towards the wall to guide the plant towards its supports.

Work fine soil around the rootball, firming well as you proceed. Climbers, especially clematis, need to be hard pruned in the spring after planting to stimulate strong new growth.

Methods of climbing

Plants have several methods of climbing. Self-clinging climbers such as ivy (*Hedera*) have aerial roots to cling to their support. Virginia creeper (*Parthenocissus*) uses sucker pads on the ends of tendrils to attach itself. These plants benefit from some initial support.

Supports on walls
Horizontal galvanised wires make good supports for climbers on walls (*below*). Use a straining bolt at one end of each wire to ensure it is tight (*left*).

Tendrils of a climber

Various adaptations are used by plants to twine through their host or up a support. Stems can twine in a clockwise direction as with honeysuckle (*Lonicera*) or anticlockwise (*Wisteria sinensis*). Twining petioles (leaf stalks) are used by plants such as *Clematis*. Climbers such as sweet peas (*Lathyrus*) also twine, but use contact-sensitive tendrils to draw them towards their support.

Wall shrubs and scrambling climbers with no natural support mechanisms need additional supports on the wall or fence and tying in at regular intervals.

Supports

Trellis and netting (wire or plastic) are suitable for twining climbers. Both are best fitted to battens to allow air circulation behind the plant.

Horizontal or vertical wires are useful for starting off self-clinging climbers, as well as for supporting other climbers. Use vine eyes at intervals to prevent sagging. Vertical wires can be used to guide plants up pergola posts.

See also Pruning clematis, p.101; Pruning honeysuckle, p.103; Passion flower pruning, p.103; Pruning wisterias, p.105; Soil fertility, p.259

Ideas for climbing plants in pots

If you think you do not have the space for climbers, try growing them in containers on the patio, terrace or balcony: annual and perennial kinds guarantee to brighten up a sunny situation in summer

Climbing plants are ideal for the many gardeners who work with limited space, as they take up such little room at ground level. Growing them in containers with a suitable support means even the smallest garden can make space for climbers, and adventurous gardeners can mix and match, experimenting with vertical plant associations that can also be moved around the plot.

Planting combinations

For maximum impact in the garden, match plants of similar vigour and flowering time with contrasting flower forms and colours. Many annual and tender perennial climbers are easy to raise from seed, and are increasingly offered as young plants in garden centres in spring.

Jasminum officinale Fiona Sunrise ('Frojas') and *Rhodochiton atrosanguineus*

A good example is *Ipomoea lobata* with small tubular flowers that open crimson and fade through orange to pale yellow. It is effective planted by itself, but interplanting with its close relative, *I.* 'Star of Yalta', a morning glory that adds dramatic splashes of purple, more than doubles the drama. An attractively planted container will produce a versatile display, which will lend height and provide colour throughout the summer.

Foliage colour can result in even greater contrasts. The jasmine *Jasminum officinale* Fiona Sunrise ('Frojas'), although rather lax in habit, has bold yellow foliage and small, subtly scented white flowers. Its medium growth habit suits a 1m (3ft) tall spiral white obelisk, all the more so teamed with the Mexican *Rhodochiton atrosanguineus*. This is a

SUPPORTS FOR CONTAINER-GROWN CLIMBERS

Supports should be an average height above the containers of about 1.5–1.8m (5–6ft). This keeps them visually in balance with the containers and provides sufficient height for the plants to mature. Proprietary supports can be used, such as wooden or steel obelisks, and the narrower designs are best for the smaller container. Home-made supports are cheaper, and may be better suited to your needs. These could include **1** a wigwam made from bamboo canes; **2** vertical plastic-coated wires similar to a maypole; **3** a cylinder of plastic-coated wire supported with canes; **4** a plastic-mesh or wire-netting cylinder supported with canes; **5** trellis formed from laths or bamboo canes and plastic mesh.

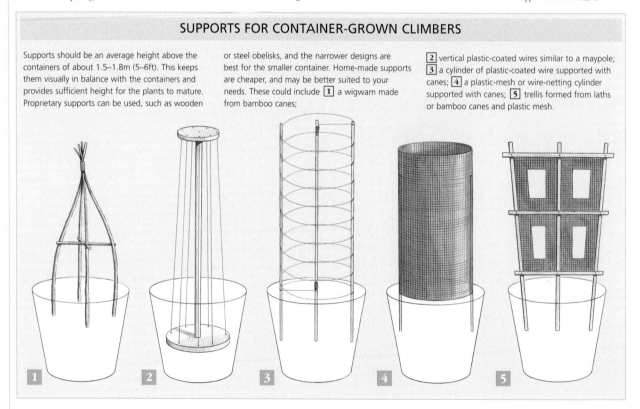

See also Planning small gardens, p.18; Ways of using clematis, pp.99–100; Planting in containers, p.161

tender perennial climber and, like several other non-hardy species, is usually grown as an annual in Britain.

A more subtle, warmer mixture results from the orange form of *Eccremocarpus scaber* (Chilean glory vine) blended with recently introduced *Thunbergia alata* 'African Sunset' (syn. 'Blushing Susie'). The Chilean glory vine is more vigorous, but it allows the *Thunbergia* (black-eyed Susan) to scramble up and through its host. Contrast is provided by the five-petalled, dark-centred blooms, predominantly red, with shades of apricot and ivory.

Simple-to-grow annual stalwarts such as *Lathyrus* (sweet peas), *Ipomoea* (morning glory), *Lablab* (Egyptian or Indian bean), *Tropaeolum majus* (nasturtium) and *Cobaea* (cup and saucer plant) are all potential container stars, but do not ignore perennial climbers, too. Many perennials may be borderline hardy but will cope if given adequate winter protection *in situ* or if moved indoors (much easier when container grown). *Dicentra macrocapnos*, which flowers from summer to autumn, produces classic locket-shaped flowers, and equally splendid is *D. scandens*, which is smaller at 3m (10ft), with a shorter flowering period. Other excellent pairings include

Good mixers

Ipomoea lubata creates drama when paired with morning glories like purple *I.* 'Star of Yalta' (*left*), or mixed with *I.* 'Cardinal Red' and black-eyed Susan, *Thunbergia alata* (*above*). Other plants also make striking combinations, as with *Senecio confusus* and *Aconitum* aff. *episcopale* (*above left*).

D. scandens and *Eccremocarpus scaber* 'Tresco Red', or *Dicentra macrocapnos* with *Tropaeolum speciosum* (flame creeper).

Moving from red to orange, *Senecio confusus* is a tender perennial climber that needs a warm, sheltered site outdoors. It has striking flame orange, daisy-like flowers and can climb 3–4.5m (10–15ft). Slightly easier to grow, and certainly more cold tolerant, is *S. hoffmannii*. Either of these two orange-flowered plants mix well with *Aconitum* aff. *episcopale*, a climbing herbaceous monkshood with deep indigo-blue flowers. This would combine equally well with tuberous-rooted *Tropaeolum tuberosum* var. *lineamaculatum* 'Ken Aslet', which grows to 1.8m (6ft), producing flared, orange, funnel-shaped flowers on long red stalks. The tall, hardy South American *Tropaeolum pentaphyllum* is even more interesting, with 2cm (¾in) long, red- or green-spurred, scarlet and purple flowers in summer.

COMBINING CLIMBERS

- Combining two or more climbers in a container can provide vivid colour without taking up too much space
- Choose plants that have similar vigour and enjoy the same growing conditions, for instance, preferring the same aspect
- Be adventurous and imaginative with your combinations

HOW TO PROPAGATE CLIMBERS

How to propagate climbers

Many climbers are easy to propagate from cuttings in summer: given adequate warmth they will root within a few weeks and you will have sturdy young plants within a year

In nature climbers root where they ramble, so it is no surprise that most are easy to propagate from cuttings. The semi-ripe wood, neither hard and woody nor soft and delicate, found in mid- to late summer, is ideal.

Leaf-bud cuttings

Many climbers can be propagated from double leaf-bud cuttings; for example, *Campsis, Celastrus, Clematis, Humulus* (hops), *Hedera* (ivy), *Lonicera* (honeysuckle) and roses.

Prepare the cuttings by cutting directly above a pair of leaves and then make a lower cut about halfway between two leaf joints. From the bottom of the cutting remove a slice

1–2cm (½–¾in) long and dip the lower part of the cutting in hormone rooting compound.

Root cuttings in a well-drained gritty compost in a heated propagator at about 20–25°C (68–77°F). However, a pot or seed tray of cuttings placed in a clear plastic bag on a windowsill will often do well. Be assiduous in picking over the cuttings for dead material.

Nodal cuttings

Alternatively, if plenty of propagating material is available, ordinary nodal cuttings can be used. Any climber that can be propagated by leaf-bud cuttings is easy to raise from nodal cuttings. Try *Akebia, Ampelopsis, Fallopia*

baldschuanica (Russian vine), *Jasminum* (jasmine), *Parthenocissus, Passiflora* (passion flower) and *Trachelospermum* (star jasmine).

Make the cuttings 8–15cm (3–6in) long, depending on subject, cutting just above and just below a node (leaf joint), remove lower leaves, dip bases in hormone rooting powder and root as for leaf-bud cuttings.

Growing on

Rooting is usually quick, six to eight weeks, particularly in a heated propagator, but it is best to leave the cuttings until spring in an unheated greenhouse or cold frame before moving into separate pots.

PROPAGATION FROM SEMI-RIPE DOUBLE LEAF-BUD CUTTINGS

Select a length of semi-ripe stem (here, clematis) with several pairs of leaves. **1** Cut slightly above a pair of leaves (just above a node or leaf joint), using a sharp knife; make a lower cut about halfway between two leaf joints. **2** This
gives you cuttings each with a pair of leaves and a length of stem. Reduce each leaf to two leaflets. **3** Remove a slice of bark, 2cm (¾in) long, from the base of each cutting to encourage rooting. **4** Dip the base of each cutting in
hormone rooting compound. **5** Insert up to the node in a pot of well-drained, gritty compost. **6** Water well, then place in a heated propagator or a clear plastic bag on a windowsill to root. Pot off separately when well rooted.

See also Multiplying perennials by division, pp.128–129; Dividing bulbs, pp. 154–155

PRACTICAL ADVICE

Climbers for fragrance

Choose scented climbers to add more atmosphere to your garden

Most gardeners like fragrant plants as they add atmosphere and romance to a garden, whether it is in the cottage style or a modern design. You need to choose climbers carefully, however, as not all of them by any means have fragrant flowers. The list below includes some of the most popular climbing plants with fragrant blooms.

Scent is most noticeable in calm conditions, not when it is windy or breezy when the scent is quickly carried away on the air. So try to plant fragrant climbers in a position that is sheltered from the wind. The perfume of flowers is probably best captured in a courtyard or partially enclosed patio where, of course, climbers are particularly useful for covering the surrounding walls.

FRAGRANT FLOWERS

Clematis armandii ‡ 3–5m (10–15ft) E ⬜ ◊ ✲✲

Clematis montana var. *rubens* ‘Elizabeth’ ♀ ‡ 7m (22ft) ⬜ ◊ ✲✲✲

Clematis rehderiana ♀ ‡ 6–7m (20–22ft) ⬜ ◊ ✲✲✲ [1]

Jasminum officinale ♀ ‡ 12m (40ft), ⬜–◙ ◊ ✲✲

Lonicera x italica ♀ ‡ 7m (22ft) ⬜–◙ ◊ ✲✲✲

Trachelospermum jasminoides ♀ ‡ 9m (28ft) E ⬜ ◊ ✲✲ [2]

Wisteria floribunda ‡ 9m (28ft) ⬜ ◊ ✲✲✲

Wisteria sinensis ♀ ‡ 9m (28ft) ⬜ ◊ ✲✲✲

See also Planning small gardens, p.18

PLANTING IDEAS

Ways of using clematis

Combining clematis with other choice plants brings a more daring edge to these enduring garden favourites

The light purple *Clematis* ‘Prince Charles’ in combination with *Rosa* Berkshire (‘Korpinka’)

The natural habit of clematis is to scramble over or wrap around their supports or host plants. This habit, when utilized in the garden, allows their glorious blooms to combine with the flowers and foliage of other plants to enhance any planting scheme.

Perfect partners
Roses and clematis are often seen happily entwined, thanks in part to their similar feeding and cultivation requirements.

These two plants have flower shapes and colour ranges that can contrast, yet combine effectively together. Early-season clematis, such as *C. alpina* and *C. macropetala*, with their bushy habits, are naturally suited to training up and masking the bare stems of climbing or rambler roses.

Early- to midsummer-flowering clematis, including *C.* ‘Lasurstern’, *C.* ‘Marie Boisselot’ and *C.* ‘Nelly Moser’, benefit from being thinned to five or six shoots before they are tied into a rose; fewer flowers may result, but these will be larger, better formed and more evenly spaced, resulting in a more balanced overall display.

Shrubby companions
Most large-flowered hybrids, Viticellas and compact species clematis, that flower from midsummer to autumn, make good partners both for evergreen and deciduous shrubs. However, before planting any combination, take into consideration: the flowering time of each plant; how they will complement one another; and any pruning methods involved. These clematis need hard pruning in early spring and, for a successful display, all types need their young shoots tying in.

Large-flowered, mid-season hybrids are well adapted to growing through large evergreen shrubs, such as ▷

See also How to plant climbers, p.95; How to prune clematis, p.101

WAYS OF USING CLEMATIS

Inspiring combinations
Top left: *Clematis* 'Pink Fantasy' looks fabulous planted with *Rosa* 'Agnes'. *Top right*: *Clematis* Arctic Queen ('Evitwo') sets off the delicate pink of *Rosa* 'Cornelia'. *Bottom right*: *Clematis* 'Ascotiensis' combines beautifully with *Rosa* 'Ballerina'.

species rhododendrons and their cultivars. Ideal cultivars include deep pink *Clematis* 'Kakio' (syn. 'Pink Champagne') or soft blue *C.* 'Will Goodwin'; the stems of these cultivars have a naturally open habit and can meander over and through their supporting plant.

Smaller, medium-sized shrubs, which have compact crowns and offer shelter from the wind, are more appropriate for the early- to late-summer blooming clematis cultivars. These generally have shorter stems and closer flowers and include mid-blue *Clematis* 'Fuji-musume', double *C.* Arctic Queen ('Evitwo') and lilac *C.* Josephine ('Evijohill').

The sporadic flowers and rather sombre greenery of evergreen shrub *Choisya ternata*, which tolerates regular trimming, can be elevated by the deep red velvety flowers of *Clematis* 'Niobe' or dark blue *C.* Petit Faucon ('Evisix') spilling over it. Many hebe cultivars also offer a good foil for clematis, particularly *C.* 'Royal Velours'.

Purple-leaved cultivars of shrubs such as *Acer palmatum*, *Corylus*, *Cotinus* and *Physocarpus* pose a challenge to find suitable contrasts or even neutral colours with which to successfully combine. *Clematis* 'Etoile Rose' and *Cotinus coggygria* 'Royal Purple' are a subtle match. So, too, is less-vigorous *Clematis* Arctic Queen ('Evitwo') beside the fine-cut foliage of *Acer palmatum* var. *dissectum* Dissectum Atropurpureum Group. Other companions might include *Corylus*

maxima 'Purpurea' and deep pink *Clematis* 'Carnaby' or ruby red *C.* 'Madame Edouard Andre' against *Physocarpus opulifolius* 'Diabolo'.

Sun-tolerant *Sambucus racemosa* 'Sutherland Gold' provides natural staking for *Clematis* 'Perle d'Azur' in the Mixed Borders at RHS Garden Wisley. The strong golden foliage and soft blue flowers contrast well together. Nearby, *Paeonia delavayi* x *delavayi* var. *lutea* supports mid- to late-season *C. flammula*.

See also Choosing plants for ground cover, pp.26–27; How to plant climbers, p.95; How to prune clematis, p.101

Smothering the ground

Herbaceous *Clematis x jouiniana* 'Praecox' has a vigorous nature and is simply too much for most planting partners to cope with. Yet, in a space of its own, it can make an excellent ground-cover plant.

Many other clematis, however, can be used for low-level combination plantings, especially the Texensis or Viticella types; they do not smother the support plant and grow well over the soil surface.

When planting heathers and clematis together, the season of interest of both can be greatly extended. Winter-flowering heathers planted with *C.* 'Etoile Violette' or *C.* 'Madame Julia Correvon' are striking combinations and, conveniently, both plants can be pruned at the same time.

CHOOSING CLEMATIS

Early spring flowers

C. alpina ♀ ‡ 1.8–3m (6–10ft) ↔ 1.5m (5ft) ✳✳✳

C. armandii ‡ 3–5m (10–15ft) ↔ 1.8–3m (6–10ft) E ✳✳

C. macropetala ‡ 1.8–3m (6–10ft) ↔ 1.5m (5ft) ✳✳✳

C. montana ‡ 5–14m (15–46ft) ↔ 1.8–3m (6–10ft) ✳✳✳

Late spring or early summer flowers

C. 'Lasurstern' ♀ ‡ 2.4m (8ft) ↔ 90cm (36in) ✳✳✳

C. 'Marie Boisselot' ♀ ‡ 3m (10ft) ↔ 90cm (36in) ✳✳✳

C. 'Nelly Moser' ♀ ‡ 1.8–3m (6–10ft) ↔ 90cm (36in) ✳✳✳

C. patens ‡ 4m (12ft) ↔ 90cm (36in) ✳✳✳

C. 'The President' ♀ ‡ 1.8–3m (6–10ft) ↔ 90cm (36in) ✳✳✳

Late summer or autumn flowers

C. 'Jackmanii' ♀ ‡ 3m (10ft) ↔ 90cm (36in) ✳✳✳

C. tangutica ‡ 5–6m (15–20ft) ↔ 1.8–3m (6–10ft) ✳✳✳

C. viticella ♀ ‡ 1.8–4m (6–12ft) ↔ 1.5m (5ft) ✳✳✳

How to prune clematis

Pruning clematis is far simpler than many people imagine, provided you know what pruning group the plant is in

For the purposes of pruning, clematis are divided into three groups. The first group, containing small-flowered species each responding to a particular kind of pruning treatment, and cultivars that flower in mid- or late spring on long shoots made in the previous year, need no regular pruning except for the removal of faded flowers.

In subsequent years some training and perhaps thinning may be necessary. If renovation is needed, plants can be cut back to 15cm (6in) from the base after flowering. This will affect flowering and should not be carried out again within three years. Plants in this group include *Clematis montana*, *C. alpina* and *C. macropetala*. *C. armandii* and *C. cirrhosa* are pruned to remove old stems after flowering.

The second group contains large-flowered cultivars that flower from late spring to early summer on short sideshoots developing from the previous year's growth. They only need to have the dead flowers removed as soon as the display is over, cutting back to a large growth bud immediately below the flower. Some plants in this group flower in the spring from the previous year's growth, then flower again later in the summer on current year's growth.

They can, if preferred, be left unpruned other than for the removal of dead shoot ends in spring. If cut hard back in late winter they may not flower that year, or flower only once, in late summer. If a proportion of the old wood is cut back to 30cm (12in) in late winter it will produce new shoots which should flower in late summer, prolonging the flowering season. Plants in this group include *Clematis* 'Nelly Moser' and *C.* 'Kathleen Wheeler'.

The third group contains those clematis that flower usually after early

Many clematis species only need thinning

summer with the flowers developing on the top 60cm (36in) or so of the current year's growth. If these clematis are left unpruned, growth will continue from where it ended the previous season, resulting in a tangled mass of growth, often flowering well above eye level and with stems bare at the base.

These late-flowering clematis are best pruned back hard, to the lowest pair of buds, in late winter each year. However, the late-flowering *Clematis orientalis* and *C. tangutica*, and the Viticella Group, can be left unpruned on pergolas or where there is space for them to scramble unchecked. Plants in this group include *C. viticella* and *C.* 'Jackmanii'.

Clematis of the Jackmanii type may be pruned by combining methods 2 and 3, to retain a basic framework while cutting older stems to the base. This extends the flowering season. Herbaceous clematis are pruned to near ground level in late autumn or early spring.

See also Ways of using clematis, pp.99–100; Clematis problems, p.102

CLEMATIS PROBLEMS

Clematis problems

Clematis have more than their fair share of ailments and unfortunately some can be fatal, but do not let them deter you from growing 'the queen of climbers'

CLEMATIS SLIME FLUX

Slime flux is believed to be caused by bacteria that enter the plant through damage to the stem and then multiply in the vessels of the stem and generate gas. The build-up of pressure causes the stems to rupture and the mixture of sap and bacteria to escape. Plants are weakened during cold winters and may suffer frost cracks, making the entry of bacteria more likely.

Symptoms

The first indication that there is a problem is usually leaves wilting and yellowing or even a complete failure to come into leaf in spring. When the base of the main stem is examined a foul smelling, whitish to pink, thick exudation is seen. This may ooze down the stem and collect in a puddle on the soil. *Clematis montana* seems to be particularly prone to this disease, although other species are occasionally affected.

Control

Unfortunately slime flux is normally fatal. Occasionally a clematis may re-shoot from below the site of the flux. However, if the plant dies it should be safe to plant a replacement in the same place, provided you remove as much as possible of the dead clematis.

Green coloured flowers

GREEN FLOWERS

The cause of green flowers is not known, but it may be due to low temperatures when the flowers are forming. Some early-flowering hybrids including 'Duchess of Edinburgh' and 'Nelly Moser' appear to be particularly susceptible.

Symptoms

Occasionally, early in the season, green flowers are found on normally colourful clematis. Symptoms range from petals tinged green along the centre line to entire petals failing to colour.

Commonly a petal will have a green, leafy tip. This seems to be linked with cold conditions and disappears as the weather warms. The blooms are perfectly formed and do not exhibit the distortion associated with green flower disease, which is caused by organisms related to viruses. In such cases the infected plant will not recover; flowers and foliage continue to be distorted.

Control

The problem of green flowers may be greatest where clematis are planted in north-facing positions. Sulphate of potash is sometimes applied as a remedy but there appears to be no real evidence for this. Plants usually revert to their normal colour later in the season as new flowers open.

Clematis affected by slime flux

CLEMATIS WILT

Spores of the fungus *Phoma clematidina* are spread by water, infecting leaves and sometimes stems. The fungus grows down stems and blocks water-conducting tissue, which causes the plant to wilt. The fungus can remain on dead clematis and probably other plant debris for many months.

Symptoms

Early flowering, large-flowered clematis cultivars are the most susceptible, others less so. Clematis species are resistant. Symptoms are sudden wilting of the upper parts of stems and, when fresh, there is internal black staining of affected water-conducting tissue.

Control

Buy healthy plants to avoid introducing the disease. Prune back promptly to unaffected tissue and destroy all traces of diseased material. Healthy buds will sometimes develop from ground level or even below. There are no fungicides available to control the disease.

Wilting and dieback are often caused by planting in unsuitable conditions. Clematis prefer deep, moist but well-drained soil. Wall-side borders are often hot and shallow, so improve conditions with organic matter and mulching.

Plant badly infected with clematis wilt

See also Avoiding pests and diseases, pp.36–37

Pruning honeysuckles

Be ruthless with pruning when honeysuckles get out of control

Tangled, woody, overgrown honeysuckles can be ruthlessly cut back in the autumn and winter, using loppers to reduce the plant to 60cm (24in) in height. In spring vigorous new shoots should be trained so the whole of their support structure is clad from base to top. Continually pinching out the growing tips stimulates bushy growth. Flowers are unlikely to develop until growth slows, but within a couple of years, perhaps sooner, flowering should be back to normal.

If this is more extreme than the situation merits, shearing over excessive growth will be sufficient, removing most of the sideshoots and

Shearing an overgrown honeysuckle
If growth is too wide and spreading, or is all at the top of a wall, shear over the excessive growth, removing most of the sideshoots. The plant will eventually become stronger and healthier.

old growth. Typically, shearing back is helpful where all the growth is at the top of a wall or fence, or where a honeysuckle is too wide and spreading. Again, flowers will be slow to form, but the plant will perform more effectively after being pruned in this way.

See also How to propagate climbers, p.90

Controlling ivy on buildings

Swift action can prevent ivy from causing structural damage

Self-clinging climbers do not usually cause damage to wall surfaces but ivy supports itself by roots on the stems and where these penetrate cracks or joints they may cause structural damage. Its dense cover can also hide defects in the fabric of the building or hinder maintenance work. Ivy may also provide access for intruders and harbour pests such as mice. Where brickwork is sound, the main task is to keep growth away from gutters and paintwork.

Large climbers can pose a risk to house foundations. This is most likely with older buildings constructed on clay soils that are prone to shrinkage.

Ivy can be killed by cutting through the stem near ground level and treating the stump with ammonium sulphamate. Top growth may be treated with a brushwood killer or a weedkiller containing glyphosate, but ivy is not easily controlled in this way because the leaves are glossy and the spray simply runs off. Repeat applications may be necessary.

Dead foliage and stems are relatively easy to remove from walls, but aerial roots are persistent and can only be removed using a hard brush, wire brush or paint scraper.

Removing aerial roots using a stiff wire brush

See also Ivy as a weed, p.33

Passion flower pruning

Restricted space leads to regular pruning for this hardy plant

Encourage low branching of *Passiflora caerulea* (blue passion flower) by pinching or cutting back all growing tips after planting. This will give plenty of shoots for training. Alternatively, cut back fairly hard in spring after a year's growth.

With unlimited space, plants can be allowed to develop fairly naturally, but where space is limited, training and regular pruning are advisable. Train several branches or shoots as a framework over the wall space and restrict any further outward development by removing the ends of the shoots in mid-spring. Sideshoots growing from these main branches can be allowed to hang down. These will produce flowers.

In early spring, as the first signs of new growth are seen, cut back to healthy growth any frost-damaged wood. Also cut back the hanging sideshoots produced the previous year to within 2.5cm (1in) or so of the main branches. Repeat this pruning annually. When the main branches have reached the limits of their allotted space, further extension growth can be left to hang loosely, cutting it back each spring as with sideshoots.

The beautiful flower of a *Passiflora caerulea*

See also How to propagate climbers, p.98

| TECHNIQUES | PLANTING IDEAS |

Renovating climbing roses

Neglected roses need some fairly drastic treatment

Neglected climbing roses sprawl with bare unproductive stems lower down and an entanglement at the top. Prune out most of the old wood in autumn or winter, aiming to promote a flush of new growth from the base.

If necessary, remove the climber from its supports and lay it on the ground for better access. After pruning, spread the new stems over the supports and, if possible, bend the branches to a more horizontal position to encourage shoots from low stems and promote flowering.

With old, fragile roses, excessive heavy pruning can harm the plant. Sometimes new growth stubbornly refuses to sprout and the rose will die. Limit the risk of this by spreading the work over several years.

Normal annual pruning

Climbers are pruned in early spring. Cut back the old flowered sideshoots by two-thirds. Prune ramblers in early autumn by cutting out to ground level all the old flowered stems. Then tie in the remaining new stems which will flower next year.

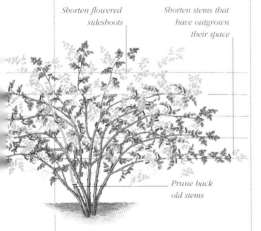

Shorten flowered sideshoots

Shorten stems that have outgrown their space

Prune back old stems

Routine annual pruning of climbing roses

See also How to prune roses, pp.90–91

Choosing climbing roses

Some climbing and rambler roses are suitable for shady, north-facing walls, while others can be used for training up pillars

Choosing roses is very much a personal matter in terms of preference for flower form and colour. Often when buying roses it is necessary to choose on the basis of a description only, particularly with species roses that are seldom illustrated in rose growers' catalogues. However, whenever possible, try to see roses in bloom before buying, by visiting rose nurseries or rose gardens during the flowering season, to avoid possible disappointment later.

SELECTING COLOURFUL CLIMBING ROSES

For north-facing walls

'Dortmund' ♥ ↕2m (7ft), Climber; single, blood-red flowers; repeat flowering ▣–▣ ◊ ✳✳✳ [1]

'Félicité Perpétue' ♥ ↕8m (25ft), Rambler; double white flowers, buds tinged red; leaves may persist into winter; one flowering period ▣–▣ ◊ ✳✳✳

'Leverkusen' ♥ ↕3m (10ft), Climber; double lightly scented, lemon yellow flowers; some repeat flowering ▣–▣ ◊ ✳✳✳

'Maigold' ♥ ↕3m (10ft), Climber; early, semi-double, fragrant bronze-yellow flowers; good foliage; some repeat flowering ▣–▣ ◊ ✳✳✳

'Madame Alfred Carrière' ♥ ↕6m (20ft), Climber; double, sweetly scented, creamy-white flowers; repeat flowering ▣–▣ ◊ ✳✳✳

'Madame Grégoire Staechelin' ♥ ↕6m (20ft), Climber; semi-double, fragrant, clear glowing pink flowers; one flowering period ▣–▣ ◊ ✳✳✳

'New Dawn' ♥ ↕2.5m (8ft), Climber; double, fragrant, apple-blossom pink flowers; repeat flowering ▣–▣ ◊ ✳✳✳

For training up pillars

'Aloha' ♥ ↕1.5m (5ft), Climber; double, fragrant, rose pink flowers; repeat flowering ▣ ◊ ✳✳✳ [2]

'Compassion' ♥ ↕4m (12ft), Climber; double, fragrant, pink shaded apricot flowers; repeat flowering ▣ ◊ ✳✳✳ [3]

Dublin Bay ('Macdub') ♥ ↕2.4m (8ft), Climber, double, slightly fragrant, deep red flowers; repeat flowering ▣ ◊ ✳✳✳

'Golden Showers' ♥ ↕3m (10ft), Climber; double, fragrant, golden-yellow flowers; repeat flowering ▣ ◊ ✳✳✳

'Morning Jewel' ♥ ↕3m (10ft), Climber, semi-double, fragrant, pink flowers; repeat-flowering ▣ ◊ ✳✳✳

See also Making pergolas and arbours, pp.28–29; How to plant climbers, p.95

How to prune wisterias

Wisterias can be trained to walls, pergolas and arches or grown as standards: but for optimum flowering they need pruning twice a year

The aim with wall-grown wisterias is to train out main branches to cover available wall space, without undue crowding. Initially space branches 45–60cm (18–24in) apart, thinning in later years, if necessary, as larger branchlet systems build up following regular pruning.

Plants often produce strong young growths from near the base, even when fairly mature, and some of these can be used to fill in bare spaces or as replacements for old, worn-out shoots which are cut out at the point of origin.

For training against a wall, vertical or horizontal galvanized straining wires spaced 30cm (12in) apart will provide support. *Wisteria sinensis* is the most suitable species for walls where its short flower trusses are displayed to advantage.

Training on pergolas and arches

Wisteria floribunda has the longest flower trusses of all the species and is shown to best effect on garden structures such as pergolas where the flowers can hang free, unimpeded by branches or foliage.

Training as a standard

Standard forms of wisteria can be grown as specimens in a border or in a large pot or tub. Start with a young, single-stemmed plant. Pot on pot-grown plants in spring, as necessary, using a container one size larger than the previous one. Use a rich soil-based potting compost as it will give the plant more stability than a lighter peat- or coir-based potting compost.

Provide a stout stake for the main stem and tie it in as necessary. Allow the main stem to grow unchecked until it reaches the height required, usually 1.2–1.5m (4–5ft). Remove the tip in late winter to encourage the formation of side shoots at the top of the stem. Prune these shoots in winter, cutting them back to 15–30cm (6–12in), repeating the process the following winter, to gradually build up a head of branches. Weaker or misplaced shoots can be cut out completely.

As the head develops, summer prune the plant by cutting out the tips of main shoots not wanted for ▷

A pergola is an ideal support for wisteria, as the flowers hang down unimpeded

See also Why do wisterias fail to perform?, p.106; How to propagate climbers, p.98

TECHNIQUES

extension after the seventh leaf, and secondary shoots (sideshoots) after one or two leaves. In the following late winter cut back all of these sideshoots to within 2.5cm (1in) of their bases.

Annual pruning

Wisterias can be left to ramble unchecked where space allows but will usually flower more freely and regularly if pruned in summer and winter to a system of branchlets. Shortening branchlets or spurs in summer, as suggested here, induces flower buds. Exactly why this happens is unknown, but this property is extremely useful to gardeners.

In late summer, shorten to 30cm (12in) from the point of origin all current season's shoots that are not needed as replacements for worn-out branches or to extend the existing

Pruning back sideshoots in late winter

branch framework. It is on these shortened shoots or branchlets, at the base of the previous year's growth, that flowers are produced, and by late winter it should be possible to distinguish the larger, plumper flower buds from the slimmer growth buds.

In late winter prune back these late-summer-pruned shoots to within 2.5–5cm (1–2in) of older wood.

PLANT PROBLEMS

Why do wisterias fail to perform?

Although wisterias are normally vigorous plants, they sometimes fail to flower, or at best flower very poorly

POOR OR NON-FLOWERING PLANTS

There are various reasons why wisterias fail to flower or produce a very poor display. It may be due to poor growing conditions or even inferior plants.

Soil conditions

Light, sandy soils can be low in potassium, making plants reluctant to flower. Apply sulphate of potash (35g per sq m/1oz per sq yd) to such soils in spring.

Wisterias need a sunny situation. Where poor or non-flowering plants are growing in some shade, flowering may be encouraged by reducing overhead shade.

Although they show good drought tolerance once they are established, it is advisable to ensure that wisterias, especially if growing against a wall, do not suffer from lack of water. Mulch in spring to conserve moisture before the onset of drier weather, and water thoroughly and regularly during periods of drought, particularly from mid-summer to early autumn when flower buds are being formed. Any plants which have not flowered for several years and which do not respond to treatment within one or two years are best discarded.

Seed-raised plants

Plants grown from seed are invariably inferior to grafted plants, are poor-flowering and may take many years to flower. It is safer to decline gifts of small wisterias.

FLOWER-BUD DROP

Flower-bud drop may occur when plants growing in dry positions, such as against a wall, have suffered from dryness at the roots during the

A well-flowered wisteria

preceding late summer or early autumn when flower buds are forming.

Flower-bud drop may also occur in early spring during periods of alternating high day temperatures and low night temperatures, or a keen late-spring frost may damage the flower trusses as they are extending, leaving them limp and lifeless on the plant. Cold winds in exposed places also cause bud drop.

Bird and rodent damage

Flower buds may be destroyed by birds searching for insects but most escape to provide some trusses of flowers. Mice have been seen collecting developing flower shoots and carrying them back to their nest. However, they do not usually cause extensive damage.

See also How to prune wisterias, pp.105–106; Soil fertility, p.259

PERENNIALS

PLAYING WITH COLOUR

Playing with colour

It is rewarding to create colour schemes with hardy perennials because you do not have to wait too long to see the results and, if some combinations do not work, they are easily changed for next season

Do not be afraid to experiment with colour – the possibilities are endless. Choose combinations that appeal to you, and use the principles of the colour wheel to explore the way in which colours are related.

The colour wheel

The wheel in its simplest form is made up of three primary colours: red, blue, and yellow, which, when blended, produce the secondary colours: purple, green, and orange. Infinite gradations of hue occur where the segments meet. The principal opposites are between primary and secondary colours: purple and yellow, red and green, and blue and orange. Such combinations can produce bold effects, and are especially impressive viewed from a distance. Some plants create their own vivid contrasts the bright green leaves and brilliant scarlet flowers of *Crocosmia* 'Lucifer', for example – but plant associations can be equally intense. Grouping blue-purple *Salvia* x *sylvestris* 'Mainacht' with yellow evening primrose, for example, accentuates the individual richness of their colours.

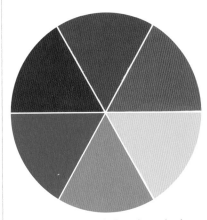

Creating harmony with the colour wheel
The wheel will help you to create pleasing colour effects in your borders. In this border, neighbouring colours on the wheel – blue, purple, and pink – have been used to create soft, gentle combinations.

RECOMMENDED HOT-COLOURED PERENNIALS

Achillea filipendulina 'Gold Plate' ♀ ‡ 1.2m (4ft) ↔ 45cm (18in) ▢ ◊ ❄❄❄

Crocosmia 'Lucifer' ♀ ‡ 1–1.2m (3–4ft) ↔ 8cm (3in) ▢–▨ ◊ ❄❄ [1]

Helenium 'Butterpat' ♀ ‡ 90cm (36in) ↔ 60cm (24in) ▢ ◊ ❄❄❄

Kniphofia triangularis ‡ 60–90cm (24–36in) ↔ 45cm (18in) ▢–▨ ◊ ❄❄❄

Lobelia cardinalis ♀ ‡ 90cm (36in) ↔ 30cm (12in) ▢–▨ ◊ ❄❄❄

Lychnis chalcedonica ♀ ‡ 80cm (32in) ↔ 45cm (18in) ▢–▨ ◊ ❄❄❄

Monarda 'Cambridge Scarlet' ♀ ‡ 90cm (36in) ↔ 45cm (18in) ▢–▨ ◊ ❄❄❄

Oenothera fruticosa 'Fyrverkeri' ♀ ‡ 30–90cm (12–36in) ↔ 30cm (12in) ▢ ◊ ❄❄❄

Papaver orientale 'Mrs Perry' ‡ 90cm (36in) ↔ 60–90cm (24–36in) ▢ ◊ ❄❄❄ [2]

Rudbeckia 'Herbstsonne' ♀ ‡ 1.8m (6ft) ↔ 90cm (36in) ▢–▨ ◊ ❄❄❄ [3]

See also Three seasons of colour, pp.110–111; Choosing ornamental grasses, pp.131–132

Using neighbouring colours on the wheel – pink *Papaver orientale* 'Mrs Perry' with purple catmint, perhaps – creates harmonious combinations. From a distance the effect may be hazy, but close-up it will be subtle. Planned colour-themed plantings can be striking, especially if you can maintain a continuity of colour through the season.

Foliage colour

Unusual leaf colour plays a part in the most intriguing combinations: gold and lime, blue-grey and silver, copper and purple. The way we perceive colour is also affected by texture and light; for example, yellow-splashed foliage, or fine golden grasses give the impression of dappled sunlight, lifting nearby colours.

Using hot colours

Even in the coolest of summers, an illusion of warmth can be produced from plantings with yellow, orange, and red flowers. Doronicums and primulas are among the first perennials to make a sunny splash in spring, but summer brings the most dazzling hues. One of the first is *Geum* 'Borisii', with its orange-scarlet flowers. Other easy choices include orange and red oriental poppies, red peonies, crocosmias in fiery red, orange, and gold, and daylilies (*Hemerocallis*) in every hue of yellow, orange, and rust-red. Shortening days encourage sedums, which bear flat, rose-pink flowerheads from late summer to autumn, and heleniums, in yellow or the bronze-red of 'Moerheim Beauty'.

Using cool colours

Spring's freshness can be emphasized and midsummer heat relieved in part by planting perennials in cool shades. White and blue schemes are obvious choices but can be stark; adding restrained hues such as pale yellows, greens, and pinks enhances the effect.

Cool schemes are easy to carry through the spring and most of the summer, starting with white and pink-flushed hellebores, supplemented with wood anemones, white and blue cultivars of *Primula denticulata*, and soft pink or white bergenias. These are followed by pink, blue, or white campanulas, blue or white monkshoods (*Aconitum*), and geraniums in shades of blue, purple, pink, and white. In late summer use plenty of foliage plants and elegant, white-flowered Japanese anemones.

RECOMMENDED COOL-COLOURED PERENNIALS

Aconitum 'Bressingham Spire' ♀ ↕ 90cm (36in) ↔ 30cm (12in) ◲ ◊ ✻✻✻ [4]

Actaea matsumurae 'Elstead' ♀ ↕ 60–90cm (24–36in) ↔ 60cm (24in) ◲ ◊ ✻✻✻

Anemone x *hybrida* 'Honorine Jobert' ♀ ↕ 1.2–1.5m (4–5ft) ↔ 60cm (24in) ◲–◲ ◊ ✻✻✻

Anemone nemorosa ♀ ↕ 8–15cm (3–6in) ↔ 30cm (12in) ◲ ◊ ✻✻✻

Bergenia 'Silberlicht' ♀ ↕ 30–45cm (12–18in) ↔ 45–60cm (18–24in) E ◲–◲ ◊ ✻✻✻

Campanula 'Burghaltii' ♀ ↕ 60cm (24in) ↔ 30cm (12in) ◲–◲ ◊ ✻✻✻

Eryngium variifolium ↕ 30–40cm (12–16in) ↔ 25cm (10in) E ◲ ◊ ✻✻✻

Geranium pratense 'Mrs Kendall Clark' ♀ ↕ 60–90cm (24–36in) ↔ 60cm (24in) ◲–◲ ◊ ✻✻✻

Helleborus foetidus ♀ ↕ 80cm (32in) ↔ 45cm (18in) E ◲–◲ ◊ ✻✻✻

Leucanthemum x *superbum* 'Esther Read' ↕↔ 50–60cm (20–24in) ◲–◲ ◊ ✻✻✻ [5]

PERENNIALS FOR SEASONAL COLOUR

Perennials for seasonal colour

When planting hardy perennials, choose those that flower early and late in the year as well as summer-flowering ones, and avoid the common mistake of having a border lacking in colour in spring and autumn

For herbaceous or mixed borders, use a selection of plants that provide interest and colour from late spring to autumn. Some may start flowering earlier than the times indicated in the list (*right*), depending on season, area, and situation; others may continue blooming into the following months. An indication of flower colour is given as a general guide.

RECOMMENDED PERENNIALS FOR SEASONAL COLOUR

Late spring

Anchusa azurea ‡ 90–150cm (36–60in) ↔ 60cm (24in), blue, ❑ ◊ ❋❋❋ [1]

Bergenia cordifolia ‡ 60cm (24in) ↔ 75cm (30in), rose-red, E ❑–❑ ◊ ❋❋❋

Dicentra spectabilis ♀ ‡ 1.2m (4ft) ↔ 45cm (18in), pink, ❑ ◊ ❋❋❋

Polygonatum x *hybridum* ♀ ‡ 1.5m (5ft) ↔ 30cm (12in), white, ❑–❑ ◊ ❋❋❋

Pulmonaria saccharata ‘Mrs Moon’ ‡ 30cm (12in) ↔ 60cm (24in), blue, E ❑–❑ ◊ ❋❋❋

Tanacetum coccineum ‘Brenda’ ‡ 70–80cm (28–32in) ↔ 45cm (18in), pink, ❑ ◊ ❋❋❋

Trollius chinensis ‘Golden Queen’ ♀ ‡ 90cm (36in) ↔ 45cm (18in), yellow, ❑–❑ ◊ ❋❋❋

Veronica gentianoides ♀ ‡↔ 45cm (18in), blue, ❑ ◊ ❋❋❋

Early summer

Acanthus spinosus ♀ ‡ 1.5m (5ft) ↔ 60–90cm (24–36in), white and purple, ❑–❑ ◊ ❋❋❋ [2]

Achillea ‘Coronation Gold’ ♀ ‡ 75–90cm (30–36in) ↔ 45cm (18in), yellow, ❑ ◊ ❋❋❋

Campanula lactiflora ‡ 1.2–1.5m (4–5ft) ↔ 60cm (24in), blue, ❑ ◊ ❋❋❋

Dianthus ‘Doris’ ♀ ‡↔ 30cm (12in), pink, E ❑ ◊ ❋❋❋

Erigeron ‘Dunkelste Aller’ ♀ ‡ 60cm (24in) ↔ 45cm (18in), violet, ❑–❑ ◊ ❋❋❋

Paeonia lactiflora ‘Sarah Bernhardt’ ♀ ‡↔ 90–100cm (36–39in), pink, ❑–❑ ◊ ❋❋❋

Papaver orientale ‘Cedric Morris’ ♀ ‡ 90cm (36in) ↔ 60–90cm (24–36in), pink, ❑ ◊ ❋❋❋ [3]

Verbascum ‘Gainsborough’ ♀ ‡ 1.2m (4ft) ↔ 30cm (12in), yellow, E ❑ ◊ ❋❋❋

Midsummer

Echinacea purpurea ‡ 1.5m (5ft) ↔ 45cm (18in), purple-red, ❑ ◊ ❋❋❋ [4]

Hemerocallis ‘Golden Chimes’ ♀ ‡ 90cm (36in) ↔ 45cm (18in), yellow, E ❑–❑ ◊ ❋❋❋

Hosta ‘Royal Standard’ ♀ ‡ 60cm (24in) ↔ 1.2m (4ft), white, ❑–❑ ◊ ❋❋❋ [5]

Iris sibirica ‘Perry’s Blue’ ‡ 75cm (30in) ↔ 60cm (24in), blue, ❑–❑ ◊ ❋❋❋

Oenothera fruticosa ‘Fyrverkeri’ ♀ ‡↔ 30–38cm (12–15in), yellow, ❑ ◊ ❋❋❋

Rudbeckia fulgida var. *sullivantii* ‘Goldsturm’ ♀ ‡ 60cm (24in) ↔ 45cm (18in), yellow, ❑–❑ ◊ ❋❋❋

Scabiosa caucasica ‘Clive Greaves’ ♀ ‡↔ 60cm (24in), blue, ❑ ◊ ❋❋❋

Solidago ‘Goldenmosa’ ♀ ‡ 75cm (30in) ↔ 45cm (18in), yellow, ❑ ◊ ❋❋❋

Late summer

Actaea racemosa ♀ ‡ 1.2–1.8m (4–6ft) ↔ 60cm (24in), white, ❑ ◊ ❋❋❋

Anaphalis triplinervis ♀ ‡ 80–90cm (32–36in) ↔ 45–60cm (18–24in), white and yellow, ❑–❑ ◊ ❋❋❋

Anemone x *hybrida* ‡ 1.2–1.5m (4–5ft) ↔ 60cm (24in), pink or white, ❑–❑ ◊ ❋❋❋

Ceratostigma plumbaginoides ♀ ‡ 45cm (18in) ↔ 30cm (12in), blue, ❑ ◊ ❋❋❋

Ophiopogon planiscapus ‘Nigrescens’ ♀ ‡ 20cm (8in) ↔ 30cm (12in), black leaves, E ❑–❑ ◊ ⊞ ❋❋❋

Persicaria affinis ‘Superba’ ♀ ‡ 25cm (10in) ↔ 60cm (24in), pink, ❑–❑ ◊ ❋❋❋

Zauschneria californica ‘Dublin’ ♀ ‡ 25cm (10in) ↔ 30cm (12in), red, ❑ ◊ ❋❋

Early autumn

Aster x *frikartii* ‘Mönch’ ♀ ‡ 70cm (28in) ↔ 35–40cm (14–16in), blue, ❑ ◊ ❋❋❋

Aster novae-angliae ‘Andenken an Alma Pötschke’ ‡ 1.2m (4ft) ↔ 60cm (24in), pink, ❑–❑ ◊ ❋❋❋

Aster thomsonii ‘Nanus’ ‡ 45cm (18in) ↔ 25cm (10in), blue, ❑ ◊ ❋❋❋

Liriope muscari ♀ ‡ 30cm (12in) ↔ 45cm (18in), violet-mauve, E ❑–❑ ◊ ❋❋❋

Nerine bowdenii ♀ ‡ 45cm (18in) ↔ 8cm (3in), pink, ❑ ◊ ❋❋❋

Schizostylis coccinea ‘Major’ ♀ ‡ 60cm (24in) ↔ 30cm (12in), red, ❑ ◊ ❋❋

Sedum ‘Herbstfreude’ ♀ ‡↔ 60cm (24in), pink, ❑ ◊ ❋❋❋

See also Colourful foliage pp57–58; Autumn colour p.62; Playing with colour pp.108–109; Choosing ornamental grasses pp.131–132

PLANT PROBLEMS

Non-flowering agapanthus

Tender loving care is needed to grow these perennials well

Border-grown agapanthus prefer a rich, well-drained soil in a warm sunny position. Mulching and supplementary feeding with a general-purpose fertilizer may help improve flowering. Keep container-grown plants in a cool, light position over winter, such as a frost-free, cool greenhouse or conservatory, avoiding excessively wet or very dry conditions. Warmth in winter may lead to early flowering, but it will be of poor quality.

Water agapanthus freely during the growing season, particularly after flowering to promote flowering for the following season. Give container plants a liquid feed fortnightly until the flowers have developed.

Too much shade can lead to lush foliage at the expense of flowering in evergreen species, and poor growth in deciduous plants. Aim for good light for at least half the day and avoid dense shade under trees.

Dividing plants may lead to reduced flowering. Divide every four to six years or when flowering begins to deteriorate. Setting seed does not appear to reduce flowering.

Agapanthus are almost always free of pests and diseases. Some of the best ones include *A. campanulatus* subsp. *patens*, a compact plant with light blue flowers, which needs an especially warm, sunny site to thrive. *A.* 'Loch Hope' has deeper blue flowers and is comparatively tall, reaching 1.5m (5ft).

Agapanthus africanus and *A. africanus* 'Albus' have deep blue flowers and evergreen foliage, but are slightly more tender. However, they make good container plants, if you can overwinter them in a frost-proof greenhouse or conservatory.

See Avoiding pests and diseases pp.36–37

PLANT PROBLEMS

Delphinium leaf spots

Drastic measures are needed to control this widespread disease

Shining, tar-like spots

Spots on the leaves are due to delphinium black blotch, a common and widespread disease, which is caused by the bacterium *Pseudomonas syringae* pathovar *delphinii*. It infects mainly *Delphinium* species but also monkshood (*Aconitum napellus*).

Symptoms

Irregular, shining, tar-like spots appear on the upper surfaces of the leaves, on stems, and flower parts. On the leaf undersides, the spots are more brown in colour rather than black. The spots may coalesce and leaves slowly turn black and die. The bacterium is spread from old, infected plant debris in the soil by water splash and infects plants via their natural openings on the leaves.

Control

Destroy affected delphiniums and replace with new stock on a fresh site. Copper-based fungicides can give control of bacterial diseases but may not legally be used for this purpose.

See Avoiding pests and diseases pp.36–37

AVOIDING DISEASE IN HELLEBORES

Avoiding disease in hellebores

Keen observation and swift action on the part of the gardener can help to save hellebores, which are among our best-loved garden plants, from being destroyed or badly affected by two serious diseases

Control

No firm recommendations on control of hellebore black death can be made until its cause is confirmed. There is no cure for virus infections and all affected plants should be destroyed as soon as symptoms are noticed to reduce the risk of spread. The mode of transmission is also unknown. The problem is known around Wisley and elsewhere in southern England, and appears to be on the increase. Based on limited observations at Wisley, affected plants do not recover.

Black streak on stem

Spots caused by black death

HELLEBORE BLACK DEATH

In recent years the Gardening Advisory Service at RHS Garden Wisley has received hellebores affected by a blackening and distortion of leaves and stems. The hellebore authorities Graham Rice and Elizabeth Strangman describe this as "black death" in *The Gardener's Guide to Hellebores* (David & Charles, 1993), and the symptoms are now well known to most hellebore growers, but the problem appears to be of recent occurrence as it is not mentioned in Brian Mathew's book *Hellebores* (Alpine Garden Society, 1989) or any earlier publications.

This serious disease of hellebores has in fact been known for at least 10 years, but its cause has been difficult to determine. Studies in 2001 detected three viruses in infected tissues. One has yet to be identified and further work is planned to try and characterize it and determine how it is transmitted. The other two are well known viruses with a wide host range, although not previously recorded in hellebores. These studies suggest that the problem

A fatal hellebore disease
Hellebore black death is a serious disease, found on *Helleborus* x *hybridus*. It is seen as black spots or streaks on leaves, stems, and flowers, and plants often become stunted and distorted. Usually they die.

is due to a viral infection, perhaps by a mixture of several viruses, although the evidence is not yet conclusive.

Symptoms

The symptoms have been found on various cultivars of *Helleborus* x *hybridus*. Too little is known about the nature and spread of the disease to comment on how susceptible other hellebore species may be, although it is likely that they are also prone to infection from this disease.

Leaves, stems, and flowers are covered in black spots or streaks which are often prominent along the veins. Plants become stunted and distorted, fail to flower, and generally die. The black marks may be in a ringspot pattern or as lines that pass down the leaf stalks into the main stem of the plant. This blackening is due to gradual destruction of plant tissue.

HELLEBORE LEAF SPOT

Hellebore leaf spot is a common and damaging disease, caused by the fungus *Coniothyrium hellebori*. It is a particular problem on the Christmas rose (*Helleborus niger*).

Large, irregular black spots appear on the leaves and stems and often coalesce, resulting in the yellowing and death of the leaves. Spots are also found on the flowers and flower stems, and infected stems may wilt above the point of attack.

To prevent the spread of the disease, pick off affected leaves and flowers and destroy them as soon as you notice the symptoms. Fungicidal treatment can be attempted using an approved fungicide.

Leaf and bud eelworms

Poor growth is the result of infestation by these pests

Microscopic nematodes known as leaf and bud eelworms (*Aphelenchoides ritzemabosi* and *A. fragariae*) attack a wide range of plants. Damage is mainly seen in late summer and autumn, especially on herbaceous plants such as chrysanthemums and Japanese anemones.

Symptoms

The eelworms live within the foliage and cause infested parts to become yellowish and later brownish-black. The spread of nematodes within a leaf is restricted by the larger leaf veins and, in the early stages, healthy and damaged zones appear as islands or wedges separated by the veins. In time, the entire leaf is invaded and becomes discoloured. Older leaves are attacked first and symptoms creep up the stems to the newer growth.

Control

None of the pesticides available to home gardeners controls nematodes, and it is best to remove completely plants that are badly infested.

Brownish-black markings

See Avoiding pests & diseases, pp.36–37

How to combat lupin problems

A giant aphid and a potentially fatal "new" fungal disease are two problems besetting lupins in our gardens

Lupin aphid infestation

LUPIN APHID

Lupin aphid (*Macrosiphum albifrons*), is a species native to North America, which attacks a range of herbaceous and shrubby lupins. The aphid is greyish-green and, being 4–5mm (⅕in) long, it is larger than most commonly encountered aphids. Dense colonies develop during early summer on the undersides of leaves and flower spikes.

Symptoms

The impact of this sap-sucking pest can be so great that the plant wilts and dies. The foliage becomes sticky with a honeydew excreted by the aphids, and a whitish, waxy deposit from their bodies also coats the leaf surfaces.

Control

Lupin aphids are present on host plants throughout the year and overwinter in relatively small numbers as nymphs on the basal buds of lupins. Their numbers steadily increase as plants come back into growth, with peak populations occurring from late May to July. Winged forms of the aphid develop in summer and fly away to find other host plants. Use an insecticide approved for use on aphids. Organic products that contain pyrethrum or fatty acids will also control aphids but may need more frequent application.

LUPIN ANTHRACNOSE

Lupin anthracnose is a fungal disease that has been recently introduced to Britain. First detected in East Anglia in 1989, it is caused by the fungus *Colletotrichum acutatum*.

Symptoms

The symptoms include dark brown dead areas on the leaf margins, dieback of the young leaves, scarring on the mature leaves and emerging flower stems, and brown staining and rotting in the crowns of small plants. Severely affected plants may die.

Control

As with other species of *Colletotrichum*, *C. acutatum* can be transmitted through seed contamination and it was probably introduced into Britain in this way. The only recommended course of action is to remove affected plants promptly to avoid spreading the disease. Do not water lupins from overhead as the fungal spores are dispersed by water splash; humid conditions encourage the development and spread of the disease.

There are no fungicides available to home gardeners that are labelled for control of this disease. To date no lupin species have been found to be resistant to lupin anthracnose.

See also Avoiding pests and diseases, pp.36–37; How to control aphids, p.42

POOR ASTER GROWTH

Poor aster growth

A mite may be the cause of stunting and poor flowering

Poor flowering due to Michaelmas daisy mite

Michaelmas daisy mite (*Phytonemus pallidus*) is a widespread pest of Michaelmas daisy (*Aster novi-belgii*); fortunately other perennial asters, such as New England asters (*A. novae-angliae*) and *A. amellus*, are not affected by this pest. The whitish mites are microscopic and feed in the flower buds as well as the shoot tips.

Symptoms

Infested plants are stunted and have brownish scarring on the stems, but the most obvious symptom appears at flowering time. Flowering is poor with many blooms being converted into rosettes of small leaves.

Control

None of the insecticides available to home gardeners is effective for Michaelmas daisy mite, so infested plants should be destroyed. They can be replaced with non-susceptible types of aster, but if you require particular *A. novi-belgii* cultivars, obtain new, pest-free plants from a reputable nursery.

See Avoiding pests & diseases, pp.36–37

Avoiding peony problems

Among our favourite perennials, peonies need tender loving care from planting time in order to perform well

NON-FLOWERING PEONIES

Peonies are vigorous plants and they require good growing conditions. They will not flower well when they are planted in poor, dry soils, or where they are competing with other plants for foods and water; nor will they tolerate wet soils.

Slow to establish, peonies may not flower until their third year. The main reason for non-flowering is planting too deep. Choose a site that is well away from the competing roots and shade of trees or shrubs and 60cm (24in) or more away from paths, walls, or a roof overhang. During the growing season their position should receive several hours of direct sunshine each day. The soil should have a neutral to

Optimum flowering results from good treatment

DIVIDING AND REPLANTING PEONIES

Although peonies dislike being transplanted, and take time to re-establish, older, congested plants may benefit from division in autumn. **1** Lift the peony clump using a fork, taking care not to damage the roots. **2** Use two forks back-to-back to separate the clump. Ensure that each division consists of one or two large fleshy roots with three to five strong buds. **3** Replant each division in a well-prepared planting hole with the crown at or up to 5cm (2in) below the soil surface. **4** Firm the soil around the plant and cover with a mulch.

See also Avoiding pests and diseases, pp.36–37; Soil pH, p.263; Why lime soils?, p.265

alkaline pH, so add lime if the pH is lower than 6.

When planting, space the plants about 1m (3ft) apart each way. Add generous quantities of well-rotted garden compost to the soil, digging it in before planting.

Excavate a good-sized hole, at least 30cm (12in) deep by 60cm (24in) wide. Set plants no more than 5cm (2in) below the soil surface; the soil will then settle to about 2.5cm (1in) above the crown. Subsequently, feed and mulch the plants in spring.

PEONY WILT

Wilt caused by the fungus _Botrytis paeoniae_ is the most common disease of herbaceous and tree peonies.

Symptoms

The fungus usually attacks herbaceous peonies at the base of the stem, causing it to collapse. A brown, dead area at soil level may become covered in grey, mouldy fungal spores. In a severe attack the leaves are also affected and the plant may be killed, or so badly weakened that it does not sprout again next spring.

Control

As soon as you detect peony wilt, cut out and destroy all infected stems, cutting well below ground level. If whole plants are badly affected it is better to destroy them in their entirety, along with the soil surrounding their roots, and replace them with new, unaffected peony plants.

Flower stem affected by peony wilt

Phlox eelworm

This tiny pest can cause big problems for border phloxes

Stunted growth

Phlox eelworms (_Ditylenchus dipsaci_) are minute and cannot be seen without the aid of a microscope.

Symptoms

The pest causes distinctive symptoms on infested plants in early summer. The young growth is stunted and swollen, with leaves at the shoot tips drastically reduced in width. Such shoots die back early, having failed to flower, and plants may be killed.

Control

No chemical controls for eelworms are available to amateur gardeners, so affected plants should be destroyed to prevent the pest from spreading. Avoid replanting the same site with phlox for at least 12 months.

Phlox eelworm infests only the leaves and stems of the plant, so it is possible to propagate new, healthy stock from root cuttings taken in autumn and rooted in a garden frame.

Phormium mealybug

Try not to introduce phormium mealybug into your garden

While phormiums are generally trouble free in Britain, since the late 1970s there has been one insect problem. This is the phormium mealybug (_Trionymus diminutus_).

The mealybugs feed by sucking sap and form dense colonies on the basal part of the upper surfaces of leaves. They have flattened bodies up to 5mm (¼in) long covered in a greyish-white mealy wax.

Symptoms

Heavy infestations cause unhealthy growth with yellowing foliage and eventually plants can be killed.

Control

Insecticides have little effect because the pest conceals itself between the folded leaf bases. Fortunately, mealybugs cannot fly, so will not easily find their way to a new host plant. When buying phormiums at a garden centre, examine the leaf bases carefully and buy elsewhere if the mealybugs are seen.

Mealybugs congregate at leaf bases

See Avoiding pests pp.36–37

Primula leaf spots

Garden primulas in particular are prone to this unsightly disease

Zoned spots on leaf

Some *Primula* species are native to Britain and attract a wide range of disease-producing organisms, including several fungi that are responsible for leaf spots.

Symptoms

Ramularia primulae is responsible for either round or angular pale brown spots surrounded by a yellow or orange border, with the fungus visible in the centre on the lower leaf surface as a white fur; the centres of the spots often fall out, leaving "shot holes". *Cercosporella primulae* causes chocolate-brown spots with centres that may become grey and papery. *Phyllosticta primulicola* forms brown spots and *Ascochyta primulae* white spots, where the fungus fruiting structures may be visible as black dots in the dead tissues at the centre.

Control

Leaf spots on primulas and other ornamentals can be controlled by spraying with appropriate fungicides approved for use on ornamental plants. As soon as you detect symptoms, remove the affected leaves and spray the plants. Dispose of the leaves; do not compost them.

See Avoiding pests & diseases, pp.36–37

Distorted houseleeks

A rust disease of sempervivums is difficult to control

Sempervivum or houseleek rust, which also occurs on echeverias, is caused by the fungus *Endophyllum sempervivi,* which enters through young leaves and growing points, penetrates the plant's centre, and grows down to the roots. Unlike many rust diseases, the fungus is not confined to just the leaves but is systemic, persisting throughout the plant as fungal strands. In spring and early summer this fungus produces small, orange, cup-like pustules on the leaves, which contain spores that spread the disease.

Symptoms

As a result of infection with the rust, the leaves of sempervivums become less fleshy, longer, and thinner, causing the rosettes to develop a more erect appearance.

Control

Because of the systemic nature of *Endophyllum,* the fungicides currently available to control rust diseases are not particularly effective and any infected plants are best uprooted and then destroyed.

Elongated, thinner leaves

See Avoiding pests & diseases, pp.36–37

Solomon's seal sawfly

Leaves can be stripped by this pest but plants still survive

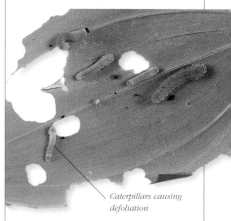

Caterpillars causing defoliation

Adult sawflies (*Phymatocera aterrima*) emerge from the soil in late spring at about the time when Solomon's seal (*Polygonatum*) is coming into flower. They have black heads and bodies up to 9mm (⅜in) long with two pairs of smoky grey wings. They fly slowly around their host plant and, after mating, the females lay batches of up to 20 eggs in vertical rows in the stems as the plants are coming into flower.

The larvae are plump, greyish-white caterpillars up to 2cm (¾in) long with black heads. There is only one generation a year and the larvae overwinter in the soil.

Symptoms

Egg laying causes purplish scars up to 2.5cm (1in) long on the stems. From late spring to midsummer the larvae can cause extensive defoliation. Defoliated plants will survive and flower the next year but may be reduced in height.

Control

Look for the larvae and either remove them by hand or spray with rotenone, pyrethrum, or bifenthrin.

See Avoiding pests & diseases, pp.36–37

PLANT PROBLEMS

Why violet leaves roll up

Grubs of a tiny fly cause this unsightly problem

Violet gall midge (*Dasineura affinis*) is a tiny fly, producing three or four generations during the summer. It lays eggs on developing violet leaves (*Viola* species). The eggs hatch into whitish-orange maggots that feed inside the rolled leaves, which give them protection. The pests overwinter as pupae inside white silk cocoons in the rolled leaves. First-generation adult flies will emerge in late spring, and newly galled leaves can be found later in the season.

Rolled basal leaf

Symptoms

The maggots secrete chemicals that cause infested leaves to become greatly thickened and unable to unfurl. The affected leaves are most clearly seen in winter once other foliage has died down. Heavy attacks reduce the plant's vigour but it will usually survive and flower.

Control

Chemical control is difficult because the larvae are protected by the curled leaves and no suitable products are currently approved for home gardeners to use. On a small scale pick off and destroy infested leaves.

See also Avoiding pests & diseases pp.36–37

PLANTING IDEAS

Plants for growing in dry-stone walls

Dry-stone walls (built without mortar) can be planted with a selection of colourful perennials and alpines

The most satisfactory approach is to plant as the dry-stone wall is being built, layer by layer. Roots can then be well spread out and covered with 2.5cm (1in) of a suitable soil-based potting compost with the addition of sharp grit or stone chips. Before adding the next layer of stones, place a few pebbles around the roots to keep the joint open.

When planting, allow for size increase and trailing habit. Some trailing plants can be allowed to ▷

Aubrieta flowering well in a dry-stone wall

RECOMMENDED PLANTS FOR DRY-STONE WALLS

Trailing plants

Acaena saccaticupula 'Blue Haze' ↕ 10–15cm (4–6in) ↔ 90cm (36in) E ☐–☒ ❋❋❋

Acantholimon glumaceum ↕ 5–8cm (2–3in) ↔ 20–30cm (8–12in) E ☐ ❋❋❋

Achillea x lewisii 'King Edward' ♀ ↕ 8–12cm (3–5in) ↔ 23cm (9in) E ☐ ❋❋❋

Aethionema 'Warley Rose' ♀ ↕↔ 15–20cm (6–8in) E ☐ ❋❋❋

Alyssum spinosum 'Roseum' ♀ ↕↔ 30–50cm (12–20in) E ☐ ❋❋❋

Anacyclus pyrethrum var. *depressus* ↕ 2.5–5cm (1–2in) ↔ 10cm (4in) ☐ ❋❋

Androsace lanuginosa ♀ ↕ 5cm (2in) ↔ 30cm (12in) E ☐ ❋❋❋

Antennaria dioica ↕ 5cm (2in) ↔ 45cm (18in) E ☐ ❋❋❋

Arabis alpina subsp. *caucasica* 'Flore Pleno' ♀ ↕ 15cm (6in) ↔ 50cm (20in) E ☐ ❋❋❋

Aubrieta ↕ 5cm (2in) ↔ 60cm (24in) E ☐ ❋❋❋

Aurinia saxatilis ♀ ↕ 20cm (8in) ↔ 30cm (12in) E ☐ ❋❋❋

Campanula cochlearifolia ♀ ↕ 8cm (3in) ↔ 30cm (12in) ☐–☒ ❋❋❋

Dryas octopetala ♀ ↕ 10cm (4in) ↔ 90cm (36in) E ☐–☒ ❋❋❋

Gypsophila repens 'Dorothy Teacher' ↕ 5cm (2in) ↔ 40cm (16in) E ☐ ❋❋❋

Helianthemum 'Amy Baring' ♀ ↕ 15cm (6in) ↔ 20cm (8in) E ☐ ❋❋❋

Iberis sempervirens ♀ ↕ 30cm (12in) ↔ 40cm (16in) E ☐ ❋❋❋

Phlox subulata ↕ 5–15cm (2–6in) ↔ 50cm (20in) E ☐–☒ ❋❋❋

Saponaria ocymoides ♀ ↕ 8cm (3in) ↔ 45cm (18in) ☐ ❋❋❋

Thymus serpyllum ↕ 25cm (10in) ↔ 45cm (18in) E ☐ ❋❋❋

Non-trailing plants

Armeria maritima ↕ 20cm (8in) ↔ 30cm (12in) E ☐ ❋❋❋

Draba aizoides ↕ 10cm (4in) ↔ 25cm (10in) E ☐ ❋❋❋

Erinus alpinus ♀ ↕ 8cm (3in) ↔ 10cm (4in) E ☐–☒ ❋❋❋

Lewisia cotyledon ♀ ↕ 30cm (12in) ↔ 25cm (10in) E ☐ ⬡ ❋❋❋

Saxifraga callosa ♀ ↕ 25cm (10in) ↔ 20cm (8in) E ☐ ❋❋❋

Sedum spathulifolium 'Purpureum' ♀ ↕ 10cm (4in) ↔ 60cm (24in) E ☐–☒ ❋❋❋

Sempervivum ↕ 8–10cm (3–4in) ↔ 30cm (12in) E ☐ ❋❋❋

Vitaliana primuliflora ↕ 2.5cm (1in) ↔ 25cm (10in) E ☐ ❋❋❋

See also Growing herbs in paving, paths, and walls pp126–127

PLANTS FOR GROWING IN DRY-STONE WALLS

Aurinia saxatilis has a trailing habit

Rosette-forming *Sempervivum montanum*

Buying and planting perennials

For a good show of perennials, start at planting time with top-quality plants and use the right planting technique to help plants establish

Most perennials are sold as container-grown plants, which can be planted at any time of year except in very frosty weather. The traditional times to plant – spring and autumn – are the best, as mild, damp weather helps plants to establish well. Avoid planting in hot, sunny weather because of the difficulty of keeping the plants watered sufficiently. If planted in adverse conditions, plants will also suffer a check to growth.

Choosing a healthy plant
Look for plants with sturdy top-growth and thick, strong stems. Do not buy perennials that are showing signs of disease or neglect, such as wilted leaves or a mass of roots appearing out of the bottom of the container. A plant growing among weeds and moss is also to be avoided – it has been in its pot too long, and you could introduce new weeds into your garden.

Lupin with sturdy top-growth and strong stems

cascade down then spread out at the foot of the wall. Do not overplant: leave spaces to be colonized by self-sown seedlings or to be planted with plants acquired at a later date.

Plant recommendations (*see p.117*) cover the more suitable species (and their cultivars), avoiding the more vigorous kinds that are less good for dry-stone wall planting. Where only the genus (for example *Sempervivum*) is given, all species within the genus are considered suitable, and where a species is listed, any of its cultivars may also be considered.

Weak top-growth

Dense, bushy, green top-growth

Good and bad choices
It is wise to assess how long a plant has been in its pot. The lupin on the left has recently been potted and has not rooted into the compost. It will be loose in its pot and the roots may not establish well if planted out now. The example in the centre is pot-bound. Although this is a fatal flaw in woody plants, it is not too serious in perennials; in fact, these plants are often ripe for division, giving three or so plants for the price of one. The plant on the right has healthy looking white roots that evenly permeate the compost.

See also Buying plants, p.10; Perennials for seasonal colour, pp.110–111

Planting container-grown perennials

Never plant in frozen or very dry soil – this usually ends in disaster. Before planting a group of plants, set them out in their pots to find the best arrangement and spacing. Water well before and after planting. To water purchased plants really thoroughly before planting, soak them in their pots in a bucket of water for 15 minutes.

Dig the planting hole twice as wide as the rootball and to the correct depth. Slide the plant out of its pot and tease out the roots with your fingers before carefully placing the plant in the hole. Backfill with soil, firm it well, and water the area.

What is the correct planting depth?

Plant most perennials, especially if in doubt, at the same depth as they are in their pots. For most perennials, planting too deeply will mean their stem bases are prone to rot. Some, however, are better with their central growths above soil level; others shoot more strongly if planted more deeply.

Shallow planting is recommended for *Sisyrinchium striatum*, pinks (*Dianthus*), milkweed (*Asclepias*), rheums, phormiums, and irises. Planting with the stem bases just below the soil is recommended for hostas, dicentras, foxtail lilies (*Eremurus*), peonies, and lily-of-the-valley (*Convallaria*). Deep planting, with the stem bases several centimetres below the top of the soil, is recommended for Solomon's seal (*Polygonatum*), crinums, monkshoods (*Aconitum*), crocosmias, and alstroemerias.

MONEY-SAVING TIP

Do not judge a herbaceous perennial by its size, as an older, bigger one may take a long time to get established. A smaller specimen with good fresh growth will be less expensive and grow away quickly. Once established, it can be divided to produce more plants.

How to support tall herbaceous perennials

Effective staking takes a little planning and preparation annually as spring fast approaches and plants burst into growth

MAKING A WIRE-MESH CYLINDER

1 Support clump-forming perennials such as delphiniums with a wire-mesh cylinder as they start to grow. Insert a 1.2m (4ft) long 2.5cm (1in) square wooden stake beside each plant.

2 Use galvanized wire mesh with a grid of 20 x 15cm (8 x 6in) to make a cylinder 1m (3ft) tall and 38cm (15in) wide. Place it over the plant, attaching it to the stake with plastic ties.

Supports should ideally be in place in spring, before plants have made too much growth. Care needs to be taken with the way supporting is carried out. Sometimes plants are staked so tightly as to appear trussed up like a sheaf of corn, and natural elegance becomes lost. Later staking is difficult as plant growth is more advanced and can easily be damaged; it can look more unsightly than no support at all.

The best materials

Traditional or modern techniques may be used, although it is mostly a question of balance and attention to detail. Effort is well repaid if it appears that plants are standing with no visible support, and keeping a neat habit no matter what the weather brings.

Garden string or twine in three-ply is suitable for most tying jobs, but be careful not to constrict plant stems, which can be damaged easily. Raffia, or soft string such as jute fillis, can be used as a lightweight tie, but may disintegrate after a year or so. Tar-impregnated string and polypropylene twine are weather resistant. Plastic-coated tying wire is strong but should be monitored as the plant grows to ensure that it does not cut into the stems. This also applies to the lighter plastic or twist-type ties. Less robust plantings can be secured to supports with wire plant rings. These are easily opened or closed around a stem and its support and are suitable for light jobs.

Upright clump-forming perennials such as delphiniums can be supported by ▷

wire-mesh cylinders, and bushy perennials including campanulas and heleniums grow well in simple circular frames. Top-heavy plants, particularly herbaceous peonies and dahlias, are well suited to grid supports. Peasticks are attractive and useful supports for front- and back-border plants. Support heavier stems of large perennials, such as *Crambe cordifolia*, with stout bamboo canes or rods.

Bamboo canes and rods

Weathered bamboo canes are a better colour in the garden than new canes, which tend to be too obtrusive and less easily disguised. They provide a practical solution when other materials may be unavailable. Black stakes and canes are available, or bamboo canes can be painted black; they look much less noticeable than green ones.

Bamboo canes should be stout, not whippy. Several canes may be needed for plants with heavier stems. Do not tie in stems too rigidly as this will only invite damage; support with movement is the order of the day. Five-ply soft twine or fillis is preferable (two- or even three-ply strands are not strong enough for large plants).

Push the thickest end of the cane into the soil – carefully, to avoid

Delphinium 'Sandpiper' staked by bamboo cane

harming plant roots – to a depth of one-quarter of its length. On heavy or compacted soils you may first need to make a hole with a narrow metal spike.

Clump-forming plants such as monardas, phlox, or achilleas will

require an outer circle of canes, with some in the centre, spaced 38–45cm (15–18in) apart. The string can then loop and criss-cross from cane to cane, thus preventing foliage from the centre falling out towards the edge.

Ensure that the tops of the canes are no higher than where the bases of the flower spikes will start and, if possible, that each cane has a discreet eye protector made of rubber or similar as a safety measure.

Modern supports and stakes

Grid or grow-through supports suit plants with soft or top-heavy growth, such as herbaceous peonies or dahlias. Link stakes are made of plastic-coated galvanized steel with a hook-and-eye system. Put them in place early in the season, positioning them around the outer edge of the plant growth and pushing them deeply into the soil. When shoots grow to the outside of the link framework, tie them lightly in place. Pull the stakes higher as plants grow. This works particularly well with bushy perennials, such as campanulas, leucanthemellas, or heleniums, all of which grow to conceal the supports.

Plastic netting

Mesh of 15cm (6in) squares is an effective support for multi-stemmed herbaceous perennials such as asters, phlox, and achilleas. The netting can be stretched horizontally between four 2.5cm (1in) square vertical stakes.

This method is cheap, but maintenance becomes awkward where there are large areas of bed or border covered. Leaving gaps between panels of plastic netting helps to provide access. Black netting is preferable as green can be too bright. During summer, carefully raise the netting as the plant grows through it, and, finally consider cutting the tops off the stakes to make them less obtrusive.

Wire mesh for delphiniums

A simple method of support for delphiniums is to create a wire-mesh

USING PEASTICKS

1 Trim your peasticks to a point at the base so that it is easier to insert them in the soil. Push them 25cm (10in) into the ground, first making a hole with a metal spike if necessary.

2 Insert the peasticks at regular intervals around a clump of plants. As the plants grow, their foliage will grow through the pea sticks and hide them completely.

cylinder around each plant (*see p.119*). This method can also be effective for similar clump-forming perennials. The foliage will fill the cylinder and support the flower spikes as they grow through, allowing them to bend and move in the breeze without the stems snapping.

Peasticks

Birch or hazel peasticks make an attractive natural framework for plant support. Consult local forestry offices and Wildlife Trusts to find sources. Birch and hazel are both good, although hazel, with a more fan-type shape to its branchlets, is slightly less noticeable than birch, and easier to work. Try experimenting with the colourful stems of coppiced dogwoods or willows as an alternative.

Start staking when new growth is 15–20cm (6–8in) high. Begin at the back of the border on taller perennials and gradually work towards the front. Weave individual twigs lightly to add strength and enhance the appearance.

Large herbaceous plants such as *Inula racemosa*, *Rudbeckia* 'Herbstsonne', and *Cephalaria gigantea* will need birch stems of at least 4cm (1½in) in diameter. Fix the stakes 25cm (10in) deep into the ground. Smaller perennials up to 90cm (36in) tall, such as phlox, heleniums, and monardas, will require smaller, finger-thick stakes of about 2cm (¾in). Trim these to a point, insert them at intervals around each plant to form a support, and, if necessary cut them down to the desired height.

Selection of modern proprietary supports

Why deadhead plants?

Removing dead blooms from perennials is well worthwhile as it improves their appearance, and often encourages more flowers

Removing faded and dead busy Lizzie flowers

Flower scissors make quick work of old blooms

Deadheading is the term used for the removal of flowers from plants when the blooms are fading or dead.

Appearance

Most flowers lose their attraction as they fade, spoiling the overall appearance of borders, bedding schemes, or individual plants – particularly where the display is in a container or extends over several weeks. The flowers of plants such as herbaceous peonies have many petals that, if allowed to drop as they fade, may scatter widely and look unsightly.

Performance

Flowers that have been pollinated by bees and other insects soon fade, shed their petals, and begin to form seedheads, pods, or capsules. Energy is channelled into the development of usually unwanted seeds, slowing down any further growth and flower development. Regular deadheading directs energy instead into stronger growth and improved performance.

Removing dead flowerheads can enhance the flowering performance and growth of many hardy perennials. If antirrhinums, delphiniums, and lupins have their dead flower spikes cut off they will often produce further, smaller spikes later in the season.

Tender perennials and other summer bedding or display plants such as pelargoniums, salvias, marigolds, petunias, stocks, dahlias, and fuchsias benefit greatly from deadheading to prolong the flower displays through the whole summer and into autumn.

All plants growing in containers and hanging baskets for summer display should be deadheaded to keep the flower display at its best.

How to do it

Dead blooms are usually cut off with some or all of the flower stem attached. Use secateurs or flower scissors. With some plants such as pelargoniums you can simply snap off dead blooms between finger and thumb. Find out simply by trial and error. Plants with masses of small flowers can be lightly trimmed over with flower scissors to remove dead blooms, rather than trying to remove individual flowers.

Cutting back perennials

Removing dead growth each year makes for a tidy border

Herbaceous perennials have persisting roots from which new foliage and flowering stems are produced annually. In late autumn, when seasonal flowering has ended, the stems and foliage can be cut down to restore tidiness. At this stage, in most cases, they are turning yellow or brown if they are not already dead.

How much to cut?

Perennials that produce leaves and flower stems from below the soil level, such as crocosmias and peonies, should be cut back to soil level. Perennials showing new basal shoot growth – for example, asters and *Sedum spectabile* – should be cut back slightly less severely. Any attractive dead stems or flowerheads can be left as an ornamental feature until early spring.

Separate and burn any diseased material (with signs of leaf spots, rusts, or mildew, for example). Add all other material, except for ripening seedheads, to the compost heap. Fork out weeds, which can be hard to control if allowed to spread, and give a light mulch and feed in early spring.

Cutting back in spring

If you wish you can leave all cutting back until early spring, working from boards if the soil is wet. In a severe winter the dead foliage and stems give protection to young basal shoots. More care is needed when cutting back in spring to avoid damaging new shoot growth. Delaying cutting back until early spring can also be helpful if you are planning to lift, divide, and replant specimens as the dead foliage marks the position and spread of plants that may otherwise be difficult to locate.

See also Dividing perennials, pp.128–129

Plants for gravel gardens

There are many plants suited to gravel gardens; since they are often drought resistant, they are a good choice for water-saving gardens

Gravel gardens are a popular choice for low-maintenance gardening, especially as plants increasingly need to meet the demands of changes in climatic conditions. The following list of plants is suitable for a gravel garden, as they are relatively drought-resistant and require little maintenance.

Most appreciate a free draining, fairly poor soil to prevent the vigorous kinds from becoming too lush and smothering some of the slower-growing plants. Additionally those plants listed as low-growing ground-cover plants or self-seeding plants would be suitable in a paved garden planting scheme.

RECOMMENDED PLANTS FOR GRAVEL GARDENS

Low-growing ground-cover plants

Acaena microphylla 'Kupferteppich' ‡ 3cm (1¼in) ↔ 60cm (24in) E ▣–▣ ❁❁❁

Arabis alpina subsp. *caucasica* 'Variegata' ‡ to 15cm (6in) ↔ 20–50cm (8–20in) E ▣ ❁❁❁ **1**

Armeria maritima ‡ 20cm (8in) ↔ 30cm (12in) E ▣ ❁❁❁

Pulsatilla vulgaris ♀ ‡ 10–20cm (4–8in) ↔ 20cm (8in) ▣ ❁❁❁

Sedum spathulifolium 'Cape Blanco' ♀ ‡ 10cm (4in) ↔ 60cm (24in) E ▣–▣ ❁❁❁

Thymus x citriodorus ‡ 30cm (12in) ↔ 25cm (10in) E ▣ ❁❁❁

Larger perennials

Acanthus spinosus ♀ ‡ 1.5m (5ft) ↔ 60–90cm (24–36in) ▣–▣ ❁❁❁

Centranthus ruber ‡↔ 90cm (36in), self-seeding, ▣ ❁❁❁

Crambe cordifolia ♀ ‡ 2.5m (8ft) ↔ 1.5m (5ft), self-seeding, ▣ ❁❁❁

Eryngium x tripartitum ♀ ‡ 60–90cm (24–36in) ↔ 50cm (20in) ▣ ❁❁❁

Kniphofia 'Atlanta' ‡ 1.2m (4ft) ↔ 75cm (30in) E ▣–▣ ❁❁❁ **2**

Limonium platyphyllum ‡ 60cm (24in) ↔ 45cm (18in) ▣ ❁❁❁

Phlomis russeliana ♀ ‡ 90cm (36in) ↔ 75cm (30in) ▣ ❁❁❁

Phormium tenax ♀ ‡ 4m (12ft) ↔ 1.8m (6ft) E ▣ ❁❁

Verbascum chaixii ‡ 90cm (36in) ↔ 45cm (18in), self-seeding, E ▣ ❁❁❁

Hummock-forming plants

Ceanothus thyrsiflorus var. *repens* ♀ ‡ 90cm (36in) ↔ 2.5m (8ft) E ▣ ❁❁❁

Cistus salviifolius 'Prostratus' ‡ 15–25cm (6–10in) ↔ 60–90cm (24–36in) E ▣ ❁❁ **3**

Cytisus x kewensis ♀ ‡ 30cm (12in) ↔ 1.5m (5ft) ▣ ❁❁❁

Hebe pinguifolia 'Pagei' ♀ ‡ 30cm (12in) ↔ 90cm (36in) E ▣–▣ ❁❁❁

Ornamental grasses

Calamagrostis x acutiflora 'Overdam' ‡ 1.2m (4ft) ↔ 60–120cm (24–48in) ▣–▣ ❁❁❁

Festuca glauca ‡ 30cm (12in) ↔ 25cm (10in) E ▣ ❁❁❁

Miscanthus sinensis cultivars ‡ 1.2–1.8m (4–6ft) ↔ 90–120cm (36–48in) ▣ ❁❁❁

Stipa gigantea ♀ ‡ 2.4m (8ft) ↔ 1.2m (4ft) E ▣ ❁❁❁ **4**

See also Drought-resistant gardening, pp.16–17; Herbs in paving, paths, and walls, pp.126–127

TECHNIQUES

Caring for frost-tender perennials over winter

Some tender perennials are easily overwintered under cover; others, such as hardy bananas, can be left outside if well protected

Frost-tender perennials are plants that grow outside in summer, but normally die back or need protection in winter. Examples include melianthus, many penstemons, and argyranthemums. It is a shame to waste those tender perennials that have flowered valiantly all summer, but finding frost-free space to keep them all is seldom possible. With planning and some simple techniques, many can be saved, albeit in a more easily stored form.

Standard fuchsias and other big, valuable plants will always have priority for any heated greenhouse or indoor space. Keep them at about 10°C (50°F) to encourage moderate growth, because at lower temperatures they may die back.

Some obliging plants such as bush fuchsias and pelargoniums will survive with minimum protection. Unheated greenhouses double glazed with bubble plastic can work well,

especially if plants and containers are wrapped with horticultural fleece in cold weather. Gardeners without a greenhouse can try glazed porches or garage windowsills.

Tender plants can be overwintered indoors on a windowsill, but it is more difficult to maintain plant health in a low light environment. Here, excess heat, a dry atmosphere, and overly wet soil are the killers. Try keeping plants in a cool room with the compost barely moist. Even so, shoots will get drawn and straggly, needing constant pinching out of the growing tips to maintain bushy growth.

Before storage, reduce the watering of plants in containers and leave them in a sunny spot so that their new growth hardens. Lift plants from the open ground before the first frosts, trim out weak, dead, or diseased shoots, shake off excess soil, and pot them up. Overwinter these plants as for pot- ▷

PROTECTING BANANAS FROM COLD, WIND, AND HAIL

1 *Musa basjoo* is an especially hardy banana that may grow outside without protection in mild districts. Overwinter tender ones in a frost-free greenhouse or conservatory or wrap them for winter. **2** Tie up the leaves, and surround each plant with a cage made from wire

netting. Pack the cage with dry straw or bracken. **3** Cover with several layers of horticultural fleece or hessian to keep out the wind, and top off with a hood of polystyrene sheet to keep the rain out. Unwrap plants in late spring to allow new leaves to unfurl.

See also Cutting back perennials, p.122; Success with tree ferns, pp.140–142

grown fuchsias (*see facing page*). Cramming them into deep trays also works well and saves space.

Overwintering fuchsia cuttings

Tender types of fuchsia need frost-free protection and careful watering over the winter. They can be overwintered as plants or cuttings, although old plants will become woodier and produce fewer flowers over several years. It is better to take cuttings from time to time and replace old plants.

For cuttings take 5–7cm (2–3in) side-shoots from midsummer to early autumn, pulling them away from the main stem with a strip of bark. Trim this so that the cut is clean, not ragged. Remove the lower leaves and dip the base in rooting powder. Fill a 10cm (4in) pot with a mixture of 1 part peat or peat substitute and 2 parts sharp sand. Using a dibber or piece of cane, make three or four 2.5cm (1in) holes around the pot edge, then place a cutting in each. Water in, plunge the pots to their rims in a box filled with insulating material, such as sand or wood fibre, and cover with clear plastic sheeting. Place in a light and airy situation at a temperature of about 10°C (50°F). As soon as rooting is underway, begin ventilating and when cuttings are well rooted pot up singly into 7cm (3in) pots, using soil-based potting compost. To keep the cuttings growing through the winter a minimum temperature of 10°C (50°F) is needed. If you are growing a young standard fuchsia through the winter 15–18°C (55–60°F) is preferable.

Pinch out the new shoots on cuttings several weeks after growth has started, to promote bushiness. Pot on again if growth is vigorous and plant out young plants or pot them on to their final pot size when all danger of frost is past.

Cut back tender perennials before lifting and storing them for winter

KEEPING PELARGONIUMS OVER WINTER

Pelargoniums can be easily overwintered even without a heated greenhouse. You can take cuttings in late summer, root them, and overwinter them in a well-lit, frost-free room. Pot them up when growth restarts in spring.

1 Old plants can be kept if they are lifted before the first frosts and stored in soil-based potting compost. Cut back top-growth in late autumn to 10cm (4in), removing leaves. **2** Place several plants into a tray of potting compost, keeping them in a light, frost-free position such as a cool greenhouse, well-lit garage, or unheated room. Very little water is needed until growth starts in spring. **3** Pot up the plants individually in mid-spring as growth restarts.

Overwintering pot-grown fuchsias

If you are able to overwinter larger, pot grown fuchsias with some warmth, reduce watering during early and mid-autumn as growth slows. Plants grown indoors for most of the season should be placed outside in late summer in a sunny situation until the first autumn frosts to ripen and harden the current season's growth and encourage the shoots to become woody. Well-ripened shoots are less likely to die back during the winter than soft, green shoots.

Keep plants over winter in good light, with a minimum winter night temperature of 7–10°C (45–50°F) and cool conditions by day. Continue the reduced watering regime, watering thoroughly but infrequently. Do not allow the plants to dry out completely.

In early spring, prune the stems to one or two buds on each shoot. Remove all weak and crossing shoots to keep a well-shaped and open bush. Repot the plants by removing much of the original compost and replacing it with fresh compost, such as moderately rich, soil-based potting compost.

Place the repotted plants in warmer conditions in good light, leaving them for a day or two then watering them in thoroughly. As growth begins, increase the frequency of watering. Start feeding six to eight weeks after repotting. Pinch out the tips of new growths, if necessary, to encourage bushiness. Plant out again in late spring after the danger of frosts is past, or use for greenhouse display.

If you are overwintering the fuchsias in a place without any additional warmth, reduce watering during early and mid-autumn. Under the influence of this regime and colder nights the leaves will turn yellow and drop. The plants can then be put in a frost-free place for the winter.

Check every two weeks or so to ensure that the compost is still moist, adding some tepid water if necessary to prevent it drying out. If the compost does dry out the roots will shrivel and the plants will become desiccated.

Acclimatizing tender plants

Gradually acclimatizing plants raised under cover to the harsher conditions of outdoors improves both growth and performance

Plants raised in protected conditions need to be acclimatized to cooler temperatures and increased air movement for about two to three weeks before they are planted outdoors. This is known as hardening off. Plants grown under warm conditions need a much longer hardening-off period. If they have been raised in a heated greenhouse and on windowsills, plants should go first into a cold greenhouse or a cold frame. After a spell in these cooler conditions, plants should be moved into a well-ventilated cold frame or placed under a cloche. Finally, after a week or two, they can be planted outside.

As an alternative to greenhouses and cold frames, cloches or horticultural fleece can be used. These do not give as much frost protection, and may need backing up in cold spells by covering the plants at night with newspaper, which is an excellent insulator.

If plants are not hardened off they may suffer a setback from which they will take several weeks to recover, or they may grow in ways that are undesirable. The effect of hardening off is to thicken and alter the plants' leaf structure and increase leaf waxiness. It will ensure new growth is sturdy. But be warned: the best hardening-off process cannot make a frost-sensitive plant into a hardy one. To be safe, do not plant out tender plants before late spring in the South of England, early summer in the North and Scotland.

WAYS TO HARDEN OFF PLANTS

Cold frames are the best choice for hardening off plants, as they are the most frost-proof option. Make sure they are well ventilated.

Cloches make a good alternative to frames, but do not give as much protection from frost; cover plants with newspaper on frosty nights.

Horticultural fleece may be used instead of a cold frame or cloche. Start with a double layer and back it up with newspaper on cold nights.

A single layer of fleece may be supported on galvanized wire hoops as the plants gradually harden up and need less protection from cold.

See also Caring for frost-tender perennials over winter, pp.123–124

Growing herbs in paving, paths, and walls

You don't need a herb garden to grow herbs: to make optimum use of space and to use herbs as a design element, try planting them in cracks in hard surfaces and walls

Using the cracks in paving and paths or the crevices in walls for growing herbs might be seen, with disapproval, as a sneaky way of cramming more plants into a garden already bursting at the seams. But the technique can be used as part of a garden's design, to soften stone structures and give the impression of nature spilling out from its restraints – in the same way that voluptuous perennials billow on to paths or rampant climbers scale walls.

Many herbs enjoy well-drained soil and full sun, and traditional herb gardens are filled with plants that originate in the dry, sharply drained soils of the Mediterranean. The small amount of soil and sharp drainage of crevices in paths or walls will mimic the natural habitat of such plants. If the site in question is in damp or dry shade then your choice of culinary herbs may be narrower, but many medicinal herbs would be suitable. In damp shade, evergreen lesser periwinkle (*Vinca minor*) and self-

seeding heartsease (*Viola tricolor*) will do well. For dry shade try purple sweet violet (*Viola odorata*) or pale pink soapwort (*Saponaria*) – but be warned that the latter is a particularly vigorous plant and can outgrow its welcome if not kept in check.

Lesser periwinkle, a medicinal herb for moist shade

Wherever space allows, improve heavy soils before planting by adding organic matter and fine gravel. Shady and dry positions are awkward but because of this they are often covered by paving, which is ideal for infilling. As with heavy soils, improve the soil in dry, shady areas before starting to plant by adding organic matter.

Traffic crossing

When choosing herbs for paving or paths, consider how often people walk across the area. If the herbs are likely to be stepped on occasionally, select those that can stand some wear and tear, such as thick mat-forming thymes, although none will flourish if crushed daily, particularly if the rooting portion as well as the edges of the plant are affected. As with any planting, consider also the qualities and combinations of colour, texture, and scent when planning which herbs to include.

Thymes are also perfect for paths because many of them spread and grow

ESTABLISHING HERBS IN PAVING

Sowing seed
Clean out the crevices on the hard surface, removing any loose mortar or soil. Sprinkle over some good-quality potting compost and brush it into the cracks before sprinkling the seed. Water gently.

Planting a plug
A plug needs a hole larger than its rootball to establish well. If you remove a paving stone, scrape out any mortar, hardcore, or soil and add new potting compost before planting. Water in well.

Transplanting into a crevice
For herbs that like sharp drainage, such as this chamomile, add some sharp sand or fine grit into the bottom of the planting hole. Cover the surface with more sharp sand, sweep away the excess, then water.

See also Plants for growing in dry-stone walls, pp.117–118; Herbs in pots, p.165

GROWING HERBS IN PAVING, PATHS, AND WALLS

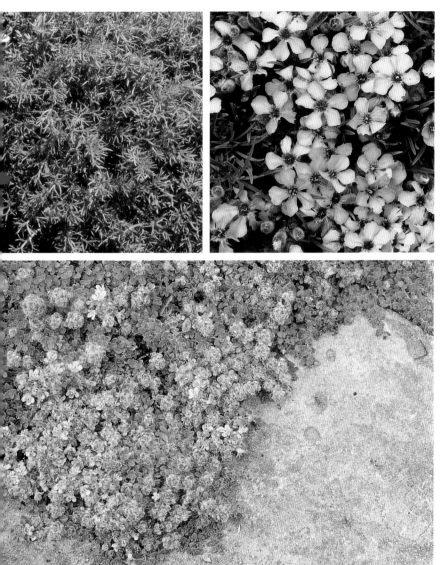

Herbs for cracks and crevices
Clockwise from top left: This highly aromatic chamomile (*Chamaemelum nobile* 'Treneague') is non-flowering; soapwort (*Saponaria caespitosa*) thrives in dry shade; wild thyme (*Thymus serpyllum*) produces purple flowers in summer.

almost cling to the ground. Pennyroyal (*M. pulegium*) also does well in damp areas and is said to drive away ants.

Herb invasion

By taking a more relaxed and selective approach to weeding the cracks in paving you can allow plants to seed themselves or creep out from beds. The spread of plants will be sporadic, giving a natural look, and plants that have found their own way in are likely to thrive. If the plants you want are herbs, this approach will be most successful when the path or terrace lies next to an established herb bed.

A more certain approach is to put the herbs in place yourself, by sprinkling seeds into a soil-filled crevice or placing a small plug plant into a gap in paving. You may need to make or enlarge the planting hole by easing or chipping out the mortar or sand. Make the hole large enough to fit the rootball comfortably (*see also box, opposite*).

Deliberately leaving open pockets of soil when laying paving slabs will give the most scope for planting. Walls can even be built especially for the purpose. Allowing some larger gaps for the plants will make planting and establishment easier and will allow you to include larger herbs, such as lavender or rosemary. Starting from scratch also means that you can plan your design more carefully, whether opting for a chequerboard or random effect, clusters of herbs in close proximity, or ribbon-like lines.

The beauty of planting in crevices is its subtlety. This is no grand design solution that will alter the look of your garden, but the right herbs in the right gaps will drag even crazy paving into the 21st century.

almost flush with the ground. They have such an array of coloured leaves and flowers that they alone can make up an intricate and fragrant tapestry. Wild thyme (*Thymus serpyllum*) forms a dense mat. Lemon thyme (*T. citriodorus*) has pale green leaves and pink flowers as well as a strong, lemony fragrance, as its name suggests. A bushier plant with an orange fragrance that would suit a wall crevice is *T.* 'Fragrantissimus'. All these thymes prefer well-drained soil and a sunny position.

Chamomile has a delicious aroma that makes it a must for any scented garden. *Chamaemelum nobile* 'Treneague' is the best cultivar for crevice planting as it is non-flowering and low-growing. It roots easily in well-drained soil. Many mints will grow in clay soil with a fair amount of shade. Growing them in small spaces will restrict root growth and prevent them becoming invasive, as they will do if allowed to. The best mint to plant in paving is Corsican mint (*Mentha requienii*), which has tiny leaves that

MULTIPLYING PERENNIALS BY DIVISION

Multiplying perennials by division

Many hardy perennials need dividing regularly to maintain health and vigour; division is also the easiest method of increasing perennials and no special conditions are needed to look after the new plants

Division involves lifting plants and splitting them into a number of pieces, each complete with roots and growth buds or shoots. This method is easy and reliable, and stops many herbaceous plants becoming overcrowded and losing vigour as they would over time if they were left undivided. Regular division, usually every three to four years, is usual, but vigorous perennials such as asters are best divided annually. Some subjects, for example peonies and red-hot pokers (*Kniphofia*), resent root disturbance and should be divided solely for propagation, unless very old and congested.

Extra plants are produced through division because smaller, young pieces of the clump are replanted, but where many are needed, plants can be split further into small or single-bud divisions.

When to divide

Divide plants when they are dormant or just starting into growth. Autumn and spring are the best times, and spring is preferable if the soil is heavy, cold, and wet, and if the plants are rather tender. Grasses, including bamboos, should be divided in early spring, when growth has just started. Perennials that flower in spring and early summer, such as epimediums, lily-of-the-valley

CLUMP-FORMING PERENNIALS FOR DIVISION

Actaea (syn. Cimicifuga)	Bamboos, many	Grasses, many	Kniphofia
Agapanthus [1]	Campanula	Helenium	Paeonia
Anemone, some	Carex	Helianthus	Phlox, border types
Artemisia	Delphinium	Helleborus	Phormium
Aster, some	Echinops	Hemerocallis	Ranunculus
Astilbe	Eryngium	Hosta, some	Salvia
Astrantia	Euphorbia	Inula	Tradescantia
	Gentiana, some	Iris, most	Veronica, some

PERENNIALS FORMING LOOSE MATS FOR DIVISION

Achillea	Corydalis, some	Hosta, some	Saxifraga, some
Ajuga	Dianthus	Lamium	Schizostylis
Alchemilla	Dicentra [2]	Liriope, some	Stachys
Anchusa	Epimedium	Lobelia	Symphytum
Anemone, some	Gentiana, some	Mimulus	Thalictrum
Aster, some	Geranium, some	Ophiopogon	Tricyrtis
Bamboos, some	Grasses, many	Primula	Trillium
Convallaria	Heuchera	Pulmonaria	Veratrum

PERENNIALS SUITED TO SINGLE-BUD DIVISION

Achillea	Bergenia	Gaillardia	Hosta
Agapanthus	Convallaria [3]	Geranium, some	Liriope, some
Aster	Eremurus	Grasses, many	Monarda
Bamboos, some	Euphorbia	Hemerocallis	Papaver orientale

See also Avoiding peony problems, pp.114–115; How to propagate grasses and bamboos, pp.138–139

SINGLE-BUD DIVISION AND "TOPPING" OF HOSTAS

[1] In spring, hostas can be reduced to single buds with roots if you want large numbers of new plants. Plant in a nursery bed. [2] Single buds of *Hosta* can quickly become multi-budded through "topping". [3] Make a small vertical cut through the base, leaving the top intact. On thicker buds a second cut at right angles may be made. After dusting with hormone rooting powder, use a stick to hold the wound open. [4] Pot or plant out each prepared division; they soon form new buds around the wound. Multi-budded plants can be divided into single buds a year later.

(*Convallaria*), and rhizomatous bearded irises, are best divided immediately after they have finished flowering.

Different methods of division

Lift plants carefully with a garden fork, working away from the crown centre to limit root damage, and split them into portions 5–8cm (2–3in) across depending on the plant, each with some roots and some shoots or buds. Larger divisions, with more shoots and roots, flower sooner than small pieces, which may take a year or more to recover. Discard the centre portion of a clump, retaining young outer parts for replanting.

Ensure all divisions have plenty of roots (which must never dry out); if there are only a few roots, trim the leaves to reduce moisture loss. Evergreen grasses benefit from leaf reduction when dividing, and stems of bamboos and grasses of a similar habit, can be cut down to 30cm (12in). However, many herbaceous plants will be dormant so excess foliage is not a problem.

Work bulky organic matter, such as garden compost or well-rotted manure, into the planting hole. If replanting into the same site then also add a balanced general fertilizer. Replant divisions to the same depth in flowering positions, and water them well to ensure they establish quickly. Plant small divisions, which require special care, in a nursery bed to grow on. Alternatively, pot them individually to build up size, overwintering pots in a cold frame or unheated greenhouse.

Many perennials such as daylilies (*Hemerocallis*) form large clumps or crowns with a mass of fibrous roots. The crown is often difficult to pull apart, so use two forks thrust back-to-back through the centre, and pull the handles apart. Repeat to divide the clump still further, using hand forks, or cut away sections, after shaking off loose soil, with a sharp knife. Plants with woody crowns, such as hellebores, or fleshy roots, such as delphiniums, need cutting with a spade or knife. Aim to produce clumps each containing three to five shoots. Divide rhizomatous, bearded irises into fans of leaves immediately after flowering. Cut the rhizome from the main clump and dust the wound with sulphur. Trim the leaves to 15cm (6in) high and plant divisions with the upper surface of the rhizome exposed.

Split asters into single, rooted shoots. Divide primulas into rosettes, bugles (*Ajuga*) into single, rooted plantlets, and sisyrinchiums and other perennials that have a similar habit, into single, rooted fans.

DIVIDING EPIMEDIUMS

Epimediums form a mass of wiry rhizomes. After lifting the whole clump, tease it apart into separate plants using your hands or a hand fork if it is particularly congested.

Split day lily clumps using two forks back-to-back

CHOOSING FRAGRANT PERENNIALS

Choosing fragrant perennials

Not all hardy perennials have scented flowers, so choose with care and complement them with other perennials that have fragrant leaves

FRAGRANT PERENNIALS

Fragrant flowers

Clematis recta ‡1–1.8m (3–6ft) ↔ 75cm (30in) ▫ ◊ ❋❋❋ [1]

Convallaria majalis ♀ ‡23cm (9in) ↔ 30cm (12in) ▨–▨ ◊ ❋❋❋

Dianthus ‡↔ variable E ▫ ◊ ❋❋❋

Hemerocallis lilioasphodelus ♀ ‡↔ 90cm (36in) E ◊ ❋❋❋

Hosta ‘Honeybells’ ♀ ‡75cm (30in) ↔ 1.2m (4ft) ▨ ◊ ❋❋❋

Iris unguicularis ♀ ‡30cm (12in) ↔ 60cm (24in) E ◊ ❋❋❋ [2]

Phlox paniculata ‡90cm (36in) ↔ 60–90cm (24–36in) ▨–▨ ◊ ❋❋❋

Primula florindae ♀ ‡45–60cm (18–24in) ↔ 60–90cm (24–36in) ▨–▨ ◊ ❋❋❋

Viola odorata ‡20cm (8in) ↔ 30cm (12in) E ▨ ◊ ❋❋❋

Fragrant foliage

Achillea filipendulina ‡1.2m (4ft) ↔ 45cm (18in) ▫ ◊ ❋❋❋

Angelica archangelica ‡1.8m (6ft) ↔ 1.2m (4ft) ▨–▨ ◊ ❋❋❋

Calamintha nepeta subsp. *nepeta* ‡45–60cm (18–24in) ↔ 60–90cm (24–36in) ▫ ◊ ❋❋❋

Chamaemelum nobile ‡30cm (12in) ↔ 45cm (18in) E ▫ ◊ ❋❋❋

Melissa officinalis ‘All Gold’ ‡60–120cm (24–48in) ↔ 30–45cm (12–18in) ▫ ◊ ❋❋❋ [3]

Mentha requienii ‡1cm (½in) ↔ indefinite ▨–▨ ◊ ❋❋❋ [4]

Monarda didyma ‡90cm (36in) ↔ 45cm (18in) ▨–▨ ◊ ❋❋❋ [4]

Nepeta x *faassenii* ♀ ‡↔ 45cm (18in) ▨–▨ ◊ ❋❋❋

See also Fragrant trees and shrubs, p.73; Fragrant climbers, p.99; Annuals for fragrance, p.159

Narrow borders

If you're stuck for space, choose restrained, small, or upright plants

SUNNY AND DRY BORDERS

Erysimum ‘Bowles’ Mauve’ ♀ ‡75cm (30in) ↔ 60cm (24in) E ❋❋❋

Geranium renardii ♀ ‡↔ 30cm (12in) ❋❋❋

Iris unguicularis ♀ ‡30cm (12in) ↔ 60cm (24in) E ❋❋❋

Kniphofia ‘Little Maid’ ‡60cm (24in) ↔ 45cm (18in) ❋❋❋

Oenothera macrocarpa ♀ ‡15cm (6in) ↔ 50cm (20in) ❋❋❋

Phlox subulata ‡5–15cm (2–6in) ↔ 50cm (20in) E ❋❋❋

Potentilla ‘Gibson’s Scarlet’ ♀ ‡45cm (18in) ↔ 60cm (24in) ❋❋❋

Rhodanthemum hosmariense ♀ ‡10–30cm (4–12in) ↔ 30cm (12in) ❋❋

Sedum cauticola ♀ ‡8cm (3in) ↔ 30cm (12in) ❋❋❋

Sisyrinchium striatum ‘Aunt May’ ‡50cm (20in) ↔ 25cm (10in) E ❋❋❋

Verbascum chaixii ‡90cm (36in) ↔ 45cm (18in) E ❋❋❋

Zauschneria californica subsp. *cana* ‡60cm (24in) ↔ 45cm (18in) ❋❋

Helleborus argutifolius is an excellent choice for a narrow, moist, shady border

See also Climbers and wall shrubs, p.94

PLANTING IDEAS

Choosing ornamental grasses

There are ornamental grasses suited to almost every part of the garden and they come in many shapes, sizes, and colours

The beauty of grasses is quite different from that of other garden plants. Rather than the static forms of strong colour created by traditional flowering perennials, grasses offer subtlety of line and texture, and a particular intimacy with the natural world. Their primary quality is their luminosity, the way they catch the light of the sky in their flowers and seedheads. Then there is the transparency – the eye can see through them to other plants and features beyond. Grasses are never static; their colour changes with the seasons, and they stir with the slightest breeze. Included here are rushes and sedges, such as *Acorus, Carex, Cyperus, Juncus* and *Luzula* – grass-like plants with similar qualities to true grasses. ▷

SUNLESS, DRY BORDERS

Anemone x *hybrida* ↕ 1.2–1.5m (4 5ft) ↔ 60cm (24in) ❋❋❋

Asplenium scolopendrium ♀ ↕ 45–70cm (18–28in) ↔ 60cm (24in) E ❋❋❋

Digitalis lutea ↕ 60cm (24in) ↔ 30cm (12in) ❋❋❋

Duchesnea indica ↕ 10cm (4in) ↔ 1.2m (4ft) E ❋❋❋

Euphorbia amygdaloides var. *robbiae* ♀ ↕ 60cm (24in) ↔ 30cm (12in) E ❋❋❋

Geranium endressii ♀ ↕ 45cm (18in) ↔ 60cm (24in) E ❋❋❋

Helleborus foetidus ♀ ↕ 80cm (32in) ↔ 45cm (18in) E ❋❋❋

Iris foetidissima ♀ ↕ 60–90cm (24–36in) ↔ 90cm (36in) E ❋❋❋

Liriope muscari ♀ ↕ 30cm (12in) ↔ 45cm (18in) E 🌱 ❋❋❋

Luzula sylvatica 'Marginata' ↕ 70–80cm (28–32in) ↔ 45cm (18in) E ❋❋❋

Polystichum setiferum ♀ ↕ 1.2m (4ft) ↔ 90cm (36in) E ❋❋❋

MOIST, SHADY BORDERS

Astilbe x *arendsii* ↕ 60–90cm (24–36in) ↔ 45–90cm (18–36in) ❋❋❋

Dicentra spectabilis ♀ ↕ 1.2m (4ft) ↔ 45cm (18in) ❋❋❋

Digitalis grandiflora ♀ ↕ 90cm (36in) ↔ 45cm (18in) ❋❋❋

Epimedium grandiflorum ♀ ↕ 20–30cm (8–12in) ↔ 30cm (12in) ❋❋❋

Gentiana asclepiadea ♀ ↕ 60–90cm (24–36in) ↔ 45cm (18in) ❋❋❋

Helleborus argutifolius ♀ ↕ 1.2m (4ft) ↔ 90cm (36in) E ❋❋❋

Hosta tardiflora ↕ 25cm (10in) ↔ 60cm (24in) ❋❋❋

Onoclea sensibilis ♀ 60cm (24in) ↔ indefinite ❋❋❋

Persicaria affinis ↕ 25cm (10in) ↔ 60cm (24in) E ❋❋❋

Primula bulleyana ♀ ↕ 60cm (24in) ↔ 60cm (24in) 🌱 ❋❋❋

Trollius x *cultorum* cultivars ↕ 90cm (36in) ↔ 45cm (18in) ❋❋❋

VARIEGATED ORNAMENTAL GRASSES

White striped

Arundo donax var. *versicolor* ↕ 1.8m (6ft) ↔ 60cm (24in) ☐ ◊ ❋

Carex riparia 'Variegata' ↕↔ 90cm (36in) ☐ ◊–◊ ❋❋❋

Holcus mollis 'Albovariegatus' ↕ 30cm (12in) ↔ 45cm (18in) ☐–☒ ◊ ❋❋❋

Luzula sylvatica 'Marginata' ↕ 70–80cm (28–32in) ↔ 45cm (18in) E ☐–☒ ◊ ❋❋❋

Miscanthus sinensis 'Morning Light' ♀ ↕ 1.2m (4ft) ↔ 90cm (36in) ☐ ◊ ❋❋❋

Phalaris arundinacea var. *picta* 'Feesey' ↕ 90cm (36in) ↔ indefinite ☐–☒ ◊–◊ ❋❋❋

Cream or yellow striped

Acorus gramineus 'Ogon' ↕ 25cm (10in) ↔ 10–15cm (4–6in) E ☐ ◊–◊ ❋❋

Alopecurus pratensis 'Aureovariegatus' ↕ 1.2m (4ft) ↔ 40cm (16in) ☐–☒ ◊ ❋❋❋

Bromus inermis 'Skinner's Gold' ↕ 90cm (36in) ↔ 60cm (24in) ☐ ◊ ❋❋❋

Carex elata 'Aurea' ♀ ↕ 70cm (28in) ↔ 45cm (18in) ☐–☒ ◊–◊ ❋❋❋ 2

Carex oshimensis 'Evergold' ♀ ↕ 30cm (12in) ↔ 35cm (14in) E ☐–☒ ◊ ❋❋❋

Cortaderia selloana 'Aureolineata' ♀ ↕ 1.8m (6ft) ↔ 1.5m (5ft) E ☐ ◊ ❋❋❋ 1

Glyceria maxima var. *variegata* ↕ 80cm (32in) ↔ indefinite ☐ ◊–◊ ❋❋❋

Hakonechloa macra 'Aureola' ♀ ↕ 35cm (14in) ↔ 40cm (16in) ☒ ◊ ❋❋❋

Molinia caerulea subsp. *caerulea* 'Variegata' ♀ ↕ 45–60cm (18–24in) ↔ 40cm (16in) ☐–☒ ◊ 🌱 ❋❋❋

Spartina pectinata 'Aureomarginata' ↕ 1.8m (6ft) ↔ 90cm (36in) ☐ ◊–◊ ❋❋❋

Banded

Miscanthus sinensis 'Strictus' ♀ ↕ 1.2m (4ft) ↔ 60cm (24in) ☐ ◊ ❋❋❋

Miscanthus sinensis 'Zebrinus' ♀ ↕ 1.2m (4ft) ↔ 60cm (24in) ☐ ◊ ❋❋❋ 3

Schoenoplectus lacustris subsp. *tabernaemontani* 'Zebrinus' ↕ 90cm (36in) ↔ 60cm (24in) E ☐ ◊ ❋❋❋

See also Getting the best from ornamental grasses, p.133; How to propagate grasses, p.138

ORNAMENTAL GRASSES

Small (60cm/24in and under)

Briza maxima ↕ 45–60cm (18–24in) ↔ 25cm (10in) ◻ ◊ ✤✤✤

Elymus magellanicus ↕ 60cm (24in) ↔ 30cm (12in) ◻ ◊ ✤✤✤

Pennisetum alopecuroides 'Hameln' ↕↔ 60cm (24in) E ◻ ◊ ✤✤

Stipa tenuissima ↕ 60cm (24in) ↔ 30cm (12in) ◻ ◊ ✤✤✤

Medium (60–90cm/24–36in)

Deschampsia cespitosa 'Goldtau' ↕↔ 75cm (30in) E ◻–◼ ◊–◊ ⌂ ✤✤✤

Luzula sylvatica 'Hohe Tatra' ↕ 70–80cm (28–32in) ↔ 45cm (18in) E ◻–◼ ◊ ✤✤✤

Panicum virgatum 'Rubrum' ↕ 90cm (36in) ↔ 75cm (30in) ◻ ◊ ✤✤✤

Tall (over 90cm/36in)

Deschampsia cespitosa 'Goldschleier' ↕↔ 1.2m (4ft) E ◻–◼ ◊–◊ ⌂ ✤✤✤

Helictotrichon sempervirens ♀ ↕ 1.4m (4½ft) ↔ 60cm (24in) E ◻ ◊ ✤✤✤

Miscanthus sinensis 'Gracillimus' ↕ 1.4m (4½ft) ↔ 1.2m (4ft) ◻ ◊ ✤✤✤

Pennisetum macrourum ↕ 1.8m (6ft) ↔ 1.2m (4ft) E ◻ ◊ ✤✤

Suitable for screening

Cortaderia selloana and cultivars ↕ 2.5–3m (8–10ft) ↔ 1.5m (5ft) E ◻ ◊ ✤✤✤ 'Silver Comet' 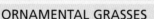 **4**

Miscanthus sacchariflorus ↕ 1.5–2.2m (5–7ft) ↔ 1.4m (4½ft) ◻ ◊ ✤✤

Molinia caerulea subsp. *arundinacea* ↕ 2.5m (8ft) ↔ 60cm (24in) ◻–◼ ◊ ⌂ ✤✤✤

Suitable for moist soils

Acorus (all) ↕ 60–90cm (24–36in) ↔ 60cm (24in) ◻ ✤✤✤ *A. calamus* 'Argenteostriatus' **1**

Cyperus eragrostis ↕ 60–90cm (24–36in) ↔ 45cm (18in) ◻–◼ ✤✤

Deschampsia cespitosa and cultivars ↕ to 1.8m (6ft) ↔ 1.2–1.5m (4–5ft) E ◻–◼ ⌂ ✤✤✤

Juncus effusus f. *spiralis* ↕ 45cm (18in) ↔ 60cm (24in) E ◻–◼ ⌂ ✤✤✤

Suitable for shade

Carex ↕ 25–35cm (10–14in) ↔ 75cm (30in) E ◊–◊ ✤✤✤ *C. flagellifera* **2**

Holcus mollis 'Albovariegatus' ↕ 30cm (12in) ↔ 45cm (18in) ◊ ✤✤✤

Luzula (all) ↕ 70–80cm (28–32in) ↔ 45cm (18in) E ◊ ✤✤✤ *L. sylvatica* 'Aurea' **3**

Milium effusum 'Aureum' ♀ ↕ 60cm (24in) ↔ 30cm (12in) ◊ ✤✤✤

Molinia caerulea subsp. *caerulea* and cultivars ↕ to 1.5m (5ft) ↔ 40cm (16in) ◊ ⌂ ✤✤✤

Drought tolerant

Festuca glauca ↕ 30cm (12in) ↔ 25cm (10in) E ◻ ◊ ✤✤✤

Helictotrichon sempervirens ♀ ↕ 1.4m (4½ft) ↔ 60cm (24in) E ◻ ◊ ✤✤✤

Leymus arenarius ↕ 1.5m (5ft) ↔ indefinite ◻ ◊ ✤✤✤

Panicum virgatum ♀ ↕ 90cm (36in) ↔ 75cm (30in) ◻ ◊ ✤✤✤

Stipa gigantea ♀ ↕ 2.4m (8ft) ↔ 1.2m (4ft) E ◻ ◊ ✤✤✤

Getting the best from ornamental grasses

Ornamental grasses, sedges, and rushes have few cultural requirements and are ideal for low-maintenance gardens; given suitable conditions, they will repay the gardener handsomely with minimum attention

Ornamental grasses are true grasses and belong to the grass family, *Poaceae*. Although they are very similar in appearance to grasses, the sedges actually belong to their own family, the sedge family, *Cyperaceae*, while the rushes belong to the rush family, *Juncaceae*. Both rushes and sedges are included here.

Siting and soil

Grasses generally grow best in full sun, although a minority require partial shade; they tolerate a wide range of soil types and pH but perform well in drier, less fertile soils.

Sedges are tolerant of full sun but prefer partial shade, require damper and more fertile soils than grasses, and some have a particular preference for alkaline or acid soils

Rushes are suited to full sun or partial shade, the soil should be wet or reliably moist, and most need a low pH, though *Juncus inflexus* will tolerate wet, alkaline soils.

Planting

Early spring is normally the best time to plant grasses, sedges, and rushes. Clear the site of any weeds and improve the drainage properties of clay soils by incorporating at least a 5cm (2in) layer of coarse grit or pea shingle into the top 30cm (12in) of soil prior to planting. Sedges and rushes prefer more moist soils so add plenty of organic matter, such as garden compost or composted bark, to help increase the water-holding capacity of the soil.

Watering and feeding

Grasses have minimum cultivation needs and usually thrive with little attention. Watering should only be necessary in the first growing season. Mulching with gravel or a shallow layer of organic matter each spring will help to reduce water loss. On average soils grasses do not need feeding, though it may help to apply a balanced fertilizer in the spring to particularly impoverished sites. The larger grasses such as miscanthus and

MULCHING

A pea-shingle, gravel, or bark mulch not only looks attractive when applied around grasses such as *Carex oshimensis* 'Evergold' in spring, but also helps to retain soil moisture.

pampas grass (*Cortaderia*) will benefit from an occasional spring feed.

Sedges and rushes have slightly higher nutrient needs than grasses and benefit from an annual spring feed. A thick spring mulch will reduce water loss, as will siting in semi-shade. Since rushes require a high level of soil moisture it is preferable to choose a wet area of the garden rather than to have to frequently water by hand.

Trimming

Grasses need only an annual tidy up to keep them in shape. For evergreens simply remove any bedraggled leaves and old flower stems in late winter. For deciduous types, such as *Stipa tenuissima*, cut back the previous year's foliage to near ground level.

Traditionally, pampas grass clumps are set on fire in winter to remove the dead foliage. However, this only really works if it is done on an annual basis in early spring, otherwise the extra heat from the blaze can cause damage to the crown of the plant. A less risky method is to cut out the dead stems by hand as far as possible without damaging new growth.

CUTTING BACK GRASSES

1 Leave the foliage of grasses over the winter to protect the crown of the plant; they often add structure to the border, too. **2** In late winter, before growth begins, cut back all the old growth to near ground level with secateurs or shears. If you leave this too late in the season, you risk damaging the emerging new foliage. **3** Rake up the dead foliage, taking care not to damage the remaining crown, and add the discarded stems to the compost heap.

See also Choosing ornamental grasses, pp.131–132; How to propagate grasses and bamboos, pp.138–139

Using bamboos in the garden

Most ornamental bamboos are not the invasive thugs that many people imagine; they have a great deal to offer in the way of attractive canes (stems) and foliage in both formal and informal gardens

In cultivation, bamboos are most often seen in isolation, as if gardeners are afraid to integrate them more fully into wider planting schemes, and while bamboos undoubtedly make fine specimen plants, they also associate well with a wide range of plants.

Plants that thrive in the dappled shade cast by specimen clumps include lungworts (*Pulmonaria*) with their speckled leaves, hardy cranesbills such as *Geranium macrorrhizum* and *G. phaeum*, *Dicentra formosa*, heucheras, and ivies. These all cope with the relatively dry shade on the edge of bamboo groves. Snowflakes, snowdrops, and wood anemones could also be scattered among the underplanting for extra spring impact.

Companion planting

Shorter ornamental grasses, sedges (*Carex*), and woodrushes (*Luzula*) can also be used to marry or contrast. Copper-coloured *Carex comans*, for example, is an excellent foil for yellow-caned bamboos. Finely divided fern species and cultivars echo the texture of smaller-leaved bamboos such as *Pleioblastus* and *Chusquea*, or these can be contrasted against the broader leaves of bergenias or hart's tongue ferns (*Asplenium scolopendrium*).

Phyllostachys aureosulcata f. *spectabilis*, *P. bambusoides* 'Castilloni', and *P. vivax* f. *aureocaulis* have golden canes striped with green. These three cultivars all work well with yellow-leaved phormiums or plain yellow and gold-variegated hostas. Alternatively they can be used to make a contrast with other foliage colours such as purple-leaved heucheras.

The black canes of *Phyllostachys nigra* look excellent complemented by the black leaves of *Ophiopogon planiscapus* 'Nigrescens' or by the shorter, variegated bamboo *Pleioblastus*

See also How to care for bamboos, pp.136–137; How to propagate grasses and bamboos, pp.138–139

5

variegatus. Many other dark-caned bamboos, such as *Semiarundinaria fastuosa*, and *Thamnocalamus crassinodus* 'Kew Beauty', are excellent behind the shiny green leaves of bergenias, ivies, or hart's tongue ferns.

Tropical planting
More robust bamboos like *Phyllostachys* and *Indocalamus tessellatus* are particularly well suited to tropical and subtropical planting schemes, and they bring the added advantage of providing a year-round, evergreen presence when other, more tender plants have to be wrapped up or taken under cover for winter. Their airy foliage creates a jungly look almost instantly when combined with hardy and half-hardy "tropical" foliage such as tree ferns, fatsias, *Trachycarpus fortunei*, gunnera, phormiums, and bananas (*Musa* and *Ensete*). Equally, plain green bamboo leaves are an excellent foil for flamboyant canna and ginger lily (*Hedychium*) flowers.

Hedges
Although not as tolerant of wind as more traditional hedging plants, several bamboo species can be used as hedges or within the garden as space dividers. Perhaps the most exposure-tolerant bamboos are *Fargesia* species.

Modern styles
The architectural qualities of the straight lines of the canes, particularly those with colourful stems, can be exploited in modern planting styles. For example, *Phyllostachys nigra* leaves stand out against its jet-black canes, and this vertical appearance can be echoed by yuccas and cordylines, and contrasted with formally clipped shrubs, such as box (*Buxus*).

Using small bamboos
Smaller species such as *Indocalamus*, *Sasaella*, *Pleioblastus*, and *Shibataea* are suitable for small gardens. They also make some of the best bamboos for pot culture.

RECOMMENDED BAMBOOS

For screens and hedging
Fargesia nitida ↕ 5m (15ft) ↔ 1.5m (5ft) ▣ ◊ ✳✳✳

Phyllostachys flexuosa ↕ 1.8–10m (6–30ft) ↔ indefinite ▣–▣ ◊ ✳✳✳

Pleioblastus gramineus ↕ 1.8–5m (6–16ft) ↔ indefinite ▣–▣ ◊ ✳✳✳

Pleioblastus hindsii ↕ 3.6m (12ft) ↔ indefinite ▣–▣ ◊ ✳✳✳

Pseudosasa japonica ♀ ↕ 6m (20ft) ↔ indeterminate ▣–▣ ◊ ✳✳✳ [5]

Sasa palmata ↕ 1.8–4m (6–12ft) ↔ indefinite ▣–▣ ◊ ✳✳✳

Semiarundinaria fastuosa ♀ ↕ 7m (22ft) ↔ 1.8m (6ft) ▣–▣ ◊ ✳✳✳

For containers
Chimonobambusa marmorea ↕ 1.5m (5ft) ▣ ◊ ✳✳✳

Fargesia murieliae 'Simba' ♀ ↕ 1.8m (6ft) ▣ ◊ ✳✳✳

Phyllostachys nigra ♀ ↕ 3–5m (10–15ft) ▣–▣ ◊ ✳✳✳

Pleioblastus variegatus ♀ ↕ 75cm (30in) ▣ ◊ ✳✳✳

Pleioblastus viridistriatus ♀ ↕ 1.5m (5ft) ▣ ◊ ✳✳✳

Shibataea kumasasa ↕ 60–150cm (2–5ft) ▣–▣ ◊ ✳✳✳

Decorative canes
Fargesia nitida ↕ 5m (15ft) ↔ 1.5m (5ft), purple-green ▣ ◊ ✳✳✳

Phyllostachys aurea ♀ ↕ 1.8–10m (6–30ft) ↔ indefinite, green to yellow ▣–▣ ◊ ✳✳✳

Phyllostachys aureosulcata f. *spectabilis* ♀ ↕ 3–6m (10–20ft) ↔ indefinite, yellow striped green ▣–▣ ◊ ✳✳✳

Phyllostachys bambusoides 'Castilloni' ↕ 5m (16ft) ↔ indefinite, yellow striped green ▣–▣ ◊ ✳✳✳ [4]

Phyllostachys bambusoides 'Holochrysa' ↕ 3–8m (13–16ft) ↔ indefinite, yellow/green ▣–▣ ◊ ✳✳✳ [1]

Phyllostachys mannii ↕ 4m (14ft) ↔ indefinite, pale green ▣–▣ ◊ ✳✳✳ [3]

Phyllostachys nigra ♀ ↕ 3–5m (10–15ft) ↔ 1.8–3m (6–10ft), black ▣–▣ ◊ ✳✳✳

Phyllostachys vivax f. *aureocaulis* ♀ ↕ 5m (16ft) ↔ indefinite, yellow striped green ▣–▣ ◊ ✳✳✳ [2]

Sasa palmata ↕ 1.8–4m (6–12ft) ↔ indefinite, bright green, streaked purple ▣–▣ ◊ ✳✳✳

Semiarundinaria fastuosa ♀ ↕ 7m (22ft) ↔ 1.8m (6ft), green, maturing to red-brown ▣–▣ ◊ ✳✳✳

Variegated leaves
Chimonobambusa marmorea 'Variegata' ↕↔ 90cm (36in) ▣ ◊ ✳✳✳

Hibanobambusa tranquillans 'Shiroshima' ♀ ↕ 2.4m (8ft) ↔ indefinite ▣–▣ ◊ ✳✳

Pleioblastus variegatus ♀ ↕ 75cm (30in) ↔ 1.2m (4ft) ▣ ◊ ✳✳✳

Pleioblastus viridistriatus ♀ ↕↔ 1.5m (5ft) ▣ ◊ ✳✳✳

Pseudosasa japonica 'Akebonosuji' ↕ 3m (10ft) ↔ indeterminate ▣ ◊ ✳✳✳

Sasaella masamuneana 'Aureostriata' ↕ 90cm (36in) ↔ indefinite ▣ ◊ ✳✳✳

How to care for bamboos

Bamboos are trouble-free and easy to grow when planted in good soil or containers and given copious watering and feeding in the growing season; choose non-invasive species to make maintenance easier

Bamboos can be divided into two main groups based on the growth habit of the root system (*see also Types of bamboo, opposite*). The largest group and the most difficult to control are the "runners" or invasive forms. When established, these plants produce long rhizomes under the soil that grow away from the main plant, enabling new territory to be colonized. In gardens this can become a major problem with some species as it is often difficult to contain them. In comparison, the second group, known as "clumpers", are non-invasive, forming tight clumps. It is therefore essential to choose carefully when selecting species.

There are usually some exceptions to the broad classification of invasive or non-invasive. It is advisable to check catalogue descriptions and, where possible, to see a mature plant to judge the suitability of the choice.

Site and soil

Bamboos enjoy open but sheltered sunny situations and most will thrive in full sun as well as dappled shade. Ideally, protect them from cold north and easterly winds and do not plant them in exposed positions, although some are commonly used for screening in mild coastal and inland regions.

Bamboos are very adaptable and will tolerate most soils and pH levels, but they prefer a soil that is loamy, rich in organic matter, and moist but free draining. Although they will grow in poor soils, they will not tolerate wet, boggy, or extremely dry conditions.

Planting

Most bamboos are sold in containers, which would suggest that they may be planted all year round as with other perennial plants. It is, however, better to plant in the first half of the year as this will ensure that the food reserves

Path cut through a stand of bamboo

Cut canes right down to create a path

stored in the rhizomes are used to produce a good flush of fresh canes in the summer. Later the rhizomes begin to develop and produce new roots before going into a resting stage that lasts from autumn through to spring.

Before planting, prepare the soil by digging to a spade's depth. This will break up any compaction and improve drainage. Add garden compost to raise the organic content and improve the water-holding capacity of the soil.

Dig out the planting hole so that the rootball sits slightly low in the hole, with 2.5cm (1in) of soil covering the original surface of the ball. During backfilling firm the soil well, taking care not to damage the young rhizomes. After planting, water well and mulch with garden compost, leafmould, or bark.

Watering and feeding

Bamboos are gross feeders and need adequate water and foods throughout the growing season. It is important to water regularly during dry periods but

vital not to overwater as this may cause rotting of the rhizomes.

Bamboos need a high level of nitrogen in the spring and a balanced fertilizer throughout the rest of the growing season. Start feeding as soon as new growth begins. Later apply a liquid fertilizer at regular intervals until late summer. Bamboos contain high concentrations of silica, a vital structural component of the cell walls. They recycle much of their silica from the fallen leaves and so these should be left to decay around the plants.

PESTS AND DISEASES

There are few pests and diseases that attack bamboo, but in very hot and dry conditions under glass, red spider mite (*Tetranychus urticae*) may become a problem, causing mottled leaves that later turn yellowish-white and eventually fall. This can be deterred by spraying the plants daily with water, using a hosepipe.

See also Using bamboos in the garden, pp.134–135; How to propagate grasses and bamboos, pp.138–139

Bamboo flowering

It is widely believed that a given species of bamboo will flower all over the world at the same time and then die. This is rarely true and the misconception probably arises from the fact that bamboos flower very irregularly, often only after many years in cultivation, and that many are derived from a single introduction, all subsequent divisions of which will tend to flower at the same time. Flowering can be spasmodic or continue for many months and weaken or even kill a clump. Flowering specimens should therefore be fed in spring with a general-purpose fertilizer. A clump that appears to have died will often shoot again from the base if cut back to ground level and fed in the spring. Many flowering species yield viable seeds that can be collected and sown.

Growing for canes

Cut canes only when they are ripe. They usually take three years to achieve maturity and it is helpful to mark each year's canes with a tiny spot of paint, using a different colour each year. The optimum time for cutting is late autumn and early winter when sap level is at its lowest. After cutting, dry the canes thoroughly before use. This

TYPES OF BAMBOO

Invasive types (runners)

Arundinaria	*Sasa*
Bashania	*Sasaella*
Chimonobambusa	*Sasamorpha*
Clavinodum	*Semiarundinaria*
Dendrocalamus	*Shibataea*
Indocalamus	*Sinarundinaria*
Phyllostachys	*Sinobambusa*
Pleioblastus	*Yushania*
Pseudosasa	

Non-invasive types (clumpers)

Bambusa	*Himalayacalamus*
Chusquea	*Schizostachyum*
Drepanostachyum	*Shibataea*
Fargesia	*Thamnocalamus*

is best done on a rack in a well-ventilated shed. Canes up to 2.5cm (1in) in diameter need around six months to dry fully, thicker canes up to 12 months.

Pruning

Although the canes live for around 10 years it is advisable to remove the older canes as they tend to lose colour after four or five years, looking ragged and becoming unattractive. It is good practice

to reduce the number of canes by 20–30 per cent, cutting away the weaker ones at ground level during the spring. This opens up the centre of the clump. Removing leaves from the lower parts of remaining stems helps to reveal the attractive canes.

Bamboo in containers

Bamboos make good subjects for containers if planted in large pots at least 45cm (18in) in diameter. The larger glazed Oriental-style pots are particularly suitable as they do not dry out rapidly. The other main advantage of container growing is that it allows the most invasive types to be grown. As bamboos are gross feeders, use a good potting compost containing a controlled-release fertilizer and water-storage granules. Additional liquid feeding during the growing season will also benefit the plant. Container-grown bamboos are more susceptible to freezing than plants grown in the open ground, to prevent this, insulate pots with plastic bubble wrap in very cold weather or move them into an unheated conservatory or greenhouse. Bamboos grown in containers need to be divided regularly, retaining the younger rhizomes and canes to ensure fresh new growth.

MAKING A BAMBOO SHELTER

1 An easy way to make more of a large bamboo, such as this *Phyllostachys violascens*, is to cut into the clump and add a seat.

2 Clear an area of the clump large enough to take the seat by severing canes at ground level using loppers.

3 You will then have a delightful, sheltered place to sit on a summer's evening. Remove unwanted new canes as necessary.

HOW TO PROPAGATE GRASSES AND BAMBOOS

How to propagate grasses and bamboos

It is easy for gardeners to propagate their ornamental grasses, bamboos, sedges, and rushes using two methods: raising plants from seed for species, and division in various forms for both species and cultivars

Grasses are an obliging group to propagate and in the main do not require sophisticated equipment. For gardeners, raising plants for home use could not be simpler, as the two methods of propagation are easy to apply anywhere.

Seed can be used for most grass species, sedges, and rushes, but not for named cultivars as their seedlings are not the same as the parent plants.

Division can be used for all grasses, sedges, and rushes, and many bamboos. As this is a vegetative propagation method, reproducing a new plant identical to the parent, it can be used for named cultivars. Rhizome cuttings, in effect small divisions, can

be used for the bamboo species that "run" rather than form clumps.

Grasses from seed

Sow seed in late winter or early spring in 9cm (3½in) pots in a cold frame or cool greenhouse to provide pots full of young grasses that can be planted out in borders by late spring.

Alternatively, make an early spring sowing in module trays; the grass should be ready for potting into 8cm (3in) pots in mid-spring, when the 2.5cm (1in) plug will be full of new growth, perhaps 6–8cm (2–3in) high. If you sow several seeds into each cell in a module, the production time is reduced and the plug can be transplanted into a 9cm (3½in)

pot. Use good-quality potting compost, which should have enough reserves of fertilizer to last the plants until planting-out time, usually in late spring. The biggest problem with young grasses is weak, straggly growth caused by low light so, shortly after potting them up, acclimatize them outside, but protect them from frost.

Dividing grasses, sedges, and rushes

Grasses, sedges, and rushes can be easily propagated by division, as can many bamboos including *Chimonobambusa*,

SOWING SEEDS OF GRASSES

1 Sow seed when fresh, no later than the spring following its formation, into modules. Here, each cell is 2.5cm (1in) square by about 4cm (1½in) deep. Fill the tray with soilless seed compost, tapping it firmly on the bench a couple of times to ensure no air pockets remain in the cells. **2** With a dibber make a 4mm (⅛in) hole in the centre of each cell. **3** Trickle one or

several seeds into the hole. Using the dibber again, gently cover the seeds with compost. Water in and then place in a cold frame or stand on a bench in a cool greenhouse. **4** Within 15 days the grass seed will begin to germinate; gentle bottom heat of 15°C (59°F) will help to speed up this process. When germinated, keep frost free and just moist.

GRASSES BY DIVISION

1 Lift the clump from the garden; here, the sedge *Carex oshimensis* 'Evergold' is used.
2 Use a knife to cut the clump, or simply pull it apart to divide it into 2.5–5cm (1–2in) pieces.
3 Maintain the balance between root and shoot. Remove any old, dead roots and foliage, and trim the remaining leaves to 10cm (4in).
4 Pot each piece into a 9cm (3½in) pot, using good-quality soilless potting compost. To aid rooting and establishment, place the pots in a humid environment such as a plastic tunnel, cold greenhouse, or cold frame. When the divisions have rooted, harden them off.

See also Choosing ornamental grasses, pp.131–132; Getting the best from ornamental grasses, p.133; Ideas for bamboo, p.135

Chusquea, *Phyllostachys*, *Fargesia*, *Pleioblastus*, *Pseudosasa*, and *Sasa*. Clump-forming plants such as *Stipa*, *Festuca*, and *Carex*, which do not grow from rhizomes (underground stems) but have light, fibrous root systems, are among the easiest to divide, and the technique also helps to maintain the health and vigour of both the root and shoot growth.

Division is best carried out in late winter or early spring, ideally just as the plants come into growth. The method of division varies depending on how you wish to grow the plants on: planted straight back into the garden, in nursery beds, or in containers.

With low grasses and sedges, pieces for growing on in pots can be as small as 2.5–5cm (1–2in) across. Divisions for immediate replanting in the garden or nursery beds should be larger – around fist-sized. Water carefully after planting as new growth often coincides with spring droughts.

Dividing large grasses and bamboos

Again, divide in early spring, using heavy-duty tools if necessary. Bamboos fall into two categories: species that are clump forming such as *Chusquea*, and those with running rhizomes that spread horizontally underground, such as *Pleioblastus*, some *Phyllostachys*, and *Sasa*. Growth patterns, however, tend to vary with climate: in temperate areas many *Phyllostachys* that are runners in the wild become clump forming.

For clump-forming types, propagation is by division of the clump, in exactly the same way as for grasses, retaining part of at least one grown cane (*see box below*). Pot such divisions into 13–15cm (5–6in) pots, and then place them in a warm, humid environment out of direct sunlight. Do not cut back the canes as this will weaken the division. When rooted, harden off and ideally grow on under protection.

Running species can be propagated by a special form of division: budded rhizome sections (*see box left*).

PROPAGATING BAMBOO FROM BUDDED RHIZOME SECTIONS

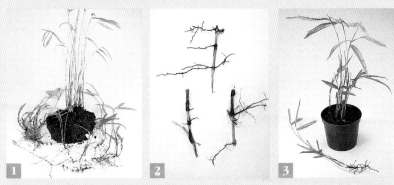

1 In early spring, just at the start of the new season's growth, lift the clump and divide it into pieces, each with a few canes, roots, and lengths of rhizome showing the buds that will form new canes. **2** Cut rhizomes into pieces containing at least one bud. Two pieces can be planted in a 9cm (3½in) pot just below the surface of the compost. **3** Divisions with three to four canes can be potted into a 13cm (5in) pot. Place newly potted bamboos into a humid environment. Water in well and new canes should emerge within about six weeks.

DIVISION OF LARGE CLUMPS

For larger grasses (such as the miscanthus shown here) and many bamboos, which form large and dense clumps of matted roots, a more drastic approach to plant propagation may be required.

1 When dividing a clump, dig it out and cut the stems back to 20–30cm (8–12in). **2** Ideally, use two forks back-to-back or a sharp knife to separate the root ball into manageable chunks.

3 Make these approximately 10–13cm (4–5in) across. **4** Clean these up and replant them immediately or pot them into a 13–15cm (5–6in) pot. **5** The sections will quickly grow away.

The best perennials for shade

There are hardy perennials for various degrees of shade; choose the right ones and they will thrive

Shade can be cast by buildings or partitions, such as walls or fences, or by trees and shrubs, which usually means additional growth restrictions such as dry soil around tree roots.

To grow healthy plants in shady areas, it is important to identify the degree of shade that a plant needs or will tolerate. Few perennials will thrive where shade is very dense, particularly when this is coupled with dry, impoverished soil. Additional organic matter and a general fertilizer will provide more suitable conditions for plants to grow.

Many hardy perennials, in addition to those listed below, will tolerate and sometimes thrive in lightly shaded areas. Plants to avoid are sun lovers originating from warm climates, or those needing a sunny site to ripen wood and induce flowering. Most midsummer-flowering perennials need good light conditions to flower freely.

DEEP SHADE

Brunnera macrophylla 'Dawson's White'
↕ 45cm (18in) ↔ 60cm (24in) ◊ ✳✳✳ [1]

Epimedium grandiflorum ♀ ↕ 20–30cm
(8–12in) ↔ 30cm (12in) ◊ ✳✳✳

Euphorbia amygdaloides var. *robbiae* ♀
↕ 60cm (24in) ↔ 30cm (12in) E ◊ ✳✳✳

Hosta (not yellow-leaved) ↕↔ variable ◊
✳✳✳

Iris foetidissima ♀ ↕ 30–90cm (12–36in)
↔ 60cm (24in) E ◊ ✳✳✳

Liriope muscari ♀ ↕ 30cm (12in) ↔ 45cm
(18in) E ◊ ﾛ ✳✳✳

Pulmonaria angustifolia ♀ ↕ 25–30cm
(10–12in) ↔ 45cm (18in) ◊ ✳✳✳

Symphytum ibericum ↕ 40cm (16in)
↔ 60cm (24in) ◊ ✳✳✳

MODERATE OR PART SHADE

In addition to those plants listed left:

Acanthus mollis ↕ 1.5m (5ft) ↔ 90cm (36in)
◊ ✳✳✳ [2]

Anemone x *hybrida* ↕ 1.2–1.5m (4–5ft)
↔ indefinite ◊ ✳✳✳

Astilbe x *arendsii* ↕ 60–90cm (24–36in)
↔ 45cm (18in) ◊ ✳✳✳

Astrantia maxima ♀ ↕ 60cm (24in) ↔ 30cm
(12in) ◊ ✳✳✳

Dicentra spectabilis ♀ ↕ 1.2m (4ft) ↔ 45cm
(18in) ◊ ✳✳✳

Geranium sanguineum ↕ 20cm (8in)
↔ 30cm (12in) ◊ ✳✳✳

Saxifraga x *urbium* ↕ 30cm (12in)
↔ indefinite E ◊ ✳✳✳

Tiarella cordifolia ♀ ↕ 10–30cm (4–12in)
↔ 30cm (12in) ◊ ✳✳✳

See also Shrubs to grow in shade, pp.83–84; Hardy ferns, p.142; Bulbs for shade, p.144

Success with tree ferns

Increasingly popular, tree ferns appear hardier than once thought

Tree ferns are found in sheltered upland forests in temperate and tropical regions of South-east Asia, Australasia, and South America. The most widely cultivated are species of *Dicksonia* and *Cyathea*. Most develop tall trunks consisting of fibrous roots (or, more correctly, rhizoids) clothed in old leaf bases, crowned with spreading fronds. Growth rates in the wild are slow, with plants growing about 3cm (1¼in) a year. Nursery-grown tree ferns may achieve up to 10cm (4in) of growth a year under favourable conditions, but this is unusual.

Very few tree ferns are likely to prove hardy out of doors in Britain. The exceptions are *Dicksonia antarctica* and *Dicksonia fibrosa* in southern and western areas. *Cyathea australis* may survive in mild areas in the south-west of England or city-centre gardens where the urban heat island effect is particularly marked.

Tree fern for the conservatory
Cyathea dealbata from New Zealand is a half-hardy tree fern, which makes it an ideal choice for growing in a tub in the cool conservatory.

See also Caring for frost-tender perennials

Dicksonia antarctica survives outdoors in southern and western areas of the UK

during the first year to encourage good rooting. The following spring plant out in the garden. Bare trunks can also be planted directly into the ground in a suitable situation when risk of frost has passed, but should be watered daily.

In the wild tree ferns are "top-feeders", catching all the moisture and foods they require in their large canopy. In the garden they benefit from a dilute liquid feed once a month, when in growth, applied to the fronds and trunk. Alternatively, apply a controlled-release fertilizer around the base. In cultivation tree ferns appear to respond to generous applications of well-rotted organic matter. Established plants will need watering on the side of the trunk in dry conditions, both summer and winter. During the growing season damaged fronds can be removed as new fronds are continuously produced. Fronds damaged in the winter by frost or wind should be removed in spring.

Winter protection

Hardiness tends to increase with the height of the growing point above the ground. Young plants with no trunk are not really suitable for overwintering outdoors except in very sheltered sites. Such plants may be best in pots, plunged in the garden for the summer, but brought into a frost-free, cool conservatory, greenhouse, or porch for the winter.

In mild winters in southern and western areas of Britain *Dicksonia antarctica* may survive planted in the garden with little, if any, protection. ▷

Evergreen under glass, tree ferns are normally deciduous outdoors in Britain, except in mild areas or mild winters.

Tree ferns are best suited to a sheltered, humid environment, protected from strong, drying winds. They will thrive in damp, poorly lit areas where few other plants will grow, but will not tolerate drying out or scorching sun. Avoid planting in a frost pocket. Plants appear tolerant of a wide range of soil types with a pH from neutral to slightly acid. These ferns are seen at their best when planted so that the tops can

spread without crowding. Fronds on mature specimens may achieve 2m (6ft) or more in length.

Growing tips

Tree ferns can be bought as container-grown plants or as bare trunks. Where they are supplied as bare trunks soak the base of the trunk and pot up into a multipurpose potting compost to encourage good rooting. Plant just enough of the trunk to ensure the plant is stable. Water the trunk every day until fronds begin to emerge. Avoid feeding

WHERE TO GROW

- In mild areas tree ferns are ideal for woodland gardens. *Eucalyptus dalrympleana* (mountain gum) is a natural companion for *Dicksonia antarctica*
- In colder areas grow tree ferns in containers in a cool conservatory with ample headroom for their far-reaching fronds

over winter, pp.123–124; Choosing conservatory plants, pp.193–194

PRACTICAL ADVICE

PLANTING IDEAS

To be safe, place 15cm (6in) of straw into the crown of the plant and fold the fronds in on themselves to protect the crown. In colder areas it is wise to cover with a hessian sack or plastic bubble wrap and additional straw. Further protection can be provided by placing a cap of polystyrene over the crown and tying polystyrene sheets around the trunk, with loose straw packed in. In very cold areas plants can be surrounded by straw bales. This protection should be applied in mid-autumn and removed in spring, before the new fronds come into growth. Even in winter it may be necessary to water the trunk during prolonged periods of dry weather, but avoid wetting the crown of the plant.

Container growing

Tree ferns make good container plants but, due to the size of their fronds, older plants are only really suitable for large conservatories or greenhouses. They will do well in an ordinary multipurpose potting compost. Alternatively, a mix of 1 part each of loam, medium-grade bark, and charcoal, 2 parts sharp sand, and 3 parts coarse leafmould or peat substitute can be used.

Under glass, plants do best in bright filtered light with moderate humidity. It is important that they never dry out so it may be necessary to water the trunk daily in summer. During the growing season apply a weak liquid feed once a week. Young plants may be stood outside in the summer, but out of direct sunlight. Indoors temperatures greater than 32°C (90°F) are likely to prove harmful. Top dress container-grown plants or pot on annually in spring.

During the winter give pot-grown plants under glass as much light as possible and keep just moist. If containers are outside over winter, move them to a sheltered position and protect both plant and container from frost, which can easily penetrate through the sides of a pot.

Choosing and growing hardy ferns

The 21st-century fern craze is satisfied by a huge range of different kinds, mostly easily grown in shady places in the garden

Most hardy ferns will thrive in any moist, shady place in well-drained, well-dug, humus-rich, neutral to alkaline soil. However, some ferns such as *Thelypteris simulata* and species of *Blechnum* prefer an acid soil, while *Osmunda* species prefer neutral to acid conditions. Lime-tolerant ferns include *Asplenium scolopendrium*, *Cystopteris fragilis*, and *Polystichum setiferum*.

Hardy species of *Asplenium*, *Dryopteris*, and *Polypodium* are tolerant of dry shade, but will need regular watering in their first season until they are established, and appreciate a mulch of leafmould, bark, or garden compost. Very wet sites can be planted with *Athyrium filix-femina* and its cultivars, *Dryopteris cristata*, *Matteuccia struthiopteris*, *Onoclea sensibilis*, and *Osmunda regalis*.

Little pruning is needed but dead or unsightly fronds should be removed before the new fronds appear. Water when necessary, but apply to the roots and not directly to the fronds or crown as this can encourage rot. If rot does develop, an approved systemic fungicide may be used and all debris cleared away to promote air circulation, while a gravel mulch may help reduce subsequent re-infection. Ferns are generally free of most garden pests, if planted in the ground, although plants grown in containers may suffer from vine weevil grubs.

Male fern (*Dryopteris filix-mas*)

RECOMMENDED HARDY FERNS

Evergreen ferns for damp situations

Adiantum venustum ♀ ‡ 15cm (6in) ↔ indefinite, evergreen in mild winters ✲✲✲

Asplenium scolopendrium ♀ ‡ 45–70cm (18–28in) ↔ 60cm (24in) ✲✲✲

Asplenium scolopendrium Crispum Group ‡ 45–70cm (18–28in) ↔ 60cm (24in) ✲✲✲

Asplenium trichomanes ♀ ‡ 15cm (6in) ↔ 20cm (8in) ✲✲✲

Polypodium vulgare ‡ 30cm (12in) ↔ indefinite ✲✲✲

Polystichum setiferum ♀ ‡ 1.2m (4ft) ↔ 90cm (36in) ✲✲✲

Polystichum setiferum Divisilobum Group ‡↔ 50–70cm (20–28in) ✲✲✲

Polystichum setiferum Plumosum Group ‡↔ 60–80cm (24–32in) ✲✲✲

Deciduous ferns for damp situations

Adiantum capillus-veneris ‡ 30cm (12in) ↔ 40cm (16in), evergreen in mild areas ✲✲

Athyrium filix-femina ♀ ‡ 1.2m (4ft) ↔ 60–90cm (24–36in) ⏚ ✲✲✲

Cystopteris fragilis ‡↔ 20cm (8in) ✲✲✲

Dryopteris affinis ♀ ‡↔ 90cm (36in) ✲✲✲

Dryopteris dilatata ‡ 90cm (36in) ↔ 1.2m (4ft) ✲✲✲

Dryopteris filix-mas ♀ ‡↔ 1–1.2m (3–4ft) ✲✲✲

Matteuccia struthiopteris ♀ ‡ 1.7m (5½ft) ↔ 90cm (36in) ✲✲✲

Onoclea sensibilis ♀ ‡ 60cm (24in) ↔ indefinite ⏚ ✲✲✲

Osmunda regalis ♀ ‡ 1.8m (6ft) ↔ 4m (12ft) ⏚ ✲✲✲

See also The best perennials for shade, p.140; Success with tree ferns, pp.141–142

BULBS

Planting dry bulbs

Good soil and the correct planting depth ensure success

Plant spring-flowering bulbs in early autumn, summer-flowering kinds in early spring, and autumn-flowering bulbs by late summer. Most bulbs are bought and planted in a dry, dormant, leafless, rootless state. Plant as soon as possible; flowering may be poor after late planting or lengthy storage.

Most hardy bulbs prefer a warm, sunny site with good drainage, but bulbs from woodland habitats need cool, moist conditions. Good soil is important, as most bulbs have only a short period in leaf before dying back. Improve light or sandy soils with bulky organic matter, such as garden compost, incorporated below bulb depth, and dig in sharp grit or sand on heavy soils.

Make a hole to the correct depth with a trowel or bulb planter and fork in some bonemeal. Plant to two or three times the bulb height – in other words, the tip of a 5cm (2in) high bulb should be 10–15cm (4–6in) below soil level. If planted too shallowly they may not flower after the first year. Carefully replace the soil over the bulbs and gently firm it with the back of a rake.

Planting depth for bulbs
Be sure to plant bulbs sufficiently deeply, because if they are planted too shallowly – a common mistake – they may not flower after the first year.

See also Multiplying bulbs by division, p.154

Bulbs in the green

Some bulbs are best lifted and transplanted while still in full leaf

Most bulbs are transplanted when they are dormant, but some resent drying out, including wood anemone (*Anemone nemorosa*), hardy cyclamen, winter aconite (*Eranthis*), snowdrop (*Galanthus*), bluebell (*Hyacinthoides*) and snowflake (*Leucojum*). Dry bulbs of these kinds are usually offered for sale in autumn and, although cheap, they often fail to establish well. Specialist nurseries that supply bulbs "in the green" offer them damp-packed, or you can buy some kinds in pots on the point of flowering from garden centres.

Bulb colonies can be increased and flowering improved by lifting and dividing overcrowded clumps in the garden shortly after flowering, but with the plant still in full leaf.

After dividing clumps, plant groups of four to six bulbs in holes wide and deep enough to spread the roots, at the same depth that they were before being lifted. This is usually made obvious by a change in stem colour from green to white. Firm the soil and water in. Keep well watered if the soil starts drying out while the bulbs are in leaf.

Transplanting in the green
Some bulbs, such as snowdrops, shown here, are planted, or lifted and divided, immediately after flowering, while the leaves are still green.

Bulbs for shade

Some bulbs grow in the shade of trees or even of buildings

RECOMMENDED BULBS

Shade can be cast by buildings or dividing partitions, such as walls or fences, or by trees and shrubs, which usually means additional problems, such as dry soil around tree roots and lack of air movement caused by overhanging branches.

Bulbs will not thrive where shade is very dense, particularly when coupled with a dry, impoverished soil. Additional organic matter and a general-purpose fertilizer will provide more suitable conditions.

A number of bulbs grow in light, partial, or moderate shade. Light shade is a site open to the sky but screened from direct sunlight. Partial shade means a site that receives sunlight for two or three hours in the early morning or late evening but not midday sun, which supplies much more light. Moderate shade is mainly reflected or diffused light, for example, below trees.

Anemone blanda ♀ ↕↔ 15cm (6in) ◊ ✳✳✳
Colchicum autumnale ↕ 10–15cm (4–6in) ↔ 8cm (3in) ◊ ✳✳✳
Cyclamen coum ♀ ↕ 5–8cm (2–3in) ↔ 10cm (4in) ◊ ✳✳✳
Cyclamen hederifolium ♀ ↕ 10–13cm (4–5in) ↔ 15cm (6in) ◊ ✳✳✳
Eranthis hyemalis ♀ ↕ 5–8cm (2–3in) ↔ 5cm (2in) ◊ ✳✳✳
Erythronium dens-canis ↕↔ 10–15cm (4–6in) ◊ ✳✳✳
Galanthus nivalis ♀ ↕↔ 10cm (4in) ◊ ✳✳✳
Hyacinthoides non-scripta ↕ 20–40cm (8–16in) ↔ 8cm (3in) ◊–◊ ✳✳✳
Leucojum vernum ♀ ↕ 20–30cm (8–12in) ↔ 8cm (3in) ◊ ✳✳✳
Muscari armeniacum ♀ ↕ 20cm (8in) ↔ 5cm (2in) ◊ ✳✳✳
Narcissus ↕ 10–50cm (4–20in) ↔ 8–10cm (3–4in) ◊ ✳✳✳
Scilla siberica ♀ ↕ 10–20cm (4–8in) ↔ 5cm (2in) ◊ ✳✳✳

See also What to plant under trees, p.64

Naturalizing bulbs

Bulbs are most often naturalized in permanent, informal drifts or groups in grass, but they can also be grown this way under trees

Naturalized bulbs give interest to areas of the garden that otherwise might not be given over to flowering plants. (Daffodils are covered on this page; for other suitable bulbs, *see p.146*.)

Under deciduous trees or shrubs use bulbs that flower in spring or autumn when there are few leaves to cast shade. Hardy cyclamen, such as *Cyclamen hederifolium* and *C. coum*, anemones, crocuses, and scillas are all suitable.

Lawns, banks, and hard-to-manage areas of turf can be transformed into a carpet of colour in spring and autumn. Bulbs for naturalizing in turf must be able to withstand competition from grass roots; ideal subjects are robust species and hybrid daffodils (*Narcissus*) or crocuses, and bulbs that complete their growth early. For a more varied display try snake's head fritillary (*Fritillaria meleagris*) and summer snowflake (*Leucojum aestivum*). ▷

GROWING DAFFOLDILS IN GRASS

Naturalized bulbs will be in place for several years, so avoid planting too close, as overcrowding will reduce flowering. ☐1☐ Scatter the bulbs randomly over the chosen area and plant them where they fall. ☐2☐ Dig planting holes with a trowel or, in grassed areas, use a bulb planter. Plant the bulbs about three times their own depth, as shallow planting leaves the bulbs more prone to drying out and tends to weaken them. If you are lifting an area of turf for planting, score the underside of the turf with a hand fork to loosen the soil before replacing it. Firm it well. ☐3☐ Remove fading blooms so that energy is not wasted producing seed; do not do this to species daffodils. ☐4☐ Leave the foliage for six weeks after flowering to nourish the bulbs before cutting back.

DAFFODILS FOR NATURALIZING

Daffodils for short grass

Narcissus assoanus ↕ 15cm (6in) ↔ 5–8cm (2–3in) ☐ ◊ ✳✳✳

N. asturiensis ♀ ↕ 8cm (3in) ↔ 5–8cm (2–3in) ☐ ◊ ☼ ✳✳✳

N. bulbocodium ♀ ↕ 10–15cm (4–6in) ↔ 8cm (3in) ☐–☒ ◊ ☼ ✳✳✳

N. cyclamineus ♀ and hybrids 'Bartley', 'Beryl', 'February Gold' ♀, 'Jack Snipe' ♀, 'Midget', and 'Peeping Tom' ♀ ↕ 15–40cm (6–16in) ↔ 8cm (3in) ☒ ◊ ☼ ✳✳✳

N. 'Hawera' ♀ ↕ 18cm (7in) ↔ 5–8cm (2–3in) ☐–☒ ◊ ☼ ✳✳

N. 'Minnow' ♀ ↕ 18cm (7in) ↔ 8cm (3in) ☒ ◊ ✳✳✳

N. nanus ↕ 15cm (6in) ↔ 5–8cm (2–3in) ☐–☒ ◊ ✳✳✳

N. obvallaris ♀ ↕ 30cm (12in) ↔ 8cm (3in) ☐–☒ ◊ ✳✳✳

N. x odorus ↕ 25cm (10in) ↔ 8cm (3in) ☐–☒ ◊ ✳✳✳

N. pseudonarcissus ♀ and its variants ↕ 15–35cm (6–14in) ↔ 8cm (3in) ☐–☒ ◊ ✳✳✳

N. 'Tête-à-Tête' ♀ ↕ 15cm (6in) ↔ 5–8cm (2–3in) ☐–☒ ◊ ✳✳✳

N. triandrus ♀ ↕ 10–25cm (4–10in) ↔ 5–8cm (2–3in) ☐–☒ ◊ ☼ ✳✳✳

N. 'W.P. Milner' ↕ 23cm (9in) ↔ 8cm (3in) ☐–☒ ◊ ✳✳✳

Daffodils for taller grass

Most of the larger Trumpet and Large-cupped daffodil hybrids naturalize well. All the following prefer the same growing conditions: ☐–☒ ◊ ✳✳✳

N. 'Actaea' ♀ ↕ 45cm (18in) ↔ 15cm (6in)

N. 'Binkie' ↕ 35cm (14in) ↔ 15cm (6in)

N. 'Charity May' ♀ ↕ 30cm (12in) ↔ 8cm (3in) ☼

N. 'Carlton' ♀ ↕ 40cm (16in) ↔ 15cm (6in)

N. 'Fortune' ↕ 45cm (18in) ↔ 15cm (6in)

N. 'Ice Follies' ♀ ↕ 40cm (16in) ↔ 15cm (6in)

N. 'Kilworth' ↕ 50cm (20in) ↔ 15cm (6in)

N. 'Merlin' ♀ ↕ 45cm (18in) ↔ 15cm (6in)

N. 'Mount Hood' ♀ ↕ 45cm (18in) ↔ 15cm (6in)

N. poeticus 'Plenus' ↕ 40cm (16in) ↔ 15cm (6in)

N. poeticus var. *recurvus* ♀ ↕ 35cm (14in) ↔ 15cm (6in).

N. 'Portrush' ↕ 45cm (18in) ↔ 15cm (6in)

N. 'Saint Keverne' ♀ ↕ 45cm (18in) ↔ 15cm (6in)

N. 'Spellbinder' ♀ ↕ 50cm (20in) ↔ 15cm (6in)

The hoop petticoat daffodil, *N. bulbocodium*

See also What to plant under trees, p.64

RECOMMENDED BULBS FOR NATURALIZING

Spring-flowering crocus

All of the following prefer the same growing conditions: ▫ ◊ ✳✳✳

Crocus ancyrensis ‡↔ 5cm (2in)

C. angustifolius ♀ ‡↔ 5cm (2in)

C. biflorus ‡ 6cm (2½in) ↔ 5cm (2in)

C. chrysanthus cultivars 'Blue Pearl' ♀, 'Cream Beauty' ♀, 'Gipsy Girl', 'Skyline', and 'Snow Bunting' ♀, all ‡ 8cm (3in) ↔ 5cm (2in)

C. etruscus ♀ ‡ 8cm (3in) ↔ 4cm (1½in)

C. flavus subsp. *flavus* ♀ ‡ 8cm (3in) ↔ 5cm (2in)

C. sieberi ♀ and cultivars 'Firefly' and 'Violet Queen' ‡ 5–8cm (2–3in) ↔ 2.5cm (1in)

C. tommasinianus ♀ and cultivars 'Ruby Giant' and 'Whitewell Purple' ‡ 8–10cm (3–4in) ↔ 2.5cm (1in)

C. vernus (larger cultivars) ‡ 10–12cm (4–5in) ↔ 5cm (2in)

Autumn-flowering crocus

Crocus banaticus ♀ ‡ 10cm (4in) ↔ 5cm (2in) ▫–◙ ◊ ✳✳✳

C. kotschyanus ♀ ‡ 6–8cm (2½–3in) ↔ 5cm (2in) ▫ ◊ ✳✳✳

C. laevigatus ♀ ‡ 4–8cm (1½–3in) ↔ 4cm (1½in) ▫ ◊ ✳✳✳

C. nudiflorus ‡ 15–25cm (6–10in) ↔ 5cm (2in) ▫–◙ ◊ ✳✳✳

C. pulchellus ♀ ‡ 10–12cm (4–5in) ↔ 4cm (1½in) ▫ ◊ ✳✳✳

C. serotinus subsp. *salzmannii* ‡ 5–8cm (2–3in) ↔ 4cm (1½in) ◙ ◊ ✳✳✳

C. speciosus ♀ and cultivars 'Aitchisonii', 'Albus' ♀, 'Artabir', 'Conqueror', and 'Oxonian' ‡ 10–15cm (4–6in) ↔ 5cm (2in) ▫ ◊ ✳✳✳

Other bulbs

Alliums All prefer the same conditions: ▫ ◊ ✳✳✳

A. hollandicum ♀ ‡ 90cm (36in) ↔ 10cm (4in)

A. karataviense ♀ ‡ 25cm (10in) ↔ 10cm (4in)

A. moly ‡ 15–25cm (6–10in) ↔ 5cm (2in)

A. triquetrum ‡ 30cm (12in) ↔ 10cm (4in)

A. ursinum ‡ 10–50cm (4–20in) ↔ 10cm (4in)

Anemone blanda ♀ ‡↔ 15cm (6in) ▫–◙ ◊ ✳✳✳

Camassia leichtlinii ‡ 60–130cm (24–54in) ↔ 10cm (4in) ▫–◙ ◊ ✳✳

Chionodoxa luciliae ♀ ‡ 15cm (6in) ↔ 3cm (1¼in) ▫ ◊ ✳✳✳

Colchicums All prefer ▫ ◊ ✳✳✳

C. autumnale ‡ 10–15cm (4–6in) ↔ 8cm (3in)

C. byzantinum ♀ ‡ 12cm (5in) ↔ 10cm (4in)

C. speciosum ♀ ‡ 18cm (7in) ↔ 10cm (4in)

Eranthis hyemalis ♀ ‡ 5–8cm (2–3in) ↔ 5cm (2in) ▫–◙ ◊ ✳✳✳

Erythronium dens-canis ♀ ‡ 10–15cm (4–6in) ↔ 10cm (4in) ◙ ◊ ✳✳✳

Fritillaria meleagris ‡ 30cm (12in) ↔ 5–8cm (2–3in) ▫–◙ ◊ ✳✳✳

Galanthus nivalis ♀ ‡↔ 10cm (4in) ◙ ◊ ✳✳✳

Hyacinthoides non-scripta ‡ 20–40cm (8–16in) ↔ 8cm (3in) ◙ ◊ ✳✳✳

Leucojum vernum ♀ ‡ 20–30cm (8–12in) ↔ 8cm (3in) ◙ ◊ ✳✳✳

Muscari armeniacum ♀ ‡ 20cm (8in) ↔ 5cm (2in) ▫ ◊ ✳✳✳

Nectaroscordum siculum ‡ 1.2m (4ft) ↔ 10cm (4in) ▫–◙ ◊ ✳✳✳

Scilla siberica ♀ ‡ 10–20cm (4–8in) ↔ 5cm (2in) ▫–◙ ◊ ✳✳✳

Crocus kotschyanus

Fritillaria meleagris

Narcissus problems

On the whole daffodils are easy, but they can attract problems

Daffodils (*Narcissus*) usually grow and flower well; a failure to thrive or produce blooms could be due to pests, diseases, poor growing conditions, or unsuitable cultivation techniques.

DAFFODIL BLINDNESS

Non-flowering or "blindness" of daffodils is generally caused by poor cultivation techniques or growing conditions. Shallow planting can lead to poor flowering, as can removing foliage too soon after flowering. In dry conditions daffodils may die down prematurely and fail to form flower buds due to insufficient food reserves. Blindness can also be caused by large narcissus bulb fly larvae (*see opposite*).

Prevention

Plant bulbs at 2–3 times their depth. For naturalising in grass, choose only recommended cultivars or species, as others may lack the vigour needed. Do not cut down daffodil foliage for at least 6 weeks after flowering, to allow bulbs to build up food reserves (*see p.145*). Knotting the leaves reduces their ability to function and should be avoided. Remove faded flowers and seed heads to divert energy to feed the bulb.

Non-flowering daffodils

See also Storage rots, p.150

Feed bulbs growing on poor soils with a general-purpose fertilizer in spring and with a high-potash fertilizer after flowering. Mulch and water bulbs in dry conditions.

LARGE NARCISSUS BULB FLY

Warm, sunny weather in late spring to midsummer increases the activity and fecundity of large narcissus bulb fly (*Merodon equestris*). Warmer summers have made this a more widespread and damaging pest. The females are about 15mm (½in) long and vary in colour but resemble small bumblebees. They lay eggs near the bulb's neck as the foliage is dying down. Newly hatched larvae crawl down to the bulbs and enter by boring through the basal plates. They grow to 18mm (¾in) long and then pupate in the soil in the following spring.

There is usually only one larva in an infested bulb. It kills the bulb by eating the centre, which becomes filled with muddy excrement. If bulbs contain many smaller maggots, these are likely to be grubs of a small bulb fly (*Eumerus* species), which feed in bulbs already damaged by another pest or disease.

Daffodils are the main host but other bulbs may also be attacked, including *Amaryllis*, *Hippeastrum*, snowdrop (*Galanthus*) and *Sprekelia*.

Control

None of the pesticides available to home gardeners controls grubs inside bulbs or prevents eggs being laid. Plant bulbs in shady places where the bulb flies are less likely to find them. Firming the soil around the necks of bulbs as the foliage dies down makes it more difficult for eggs to be laid. Valuable bulbs can be covered with horticultural fleece during the egg-laying period to exclude bulb flies, but the increased humidity may encourage fungal diseases of the foliage.

NARCISSUS BASAL ROT

One of the most serious daffodil diseases, this is caused by the soil-borne fungus *Fusarium oxysporum* f. *specialis narcissi*.

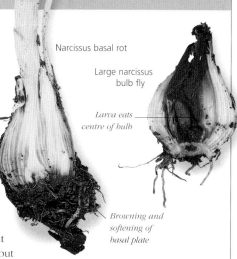

Narcissus basal rot

Large narcissus bulb fly

Larva eats centre of bulb

Browning and softening of basal plate

This occurs in most soils, even those with no record of daffodil growing. It infects bulbs through either the roots from the basal plate or small wounds, usually made at lifting time.

Symptoms may show after lifting, but are usually not seen until the bulbs have been in storage for some time. Affected bulbs develop a softening and brown discoloration of the basal plate. The rot spreads through the inner bulb scales, which turn reddish brown, often with a pink-white fungus. Eventually the bulbs become brittle, shrunken, and mummified. Basal rot occurs in bulbs stored at above 22°C (72°F).

The disease is carried over from one season to the next mainly through the bulbs. If slightly infected bulbs are planted, the symptoms are yellowing, stunting, and sparse foliage. Severely infected bulbs do not grow.

Control

There is no cure, so discard bulbs that show signs of disease. To prevent infections, lift daffodil bulbs 6 weeks after flowering, before the soil warms up in summer. Avoid bruising bulbs when handling and store them in a cool, airy place. Do not leave them exposed to hot sunshine. Dusting bulbs with sulphur before storing and planting early in autumn may reduce infection.

Losses in naturalised daffodils are likely to be noticed if bulbs fail to grow in spring. Here hygiene is key; ensure that infected bulbs are removed.

Rodent damage

Mice and voles can wreak havoc among bulbous plants

Mice and voles can help themselves to bulbs in storage and in the garden. The damage is done mainly during the autumn to spring period. Many bulbs and corms are affected, but those of crocuses and tulips seem particularly attractive to mice.

Symptoms

Distinctive teeth marks can be seen on the remains of the bulbs. If the plants were attacked while in the ground, the bulb or corm may be gone but foliage is often discarded near the holes where they were dug up, as the rodents ignore the leaves and concentrate on the more nutritious storage tissue.

Control

Store lifted bulbs and corms in rodent-proof containers. After bulb planting, firm the soil to disguise the planting holes. Place mouse traps under covers made from logs or stones to prevent pets or birds coming into contact with them.

Firming the soil
Mice love bulbs, so after planting hide the positions of the planting holes and make digging harder by firming the soil surface. If you know there are mice around, set traps nearby.

TULIP PROBLEMS

Tulip problems

If your tulips become infected with viruses or the fungal disease tulip fire you will need to take drastic action

Tulips are best lifted after flowering, partly to minimize the chances of infection with viral and fungal diseases.

TULIP VIRUSES

The most important of the 13 or more viruses affecting tulips is tulip-breaking virus, which causes the well-known and sometimes prized colour "breaking" patterns on the petals and also a gradual loss of vigour and flower production. Cucumber mosaic virus, which affects many plants, can also cause these symptoms. Tobacco necrosis virus causes Augusta disease (named after the tulip cultivar), seen as brown streaks in leaves and stems.

Control

Tobacco necrosis virus is spread by the soil fungus *Olpidium*. Planting in late autumn helps minimize infection. The other viruses are spread by aphids, but control using insecticides is not very effective. Pull up and discard tulips infected with virus. Avoid planting tulips near lilies, which may harbour a virus without visible symptoms.

TULIP FIRE

This is caused by the fungus *Botrytis tulipae*. In damp weather the fungus produces masses of grey fungal spores,

which are spread by wind or rain. Later, the fungus forms hard, black, pinhead-sized bodies, which can remain dormant in the soil for up to two years, ready to infect the next host.

Tulip fire is first seen when the tips of infected, emerging leaves appear brown and scorched and often shrivel and rot. Brown spots appear on leaves

Symptoms of tulip fire on emerging leaves

and flowers, which sometimes also rot. The foliage then becomes covered in fuzzy, grey fungal growth. Some plants may flower, but others fail to mature, and the bulbs may rot.

Control

There is no chemical treatment for infected plants in the ground. Plant only healthy-looking bulbs. Remove any infected foliage promptly, and remove and dispose of severely infected plants, together with the soil in the immediate vicinity of the roots. Late planting may decrease the chances of the disease developing.

Do not plant tulips on the same ground for more than two years in succession, and do not replant in infested soil for at least three years. At the end of the season, lift tulip bulbs and dust them with sulphur before storing them for the winter.

Tulip fire in a flower
Buff-coloured flecks

See also Lifting and storing bulbs, p.150; Storage rots, p.150

Lifting and dividing irises

Irises will be more vigorous and flower better if divided regularly

Bulbous irises produce bulbils which can be removed and replanted when dormant. They reach flowering size in 2 to 3 years. Lift, separate, and replant congested bulbous irises in early autumn. Bearded, Siberian, and Pacific Coast irises grow from rhizomes.

Lift and divide bearded irises every few years, 6 weeks after flowering. Cut away each fan of leaves with a portion of young rhizome – up to 15cm (6in) long for tall bearded irises, smaller for dwarf or miniature types. Discard smaller fans and old rhizomes and replant large fans with healthy rhizomes. Plant rhizomes at the soil surface on heavy soils, a little below on light soils. Space them 30cm (12in) apart, or 15cm (6in) for dwarf kinds.

Divide Siberian irises shortly after flowering. Use two forks back to back through the centre, avoiding breaking the clump into very small sections. Replant young outer sections. Divide the winter-flowering *Iris unguicularis* in autumn, or after flowering in spring. Split the clump into largish sections to minimize disturbance. Pacific Coast irises dislike disturbance, so lift part of the clump in late summer when new roots have been made.

Section of rhizome
Cut the leaves at about 15cm (6in)
Dividing a bearded iris

Zantedeschia care

Versatile arum lilies can be grown in mild gardens, as a pond plant, or in pots under glass

Zantedeschias or arum lilies, *Zantedeschia aethiopica*, are South African perennials with tuber-like rhizomes. In spring or summer they produce large, pure white, petal-like spathes. All parts of the plant can cause mild stomach upsets, and the sap can be a skin irritant.

Zantedeschia elliottiana is grown under glass

Growing out of doors

Zantedeschias are not generally hardy, although the cultivar 'Crowborough' will often survive outdoors in very sheltered situations in the warmest parts of the country. Grow in a sheltered position in full sun, in fertile, moisture-retentive soil, adding plenty of organic matter, such as garden compost or leafmould, before planting. Give a thick organic mulch as winter frost protection. They may also be grown in ponds as a marginal aquatic.

Growing under glass

Zantedeschias can also be grown in pots in a greenhouse or conservatory. Providing warmth will boost growth and give earlier spring flowering. Pot in early winter, 2 or 3 rhizomes to a 23cm (9in) pot in well-drained, loam-based potting compost, so that they are just showing at the surface. Water in well and keep the compost steadily moist. Provide winter night temperatures of about 16°C (60°F), increasing to around 18°C (65°F) by day, during the early stages of growth. If you do not have a warm greenhouse or conservatory, plants tolerate a night minimum of 13°C (55°F), but rhizomes should be potted in late summer or early autumn to give them a longer growing period.

Feed established plants regularly with high-nitrogen liquid feed. Provide as much light as possible in winter, but there may be a need for some shade later to protect against strong sunshine. Stop feeding plants altogether during flowering, but resume when the flowers have faded until drying off begins. Watch for greenfly, which can be troublesome.

In late spring or early summer, gradually dry off the plants and place the pots on their sides in a greenhouse or conservatory until repotting. To repot, shake out the old compost and replant in the same type of compost. You can stand pots in the open until early or mid-autumn if there is no frost, keeping the compost moist, then bring them in. Propagate by offsets, removed when the plants are repotted. If picking for displays, pull the stems rather than cutting them, to avoid stem curling, and gather just before the petal-like bract begins to turn downwards.

Aquatic basket for planting
To grow zantedeschias in a pond, plant in a 30cm (12in) diameter aquatic basket, using aquatic-plant compost. Place in water no deeper than 30cm (12in).

See also How to create a bog garden, p.274; Choosing water plants, pp.276–277

Summer bulbs

Summer-flowering bulbs add much colour to borders

RECOMMENDED BULBS

Hardy summer-flowering bulbs can be bought in the autumn, tender kinds in late winter and spring. Potted bulbs in flower can be used for gap filling or patio display and then transferred to borders. Bulbs add colour and variety to a border without using much space, and shrubs and hedges are a good backdrop for showing them off. For large bulbs that need moist soil, avoid too much competition from surrounding plants; smaller bulbs can grow through the foliage of spring flowering plants.

Allium ‡ 15–180cm (6–72in) ↔ 8–15cm (3–6in) ▢ ◊ ✳✳–✳✳✳

Camassia leichtlinii ‡ 60–130cm (24–54in) ↔ 10cm (4in) ▢–▨ ◊ ✳✳

Cardiocrinum giganteum ‡ 1.5–4m (5–12ft) ↔ 45cm (18in) ▨ ◊ ✳✳✳

Crocosmia 40–120cm (16–48in) ↔ 8cm (3in) ▢–▨ ◊ ✳✳–✳✳✳

Dierama pulcherrimum ‡ 90–150cm (3–5ft) ↔ 60cm (24in) ▢ ◊ ✳✳

Eucomis autumnalis ♀ ‡ 20–30cm (8–12in) ↔ 20cm (8in) ▢ ◊ ✳✳–✳✳✳

Galtonia candicans ♀ ‡ 90–120cm (3–4ft) ↔ 10cm (4in) ▢ ◊ ✳✳✳

Ixia hybrids ‡ 40cm (16in) ↔ 8cm (3in) ▢ ◊ ✳

Nectaroscordum siculum ‡ 1.2m (4ft) ↔ 10cm (4in) ▢–▨ ◊ ✳✳✳

Watsonia pillansii ‡ 50–120cm (20–48in) ↔ 10cm (4in) ▢ ◊ ✳

Cardiocrinum giganteum

See Three seasons of colour, pp.110–111

TECHNIQUES

Lifting and storing bulbs

Saving bulbs for another year often means storing them

Bulbs grown in containers are often lifted so that the container can be planted with other plants for summer bedding. Many summer-flowering bulbs are tender and in frost-prone gardens need to be lifted in autumn and stored for the winter. Other bulbous plants, such as tulips, need exposure to high summer temperatures to ripen the bulbs for the following year.

It is essential not to lift bulbs too early. Leave at least 6 weeks between flowering and lifting, watering and feeding the bulbs with liquid tomato fertiliser to prolong the life of the foliage, which needs to manufacture and store sufficient reserves to enable the bulbs to flower next year.

When the foliage has died down, carefully lift and clean the bulbs.
[1] Roots can be trimmed back and the "tunic", the outer layers of loose, flaking skin, removed. Keep only healthy bulbs of a good size and discard damaged or diseased bulbs.
[2] Lay the bulbs on a tray to dry for 24 hours, then dust with sulphur, place in labelled paper bags or nets and store in a dry, airy, and cool but frost proof place.

See also Tulip problems, p.148

PLANT PROBLEMS

Storage rots

Stored bulbs, corms, and tubers can be susceptible to rots

Rotting is mainly caused by soil-borne fungi and bacteria that enter tissues through wounds made at lifting. Some may also have attacked the leaves during growth, then spread back to the storage tissues. The hard, black resting structures of botrytis fungi remain in the outer scales of the bulb and germinate to produce infective spores in the spring. Begonias, tulips, daffodils (*Narcissus*), and gladioli are particularly prone to rots.

Healthy tissues are firm and white or pink when outer scales are removed; infected tissues can be hard, brown, and shrivelled, or soft and discoloured. In damp conditions, grey (*Botrytis*) or blue-green (*Penicillium*) fungal growth may be seen. Once the storage organ is damaged, bacteria may enter and grow, emitting unpleasant smells.

Control

Lift carefully and clean off soil as far as possible without damaging the bulb. Remove outer, dead scales carefully and discard any bulbs with signs of softening or black, seed-like structures in them. Dust bulbs with sulphur dust and store in dry, cool conditions in clean and disinfected storage trays. Rots spread by contact, so leave space between bulbs. Check regularly for any sign of rot and remove affected bulbs promptly.

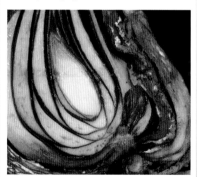
Blue mould enters through bulb wounds

See also Narcissus problems, p.146

TECHNIQUES

Dahlias and cannas

These tender perennials are grown for summer display

Dahlias and cannas are among the easiest tender plants for summer display. Dahlia tubers and the fat rhizomes of cannas are lifted and stored in winter.

Raising bedding dahlias

These dwarf dahlias are easily grown from seed. Sow in multi-purpose compost in early spring at 16°C (60°F). Prick out seedlings into individual pots and grow on under glass. Spray for aphids with insecticidal soap and trap earwigs in upturned, straw-filled pots on canes. Control powdery mildew by spraying with an approved fungicide. Lift the tubers before the first frosts, and store (*see opposite*).

Growing cannas

Cannas grow from fleshy rhizomes. In mid-spring start dormant rhizomes into growth in a frost-free greenhouse with a minimum temperature 10°C (50°F). Divide congested clumps into sections with two or three growing points. Plant into 15–20cm (6–8in) pots, using any good potting compost, so that the crown is just below the surface. Water sparingly until shoots and roots are well established, then increase watering and apply a balanced liquid feed fortnightly. Good light is vital for sturdy growth. Ideally keep at 16°C (61°F), although plants tolerate cooler conditions.

Plant out when risk of frost has passed in an open, sunny site. Enrich the soil well with organic matter and a general-purpose fertilizer before planting, and water in well. Keep well watered and apply a balanced liquid feed fortnightly throughout the season. After the first frosts, cut down the stems, lift the rhizomes and store in a frost-free place over winter. Store them in pots, covered with compost or bark, and keep just moist.

SEASONAL GUIDE TO GROWING DAHLIAS

Dahlias will grow in a wide range of soil types and situations. The best position has well drained, open-textured soil in full sun where plants do not have to compete with other bedding plants for root space; a bed specially for dahlias is ideal.

Mid- to late winter

Enthusiasts start tubers into growth in a heated greenhouse at this time. Place tubers in loam-based or soilless potting compost, with the crown above the soil surface. Water well and maintain a temperature above 10°C (50°F). Tubers take two to three weeks to produce the first shoots.

Early and mid-spring

Divide clumps if necessary when shoots are 2.5cm (1in) tall. Remove them from the compost. Each portion of split clump must contain a growing point, so separate into portions with roots, tubers, and shoots. Pot each division into a separate pot.

Alternatively, take cuttings of the new shoots. Use a sharp knife to remove the cuttings from as near to the crown as possible, dip the bases into hormone rooting powder, and insert in a mixture of equal parts peat substitute and vermiculite or perlite. Root the cuttings at 21°C (70°F), using a propagating case. Pot them individually when they have produced roots, in about two weeks.

By mid-spring begin to acclimatize plants in a cold frame ready for planting out when the frosts

Pinch out the growing tip of young plants

are over. Dormant tubers can also be planted straight into their flowering position at this time, set 10–15cm (4–6in) deep.

Late spring to early summer

When frosts are no longer a danger plant out the dahlias. About 10 days before planting, apply general-purpose fertilizer at approximately 34g per square metre (2oz per sq yd). Set out small bedding dahlias close together so they blend in with one another, but it is advisable to leave at least 60cm (2ft) between taller growing cultivars. Encourage young plants to bush out by removing the growing tip. This will promote formation of flower buds on side shoots. Support tall-growing dahlias by tying in stems to a wooden stake.

Midsummer to early autumn

Throughout the flowering season regularly remove dead and dying flowers. Mulch the soil to conserve moisture in hot and dry weather, and apply a high-potash liquid fertilizer to moist soil around the plants every fortnight.

Apply the last high-potash liquid feed at the onset of autumn. Reduce feeding and watering, to make sure that the tubers are robust enough to store well.

Mid- to late autumn and winter

Lift the tubers after the first frost, dry them and store in a cool, dry, frost-free place (see below). If dahlias are stored in a garden shed, cover the trays with a layer of sacks or newspaper when hard frost is predicted. Check the condition of the tubers every fortnight throughout the winter, and discard any that are rotting.

Leaving dahlias in the ground

For a colourful display where show-class blooms are not essential, plant tubers 10–15cm (4–6in) deep in their flowering position in late spring. After the first light frost, cut the plants back close to ground level and then leave the tubers in the ground, covered with a deep layer of bracken to protect them from the worst of the cold. This can be a risky strategy in a very cold or wet winter, but should work in the average winter, especially in milder areas or on light, well-drained soils.

Lifting and storing dahlia tubers for the winter

[1] When the first autumn frosts have blackened the foliage, cut down the stems down to about 15cm (6in) above ground level. Loosen the soil and carefully ease the tubers out.

[2] Remove excess soil from the tubers and label them. Place the tubers upside down for about three weeks in a cool, dry, frost-proof place, so that they dry off thoroughly.

[3] Store tubers in a box, covered with bark or peat substitute in a cool, dry, frost-proof place. Keep tubers dry until spring. Start under glass, or plant out when frosts have passed.

Lilies in pots

Lilies grown in pots can be used to decorate the greenhouse, conservatory, living room, or patio

Most lilies grow well in pots, although the taller types will need some support. Suitable species for containers include *Lilium auratum*, *L. formosanum*, *L. longiflorum* and *L. speciosum*. Among the hybrids, the short-growing, Asiatic Hybrids, such as 'Apollo' and 'Côte d'Azur' at 60cm (24in), and the 'Pixie' series, at just 50cm (20in) tall, are also suitable.

Planting up

Bulbs with a diameter of 10–12cm (4–5in) should be planted singly in 20–23cm (8–9in) pots; bulbs with a diameter of 5–8cm (2–3in) can be planted three or four to a 23–25cm (9–10in) pot. Always allow 5cm (2in) between the bulbs and use deep pots.

Rich, loam-based potting compost, with 20 per cent by volume each of horticultural grit and ericaceous compost or leafmould added, is suitable for most lilies. There are a few lime-haters, such as *L. auratum* and *L. speciosum*, which must have lime-free compost.

Ideally plant in early autumn, although bulbs can be planted until spring. Place a 5cm (2in) layer of drainage material, such as broken clay pots or small stones, in the bottom of the pot before starting to fill with compost. Place bulbs half-way up the pot, just covering them with compost. When their stems begin to grow, gradually fill the pot with compost to within 2.5cm (1in) of the rim.

Caring for lilies

Keep the pots in a cool but frost-free, airy place with strong light, such as a well-ventilated cold greenhouse, especially if the pots are required for indoor use. Many lilies are hardy enough to be left outside all winter in mild areas, but it may be necessary to wrap the pots with bubble plastic in severe weather.

Forcing Easter lilies
The fragrant flowers of the Easter lily (*L. longiflorum*) can be enjoyed early in the year by forcing the bulbs in heat. However, do not try to force them for a second year.

Keep the compost moist at all times, but not wet. Lilies are demanding feeders, so use a tomato fertilizer every fortnight during summer. Stake pot-grown lilies when the stems reach about 30cm (12in) high.

Following flowering, repot or transfer bulbs to the garden when the stems begin to wither, because some lilies begin new root growth after only a very short period of summer dormancy. Lilies can be grown on for a second season in larger pots but they should be top-dressed with fresh compost while dormant.

Forcing for early flowers

Some lilies are suitable for forcing into flower early, but this should only be done once. They include *L. auratum*, *L. longiflorum*, *L. speciosum*, and the Asiatic Hybrids. When shoots appear, move into the warmth of a greenhouse or conservatory. A temperature of 18–21°C (65–70°F) will ensure a good rate of development, but 13–16°C (55–60°F) is acceptable. Flowering will usually take place a few weeks after the buds appear. Bring pots into the room where you want them as soon as the first flower buds show colour.

See also Planting bulbs, p.144

Lily pests and diseases

Viral diseases, fungal rots, and pests can all attack lilies

Lilies are not difficult plants, but keep an eye on them in case they develop problems, and deal with infections and infestations early to stop their spread.

Lily beetle

Bright red lily beetles 8mm (⅜in) long (*Lilioceris lilii*) and their orange-red grubs strip the leaves of lilies and fritillaries in late spring and summer. The grubs are camouflaged by a covering of wet, black excrement. Lily beetles are best controlled on a small scale by hand picking, or where many plants are affected by applying an approved insecticide.

Lily disease

This disease is caused by a fungus, *Botrytis elliptica*, which appears as elliptical brown spots that develop on leaves during wet weather. These spots can spread and kill the leaf if the conditions remain wet. The fungus remains present in the dead leaves as

Lily beetle and grubs
During spring and summer, the bright red adults and the orange-red grubs defoliate lilies and fritillaries. The grubs camouflage themselves with excrement. Hand pick to control small numbers.

See also Avoiding pests and diseases, pp.36–37

Distortion caused by lily virus

Lily disease

black resting bodies, which produce spores the following year to re-infect lilies. Remove and destroy infected leaves promptly and avoid planting lilies where the disease has occurred. No fungicides are available to control lily disease.

Lily viruses

Several viruses attack lilies, including the widespread cucumber mosaic virus, lily mosaic and mottle viruses, and tulip-breaking virus, which also causes colour streaking in tulip flowers (*see p.148*). The symptoms of viral attack include streaking and mottling of leaves and loss of vigour in the plants.

There are no treatments for viral diseases. To minimize infections, buy only good-quality bulbs, avoid growing lilies near tulips, do not handle healthy plants after ones that may be diseased, and destroy affected plants.

TECHNIQUES

Propagating lilies

Raise species from seeds – slow but ensures vigorous, healthy plants – and hybrids from bulb scales – a quicker and easier method

All species lilies can be raised from seeds, but the garden hybrids have to be propagated vegetatively from bulb scales (*see box below*). Raising lilies from seeds is slow and requires care, but it yields vigorous and virus-free plants. Seed-raised plants take four to five years to reach flowering age.

Collect seed pods in autumn when the tops split open. Separate them from the crushed pods and sow immediately. Use a deep pot and sow thinly into a loam-based seed compost, or an ericaceous compost for lime-haters.

Cover the seeds with a layer of fine grit and stand the pots in a shaded place out of doors. Keep the seeds moist. Seeds of some lilies germinate straight away, sending up a shoot, but other lilies first form roots and then send up shoots the following spring, following a cold spell, so do not discard apparently failed pots. If germination does not take place by the following spring, keep the pots, moist and lightly shaded, for at least two years. Pot on seedling bulbs regularly when dormant, to encourage vigorous growth.

SCALING LILIES

Most lilies, particularly the hybrids, are increased by this method. It is quite easy if done in late summer so that growth can be achieved before winter.

Lift and clean a mature bulb. Discard any damaged outer scales. [1] Snap off a few scales from the bulb as close as possible to the base. [2] Shake the scales in a bag with fungicidal powder to coat them thoroughly. [3] Place the scales in a plastic bag with a mix of equal parts moist peat substitute and perlite. Fill the bag with air, seal and label it. Keep in a dark place for 6 weeks at 21°C (70°F). Some lilies, such as

Lilium martagon and North American lilies, need a further 6 weeks at 5°C (41°F) to simulate winter and stimulate bulblet production.
[4] Check regularly for new bulblets at the base of the scales. [5] Pot bulblets on individually (do not remove the scale if it has roots from the base) and cover with their own depth of compost. Use a mix of equal parts loam-based potting compost and 5mm (¼in) grit for most lilies, and ericaceous compost for lime-hating species. [6] Top the pots with grit, label, and grow on in a cool, shady place over summer, and overwinter in a cold frame.

See also Multiplying bulbs by division, pp.154–155

Multiplying bulbs by division

Division is a quick and easy method of obtaining more bulbous plants if carried out at the right time, and the offsets soon start producing flowers

The most economical way of obtaining bulbous plants is to propagate your own. Species can be raised from seeds, but vegetative propagation is best for cultivars and hybrids, to ensure they remain true to type, and for plants that do not produce seed. Divisions often give quicker results than seed-grown plants – snowdrops (*Galanthus*) and lilies can flower in two years, daffodils (*Narcissus*) and hyacinths in three.

Differing methods of propagation

Bulbs, corms, and tubers are types of underground storage organ, which enable plants to withstand a seasonal dormant period. While in growth, the leaves manufacture food to swell the storage organs and provide energy for the plant to emerge from dormancy.

Some propagation methods involve wounding or cutting up the bulb (*see p.156*), and are used when large numbers of new plants are needed.

Division, which gives fewer plants more quickly, is simpler and can be done with all plants that produce offsets, including many crocuses, daffodils,

Different types of underground storage organs

A bulb has a basal plate, in fact a compressed stem, from which roots grow, and a flower bud enclosed by fleshy, modified leaves known as scales. "Non-scaly" or "tunicate" bulbs, such as daffodils, have tight scales and a protective, papery tunic. "Scaly bulbs", such as lilies, have loose scales with no tunic. Corms, such as crocuses, are thickened stems with buds at the top, often covered with thin, fibrous scales. A new corm usually forms on top of the old one annually. Root tubers, such as dahlias, are swollen roots with buds only at the stem base. Stem tubers, such as cyclamen, are modified stems with buds on the surface. Fleshy rhizomes, for example bearded irises and cannas, are also storage organs.

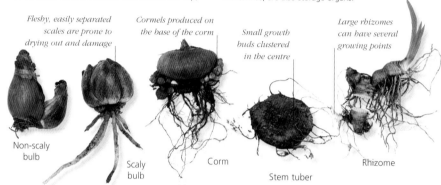

Fleshy, easily separated scales are prone to drying out and damage

Cormels produced on the base of the corm

Small growth buds clustered in the centre

Large rhizomes can have several growing points

Non-scaly bulb

Scaly bulb

Corm

Stem tuber

Rhizome

muscari, and tulips. Offsets are miniature bulbs or corms that develop while attached to the parent plant, and which can be separated to form new plants.

A similar, easy, fairly quick method is to grow on either bulbils formed on stems and in flowerheads, or bulblets formed on stems underground (*see opposite*).

When to divide

Lifting and dividing overcrowded, poorly-flowering clumps of bulbs and corms is a way of maintaining their performance, as well as a means of obtaining more plants by removing small offsets. However, some plants, such as nerines and hippeastrums, only flower well when the bulbs are tightly packed and so should only be divided for propagation.

The best time to divide most subjects is at the start of the dormant period, when leaves turn brown and die back – when this occurs varies with the type of plant – but some bulbs are best lifted when the leaves are still in growth (*see p.144*). Nerines are best divided in spring rather than after the leaves die down, to avoid damaging the flower buds. Evergreens, such as *Dierama* and *Cyrtanthus*, should be dug up straight after flowering.

Detaching offsets and growing on

After lifting the bulbs or corms, detach offsets carefully. With bulbs, offsets are usually found beneath the flaky outer

---

DIVIDING CLUMPS OF CROCOSMIA

Crocosmias form congested mats or "chains" of corms, with younger corms on top of the older ones. **1** When the foliage has died down after flowering, lift mature clumps. Dig at least 30cm (12in) down to avoid damaging the corms or roots. **2** Carefully pull the clump apart; if it is very congested, prise it apart with two forks driven in back-to-back. Remove any dead or diseased matter. **3** Tease the chains of corms apart. Pot up smaller corms in soilless potting compost to grow on for a year. Replant larger chains of corms at the same depth as before, at least 8cm (3in) apart, and water in thoroughly.

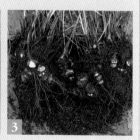

See also Bulbs in the green, p.144; Dahlias and cannas, pp.150–151; Propagating lilies, p.153; Scoring, scooping, and chipping bulbs, p.156

DIVIDING BY BULBLETS

Some lilies and many alliums produce bulblets. These are small bulbs that develop on sections of the stem beneath the soil surface. [1] Lift the parent bulb in early spring while it is dormant and remove the bulblets. [2] Plant in loam-based potting compost at twice their own depth and grow them on as for offsets. Young plants should flower in a few years.

DIVIDING BY BULBILS

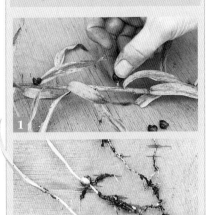

Bulbils can be found on some alliums, lilies, *Calochortus*, *Lachenalia*, and *Notholirion*. They develop in the leaf axils or on the flowerheads. [1] Gather bulbils only from disease-free plants before they fall, usually in late summer or early autumn. Pot and grow on in a cold frame until the following autumn. [2] The bulbils quickly develop roots and shoots; grow on as offsets.

THE BEST TIME TO DIVIDE

Hardy and tender plants grouped by type of underground storage organ

Bulbs

Allium late summer
Amaryllis spring
Camassia autumn
Chionodoxa autumn
Cyrtanthus spring after flowering
Erythronium autumn
Fritillaria autumn
Galanthus (in the green) spring
Hippeastrum late winter or early spring
Hyacinthus autumn
Ipheion autumn
Iris (Reticulata and Xiphium types) autumn
Lachenalia late summer or early autumn
Leucojum late summer or early autumn
Lilium (some species) early spring or autumn
Muscari autumn
Narcissus autumn
Nerine spring
Ornithogalum autumn
Scilla early autumn
Tulipa autumn
Veltheimia autumn

Corms

Colchicum late summer to autumn
Crocosmia late summer
Crocus late summer
Dierama late summer after flowering
Gladiolus autumn

Tubers

Alstroemeria late summer to autumn
Anemone mid- to late summer
Arum early summer
Corydalis (some species) autumn
Dahlia spring
Eranthis (in the green) spring
Tropaeolum spring

When to propagate by bulbils

Allium (some species) late summer
Begonia late summer or spring
Calochortus autumn
Lachenalia late summer
Lilium (some species) late summer
Notholirion (some species) late summer

When to propagate by bulblets

Allium late summer
Lilium (some species) early spring or autumn

skin and always attached to the basal plate (from which roots grow) – either around its circumference or sometimes underneath, as with tulips. Tiny corms, known as cormels, generally form around the base of the parent corm, or in long chains as with crocosmias. Bulbs and cormels are prone to rot, so dust any wounds with sulphur dust.

Sort the offsets according to size. The largest offsets, those that are already of almost flowering size, can be replanted where they are to flower, or if tender repotted one per pot. These will almost certainly flower within the year.

Grow on smaller offsets under nursery conditions. Hardy subjects can be planted in a nursery bed outdoors, but you will achieve greater control by growing them on in pots until large enough for planting out. Plant about five small offsets in a pot that will allow for some growth. They may flower within two years. Use well-drained, gritty, soil-based compost and cover most bulbs and corms with a layer of compost equalling twice their own depth. Stand hardy subjects in a cold frame, ideally with the pots plunged to their rims in coarse sand or grit. Keep well ventilated in summer. Frost-tender offsets need to be kept in a heated greenhouse or indoors over winter.

Increasing cormel production

The commercial technique of shallow planting mature corms, such as gladioli and crocuses, to increase cormel numbers is useful if many new plants are needed. Plant parent corms 2.5cm (1in) deep in a nursery bed. Cut back all flowering stems. Lift in autumn and remove all the cormels.

Store gladiolus cormels in dry compost in a frost-free place over winter and plant them 5cm (2in) apart in 2.5cm (1in) deep drills in spring. Plant crocus cormels immediately, either in a nursery bed or in pots in a cold frame. Cormels of both will reach flowering size in two to three years.

Scoring, scooping, and chipping bulbs

If you need lots of bulbs for a mass display then try these easy vegetative methods of propagation, which involve cutting bulbs into segments or cutting their bases to encourage bulblets

Bulbous plants are often needed in large numbers for impact. Scooping, scoring, and chipping are ideal for this; they are also quick, easy methods for those bulbs that do not produce many offsets for division (*see pp.154–155*).

Ensuring success
Use only disease-free bulbs, either newly bought or freshly dug from the garden. Work in hygienic, controlled conditions under cover, and clean knives regularly (*see box, right*).

Bulbs, corms, and tubers are prone to rotting, so coat with sulphur dust if fungicidal treatment is recommended during propagation to help prevent rot, particularly on wounds and cut surfaces.

Scoring and scooping
Both these methods involve wounding the basal plate of a bulb to encourage bulblets (tiny bulbs) to form; the easier

of the two is scoring. They are both suitable techniques for propagating fritillaries, hyacinths, and scillas.

These methods are carried out in late summer. To score, hold the bulb upside down and cut a V-shaped groove across it, right through the basal plate, using a sharp knife. Make one or two further criss-crossing grooves. Dust wounds with sulphur dust. Fill a small pot with moist sand and gently push the bulb into it upside down, just far enough for the sand to hold it upright. Scooping is more tricky. The centre of the basal plate is scooped out with a sterilized cutter, such as a sharpened spoon or scalpel, leaving the rim intact. Support the scooped bulb upside down in sand.

Place the pot in a warm, dry, dark place such as an airing cupboard, and bulblets will appear in two to three months. When they have formed, pot the bulb – still upside-down – in soilless

IMPORTANCE OF HYGIENE

Scrupulous hygiene is essential to prevent disease from entering the cut segments. Wear thin rubber gloves or wash your hands thoroughly, and use a sterile cutting board. The knife or scalpel should be wiped with surgical or methylated spirit, or held in a flame, between each cut.

potting compost, covering the bulblets with a thin layer of compost. Grow on in a well-ventilated cold frame. After a year, separate the bulblets and pot them individually.

CHIPPING BULBS

This involves cutting a non-scaly bulb (*see p.154*) into segments, each of which produces bulblets. It is carried out in early summer for snowdrops (*Galanthus*), late summer for alliums, daffodils (*Narcissus*), iris, nerines, and scillas. Remove the outer skin or tunic of the bulb. **1** Cut back the roots leaving the basal plate intact, then cut off the top ("nose") of the bulb. **2** Turn the bulb upside down and cut it vertically into 8 to 16 segments ("chips"), depending on the size of the bulb; each segment must have a piece of basal plate attached. **3** Shake the chips in a bag containing sulphur dust, then place them in a bag of moist vermiculite, mixing them well with the rooting medium. Keep in a warm, dark place, at a temperature of 20°C (68°F). **4** Within about three months, bulblets will form just above the basal plate. **5** Pot these up separately, covering them with about 1cm (½in) of compost. **6** Grow on in a well-ventilated cold frame or, for tender bulbs, in slightly warmer conditions under glass. Flowers should appear after two to three years.

See also Multiplying bulbs by division, pp.154–155

ANNUALS, BEDDING &
CONTAINERS

SOWING HARDY ANNUALS

Sowing hardy annuals

Hardy annuals are easy to grow and are sown where they are to flower, but you need to prepare the soil well for good results

Sow hardy annuals directly in the soil where they are to grow. They will withstand frost without protection. Most need an open, sunny position; in shade they will come into flower more slowly and flower less freely.

Annuals are most successful on medium to light soils, which warm up early in spring. They can be slow to germinate and grow away on heavier, poorly drained soils, which take longer to warm up. Annuals are not as successful on rich soil as it encourages lush growth and fewer flowers.

Start soil preparation in autumn. Roughly dig the area to be sown then leave it over winter for the weather to break the soil down. In spring fork over the area, remove any weeds, then tread lightly to settle the soil. Rich soils do not need any fertilizer, but for other soils, sprinkle 70g per sq m (2oz per sq yd) of general-purpose fertilizer over the soil and rake it in. Level the soil to make a good sowing surface.

Sow from early to late spring, depending on the area – early sowing in mild areas, later in colder regions. In milder gardens sowing may begin early and spread over several weeks; in colder gardens begin sowing later and make fewer successional sowings. If conditions are dry, water thoroughly before sowing and allow to drain.

HOW TO SOW AND THIN HARDY ANNUALS

During winter, prepare a plan for the positions of the different varieties of annuals within the area to be sown.

1 Mark out these positions on the soil just before sowing. Do this by sprinkling sand or scratching the soil with a cane to outline each sowing area. Make shallow furrows within each area with the corner of a draw hoe blade or with a cane. Vary the direction of the furrows for each variety to avoid a regimental appearance. Make the furrows 0.5–1cm (¼–½in) deep, depending on the size of the seed. Smaller seeds need to be lightly covered. Spacing between furrows depends on the eventual size of the plants, but an average of 15cm (6in) is about right.

2 Space out large seeds individually by hand. When sowing very small seeds first add some fine sand to the packet, shake well, then sow. This helps to achieve more even distribution. After sowing, rake fine soil into the furrows and firm it gently with the back of a rake.

3 Thin out seedlings as soon as they are large enough to handle, to one-quarter of their final distance apart. After a week or two thin again, to half the final spacing, and later to their final distance. If lifted carefully with a small hand fork, thinnings can be used to fill any gaps.

See also Harvesting seeds, p.174

Sowing for early blooms

Autumn-sown hardy annuals flower before spring-sown ones

If you want an early display of hardy annuals, there are some that will successfully overwinter from an early autumn sowing. Some can be sown directly in the open ground (*see box, left*), where they will withstand most frosts. Others are not quite so robust and can be sown direct in their flowering positions and covered with cloches when there is a risk of frost; alternatively, sow in pots and keep in a cool but frost-free greenhouse over winter. Unless you have a heated greenhouse, half-hardy and tender annuals are best sown in spring.

AUTUMN-SOWN ANNUALS

No protection needed in mild areas

Briza maxima, B. minor
Calendula officinalis
Centaurea cyanus
Consolida ajacis
Hordeum jubatum
Limnanthes douglasii ♀
Linum grandiflorum ♀
Nigella damascena

Some protection needed

Adonis aestivalis
Cerinthe major 'Purpurascens'
Eschscholzia californica ♀
Gypsophila elegans
Lathyrus odoratus (best sown in pots)
Lavatera trimestris
Lunaria annua
Matthiola longipetala subsp. *bicornis*
Nemophila menziesii
Papaver commutatum ♀, *P. rhoeas, P. somniferum*
Salvia viridis (best grown in pots)
Viola

Annuals for shade and fragrance

Comparatively few annuals have fragrant flowers or thrive in shade; those that do make beautiful and valuable additions to the garden

ANNUALS AND BIENNIALS FOR FRAGRANCE AND SHADE

Fragrant annuals and biennials

The few annuals that are fragrant are much sought-after and popular ingredients of cottage gardens, although they are also at home in more modern settings. Some are particularly scented in the evening, including tobacco plants (*Nicotiana*) and evening primrose (*Oenothera*).

The most fragrant of the annuals are sweet peas (cultivars of *Lathyrus odoratus*), although not all of them have scented blooms. Old-fashioned sweet peas are particularly noted for their delicious perfume.

Amberboa moschata hardy annual

Erysimum x allionii, *E. cheiri* biennial

Lathyrus odoratus hardy annual

Lobularia maritima hardy annual

Matthiola hardy annuals and biennials

Nicotiana affinis, *N. sylvestris* ♥ half-hardy annuals

Oenothera biennis hardy annual or biennial [1]

Reseda odorata hardy annual

Annuals and biennnials for shade

Several annuals and bedding plants can be grown in moderate shade, such as the dappled shade found under trees. Areas of partial shade receiving sunlight for two or three hours a day, either in the early morning or late evening, are suitable, too. However, the midday sun supplies considerably more light and therefore the conditions it creates are not ideal for these annuals.

Begonia semperflorens tender annual

Bellis perennis biennial

Campanula medium biennial

Impatiens tender annuals

Limnanthes douglasii ♥ hardy annual [2]

Linum grandiflorum ♥ hardy annual

Lunaria annua biennials

Myosotis biennials

Nemophila menziesii hardy annual

Nicotiana half-hardy annuals

Schizanthus half-hardy annuals

Tropaeolum peregrinum half-hardy annual

Viola hardy annuals and biennials

See also Raising plants from seed, pp.20–21

Buying bedding plants

Buy healthy plants and plant out when frosts are over

If you do not raise your own summer bedding plants from seed, the alternative is to buy them as young plants in trays or pots from a garden centre, ready for planting out and on the point of flowering. You can also buy bedding as smaller plants or plugs from seed companies, and you will need to pot these up when you receive them and grow them on in a frost-free greenhouse.

When buying, make sure the plants are in good condition – sturdy, well branched, with short-jointed shoots, and with healthy foliage. Also ensure that the compost is moist. Buy only plants with well-developed roots, but not those that are pot bound.

Summer bedding plants are offered for sale well before it is safe to plant them out. Before buying, ensure that you can provide suitable conditions for growing them on under cover until the danger of frost has passed. You will need to gradually acclimatize young plants to outdoor conditions, using a cold frame for several weeks before planting them out. Otherwise, delay buying.

Good and poor examples
The sturdy pansy on the left has healthy foliage and is developing flower buds. This is the one to buy. The plant on the right has fading flowers and yellowing foliage – both signs that the plant is past its sell-by date.

See also Acclimatizing tender plants, p.125

Ideas for tropical bedding displays

Planting schemes using subtropical, tender subjects, popular in Victorian times, are enjoying a resurgence in interest; there are no hard and fast rules for designing these schemes, so let your imagination run wild

You can re-create memories of a far-flung subtropical paradise in the seclusion of your own back garden. All manner of plants, tender and hardy, can be used to dramatic effect. Milder winters and the explosion in the range of tender exotics now available has enabled this style of gardening to reach new heights. Most tender subjects need planting in late spring or early summer after the risk of frost has passed, so will come into their own in summer, providing interest to mid-autumn.

There are so many ways of creating the subtropical style and the techniques can be tailored to meet your needs. You could have a small collection of potted cannas, for example, or a large-scale scheme with structural plantings of hardy ornamental trees such as catalpa and paulownia. In autumn cut these trees down so that by next summer they sprout vigorous shoots with outsized leaves. Remove weak shoots to leave the most dramatic.

Planting plans
Before planting your summer border, arrange the plants in their pots on the soil surface. This will provide a clearer idea of how the display will look when mature, and gives you the opportunity to make any adjustments to the design without disturbing the plants. Some tender plants like bananas will be quite happy if plunged into the border in their pots.

Winter planning

Plan according to the size of your plot, budget, the time available to grow and tend your material, and facilities at your disposal such as a frost-free greenhouse, conservatory, or frames to overwinter tender plants. You can still create drama by growing bulbous ginger lilies (*Hedychium*) and cannas with annuals such as spider flowers (*Cleome hassleriana*), *Nicotiana tabacum* and *N. sylvestris*, and castor oil plants (*Ricinus communis* 'Carmencita').

Tender climbers grown as annuals, such as *Cobaea scandens*, *Ipomoea lobata,* and *Dicentra scandens*, can be grown over a framework either as a backdrop or as a feature in the planting. Vegetables like aubergines, variegated maize, Swiss chard, or even some of the heirloom tomatoes with strange-shaped, odd-coloured fruit can also be used. Be bold and don't be afraid of combining strong colours. Mix foliage shapes and textures with flowers to provide structure and continuity throughout the season.

Tips for success

Choose a sunny, sheltered site. Plants perform best given warmth and water; the soil need not be too rich or fertile. Choose large specimen plants for the structural planting; small plants will not achieve sufficient stature in one season. Fill gaps with rooted cuttings or annuals to suppress weed growth. Harden off all tender plants before planting out after the last frost has passed. Water as required, daily in hot weather, and apply general-purpose fertilizer before planting to encourage growth. Remove spent flowers and support tall plants as they develop.

Hot plants
Clockwise from top left: Cleome hassleriana 'Colour Fountain', Ricinus communis 'Carmencita Pink', and Canna 'Verdi' are great for the tropical look.

Foliage effects
Mix interesting foliage shapes and textures, such as bananas (*Musa* and *Ensete*) with paddle-like leaves and *Plectranthus argentatus* with silvery-grey foliage.

See also Caring for frost-tender perennials over winter, pp.123–125; Acclimatizing tender plants, p.125

Planting in containers

When it comes to containers, size matters, as does the type of compost used and the planting time; all of these elements encourage optimum growth of your plants, provided you water and feed them regularly

Container-grown plants need more care than those grown in the open ground. Tubs restrict root growth and stronger-growing plants such as trees, shrubs, and climbers may soon show signs of this, with limited growth, smaller leaves, and below-average flowering. On the other hand, vigorous plants may flower and fruit earlier due to the restriction. With care, many plants may be grown reasonably well in containers for many years, although performance may not match those in open ground.

Containers

Many types of tubs, pots, and other containers are available and larger ones may hold several plants. When planting single plants in tubs or pots, choose a container just large enough to hold the roots without them being cramped. Small pots hold relatively little compost and tend to dry out rapidly, so move the plant on to a pot or tub one size larger as soon as the compost is well filled with roots, but only at the start of a growing season or when there are several weeks of growth ahead. Final containers of 30–45cm (12–18in) in diameter are suitable for developing shrubs and climbers. A diameter of 60cm (24in) is about the largest movable size, but permanent planters may be much larger.

Ensure there are plenty of drainage holes in the base of containers and raise them off the ground slightly on small blocks to ensure good drainage.

CONTAINER COMPOSTS AND FERTILIZERS

All proprietary potting composts contain sufficient foods for a limited period of growth. Check the maker's recommendations for feeding as some composts may include slow-release fertilizers. If there are no feeding recommendations, begin feeding four to six weeks after planting in soilless composts, or no earlier than eight weeks if using soil-based compost. From mid-spring to late summer use a general-purpose proprietary liquid fertilizer or, even better, a high-nitrogen liquid feed from mid-spring to early summer, then a low nitrogen/high potash feed in mid- and late summer. With soilless composts make sure that the liquid feed includes essential trace elements. For lime-hating plants use ericaceous fertilizer.

Soilless
Soilless compost, based on peat or peat alternatives, is ideal for short-term plantings like busy Lizzies.

Soil-based
For plants that will stay in pots for more than a year, such as hostas, use soil-based potting compost.

Ericaceous
Lime-haters like camellias need ericaceous compost. Most are soilless, but use soil-based types for permanent plantings.

Planting and aftercare

Plant permanent plants such as trees, shrubs, climbers, and hardy perennials in early spring so that they quickly put out roots and become established.

Check for moisture daily, or twice daily in hot weather, from mid-spring to early autumn and check evergreens and conifers at least weekly during the winter. Water thoroughly, filling the container to the rim and allowing the water to drain, then filling it a second time to ensure that the whole depth of compost is thoroughly moistened.

In severe winter weather the compost may freeze solid and plants may be killed unless the containers are well protected with bubble plastic or brought under temporary cover. In hot, sunny conditions containers can be wrapped with moist sacking to slow down drying out. In very wet weather move them under temporary cover if the compost becomes sodden, until it has dried out a little.

Bedding plants and annuals will benefit from feeding right through to early autumn. Feeding is not necessary during the winter and can in fact be harmful. Apply fertilizer only when the compost is moist.

Unusual containers
Plants can be grown in just about any container provided it can hold compost and allows free drainage. For example, a kitchen colander can easily be converted into a hanging basket.

See also Roof gardens and balconies, p.18; Trough and sink gardening, pp.22–23; Repotting and topdressing, pp.162–163

Repotting and topdressing

The explosion in container gardening means more plants are spending their whole lives in containers, both outdoors and indoors; you need to know how to keep them vigorous, free-flowering, and looking their best

Potting on and repotting are necessary periodically to avoid plants becoming pot-bound. This occurs when their roots have completely permeated the compost and are densely packed in the pot. The signs of a pot-bound plant are retarded and sickly looking growth, yellowing leaves, and, in the worst cases, near-permanent wilting despite regular watering. A plant pot full of roots can hold little moisture, and the irrigation water can fail to penetrate what compost is present, instead running straight down the sides of the rootball. What plant foods there are in the small volume of compost will not be available to the plant if it remains dry, leading to signs of food deficiency such as yellowing or reddening of the leaves. Ideally, potting on or repotting should be carried out before plants show these symptoms.

Potting on and repotting also provide a plant with fresh compost and a new food supply. Composts based on organic materials such as peat, peat substitutes, or bark break down into smaller pieces, which can pack together tightly. This reduces the air that the compost can hold and impedes drainage.

POTTING ON

1 Remove the plant to be potted on from its pot, here a variegated weeping fig (*Ficus benjamina*). Tease out any roots circling the base of the rootball.
2 Add fresh compost to the new, larger pot. Place the old pot inside the new one and add compost around the sides to produce a cavity the size of the rootball. 3 Remove the old pot and seat the plant in the cavity. Firm the compost around the rootball and top up with more compost if necessary.
4 When potting on is complete, mulch the surface of the compost if required (*see box, opposite*).

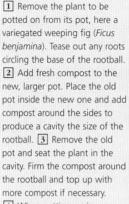
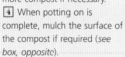

Going up

Potting on involves transferring a plant from its existing pot to a larger one, with minimal disturbance to the rootball. When potting on, select a new pot only one or two sizes bigger. Too big a pot provides a large volume of new compost that will only slowly be penetrated by roots and therefore will remain wet. This can lead to root rots. Use half pots for shallow-rooting plants such as house plants like columneas, fittonias, marantas, and pileas; for low-growing species of cacti, succulents, and alpines;

REPOTTING

1 If a larger-sized pot is unfeasible, repot into the same-sized container to help maintain vigour in mature plants. Firstly, remove the plant from its pot.

2 Gently remove outer layers of the old compost from the rootball and tease out circling roots. Prune back overlong and old roots to leave a more compact rootball.

3 Place a layer of fresh compost in the base of the pot and return the plant to it. Trickle fresh compost around the sides of the rootball and work it in well between the roots.

Standard bay tree in its final pot

See also Planting in containers, p.161; Herbs in pots, p.165; Meadows in containers, pp.166–167; Evergreens in pots, pp.168–169 and for those with naturally compact root systems such as bromeliads, orchids, ferns, and rhododendrons.

Stick to terracotta or plastic pots throughout the life of individual plants. Changes produce different growing conditions and cause a check to growth. The same applies to composts, either soilless or soil-based.

House and greenhouse plants can be potted on at virtually any time of year, but the ideal time is the start of the growing season, usually spring. Outdoor plants should be potted on in early spring, just before growth starts. Young, vigorous plants need potting on more frequently (often several times a year) than older, slower-growing ones such as cacti, succulents, and many conifers: move these on annually or biennially. To judge when to pot on, keep an eye on the plant, if necessary removing it from its pot to check the roots. Pot on when roots have completely permeated the compost but before they start to circle the pot, which can retard growth, even if the plant is not pot-bound.

Do not pot on when plants are dormant as the new compost will stay wet, which may lead to rotting of inactive roots. Aim for minimal root disturbance but tease out any spiralling roots at the bottom of the rootball.

Same-size pots

In repotting, plants are removed from their pots and a proportion of the old compost is teased from their roots (which may also be trimmed), before replanting into the same-sized pot. Repotting is particularly useful when it is impractical to pot on specimen plants due to the size of container needed. Carry out repotting at the same time of year as potting on. Aim to remove as much of the old growing medium as possible, to make room for fresh compost, while minimizing root damage. Tease out encircling roots.

Root pruning may be needed if, after untangling, the roots make repotting difficult. Pruning out some of the older,

Topdressing an established plant
Plants in larger containers can have old surface compost scraped away and replaced with fresh compost. This is best done in spring.

thicker roots leads to the production of finer, fibrous roots that absorb moisture and foods better. Between a quarter and a third of the rootball can be removed.

Frequency of repotting depends on the vigour of plants: annually for fast growers such as some bamboos, angels' trumpets (*Brugmansia*), and *Sparrmannia*, biennially for slower growers such as holly (*Ilex*) and yew (*Taxus*). Large trees and shrubs, and large, tall cacti and succulents are best grown in soil-based composts, the extra weight of which aids stability.

On the surface

Topdressing is done at the start of the growing season by replacing the top 2.5–5cm (1–2in) of compost. Small, easily handled plants can be removed from their pots and the top layer of old compost rubbed off. Return them to their pots and fill up with fresh compost. Plants in larger containers can have old compost scraped away with a spoon or narrow-bladed trowel and then replaced. A generous layer of mulch can be added at this stage (*see box, right*).

MULCHES

Mulches can be organic or inorganic, and a wide and varied range of both sorts is available. They provide an attractive finish and help to retain moisture in the compost and deter weeds. Decorative mineral mulches offer the widest choice. Once limited to gravels, which vary in colour and texture according to their geology, decorative minerals now include more unusual products such as painted gravels and coloured chippings. The newest type is glass "gravel", available in various colours.

Bark mulch is available in several grades and looks natural. It needs to be replaced when repotting as it breaks down over time.

Proprietary baked-clay granules make an attractive mulch for cacti and succulents, and ensure good drainage around the stem bases.

Moss (raked from the lawn) is an appropriate mulch for epiphytic plants such as many orchids, bromeliads and forest cacti.

Gravel ensures good drainage around the neck of plants; this is vital for plants prone to rot such as cacti, succulents, and many alpines.

Plants for patios

Many plants are ideal for growing in patio tubs and for planting in small patio beds, but as with anywhere in the garden, you need to choose plants suited to the conditions

SUNNY, DRY CONDITIONS

Shrubs

Artemisia 'Powis Castle' ♀ ‡ 60cm (24in) ↔ 90cm (36in) E ✳✳

Caryopteris x *clandonensis* 'Heavenly Blue' ‡ 90cm (36in) ↔ 1.5m (5ft) ✳✳✳

Ceanothus 'Blue Mound' ♀ ‡ 1.5m (5ft) ↔ 1.8m (6ft) E ✳✳

Cistus x *pulverulentus* 'Sunset' ♀ ‡ 60cm (24in) ↔ 90cm (36in) E ✳✳

Convolvulus cneorum ♀ ‡ 60cm (24in) ↔ 90cm (36in) E ✳✳

Hebe pimeleoides 'Quicksilver' ♀ ‡ 30cm (12in) ↔ 60cm (24in) E ✳✳

Lavandula angustifolia 'Hidcote' ♀ ‡ 60cm (24in) ↔ 75cm (30in) E ✳✳✳

Phormium cookianum subsp. *hookeri* 'Cream Delight' ♀ ‡↔ 90cm (36in) E ✳✳

Potentilla fruticosa 'Primrose Beauty' ♀ ‡ 90cm (36in) ↔ 1.5m (5ft) ✳✳✳

Artemisia 'Powis Castle'

Perennials

Dianthus 'Doris' ♀ ‡ 30–45cm (12–18in) ↔ 23–30cm (9–12in) E ✳✳✳

Geranium x *oxonianum* cultivars ‡ to 80cm (32in) ↔ 60cm (24in) E ✳✳✳

Oenothera macrocarpa ♀ ‡ 15cm (6in) ↔ 50cm (20in) ✳✳✳

Penstemon barbatus ‡ 1.8m (6ft) ↔ 30–50cm (12–20in) ✳✳✳

Sedum spathulifolium ‡ 10cm (4in) ↔ 60cm (24in) E ✳✳✳

Bulbs

Crocosmia 'Lucifer' ♀ ‡ 1–1.2m (3–4ft) ↔ 8cm (3in) ✳✳

Nerine bowdenii ♀ ‡ 45cm (18in) ↔ 8cm (3in) ✳✳✳

Sternbergia lutea ‡ 15cm (6in) ↔ 8cm (3in) ✳✳

SHADY, DRY CONDITIONS

Shrubs

Berberis buxifolia 'Pygmaea' ‡ 30cm (12in) ↔ 45cm (18in) E ✳✳✳

Cotoneaster horizontalis ♀ ‡ 90cm (36in) ↔ 1.5m (5ft) ✳✳✳

Euonymus fortunei 'Silver Queen' ‡ 2.4m (8ft) ↔ 1.5m (5ft) E ✳✳✳

Hedera helix cultivars ‡ 10–15cm (4–6in) ↔ indefinite E ✳✳–✳✳✳

Mahonia aquifolium ‡ 90cm (36in) ↔ 1.5m (5ft) E ✳✳✳

Prunus laurocerasus 'Otto Luyken' ♀ ‡ 90cm (36in) ↔ 1.5m (5ft) E ✳✳✳

Vinca minor cultivars ‡ 10–20cm (4–8in) ↔ indefinite E ✳✳✳

Mahonia aquifolium

Perennials

Alchemilla mollis ♀ ‡ 60cm (24in) ↔ 75cm (30in) ✳✳✳

Bergenia purpurascens ♀ ‡ 45cm (18in) ↔ 30cm (12in) E ✳✳✳

Brunnera macrophylla ♀ ‡ 45cm (18in) ↔ 60cm (24in) ✳✳✳

Campanula portenschlagiana ♀ ‡ 15cm (6in) ↔ 50cm (20in) E ✳✳✳

Epimedium perralderianum ‡ 30cm (12in) ↔ 60cm (24in) E ✳✳✳

Euphorbia amygdaloides var. *robbiae* ♀ ‡ 60cm (24in) ↔ 30cm (12in) E ✳✳✳

Geranium macrorrhizum ‡ 50cm (20in) ↔ 60cm (24in) ✳✳✳

Lamium maculatum cultivars ‡ 15–20cm (6–8in) ↔ 90cm (36in) ✳✳✳

Liriope muscari ♀ ‡ 30cm (12in) ↔ 45cm (18in) E ✳✳✳

Pulmonaria saccharata ‡ 30cm (12in) ↔ 60cm (24in) E ✳✳✳

Lamium maculatum

SHADY, MOIST CONDITIONS

Shrubs

Acer palmatum var. *dissectum* ♀ ‡ 1.8m (6ft) ↔ 3m (10ft) ☼ ✳✳✳

Camellia x *williamsii* 'Anticipation' ♀ ‡ 4m (12ft) ↔ 1.8m (6ft) E ☼ ✳✳✳

Fatsia japonica ♀ ‡↔ 1.5–4m (5–12ft) E ✳✳

Hydrangea macrophylla 'Altona' ♀ ‡ 90cm (36in) ↔ 1.5m (5ft) ✳✳✳

Perennials

Ajuga reptans ‡ 15cm (6in) ↔ 60–90cm (24–36in) E ✳✳✳

Alchemilla mollis ♀ ‡ 60cm (24in) ↔ 75cm (30in) ✳✳✳

Anemone nemorosa ♀ ‡ 8–15cm (3–6in) ↔ 30cm (12in) ✳✳✳

Astilbe x *arendsii* 'Fanal' ♀ ‡ 60cm (24in) ↔ 45cm (18in) ✳✳✳

Convallaria majalis ♀ ‡ 23cm (9in) ↔ 30cm (12in) ✳✳✳

Helleborus x *hybridus* ‡↔ 45cm (18in) ✳✳✳

Hosta species and cultivars ‡↔ variable, ✳✳✳

Tolmiea menziesii 'Taff's Gold' ♀ ‡ 30–60cm (12–24in) ↔ 90cm (36in) E ✳✳✳

Tricyrtis formosana ♀ ‡ 80cm (32in) ↔ 45cm (18in) ✳✳✳

Viola cornuta ♀ ‡ 15cm (6in) ↔ 40cm (16in) E ✳✳✳

Ajuga reptans

Bulbs

Eranthis hyemalis ♀ ‡ 5–8cm (2–3in) ↔ 5cm (2in) ✳✳✳

Galanthus nivalis ♀ ‡↔ 10cm (4in) ✳✳✳

Muscari armeniacum ♀ ‡ 20cm (8in) ↔ 5cm (2in) ✳✳✳

Narcissus cyclamineus hybrids ‡ 20–30cm (8–12in) ↔ 8cm (3in) ☼ ✳✳✳

See also Trees in containers, p.59; Climbers in pots, pp.96–97; Meadows in containers, pp.166–167; Evergreen shrubs in pots, pp.168–169

Herbs in pots

A few fresh herbs within easy reach of the kitchen can make a big difference to cooking; try growing herbs that will be used in the same saucepan together in one patio container

While most gardeners and all keen cooks know which herbs to use for a chilli con carne, a curry, or a pasta dish, few grow them together. By planting the herbs used in Mexican, Indian, or Italian cookery in one container they become even more convenient for cooks and make an attractive patio feature.

Most herbs are perfect container plants; they love the free-draining conditions that can be created and many are happy to nestle up to other plants. Regular clipping will keep them small and bushy.

The vigour of the plants in these pots is not perfectly matched; some will grow faster than others and need cutting back more often. Any that do not like competition or are particularly vigorous (such as mint) can be planted in separate pots to be placed alongside or plunged into the main herb container. All these pots will need replanting after a few years, and some plants such as coriander will need annual replacement.

Mexican

The most important ingredients in Mexican cookery are fresh coriander (*Coriandrum sativum*) and chilli (*Capsicum annuum*). Other well-known herbs widely used to flavour Mexican dishes include basil (*Ocimum basilicum*), tarragon (*Artemisia dracunculus*), and bay (*Laurus nobilis*).

Some less well-known herbs will add unusual tastes of Central America. Trailing *Satureja douglasii* is known as *yerba buena* ("good herb"), and has a mint-like taste that is particularly good with beans and onions or made into a tea. As lots of chocolate is used in Mexican cooking you could include Mexican marigold (*Tagetes lucida*), which has a sweet, liquorice taste and is used in chocolate dishes. It can also be used instead of tarragon.

Indian

As in Mexican cooking, Indian cooking is dominated by coriander and chilli. The strong aniseed flavours of fennel (*Foeniculum vulgare*) are also important,

Hot and spicy: an Indian pot

as is bay. Golden-leaved *Laurus nobilis* 'Aurea' adds a splash of colour but is vigorous, so could be grown in its own container. Curry leaf (*Murraya koenigii*) is an essential part of cookery in India, where the fresh leaves are almost always used in preference to dried powder. It is not often grown in Britain, perhaps because it needs a really warm, sheltered spot to thrive. Ordinary basil could be used, but holy basil (*Ocimum tenuiflorum*) is native to India and has a hot, spicy flavour.

Italian

Rosemary (*Rosmarinus officinalis* Prostratus Group) and Spanish sage (*Salvia lavandulifolia*) will trail over the sides of a pot. Basil (*Ocimum basilicum*) has a reputation for being a difficult plant so may need to be grown in its own pot and watered carefully in the morning. *Origanum vulgare* subsp. *hirtum* 'Greek' is a particularly strong-tasting oregano with a compact habit that makes it perfect for containers. Flat-leaved parsley (*Petroselinum crispum* var. *neapolitanum*) is also widely used in Italian cookery.

PLANTING AN ITALIAN HERB POT

1 Herbs need plenty of drainage, but pots can dry out quickly. Put pieces of broken clay pot into the base of the container and fill with soil-based potting compost. Add the plants and firm the compost around them. **2** Add a mulch of gravel to stop the crowns of the herbs from rotting off. **3** Keep the pot in a sheltered, frost-free spot in full sun. Make sure it is watered regularly – sparingly at first, then more thoroughly. Clip plants regularly.

See also Growing herbs in paving, paths, and walls, pp.126–127; Planting in containers, p.161

Meadows in containers

Capturing the diversity and informal beauty of wild meadows is a challenge on a large scale, let alone in pots, but micro-meadows of annuals and grasses with a range of characteristics can be achieved

Ever since people first tilled the soil and cultivated land to feed family and stock, meadows have been an integral part of human civilization. Their agricultural origins and purpose aside, meadows have also long been valued for their intrinsic beauty, inspiring artists, musicians, and gardeners alike. Who has not been captivated by the exuberance of old hay meadows, or been dazzled by red rashes of poppies welling up through verdant seas of corn? Over millennia we have built a strong spiritual affection for meadows of all kinds, and recently have acknowledged their importance as a refuge for wildlife.

Lamentably these complex communities of grasses and associated flowering plants are fast disappearing. It is not surprising then that gardeners might wish to capture a little of their essence in towns and cities, perhaps as a romantic notion of a cherished bygone age, or as an attempt to connect with nature as we see it from our doorstep.

In recent years there has been significant interest in creating meadow-like plantings in domestic spaces. But not all gardeners have the room or inclination to devote garden space to permanent mass plantings of this kind.

Annuals can short-circuit the process, being ideally suited to container work.

A study in electric green and blue
This beautiful and natural-looking container includes *Cerinthe major* 'Purpurascens', *Centaurea cyanus* 'Blue Diadem', *Salpiglossis* 'Kew Blue', *Delphinium ajacis* 'Frosted Skies', *Anagallis monellii*, *Elymus magellanicus*, *Bupleurum rotundifolium* 'Green Gold', and *Nicotiana* 'Lime Green'.

By mixing suitable species and cultivars of hardy and half-hardy flowers and grasses you can create dazzling combinations that simply mimic a cornfield or meld together exhilarating colours, shapes, and textures. All can be retuned or substituted each year to suit your changing needs. Why not try the micro-meadows shown here?

Plants to try

To look natural, think natural. Choose, in the main, hardy and half-hardy annuals that have not had their wild ancestry and character bred out of them. Avoid dwarf or compact types, variegated leaves, or over-enlarged or fussy double flowers. Mixtures can work, their differing heights and colours reflecting the diversity of nature, but their suitability will depend largely on the plant in question.

Ornamental annual grasses in individual rather than mixed packets are better for this purpose as mixtures often contain too many species and hold the risk of being visually unpredictable.

Think through your idea first and set a brief defining your objectives – do you want to create a cornfield or something more ambitious using colour, form, or texture? Some grasses and flowers will form the backbone of the scheme and define its character, while others will be used more sparingly as highlights. Then decide when you want the plants to bloom: together in a splash of colour, or at different times to prolong the season of interest? Some grasses and annuals also produce beautiful seedheads or burnished tones as they die in autumn; these are dramatic backlit by sunlight.

Meadow schemes to provide colour and interest from spring to autumn
Above left: Normal and compact forms of *Lagurus ovatus* with dwarf *Helichrysum monstrosum* 'Bright Bikini Mixed'. *Above centre:* An emerging cornfield of *Triticum spelta* (wheat) blazes from late spring with *Roemeria refracta*, *Lupinus aridus* 'Summer Spires', and *Scabiosa stellata*. *Above right:* This mix includes *Panicum miliaceum*, *Agrostis nebulosa*, *Cosmidium burridgeanum*, and *Rudbeckia* 'Cherokee Sunset'.

Try to match the vigour of the plants; mass less competitive subjects in larger numbers, and position small and trailing types at the edge of arrangements. Search through many different seed catalogues, listing choices that meet your needs. The overall number of plants used will depend on the size of pot and the objective. Smaller or simple plantings may have two to three subjects, while larger plots or half-barrels may take six different plants or even more.

Ideas you could try in containers include: a corn meadow with poppies and wild lupins; a planting with electric-blue and green foliage and flowers (you could cheat a little here and include clumps of *Elymus magellanicus*, a perennial blue grass); a high-summer and autumn meadow with golden and russet tones; a feature comprising white flowers and pale seedheads; and a vegetable meadow featuring tomatoes, beans, and strawberry spinach.

Growing techniques

Sowing in modules is much easier than direct sowing, allowing plugs of young plants to be arranged to create specific effects. Smaller or slender annuals including anagallis or cosmidium can be patch sown or planted in clumps to form more substantial displays.

Don't be too ambitious with the number of plants grown; a propagator full of seedlings soon becomes a greenhouse bursting at the seams. Start hardy annuals from late winter onwards,

Dying splendour in late summer
In late summer the globular papery seedheads of *Scabiosa stellata* counterpoint the whiskered ears of wheat, both in faded, mellow colours and backlit by low evening sunlight (*see scheme opposite, centre*).

while you probably need to start half-hardy types such as salpiglossis later if there is not the warmth to sustain them early in the year. Avoid overfeeding as this will result in leggy, weak growth that is prone to collapse.

For best results use a soilless compost rather than soil-based, which is too heavy in texture. Improve the drainage of large volumes of compost in tubs and barrels by mixing in horticultural grit or

perlite and drill out drainage holes in barrels with a router drill, making six or eight holes per barrel. Position them empty as they will be too heavy to move when planted. Fill the container and lightly firm the compost.

When the planting is complete, water the plants in and keep them moist, especially those in smaller pots because they dry out more quickly. As at the growing on stage, avoid overfeeding, but if some plants look starved, dribble in small quantities of dilute (quarter-strength) tomato fertilizer.

Most plants will support each other, but tall plants at the edges of containers will need staking, or strong winds and rain will eventually take their toll, leaving tubs of bedraggled plantings in their wake. Pea sticks of willow or hazel will hold the plants more securely and less obtrusively than cane and twine. If you are not growing plants for their seedheads, pick off spent flowers to encourage the plants to flower again, continuing the display.

ARRANGING PLANTS IN A MICRO-MEADOW

Position the backbone plants of your composition, such as the main flowering plants or grasses, in clumps or as individuals, allowing others to be woven in. Keep the most vigorous and tallest towards the centre of the container and work in the smaller and weakest plants towards the outside, where they will have more space and receive more light to perform. Thin, adjust spacing, and add spares if necessary as the plants begin to mesh together.

EVERGREEN SHRUBS IN POTS

Evergreen shrubs in pots

Some of the most beautiful evergreen shrubs can be grown in containers on the patio or terrace, giving permanent structure to the garden and overcoming problems with unsuitable garden soil

Evergreen shrubs can bring an added dimension to the garden when used in containers, particularly on patios where they help to soften the hard geometry of the paving.

Flowering evergreens

Evergreen shrubs that also produce displays of flowers are really treasured. Many of the most attractive and valuable flowering evergreen shrubs belong to the heather family, *Ericaceae*. For the most part they prefer to have their fine, fibrous roots in moist, acid, peaty soils. Lime or chalk in the soil will produce a characteristic yellow pallor to the leaves, and weak, sickly growth. This makes many of them ideal for growing in pots of lime-free (ericaceous) compost – a real bonus if you have limy or chalky garden soil.

Of the many rhododendrons that are worth trying, hybrids of *R. yakushimanum*, such as 'Aloha', are some of the best for pot culture. Most "yaks" have a compact, mounded habit with dark leaves, some cobwebby, others with a rusty, felty surface on the reverse. In late spring and early summer they burst into blossom with clusters of bell-like flowers in shades varying from red and pink through to cream and white.

Recent breeding work on the calico bush (*Kalmia latifolia*) has seen an increase in the range of flower colours, from the rich maroon of *K. latifolia* 'Ostbo Red' to the banded white flowers of 'Bullseye'. All produce heads of chalice-shaped flowers.

Of all the members of the heather family with white pitcher-shaped flowers, the strawberry tree (*Arbutus unedo*) is one of the best. It produces peeling red bark on gnarled, twisted branches, and is sprinkled with white blossom and spherical red, marble-like fruits in mid- to late autumn when little

Quality flowering evergreens
Hybrids of *Rhododendron yakushimanum*, such as 'Aloha' (*far left*), are excellent for pot culture as they have a compact, mounded habit and flower in late spring and early summer. The dwarf *Arbutus unedo* 'Compacta' (*left*) has real presence and quality, with both white, pitcher-shaped flowers and red fruits in mid- to late autumn.

else is performing. If possible, choose dwarf cultivars such as *A. unedo* 'Compacta' or the even daintier but rarer *A. unedo* 'Elfin King'.

The secret to success with all lime-hating evergreens grown in containers is to keep the compost moist at all times (but not waterlogged) and use an ericaceous fertilizer. All prefer to grow in semi-shade, rather than hot, dry places.

Camellias also love moist, acid soils and dappled shade and, when happy, will reward with a wonderful display early in the year. For the best results, avoid placing them in an exposed or bright, sunny position where frosted flowers will be more easily damaged. *Camellia x williamsii* cultivars such as 'Anticipation' are recommended.

Evergreens for sun

Berry-bearing hollies can make valuable container plants (as long as you place them in a position where they are not brushed against) and grow in sun or shade. Choose robust, ideally compact-growing cultivars and remember that most hollies are separate-sex plants, and that females need a male tree nearby to cross-pollinate. To confuse things further, those with female names are not always female, so check before buying. Variegated cultivars give colour all year round. Female cultivars to use include *Ilex aquifolium* 'J.C. van Tol' (elliptical leaves) and 'Alaska' (spiny leaves), and *I. x altaclerensis* 'Golden King' with gold-margined leaves. *I. x altaclerensis* 'Lawsoniana' is an

Magnolia grandiflora 'Little Gem'

Daphniphyllum teijsmannii

See also Growing trees in containers, p.59; The best evergreen shrubs, p.78; Planting in containers, p.161; Repotting and topdressing, pp.162–163

Viburnum odoratissimum

attractive variegated female holly, relatively non-spiny, and, like most hollies, can be trained and clipped into shapes from cones and pyramids to standards. Containerized hollies should be kept moist in summer and given controlled-release fertilizer each year, but are best kept for only a few years in a pot then planted out.

For a hot, sunny spot, try floriferous and durable Mexican orange blossom (*Choisya ternata*), with glossy, three-fingered leaves and sweetly scented white flowers. Golden-leaved *C. ternata* Sundance ('Lich') glows with colour in summer and turns lime-green in winter. *Choisya* 'Aztec Pearl', a cross with *C. arizonica*, is more delicate in appearance and produces abundant white flowers over a long period. Dainty, glossy pittosporum leaves, in colours from yellow to near black, are another alternative for pots in full sun.

Unusual evergreens

A legion of beautiful evergreens from around the world is available from specialist nurseries. Some are tender and only suitable for mild climates, or need winter protection or a sheltered position against a wall, all facilitated by growing them in pots. Others are fully hardy but because they look exotic and tender, remain rarely grown.

Among magnolias is a small cultivar of North American *M. grandiflora*. Slow-growing 'Little Gem' ultimately reaches only 1.8m (6ft) high – less in a pot – and sporadically produces characteristic white flowers in high summer with a captivating lemon scent. It loves to bask in full sun in a sheltered position.

Once seen, *Crinodendron hookerianum* is never forgotten. Hailing from Chile, the whole shrub becomes festooned with waxy red lanterns in late spring – a plant in full flower is an awe-inspiring sight. To get the best from it, grow it in lime-free compost, keeping the roots moist, and place the pot in a semi-shaded site.

Also from South America is *Drimys winteri*, commonly known as Winter's bark. This stately, frost-hardy evergreen has leathery, lance-shaped leaves and umbels of sweetly scented white flowers nestling among the foliage over a long

season from spring onwards. The slow-growing, dwarf, high-altitude variety *D. winteri* var. *andina* is a better prospect for more general use.

More substantial in leaf and effect, *Daphniphyllum himalaense* subsp. *macropodum*, from Japan and China, is a first-class shrub of rounded form with whorls of red-stalked, oval, dark green leaves. From higher elevations is *D. teijsmannii*, which, given shelter, is fairly fast growing.

From closer to home, mock privet (*Phillyrea angustifolia*) is an attractive, small Mediterranean shrub that produces tiny, sweetly scented green flowers in spring.

Strong-growing *Viburnum odoratissimum*, whose distribution includes India and China, is ultimately a large shrub with thick, glossy leaves, but can be kept in a pot for several years. It has scented white flowers.

UNDERPLANTING EVERGREENS

The surface of the compost of potted plants can look unsightly. Although it is a useful visual indicator for watering, the compost can become colonized by weeds, moss, or liverworts. Underplanting is one option, but its success hinges on balancing the growth characteristics of the plants being partnered, the aspect of the pot, and the amount of space available in the container. Whether for sun or shade, the ideal perennial ground cover will be low growing, tufted without being too dense or vigorous, and, ideally, shallow rooting.

Planting partners
This clipped box is festooned with a nasturtium. Although vigorous, nasturtiums tolerate drought, thrive in poor soils, and provide a splash of colour.

Black-leaved *Ophiopogon planiscapus* 'Nigrescens' can be planted under *Chamaerops humilis* var. *argentea*. Both revel in sunny conditions.

Windowbox and hanging basket plants

Try some new and different plants in your windowboxes and hanging baskets to give you colour and interest all year, or even an edible display

IDEAS FOR SUMMER HANGING BASKETS

Although hanging baskets can be permanently planted with dwarf shrubs, or with winter- and spring-flowering perennials and bulbs, they are most often used for summer-flowering half-hardy annuals and tender perennials, and sited in sunny, sheltered positions.

Centre of basket

Antirrhinum majus, *Begonia* (tuberous cultivars), *Dahlia* (dwarf bedding cultivars), *Dianthus chinensis*, *Diascia*, *Fuchsia* (upright habit), *Gazania*, *Iberis umbellata*, *Nemesia strumosa*, *Nicotiana alata* (dwarf cultivars), *Osteospermum*, *Pelargonium* (zonal), *Salvia splendens*, *Zinnia elegans* (short cultivars)

Middle of basket

Ageratum houstonianum, *Anagallis* 'Skylover', *Begonia* Illumination Series, *Begonia semperflorens*, *Brachyscome iberidifolia* 'Purple

Splendour', *Erigeron karvinskianus* ♀, *Impatiens walleriana*, *Isotoma axillaris*, *Linaria maroccana*, *Lobularia maritima*, *Matthiola longipetala* subsp. *bicornis*, *Portulaca grandiflora*, *Solenostemon*, *Tagetes patula*, *T. tenuifolia*, *Verbena* x *hybrida* (trailing cultivars), *Viola*

Outside edges

Fuchsia (trailing cultivars), *Glechoma hederacea* 'Variegata', *Hedera helix*, *Helichrysum petiolare* ♀, *Lobelia erinus* cultivars, *Lysimachia nummularia* 'Aurea' ♀, *Pelargonium* (ivy-leaved and balcony types), *Petunia* Surfinia Series, *Sanvitalia procumbens*, *Scaevola*, *Sutera cordata* 'Snowflake', *Thunbergia alata*, *Tropaeolum majus*

Hot basket
Above right: This basket is packed full of summer colour, provided by such plants as mimulus, *Tradescantia zebrina*, pansies, and *Lobularia maritima*. The secret of creating such a ball of colour is to plant closely and in the sides of a wire hanging basket.

Pink scheme
Above left: To create this colourful scheme in bright and pale shades of pink you will need diascias, annual phlox, verbenas, lobelias, and ivy-leaved pelargoniums. As with the hot basket, plant generously in the top and through the sides.

IDEAS FOR WINDOWBOXES

Planting for winter and spring

Plant out winter windowboxes as soon as the first frosts have damaged summer bedding, or up to mid-autumn. Prolonged frost will freeze the compost, preventing water uptake by plants and causing desiccation. Under prolonged wet conditions, particularly with inadequate drainage, roots may rot, which will cause the plants to die. In extreme conditions move the boxes to a greenhouse if possible.

HARDY PERENNIALS

Aubrieta (trailing) ▣, *Bellis perennis* cultivars ▣–▧, *Lysimachia nummularia* 'Aurea' ♀ ▣–▧, *Myosotis alpestris* ▣–▧, *Primula denticulata* ♀ and cultivars ▣–▧, *Primula* 'Wanda' ♀ ▣–▨, *Pulmonaria angustifolia* ♀ ▣–▨, *Viola* 'Prince Henry' ▣–▧, *V.* 'Prince John' ▣–▧

HARDY BULBS

Dwarf daffodils ▣–▧, crocuses ▣, winter aconite ▣–▧, dwarf irises ▣, tulips ▣, hyacinths ▣–▧, grape hyacinths ▣

HARDY SHRUBS AND CLIMBERS

Erica carnea cultivars ▣, *Euonymus fortunei* 'Emerald Gaiety' ♀ ▣–▧, *E. fortunei* 'Emerald 'n' Gold' ♀ ▣–▧, *Hedera helix* cultivars ▣–▨, *Santolina rosmarinifolia* ▣

SHORT-TERM BEDDING PLANTS

Erysimum cheiri and cultivars ▣, *Myosotis sylvatica* ▣–▧, *Primula* Crescendo Series (polyanthus) ▣–▧, *Viola* (winter-flowering cultivars) ▣–▧

Planting for summer

Plant out as soon as danger of frost is past: late spring in mild areas, early summer in colder ones.

PLANTS 20–30CM (8–12IN) TALL

Antirrhinum majus ▣ ☀, *Dahlia* (dwarf bedding cultivars) ▣ ☀, *Fuchsia* (many) ▣–▧ ☀, *Gazania* ▣ ☀, *Nemesia strumosa* ▣ ☀, *Osteospermum*

Winter windowbox
This box features ornamental cabbages with showy red centres, interplanted with winter-flowering pansies. Variegated ivies trail over the edges.

Summer window box
In this windowbox black-flowered pansies contrast with a white *Sutera cordata*, which spills over the edges. *Stachys byzantina* is used in the centre.

See also Care of container and hanging basket plants, p.172; Environmentally friendly basket liners, p.173

GOOD ENOUGH TO EAT

Herb baskets

A selection of less vigorous herbs in a basket is ornamental and useful. Include chives, summer savory, parsley, winter savory, thyme, sage, feverfew, oregano, pennyroyal, lemon balm, hyssop, salad burnet, and rosemary.

Vegetable baskets

A selection of dwarf, trailing vegetables is the most useful in the limited root space. Try dwarf French beans, cherry tomatoes, ridge cucumbers, courgettes, and mangetout.

Fruit basket
Almost any cultivar of strawberry crops well in hanging baskets. Plant in late summer and overwinter plants in a cool greenhouse.

◻ ✳, *Pelargonium* (zonal, regal, ivy-leaved) ◻–◻ ◈, *Petunia* ◻ ✳, *Salvia splendens* ◻ ✳, *Zinnia haageana* 'Persian Carpet' ◻ ✳

PLANTS 10–20CM (4–8IN) TALL

Ageratum houstonianum ◻ ✳, *Begonia semperflorens* ◻–◻ ◈, *Impatiens walleriana* ◻ ◈, *Limnanthes douglasii* ♀ ◻ ✳✳✳, *Linaria maroccana* ◻ ✳✳✳, *Lobelia erinus* ◻–◻ ✳, *Lobularia maritima* ◻ ✳✳✳, *Malcolmia maritima* ◻–◻ ✳✳✳, *Matthiola longipetala* subsp. *bicornis* ◻ ✳✳✳, *Phlox drummondii* ◻ ✳✳, *Tagetes patula* ◻ ✳, *T. tenuifolia* ◻ ✳, *Tropaeolum majus* ◻ ✳, *Verbena* x *hybrida* ◻ ✳, *Viola* (pansy) ◻–◻ ✳✳✳

TRAILING PLANTS

Fuchsia (many) ◻–◻ ◈, *Glechoma hederacea* 'Variegata' ◻–◻ ✳✳✳, *Hedera helix* cultivars ◻–◻ ✳✳–✳✳✳, *Helichrysum petiolare* ♀ ◻ ✳, *Lobelia erinus* (some) ◻–◻ ✳, *Lysimachia nummularia* 'Aurea' ♀ ◻–◻ ✳✳✳, *Pelargonium* (ivy-leaved) ◻ ◈

Sowing and training sweet peas

Sweet peas are easy to raise from seeds in autumn or spring; autumn-sown ones, if grown well, will make robust, early-flowering plants

SOWING SWEET PEAS

Sweet peas may be sown in pots in autumn, but if you miss this period sow during mid- or late winter. Alternatively, sow them in their final flowering positions in late spring.

1 Sow seeds at intervals in a tray, or five seeds in a 13cm (5in) pot, or individual seeds in modules. Use multipurpose compost, or soil-based potting compost with added perlite. Firm the compost, press the seeds in to a depth of 2.5cm (1in), and water in. Keep at 12–18°C (54–65°F) until the seeds germinate. To assist germination where the seed coat is hard, chip or soak the seeds: use a sharp knife to nick the seed coats or leave them overnight on damp kitchen paper prior to sowing.

2 When seedlings are about 3.5 cm (1½in) high move to individual 7cm (3in) pots, using soilless or soil-based potting compost. Keep seedlings in a well-ventilated cold frame. Pinch out the growing tips of autumn-sown seedlings when they are about 10cm (4in) high to encourage branching. Pinch spring-sown seedlings just above the first pair of leaves. Plant out overwintered plants in mid-spring, and spring-sown plants in late spring. Choose a sunny, open, well-drained, humus-rich site.

3 For garden display or cutting, use traditional pea sticks, or construct wigwams from canes, and encourage the plants to scramble up and over their supports.

Training sweet peas
For top-quality blooms, train plants as cordons. This involves training them as single-stemmed plants to individual canes, and removing sideshoots and tendrils.

CARE OF CONTAINER AND HANGING BASKET PLANTS

Care of container and hanging basket plants

Bedding plants in containers rely on you totally for water, foods, and general good health; they will repay your care by blooming prolifically throughout the summer and into autumn

The bigger the leaf area of the plants in your containers, the more water they need. Windy and sunny conditions increase the amount of water loss from foliage. Porous terracotta pots also lose water through their sides. Lining them with plastic sheeting reduces this loss, but the amount of water saved is insignificant compared to losses through foliage.

Fine composts hold on to more water than coarse ones. Water-holding gels are unlikely to increase the moisture content of fine composts by very much, but they will help where coarser ones are being used.

Composts and feeding

Soil-based composts are heavy and ideal where tall plants are being grown as they provide stability. Their clay content helps them to hold on to moisture and foods, resulting in better plant growth. Soilless multipurpose composts tend to be fine and may pack down in large containers, leading to airless, soggy soil that cannot support good root growth. You could try adding up to 25 per cent by bulk of coarse grit or fine gravel.

Composts lose their structure over time as the organic ingredients decay. They may support one season's growth, but plants may fail later. Shrubs and trees that stay in a pot for months or years are especially vulnerable. When it is no longer convenient to repot them every year into a bigger pot, they should be removed from their pots, up to one-third of compost and roots removed, and each repotted in the same pot using fresh compost.

Compost can hold only a certain amount of fertilizer. Adding more in the growing season tops up plant foods, but you may find it more convenient to use a controlled-release fertilizer at the start of the season.

CREATING GOOD DRAINAGE

Use open composts and containers with plenty of drainage holes. An electric drill with a wood or masonry bit can be used to make more holes in plastic or earthenware pots. Broken clay flower pots in the bottom of containers don't help with drainage but may help to prevent compost from being washed out. Layers of gravel interrupt the upward flow of water in the pot and may actually decrease drainage and reduce available water. It is better to use compost throughout the depth of the pot and prevent soil from being washed out with a layer of fine mesh or old fleece over the drainage holes. Where water lies on the ground, keep the bottom of the pot out of the water by standing it on pot "feet".

Pot feet

Broken pot pieces to stop compost washing away

Keep hanging baskets flowering

If your hanging baskets become thin, straggly, and lacking in flowers by late summer aim to improve plant growth and encourage more flower buds.

If you have not deadheaded your plants, the development of seedheads will have seriously hampered the growth of further flower buds. So trim back the

Deadheading to encourage flowers
Rather than waiting for flowering to cease, carry out regular deadheading of plants such as petunias to encourage more flower buds and therefore continuous flowering. Cut or pinch off the spent flowerheads.

plants to remove all seed-bearing growth. Then feed them weekly with a balanced liquid fertilizer to stimulate new growth and keep it healthy. Later, switch to a high-potash liquid feed, such as tomato fertilizer, to encourage the production of flower buds.

Well-fed, vigorously growing plants are better able to cope with pests and diseases. Removing old and dying foliage also helps reduce troubles and improves growth.

If you cannot keep up with watering, try moving hanging baskets to a shadier spot. Use cut-down plastic drinks' bottles as funnels to direct water down into the soil of the basket, preventing it running off the surface. These can be hidden in the foliage at the top of the basket.

Finally, look at the causes of hanging baskets failing to perform well and make a note of preventative action for next year, such as using larger baskets, adding controlled-release fertilizer, choosing plants that need less water, and deadheading regularly.

See also Repotting and topdressing, pp.162–163; Water-storing gels, p.174; Controlled-release fertilizers, p.174

Environmentally friendly basket liners

Traditional wire hanging baskets have to be lined to retain the compost, and sphagnum moss has long been the first choice of lining, but there are lots of other more interesting materials that can be used

Many gardeners find that moss raked from the lawn is ideal for lining hanging baskets. It is just as effective as shop-bought sphagnum moss. Other materials can also be used to create different effects. Straw mellows to a golden-brown colour with age and has a rustic appeal. Maple leaves turn to a chestnut-brown colour.

Leaves to try
Foliage of broad-leaved bamboos, such as *Sasa palmata* (*far left*) mellow in colour over the summer. Fern leaves (*centre*) offer an intricate and flexible lining. Fatsia leaves (*left*) turn a pleasing light brown shade.

Bright ideas

Be creative and bold with your choice of leaves and you may be surprised at their performance as environmentally friendly and natural basket liners, although the baskets may require more frequent watering. You may even find you set a trend in your neighbourhood for intriguing and unusual hanging basket displays.

Leaves are first arranged inside the baskets to provide a layer of lining without gaps. Then a circle of plastic sheeting needs to be placed in the base to help retain water, as leaf-lined

baskets dry out more quickly than those with more solid liners. Mix water-retaining granules with the compost to reduce this problem. Leaves hold the compost well but it is not usually possible to plant through the sides of the basket as it is with a traditional moss liner. Each leaf will age differently, creating enough interest over the season to compensate for the lack of planting in the sides of the basket.

Bamboo, fern, fatsia, phormium, and *Gunnera manicata* leaves can all be used as liners for hanging baskets, along

with numerous others, each offering different combinations of shape, strength, flexibility, and colour.

Leaves of the bamboo *Sasa palmata* soften to pale beige over summer and they soon perfectly complement the pastels of a planting of lavenders, phlox, lobelias, and petunias.

Only fern leaves are flexible enough to allow planting through the sides of the basket. Start by putting a few leaves across each other at the base of the basket. Place a circle of plastic sheeting on top of the basket base to act as a water reservoir and weigh it down with a couple of handfuls of compost. Then plant a layer of trailing plants such as lobelias. Gradually build up around the side of the basket using further alternate layers of fern leaves and trailing plants. Alternatively, use the fern leaves to create a solid basket liner and plant it up with autumnal colours. These will complement the fern leaves, which turn a rich brown as they age.

CREATING A PHORMIUM LINER

1 Place phormium leaves at right angles to each other to form a good coverage for the basket. The strong, fleshy leaves contain so much water that they shrink as they dry, which can leave soil exposed and prone to drying out. To counteract this, place a plastic

liner inside the layer of leaves before adding the compost. **2** Cut off overlong ends of the leaves, but allow extra for shrinkage. **3** Phormium-lined baskets look good when planted with bold colours to echo the strong variegation of the leaves.

Leaves can make a woven liner

Trimming gunnera
Gunnera leaves can be fed through the wire basket then have their stems cut off. These leaves are fairly brittle when dry, but their distinctive dark brown veins provide interest throughout summer.

See also Water-storing gels, p.174; Controlled-release fertilizers, p.174
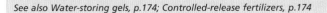

WATER-STORING GELS

Water-storing gels

Ensure sufficient moisture in composts by adding special gels

Water-storing gels are used for their ability to absorb and release many times their own weight in water and are added to potting composts and soil to provide an extra reservoir of moisture for the plants. They are able to absorb and release water over many seasons. Gels are also able to absorb plant foods and reduce leaching of these in poor soils.

Gels are of most benefit where evaporation of moisture from the soil is high, soil moisture-holding capacity is low, and plants are growing rapidly. They increase the supply of available moisture and make watering easier. However, where water is readily available for watering, and plants and soils are already well developed, gels will have less impact.

Gels are therefore worth mixing into the compost used for filling hanging baskets, windowboxes, and patio containers, which are liable to dry out rapidly in hot weather.

USING GELS

- Water-storing gels come as granules that swell when they absorb water
- Follow the manufacturer's instructions on use, especially how much gel to mix with the volume of compost used
- Granules must be evenly distributed, so thoroughly mix them into the compost while still dry

See also Planting in containers, p.161

Controlled-release fertilizers

Don't panic if you see egg-like objects in your pots

You may be puzzled by the discovery of yellowish-brown or bluish-green round objects, about 1–3mm (⅛in) in diameter, found among the roots of plants in containers. They are controlled-release fertilizer pellets that were added to the compost by the nursery that grew the plants.

The pellets have the ability to absorb water from the soil, and their permeable outer membrane allows plant foods to seep out slowly, over a period of many months. Adding them to compost in a container makes feeding plants less laborious as they often last for the growing season.

When squeezed, the pellets burst like an egg. This leads to fears that plants are infested with pest eggs, such as those of the vine weevil. Eggs of this pest are brown and spherical but less than 1mm (¹⁄₁₆in) in diameter and so very difficult to see in the soil.

Using controlled-release fertilizer
Controlled-release fertilizer pellets are useful for plants in containers. Insert them in the compost in spring; as long as the soil is moist no more feeding should be needed in the growing sesason.

See also Choosing fertilizers, p.267

Harvesting seeds

It is easy to save seeds from your annuals and biennials

In late summer seeds of many annuals and biennials are ready for collecting, including those of honesty (*Lunaria*), pot marigold (*Calendula*), poppy (*Papaver*), and love-in-a-mist (*Nigella*). The offspring of cultivars will not be exactly the same as their parents, whereas species will be.

Collect seeds immediately they are ripe. This is usually indicated by a colour change of the pods from green to brown.

Leave the seeds to dry for a few days, then remove them from their pods, by crushing the latter if necessary. Then you will need to separate the chaff (crushed pods), which can generally be done by gently blowing over the mixture of seeds and chaff.

Store seeds in an airtight container with some silica gel or even rice to absorb moisture from the air. Keep them in a cool, dry place until sowing time in spring.

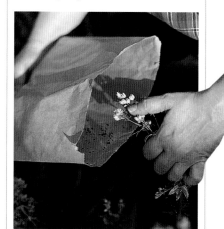

Collecting your own seeds
Collect seed pods and capsules just before they split open and shed their seeds and place them in a paper bag, one type per bag. If the bags are put in a warm place for several days, the seeds will be released into them.

See also Sowing hardy annuals, p.158

LAWNS

Choosing grass-seed mixes

Recent years have seen a vast improvement in cultivars of lawn grasses; make sure these are included in lawn-seed mixes when you are looking to create a new lawn

Coarse lawn mixture

Fine lawn mixture

Grass-seed mixes

Lawn-seed mixes are best sown in warm, moist conditions so that the seed can germinate and establish quickly (*right*). When choosing a mix, decide what sort of grass you want by how you will use the lawn.

Grass-seed mixes are mainly based on the species of four grasses: *Agrostis* (bent grasses), *Festuca* (fescues), *Poa* (meadow grasses) and *Lolium* (ryegrass). Fescues and bent grasses traditionally make up fine lawn mixtures. Perennial ryegrass is a coarse grass that is very quick to establish, is extremely hard-wearing, and will also tolerate a wide range of different soil types. It is widely used in utility lawns, combined with a mixture of bent grasses, fescues and *Poa pratensis* (smooth-stalked meadow grass).

When buying a lawn-seed mix make sure it contains not only the most appropriate species but also the latest strains and selections. Breeding and trials have provided named cultivars to cope with most situations. Mixtures should include these and not older or agricultural types of *Lolium perenne* (perennial ryegrass). In the past, cultivars of *L. perenne* made a coarse lawn that was intolerant of close mowing, but new types with a finer leaf and more compact growing habit have been bred.

Bent grasses produce a fine-leaved lawn tolerant of close mowing due to their low growth habit. They can be harder-wearing than fescues although they are slow to establish. *Agrostis capillaris* (syn. *A. tenuis* – browntop bent) grows on most soils, preferring acid ones, and it is tolerant of damp shade. *Agrostis castellana*, usually represented by the cultivar 'Highland', tolerates dry shade, and performs well under most conditions. *Agrostis stolonifera* (creeping bent) is best in moist, fertile soils, but can produce large amounts of thatch (mats of dead leaves).

Fescues are fine-leaved grasses, establishing reasonably well and tolerant of close mowing. They can be hard-wearing with some species tolerating poor soils. *Festuca rubra* subsp. *rubra* (creeping red fescue) does well in dry shade but will put up with moist shade. *Festuca rubra* subsp. *commutata* (Chewing's fescue), *Festuca ovina* (sheep's fescue) and *F. rubra* subsp. *litoralis* (slender red fescue) all grow satisfactorily in dry shade. *F. ovina* subsp. *tenuifolia* (fine-leaved sheep's fescue) is less tolerant of low cutting, but will grow in dry, infertile soils, as does *F. longifolia* (hard or blue fescue), but this is not hard-wearing under low cutting.

Many grasses tolerate shade, but may be sparse or of poor quality. Greater attention to watering and feeding will be needed. *Poa nemoralis* (wood meadow grass) and *P. trivialis* (rough-stalked meadow grass) are well suited to moist shade, but are not tolerant of close mowing or heavy wear. *Poa pratensis* (smooth-stalked meadow grass) has better drought and wear tolerance, but tends to perform badly in shady areas.

Under unfavourable conditions, some less competitive fine grass species may die out allowing coarse lawn grasses, weeds and weed grasses such as *Poa annua* (annual meadow grass) to take over.

SEEDING LARGE AREAS

For seeding a larger area, check details of available mixes from specialist seed suppliers. Mix the seed thoroughly before sowing, because the smaller and heavier seeds will settle in storage and distribution will be patchy. Keep some seed back for later overseeding of any patches that do not establish well.

See also Creating a lawn from seed, pp.177–178; What is thatch?, p.183

Creating a lawn from seed

Seeding is less expensive than turfing and it is easier to choose suitable seed mixtures, but patience is needed as you won't be able to use the new lawn much for the first season

CREATING A LAWN FROM SEED

A fine lawn, grown from seed
To achieve the aim of a new, seed-grown lawn takes a good deal of preparation, perseverance and patience, but the end result more than makes up for the time and effort involved.

- General-purpose or utility lawns (with rye grass) – 15–20g per sq m (½oz per sq yd).

When sowing by hand divide the correct seed quantity in half. Divide large areas into small sections, or small plots into square metres (or square yards). Sow half the seed over the whole area by working in parallel rows lengthways. Repeat the process with the remaining seed, working in parallel rows widthways.

If you are using a seed distributor, it needs to be set to the correct sowing rate, so mark out two separate test plots of a square metre (or square yard) each. Scatter the appropriate amount of seed by hand on one plot as a visual guide and run the distributor over the other square to distribute the same amount of seed, adjusting it until the correct rate is obtained. Sow seeds in two portions as for hand sowing, ▷

The most suitable times to sow a lawn are early autumn and mid-spring. Late summer in colder regions and early autumn in mild areas are the best periods, as the soil is still warm, there is plenty of moisture and temperatures are generally cool. Under these conditions germination occurs between seven and ten days and seedlings will become established before the first severe frosts in autumn.

After early autumn seeds will take longer to germinate and germination will be reduced. Seedlings will develop more slowly and may not survive prolonged cold and wet weather. Sowing before mid-spring may mean soil temperatures are still low and germination is likely to be poor.

Ground preparation

This is the same as for turf (*see p.178*). Before the final raking apply 30g per sq m (1oz per sq yd) of superphosphate to help rooting (important if the soil is poor). When sowing in autumn also apply 10g per sq m (⅓oz per sq yd) of sulphate of potash to ensure early growth is not too soft and susceptible to winter damage. When sowing in spring also apply sulphate of potash at the same rate and 15g per sq m (½oz per sq yd) of sulphate of ammonia.

Sowing

You can sow seed by hand or with a seed distributor. Calculate the correct seed quantity for the area to be sown. Seed suppliers' recommended sowing rates may vary, so check before buying proprietary mixtures. Where there are no recommendations, sow as follows:
- High-quality ornamental lawns – 30g per sq m (1oz per sq yd).
- General-purpose ornamental lawns – 20–25g per sq m (¾oz per sq yd).

PREPARING THE GROUND

Preparation is all important when you are growing a lawn from seed. Forking organic matter into the soil prior to sowing will help to give the lawn a good start.

See also Choosing grass-seed mixes, p.176; Creating lawns from turf, pp.178–179

TECHNIQUES

CREATING A LAWN FROM SEED

Raking soil over scattered grass seed

working over the plot lengthways, then again widthways.

Lightly rake over the sown area to incorporate the seeds into the surface of the soil – it is sufficient if most seeds are covered. If the weather remains dry for two or three days, water gently with a light sprinkler. If dry conditions persist, repeat watering as necessary while the seeds are germinating and the seedlings are becoming established. If birds have been a problem in the past or are a problem in neighbouring gardens, use seed that has been treated with a bird deterrent. To help prevent birds dust bathing, cover with horticultural fleece until seeds have germinated.

Aftercare

When the seedling grasses are 5–7.5cm (2–3in) high, lightly roll the lawn using the rear roller of a cylinder mower, lifting the front roller and blades away from the surface. Two or three days later, cut the grass down by about one-third of its height. Use a cylinder-bladed mower and ensure that the blades are really sharp. Before mowing, remove the front roller to prevent flattening the grass. For an autumn-sown lawn no further mowing is usually necessary until the following spring, but for a spring-sown lawn progressively reduce the height of cut to that suitable for mature lawns.

See also Mowing techniques, p.182

Creating a lawn from turf

Laying turf is the quickest way to create a new lawn, although it is more expensive than seed and probably harder work

Lay turf at any time between early autumn and late winter when the soil is not frozen or too wet. The best time is usually during early to mid-autumn when the soil is moist but the ground is still warm, which will encourage quick rooting. If you lay turf in spring, water it thoroughly if a dry spell occurs early on before it has fully rooted. Mowing is minimal in spring and autumn, so after the turf has been laid it can be left relatively undisturbed for several weeks.

You can lay turf in summer provided you water it well, but rooting will be hampered by the need for regular mowing, and in hot weather it may be subject to considerable stress and be slow to take root.

Ground preparation

Dig the lawn site and add well-rotted manure, garden compost, peat substitute or leafmould to the trenches, especially on sandy soil, to hold moisture. Do not use fresh manure or the ground may settle too much as the manure rots. Clear the ground of perennial weeds, either by applying glyphosate weedkiller before digging or by removing them during digging.

When the area has been dug leave it for several weeks or even months to settle – the longer the better, ideally five to six weeks at least. Before laying the turf tread the area several times in different directions to obtain a firm, even bed. After firming rake the soil several times in different directions, and before

LAYING A TURF LAWN

1 Having prepared the ground, lay the first roll of turf alongside a straight edge, such as a path or patio, and continue each new turf flush with the previous one. **2** Place a plank on the first row of turves to kneel on, then lay the next row with the turf joints staggered, similar to the pattern of a brick wall. **3** Tamp down the turves with the back of a rake to ensure there are no air pockets. Rolling the lawn with a light roller is equally effective. **4** Apply a topdressing of sandy loam and brush well in. Make sure that any gaps between the turves are filled in.

See also Creating a lawn from seed, pp.177–178; Fun ideas for turf, p.180

the final raking apply 70g per sq m (2oz per sq yd) of superphosphate to help rooting. This is essential if you have poor soil. It is also important that the area to be turfed is firm and that the levels are correct so that the finished site is, and remains, absolutely level.

Preparing the turf

Bought turves may vary in size and thickness. Common sizes are 40cm x 2m (16in x 81in) and 30cm x 90cm (12in x 36in). For ease of transport and convenience the turf is usually rolled up. Sometimes the turves may be only 30cm x 30cm (12in x 12in) or 30cm x 60cm (12in x 24in) and these are usually delivered flat. Machine-lifted turf will usually be around 2cm (¾in) thick.

If you use turf from another site instead of buying it in you will have to lift it with a turfing iron (also known as a turf race) and cut it into suitably sized turves with a half moon (edging iron). Suitable alternatives are a spade and an old knife respectively. You will find it more practical to cut turf about 5cm (2in) thick, levelling each turf to the same thickness using a turf box and knife. To do this, place the turf upside down in a prepared box of the required depth and slice off the soil until it is the correct depth. The thinner the turf (within reason) the better the rooting; thus a 2cm (¾in) turf roots better than a 7.5cm (3in) turf.

Any turf that contains a lot of weeds should not be used. If buying, avoid turves that easily disintegrate when handled. If you have to delay laying the turves, place them flat to avoid any

As soon as the grass is about 5cm (2in) high, give it its first light cut with the mower blades set high

discolouring and weakening, but where possible they should be laid within 24 hours of delivery.

Laying the turf

Begin at one side or one end of the area and work across in a forward direction so that when you are laying the turves you are facing the bare soil. Work from a board so that your feet do not make indentations in the newly laid turf. Lay the turves with staggered joints as in the pattern of a brick wall and closely butt them together so that there are no gaps. Lay all the turves at the same level. This is done by having a bucket of sandy soil at hand and adding or removing a little soil as necessary.

If you are turfing an old flower bed in a lawn, lay the turf slightly higher than the rest to allow for settlement of the soil and prevent a hollow developing.

When you have laid all the turf, it can be rolled lightly to firm it, although this is not essential, but the roller must not be too heavy. An alternative is to firm each turf gently after laying, using a piece of flat wood attached at right

angles to a broom handle, or pat each turf with the back of a spade.

Topdress the newly laid turf with a mixture of sand and fine soil, and work this mixture well into the joints, using a rubber rake or stiff broom. This topdressing helps to fill any minor hollows over the area and also helps the turves knit together and therefore become established more quickly.

Aftercare

After topdressing leave the turf undisturbed. The first few days are critical for new root growth and in dry weather you may have to keep the new turf well watered for the first week or so after laying. Subsequently during dry periods water the new lawn every seven days during the summer. At other times of year apply water during dry periods every 14 days. Excessive or prolonged watering can result in shallow rooting and encourage annual meadow grass (a weed). When watering, 12–15 minutes' sprinkling with a garden sprinkler at normal water pressure should be adequate.

MOWING A NEW LAWN

Once you have given the new lawn its first light cut with the blades set high, you should resume normal cutting height gradually until the lawn is well established. Thereafter, the frequency and height of cut will depend on the type of grasses grown, how the lawn is used and the time of year. The general rule is little and often.

FUN IDEAS FOR TURF

Fun ideas for turf

The perfect traditional two-dimensional lawn may be discouraging us from experimenting with turf: altering the way we lay out and mow lawns, and thinking in three dimensions, could open the way for innovation

The term *tapis vert* is used to describe grass areas mown at various heights to produce patterns and it is here that the lawn could enjoy a degree of reinvention, assisted by advances in technology – most mowers can be adjusted by the flick of a lever to give various cutting heights. In areas of a modest size, rotary mowers would be ideal for this purpose.

The most simple patterns create the best effects, especially in small spaces. To maintain the crispness of the pattern, place pegs around the edge of the grassed area to provide sight-lines when mowing. Alternatively, use statuary or pots to act as guides to the boundaries of different grass heights. When the design has been fixed, mow every week or fortnight, depending on the required effect.

Designs can be permanent or renewed each spring when the grass starts to grow.

Building with turf

With a little ingenuity turf can be used for a range of interesting three-dimensional features. Turf seats can be created, for example. Use wooden or metal frameworks for three-dimensional features, filled with soil or potting compost to support a cladding of turf. Any structure should be free-draining and at least 5cm (2in) of space allowed for soil or compost

Green plant pots

Turf can be used to make living, growing plant containers. The basic construction uses two lengths of galvanised wire netting and a square base of marine-grade plywood. Place the strips of wire netting, both three times the length of the base, on top of each other, at right angles, so that they form a cross. Place the wooden base underneath, in the square-shaped area where the wire netting overlaps, and staple the netting to it. Turn the structure over and, with the wooden base now inside, fold the wire netting up to form the sides of the container and tie the edges together with nylon twine.

Small containers of about 30cm (12in) square are easier to move around but dry out more quickly. Larger sizes of 45cm (18in) or more square give more

Turf chairs and a table can be easily created

planting space, but are too heavy to move; they must be built where they are intended to remain. Lay turf within the containers, against the wire-netting sides, with the grass facing outwards. Hold each layer in place with compost, first packed firmly into the corners to establish the shape, then not so tightly into the centre of the container so as to avoid the sides bulging out. Use light, soilless potting compost and water it well to help it settle.

Grass needs even sunlight to grow healthily – not easy to achieve when used three-dimensionally. Turn the pots every few days to overcome this. When established, the grass grows well all summer, but needs to be kept moist with a daily dousing while watering the plants within. Keep the grass clipped or leave long, but if it is allowed to grow lank and then cut, it will need time to recover – just like a lawn.

Earthy advice

Make sculptural features from turf in spring to allow it time to establish and produce roots. To prevent the joins between strips of turf drying out and shrinking, make sure the turf is in contact with the soil or compost, avoiding air pockets and keeping the whole structure well watered.

A living turf plant container

A turf pyramid as a focal point

See also Creating a lawn from turf, pp.178–179

Greening up the lawn

For a vigorous lawn able to compete with weeds and moss, feed regularly each year, and start watering at the right time if you want to avoid a brown sward in dry periods

Feed lawns annually in spring to maintain vigour as weeds and moss quickly take over where vigour is low. Apply fertilizer when the soil is moist, during showery weather, or water in after application.

Apply fertilizer in early to mid-spring using a complete fertilizer comprising sulphate of ammonia at 15g per sq m (½oz per sq yd), superphosphate at 50g per sq m (1½oz per sq yd), and sulphate of potash at 8g per sq m (¼oz per sq yd). Bulk up low doses of fertilizer with coarse washed sand (not builder's sand) or dry soil to give an even distribution. If the turf colour is poor it can be improved by adding 5g per sq m (¼oz per sq yd) of sulphate of iron to this mixture.

Alternatively, use a proprietary spring/summer lawn fertilizer.

From late spring to late summer, if you notice a decline in vigour or loss of colour, apply 15g per sq m (½oz per sq yd) of sulphate of ammonia bulked up with four times its weight in dry soil or sand to ensure even distribution. Or, again, use a proprietary spring/summer lawn fertilizer.

If your lawn has suffered from drought or compaction (both conditions causing root deterioration), apply an autumn lawn fertilizer in early autumn after raking and aerating, and before topdressing. Use a proprietary autumn lawn fertilizer, high in phosphate and low in nitrogen.

Watering

Grass can turn brown and stop growing in dry spells. Although unsightly it is not serious as grass re-grows strongly when rain resumes. In most gardens, lawns are not a high priority for watering.

However, if you want continuously green grass you must water the lawn

HOW MUCH WATER?

A clever way to find out if sufficient water is being applied is to make a small test hole, for example, in a border at the side of the lawn, to see how deep the water has penetrated. By noting the duration of watering needed, future waterings can be more accurately applied and excessive evaporation avoided.

during dry periods. Watering is needed when the grass no longer springs back up after it has been stepped on.

You must apply the right amount of water. Too much is wasteful and encourages shallow rooting, which makes the lawn drought susceptible, as well as encouraging the weed, annual meadow grass.

Apply a sufficient amount of water each time to wet the top 10–15cm (4–6in) of soil. On most soils this will be about 25 litres of water to 1sq m (4½ gallons to 1sq yd), which equals 2.5cm (1in) of rain.

The average hosepipe will deliver up to 900 litres (200 gallons) of water per hour through a sprinkler. If it is assumed that the sprinkler covers 9sq m (97sq ft), in one hour it will deliver about 100 litres per sq m (22 gallons per sq yd). Even in early to midsummer, 1sq m (1sq ft) will need only 20 litres (4½ gallons) every seven days. On that basis, 12 minutes' steady sprinkling should easily fulfil the lawn's requirement.

However, sprinklers may vary considerably in area of coverage. Check by buying a rain gauge and measure how much water is delivered in a given period. Sprinkler patterns may be uneven, so take several measurements over the wetted area. You then just calculate the time it takes to deliver 2.5cm (1in) of water.

Water lawns regularly with a sprinkler to keep them in the best possible condition

See also Lawn care in dry weather, p.182; Autumn lawn maintenance, pp.182–183

TECHNIQUES

Mowing techniques

Get the best from mowing by following these techniques

A cylinder mower gives the best cuts

Height
Start the season on a high setting and gradually lower it. For fine lawns, the height is 6mm (¼in) to 13mm (½in). For ornamental lawns, heights vary from 13mm (½in) to 4cm (1½in).

Frequency
On average mow twice weekly in summer, and once a week in spring and autumn, or during dry spells in summer. Remove up to one-third of the leaf at each cut.

Quality
The highest quality cuts are achieved with cylinder mowers with a large number of blades. Rotary and hover mowers are suitable for ornamental rather than fine lawns.

Clippings
Remove clippings except in spells of hot dry weather, when they can help reduce water evaporation.

Mowing problems
Scalping can occur:
• On soft ground, as the wheels of mowers may sink in.
• On turns, if they are taken too fast.
• If ruts form through not varying the direction of the cut.
• If the height of the cut is too low.

See also Fun ideas for turf, p.180

PRACTICAL ADVICE

Lawn care in dry weather

Regular care can help increase a lawn's drought tolerance

Lawns can die back in dry weather, resulting in brown patches. The grass will grow again when rain starts, but it can be slow, allowing drought-resistant weeds such as yarrow (*Achillea millefolium*) and hawkbit (*Leontodon* species) to establish.

In dry periods lawns may begin to suffer after seven to ten days. First they lose their ability to spring back after being walked on, then the grass discolours. Raise the cutting height of the mower to help reduce drought stress and do not mow during drought. Water the lawn thoroughly during dry or drought periods to saturate the top 10–15cm (4–6in) of soil (*see p.181*).

To increase a lawn's drought tolerance scarify in autumn to remove thatch (*see p.183*). Although a thin layer of thatch can act as a mulch and make the turf more resilient, a layer greater than 1cm (⅜in) can impede water penetration.

Regular aeration is important for moisture to penetrate the root zone. Aerate in autumn, concentrating on worn areas (*see p.187*). After aerating apply a high-phosphorus, low-nitrogen autumn lawn fertilizer to encourage strong root growth (*see p.181*). Apply a topdressing to improve surface drainage (*see p.183*).

TIPS FOR DRY WEATHER
• Only water important areas regularly. Too much results in shallow rooting and may encourage annual meadow grass
• Feed the lawn to help it through the extreme conditions
• Keep daily wear and tear to a minimum during drought conditions

See also Greening up the lawn, p.181

TECHNIQUES

Autumn lawn maintenance

Lawn care in autumn ensures good growth the following year

At its most basic, lawn care comes down to mowing one to three times a week and perhaps watering in dry spells in summer. Yet early in autumn a more rigorous programme is needed for the sward to grow away strongly in spring and maintain healthy growth through the season.

Scarifying
Over time a layer of fibrous material called 'thatch' builds up in lawns (*see p.183*), impeding penetration of moisture and fertilizers and making turf less resistant to disease and drought. To remove thatch, scarify (rake vigorously) in autumn with a spring-tine rake. Scarifying machines are available and can be hired on a daily basis. Use with care as over-enthusiastic use can damage the turf.

Aerating
The process of spiking or slitting a lawn to relieve compaction is called aerating. You need only aerate the whole lawn every two or three years, but most lawns will have some areas that need more frequent attention, for example, where garden seats are used or where short cuts to another part of the garden are taken over the grass.

Aerate after scarifying when the soil is moist. For small areas use a garden fork, spacing sets of 10–15cm (4–6in) deep holes about 10cm (4in) apart. If buying or hiring aerators choose those that give at least 7.5cm (3in) penetration.

If your soil is heavy use a hollow-tine aerator, which extracts plugs of soil. Afterwards sweep up the plugs and topdress with sandy soil. This improves air and moisture penetration and stimulates root growth. Repeat every third or fourth year.

See also Controlling moss, p.186

BASIC LAWN CARE

Scarifying the lawn with a spring-tine rake to keep the grass clear and unhampered by both moss and thatch.

Aerate the lawn after you have scarified it and the soil is moist. A hollow-tine aerator (shown) removes plugs of soil. Fill with topdressing.

If you need to apply fertilizer to the lawn after raking and aerating, using a fertilizer spreader is the easiest method.

Feeding

Apply fertilizer in early autumn after raking and aerating and before applying a topdressing mixture. Use a proprietary autumn lawn fertilizer with high phosphate and low nitrogen content. For even coverage use a fertilizer spreader.

Topdressing

Topdressing is the application of a mixture of loam (soil), sand and organic matter to a lawn to correct surface irregularities and encourage thickening of the turf. A simple formula is 3 parts sandy loam, 6 parts sharp sand and 1 part peat substitute, parts by bulk. Apply at 2kg per sq m (4lb per sq yd) but on irregular turf this can be increased to 3kg (7lb). Work the dressing in with the back of a rake. Do not attempt to correct major irregularities in a single season by topdressing, because this will smother finer grasses.

Repairing damage

Damaged areas of turf can be replaced or re-seeded by lightly forking over the area and sowing at 15–35g per sq m (½–1oz per sq yd) before applying a topdressing.

Moss control

Poor growing conditions – such as low fertility, compaction, over-acidity, poor drainage and excessive shade – favours moss. Encourage vigour in the turf by feeding and regular lawn care. Avoid mowing the grass too short.

For moss control use a proprietary lawn moss killer and scarify two weeks later when the moss is dead (it turns black). Control with a moss killer will only be temporary unless the conditions which allowed the moss to become established are improved.

A better, more permanent control is to avoid close mowing and to improve growing conditions by following the maintenance steps outlined above, and thereby preventing the moss from becoming established (*see also p.186*).

What is thatch?

For a healthy lawn, this layer of dead material is best controlled

Thatch: a layer of organic debris

Thatch is the term used for the accumulation of organic debris and fibrous material that occurs on the surface of many lawns. Dead basal leaves of grasses, grass clippings that elude the mower collection box, mosses, wind-blown debris, and organic material from topdressings all add to the gradual build up. In time grass roots may grow in it and the surface of the lawn becomes matted and consolidated, and spongy underfoot in wet weather.

Where a build up of thatch occurs on small lawns use a spring-tine lawn rake to control it. For larger areas use a powered scarifier. Treat thatch in early autumn, which allows time for recovery in cool, moist conditions.

Rake or scarify with caution because deep penetration may damage grass roots. With a powered scarifier work over the area lightly, several times at different angles. Put the raked thatch on the compost heap. Then assess the condition and density of the de-thatched lawn – if it is sparse, topdress immediately with a sandy soil compost containing a little grass seed.

To guard against excessive thatch, remove lawn clippings and spike the lawn regularly to ensure good aeration and surface drainage.

See also Autumn lawn maintenance, p.182

Fairy rings

A neat lawn can be ruined by this serious disease

Toadstools appear in summer and autumn

Fairy rings on lawns are caused by toadstool fungi that live in the root zones of the grass and spread outwards. The fungi help to make foods available to the grass roots, hence the darker green colour of the grass, but they can starve roots of moisture, leading to short-term dieback or even death (type 1 rings only, *see below*). The toadstool *Marasmius oreades* causes type 1 rings; the others can be caused by a wide variety of fungi.

Symptoms

Rings or crescents of darker green grass with zones of dead turf either in the centre or around the inner edge of the ring (type 1 rings); or dark green rings without zones of dead grass (type 2 rings); or simply patches of darker green grass (type 3 rings). Toadstools of various fungi appear in the dark patches throughout summer and autumn.

Control

There are no fungicide treatments available to amateurs. Digging out the affected grass and soil is unlikely to be successful because the fungi spread extensively around the roots.

Turf snow mould

Aim to prevent this disease from occurring on your lawn

Turf snow mould (also known as fusarium patch) is caused by the fungus *Monographella nivalis* and occasionally other fungi. It is often encouraged by poor aeration and damp conditions. If the grass is walked on in winter after a fall of snow, the disease frequently develops in these areas.

Symptoms

Early symptoms are small patches of yellow, dying grass that join together into larger, brown areas. Under moist conditions the dead area may be covered by threads of white or pale pink fluffy fungal growth. The disease occurs at any time of year, but autumn and mild spells during winter are the usual times.

Control

Lawns containing a lot of *Poa annua* (annual meadow grass) are most susceptible so try to prevent or eradicate this weed. Scarify the lawn to remove dead material and carry out spiking or aeration, followed by topdressing, to reduce surface moisture (*see pp.182–183*). Sweep off heavy morning dew with a bamboo cane or besom; do not use high-nitrogen fertilizer in late summer and early autumn.

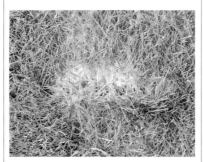

Turf snow mould

See also Autumn lawn maintenance, p.182

Worm casts

Some earthworms produce little piles of mud on lawns

Worm casts create muddy conditions

Earthworms are generally beneficial garden creatures because their soil-burrowing activities help aerate and drain the soil. They also pull dead leaves into their tunnels and so help incorporate organic matter into the soil.

Symptoms

Earthworms feed on decaying vegetation and produce a muddy excrement which some species deposit on the soil surface, known as worm casts. This causes problems on fine ornamental lawns, where large numbers of worm casts make the turf muddy and slippery. The casts can become smeared by lawn mowers or feet, creating muddy spots where moss and weeds can develop. Worm activity is greatest in autumn and spring, and also in mild weather during winter.

Control

Dry worm casts can be dispersed with a besom, stiff broom or up-turned wire lawn rake. Carry this out before mowing the lawn. There is no chemical control available, so, in wet periods, little can be done about worm casts.

Eliminating lawn weeds

Most lawn weeds can be controlled by using lawn weedkillers, but first try cultural measures to improve the growth of the turf

Lawn weeds can be attractive but also a pest if you are aiming for a 'bowling-green' lawn

Carry out hand weeding with a 'daisy grubber' or hand fork if there are only a few rosette-forming weeds such as daisy (*Bellis perennis*), dandelion (*Taraxacum officinale*) and plantain (*Plantago* species).

Rake the lawn to help check the spread of creeping weeds such as speedwells (*Veronica* species), white clover (*Trifolium repens*), silverweed (*Potentilla anserina*) and sorrels (*Rumex* species). Follow immediately by mowing.

If your soil is acid apply lime in winter at 50g per sq m (1½oz per sq yd) as a deterrent against weeds that prefer acid conditions, such as sorrels (*Rumex* species), field woodrush (*Luzula campestris*) and mosses.

Feed, aerate and scarify at the correct time of year (*see pp.182–183*) to encourage vigour in grasses and more resistance to invasive weed growth.

Avoid close mowing, particularly if you have parsley piert (*Aphanes arvensis*), pearlwort (*Sagina procumbens*) and mosses in your lawn.

Using weedkillers

Lawn weedkillers spread through the plant. Typical effects are twisting and contortion of weed stems and foliage, occurring within a few days of application. They do not harm grasses at normal dilution rates but should not be used on seedling grasses. Allow one growing season to elapse before using on new lawns.

There is a good range of proprietary lawn weedkillers in various forms: concentrated liquids for dilution, applied with a garden sprayer or watering can fitted with a fine rose or dribble bar; soluble powder for dilution, applied as above; wax solid, a stick or bar to wipe over weeds for spot application; granules, applied with a fertilizer spreader, or carefully by hand; and ready-to-use sprays, already diluted and suitable for spot treatment. Sometimes lawn fertilizers contain weedkiller and/or a mosskiller.

Always read the label before you buy, and apply strictly according to the maker's recommendations.

See also Autumn lawn maintenance pp.182–183; Methods to control moss p.186

Controlling yarrow

You need to be persistent to get rid of this weed

Yarrow (*Achillea millefolium*) is a common plant of dry grassland on gravel and chalk, in summer producing flat-topped heads of small, usually white flowers on 60cm (2ft) stems.

In lawns, where it can establish from seed in bird droppings, yarrow survives close mowing, but will not reach flowering height. The branching stems become prostrate, extending 15cm (6in) or more a year at ground level and rooting at the leaf joints. Its soft, grey-green leaves create spreading patches, which are moss-like in appearance.

Yarrow thrives where lawn grasses are undernourished and weakened by drought, so strengthen turf by feeding in spring and autumn. Weed it out by hand if feasible. It is fairly resistant to lawn weedkillers but can be progressively controlled by repeat applications of products containing 2,4-D combined with mecoprop-p or dicamba. Carefully read the manufacturer's recommendations for use on the label before buying.

Yarrow survives close mowing

Controlling moss

Try to correct the conditions in your lawn that favour moss before resorting to the use of chemicals

A serious case of moss invasion on a neglected lawn

Many types of moss may invade lawns and they are likely to be the result of one or more of the following conditions, which may simply be corrected by following the treatment suggested:

• Lack of soil aeration/compaction – spike or hollow-tine the lawn in early autumn.

• Low fertility – use a lawn fertilizer in spring and autumn.

• Over-acidity of the soil – for soils below pH 5.5 apply ground chalk or ground limestone at 50g per sq m (1½oz per sq yd) in winter.

• Waterlogged soils – improve the surface drainage of the lawn by hollow-tining and the application of sharp sand. In very wet areas consider laying land drains.

• Excessive shade – cut back, remove or thin the crown of overhanging trees if possible.

• Mowing too closely – during the growing season keep fine ornamental lawns to 6–13mm (¼–½in), average

ornamental lawns to 13mm (½in) and utility lawns to 2.5cm (1in) in height.

• Drought/disease/pests – feed, aerate and re-seed sparse turf.

Try to remedy the causes without resorting to chemicals, which only give temporary control. However, when the conditions that allowed the moss to become established have been improved, you can apply a proprietary lawn moss killer before feeding and, if necessary, oversowing thin areas. Rake out the blackened, dead moss with a spring-tine lawn rake.

METHODS OF CONTROL

• Apply lawn sand in place of spring feed in mid- to late spring

• Treat moss again with lawn sand in early to mid-autumn if it persists

• If the lawn is occasionally affected, treat with a chemical moss killer only after having tried lawn sand, and scarify regularly

See also Autum lawn maintenance, pp.182–183

What causes dead patches?

Many things, from diseases to petrol spills, can harm a lawn

Leatherjackets

Dead patches in lawns are unsightly and can be caused by pests, diseases or even careless maintenance. Turf snow mould (*see p.184*) is prevalent during cold weather, while brown and yellow patch (*Rhizoctonia* species), turf dollar spot (*Sclerotinia homoeocarpa*) and turf ophiobolus patch (*Gaeumannomyces graminis*) develop when it is warmer.

Some pests eat grass roots and cause turf discolouration, including leatherjackets, the larvae of daddy-long-legs or crane flies (*Tipula* and *Nephrotoma* species). These greyish brown, legless maggots up to 45mm (1¾in) long are most damaging in midsummer. Chafer grubs, such as garden chafer (*Phyllopertha horticola*) and Welsh chafer (*Hoplia philanthus*), cause problems between autumn and spring. The fat grubs are creamy white with brown heads and legs.

There are many causes of dead patches on lawns that are not pest- or disease-related. The most common are the result of spilled or leaked petrol from the mower, or uneven application of weedkiller or fertilizer.

Control

No pesticides available to amateur gardeners are approved for use against lawn pests and diseases. Prevent damage through good lawn maintenance to encourage vigorous turf. However, biological control of leatherjackets and chafer grubs is available in the form of pathogenic nematodes (*Steinernema feltiae* and *Heterorhabditis megidis* respectively).

See Using biological controls, pp.40–41

TECHNIQUES

Repairing worn lawns

Fill bare or dead patches with new turf or grass seed

Before attempting to repair a worn lawn, find out why the patches have died and remedy the problem first, otherwise it will recur. Carry out repairs in cool, moist weather in autumn or spring. Fork over bare areas, taking care to break up hard, compacted ground, and apply slow-release fertilizer before re-seeding. Lift brown, dead turf in squares, disturbing as small an area as possible. Again, loosen the soil with a fork and apply fertilizer, then lay new turf. Alternatively, after removing the affected turf, fill the patch with topsoil to the same level as the rest of the lawn, then sow grass seed, lightly raking to cover the seed. Use the same type of turf or seed mixture as the original lawn, so it will blend in seamlessly.

For broken edges, cut out a square of turf adjacent to the edge and move the whole piece across to reform the margin. Then fill the gap left in the lawn with turf or grass seed. If the weather becomes dry, water well.

PATCHING A LAWN

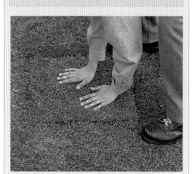

When applying a turf patch to an area of lawn that is not performing well, ensure the new turf is level with the rest of the lawn before firming in and watering well.

See also What causes dead patches, p.186

PRACTICAL ADVICE

Reinforcing turf

Keep your lawn looking good even with heavy summer use

Lawns can wear out, even if good practice is followed, such as avoiding close mowing and improving drainage and aeration by hollow-tining or spiking, followed by topdressing (*see pp.182–183*). Laying paths or stepping stones are one answer, but embedding rubber meshes and interlocking plastic or concrete blocks in the soil are another option you may like to consider.

Grass grows in soil between the grids and meshes with a lawn-like appearance, disguising the reinforcements. Blocks or grids are able to support vehicle wheels and protect tree roots from compaction, while meshes are adequate for pedestrian wear.

Lawn edges are especially vulnerable unless reinforced with timber or metal edging.

Although mowing and feeding reinforced turf are possible, other practices are not, so if necessary remedy drainage and aeration of the soil beforehand.

AVOIDING WEAR

You can help to prevent turf from wearing out simply by laying paths or stepping stones in the parts of the lawn where it is getting the most wear and tear.

See also Autumn maintenance, pp.182–183

PLANTING IDEAS

Create a non-grass lawn

You don't need grass to make a lawn: try other dwarf plants

Chamaemelum nobile 'Treneague'

There are no other plants with the qualities that make grass the ideal close-growing, surface-covering plant for ornamental and utility use. The resilience of grass, despite heavy use, is unsurpassed. Its habit of growth, whereby it is constantly renewed from the base, allows frequent mowing, which maintains its freshness of texture and colour through the year.

If you walk on low-growing herbaceous plants their fleshy stems and leaves will quickly become bruised and crushed. The woody stems of low-growing shrubby plants would be broken and growth shoots damaged, leading to disease.

Where use is light, a few plants can be grown on suitable sites as grass alternatives. To be effective, such plants must tolerate being walked on occasionally. They must remain neat and attractive throughout the year and form a low-growing cover sufficiently dense to be a good weed deterrent, particularly important as selective lawn weedkillers cannot be used. For this reason you should kill off all perennial weeds before planting.

Acaena novae-zelandiae
This vigorous, creeping evergreen perennial is a useful grass substitute ▷

Trifolium repens (white clover) makes a good alternative to grass for a lawn

in sunny, well-drained sites. It forms a rather thick, 10cm (4in) high carpet, has soft, rich green, feathery leaves and spreads rapidly by means of slender rooting stems. It is a useful plant for sunny banks bordering driveways, or any area where grass is difficult to mow and the presence of taller plants would spoil a view. You could also try other acaenas, such as *A. buchananii*.

Chamaemelum nobile (chamomile)

Chamomile is a good ground-cover plant for infrequently used paths or small areas that are difficult to mow. It is a low-growing evergreen perennial with creeping stems that root as they spread. The dark green, finely divided leaves are aromatic when crushed underfoot, the flowers are small, white and daisy-like. The plant prefers open, sunny sites and light, but not dry, soils. It dislikes shade, although it may grow reasonably well in broken shade. It tends to die out in patches and is not weed proof, therefore you will need to handweed from time to time.

Trim with a mower or shears in late summer to remove dead flowerheads

and the occasional straggly shoot. The best form of ground cover is the cultivar 'Treneague', which does not flower and reaches only 10cm (4in) in height.

Plants of the species are raised from seed. Sow the seed in early spring in a greenhouse; transplant the seedlings into seed trays and then harden them off in a cold frame. Plant out in late spring about 23cm (9in) apart. 'Treneague' does not produce seeds, so you will have to propagate it by division or cuttings.

Leptinella squalida

This is an attractive, fairly dense plant that forms a close carpet of creeping stems. It can be grown in sun or light shade and prefers reasonably moist conditions, although it is fairly tolerant of direct sun. The foliage is soft, fern-like and bronze-green. Yellow, button-like flowers appear in summer. It can be used for narrow borders next to walls and for planting occasional squares to break the formality of paved areas.

Thymus serpyllum (wild thyme)

This is an evergreen perennial with tiny dark green leaves and matted prostrate

stems. Many small lavender-pink flowers appear in summer. Thyme needs full sun and well-drained soil. It is not so successful on poor, light soils.

Thyme makes an attractive close cover for undulating surfaces where the soil is stony and it can also be used to provide access to informally planted areas of low-growing plants, known as alpine lawns. There are several attractive varieties and cultivars including *Thymus sserpyllum* var. *albus* and 'Pink Chintz'.

Trifolium repens (white clover)

White clover is often considered a weed in lawns, but it is sometimes used as a lawn in its own right, particularly on poor chalky or alkaline soils. Clover needs relatively little mowing but it can grow quite lushly in mild, moist weather in the spring, when it is easily bruised and blackened underfoot.

It does not need much feeding. Bacteria in its root nodules produce nitrogen (an important plant food) but a dressing of superphosphate at 50g per sq m (1½oz per sq yd) in early spring will stimulate growth. As clovers are susceptible to most lawn weedkillers, stronger growing rosette-type weeds such as dandelion, as well as grass weeds, may become troublesome. Clover can be introduced to an established grass lawn by over-sowing in mid- to late spring, using a dwarf agricultural cultivar or strain, such as 'Kent Wild White' or S184, sowing at the rate of 5g per sq m (1oz per 5sq yd).

NON-GRASS LAWNS

- Be careful when deciding to create a non-grass lawn – they are not always as hard-wearing as they might be
- Some alternative plants to grass will require a great deal of maintenance
- Choose a plant that will look good all year round, for example *Trifolium repens* (white clover)

GREENHOUSES &
GREENHOUSE PLANTS

How to heat a greenhouse

Heating a greenhouse is an expensive business, so do not be too ambitious unless you can afford to do so: you can actually achieve a lot in a frost-free or cool greenhouse

Electricity is the most convenient fuel if you have a small greenhouse and is ideal for providing frost protection. An electric heater is the most efficient means of maintaining a particular temperature, or range of temperatures. Installing an electricity supply also enables you to use a variety of electrical appliances.

There are element and tubular heaters to choose from. Tubular heaters are rated in watts per unit length of the tube. They can become quite hot, so to avoid accidental contact, fit a guard. Some may not have a built-in thermostat – adding one would considerably improve economy.

Element heaters may have a fan to aid heat circulation. In some models the fan is continuous whether the heat is on or not. In others the fan cuts in with the thermostat. If the fan is independent of the thermostat it uses slightly more electricity but circulates air to keep an even temperature. Fan heaters can give poor distribution of heat, particularly in large greenhouses.

Get a qualified electrician to lay a mains cable of suitable capacity in a trench to the greenhouse for running electrical equipment. Do not use an extension cable from the house.

Paraffin

This is the most basic method of heating. The heater needs frequent filling and the wick must be trimmed periodically. Generally, paraffin is considered only as a useful standby because smaller heaters can be unreliable in maintaining a reasonable temperature in cold weather. The choice is between a heater with a flue and a direct discharge heater.

Flued heaters distribute heat through hot-water pipes and discharge the exhaust fumes through a flue, so none of the exhaust gases come into contact

Brugmansia x *candida* 'Grand Marnier' flowering happily in a cool greenhouse

with plants. With direct discharge heaters, the exhaust fumes are released into the greenhouse.

Use premium-grade paraffin (blue or pink paraffin) with a guaranteed sulphur content of no more than 0.06 per cent. Provided temperature lift is low – no more than 4°C (40°F) – there is unlikely to be any serious damage from the waste products.

Blue-flame heaters are better for plants than yellow-flame models. Water vapour is one by-product of burning paraffin

INSULATION

In winter, to try and cut back on additional costs, insulate a heated greenhouse on the inside with bubble plastic to help retain heat and so make for more economical heating. Special fittings are available for attaching it to metal greenhouses. Insulate ventilators independently so that they can be opened.

and humidity can be very high on still, cold nights.

Burning fuels such as paraffin, bottled gas and natural gas generates a mixture of gases that are potentially toxic to plants if they build up to high levels, so even in the coldest weather provide top ventilation so that damaging fumes do not accumulate. Ventilate fully in the morning to release trapped gasses.

Oil

Oil-fired heaters are based on indirect burners with a flue and are used in conjunction with a thermostat.

Natural gas

Natural gas probably provides the cheapest method of heating and is a relatively reliable source of heat for greenhouses. A pilot flame ignites the gas when the thermostat indicates that heat is needed. Make sure the heater is approved for greenhouse use. When burned, natural gas produces water

See also Caring for frost-tender perennials over winter, pp.123–124; Choosing conservatory plants, pp.193–194

PRACTICAL ADVICE

Greenhouse preparation for the springtime

In spring, especially when plants are being raised, high light transmission and heat retention help to ensure good results

vapour and carbon dioxide. At very high flame temperatures plant-damaging gases can be formed. Therefore, ventilate as recommended for paraffin.

Bottled gas

This is a useful standby; however, bottled gas (propane) is expensive and bottles need frequent replacement. Bottled gas may contain propylene, which acts as a plant hormone, damaging plants. Ventilate freely, as recommended for paraffin, and be careful to avoid gas leaks.

Soil warming

Soil-warming cables to heat the staging for propagation are an economical way of using electricity and can be controlled by a thermostat. A section of bench can be partitioned, using clear or bubble plastic.

Heating costs

One of the main decisions when considering heating costs is what minimum temperature is to be maintained in winter. The cheapest greenhouse to run is frost free, with a minimum winter temperature of 4°C (40°F), suitable for pelargoniums, fuchsias and cacti, for example. Next is the cool house, with a minimum winter temperature of 7°C (45°F), ideal for cinerarias and primulas, for example.

The intermediate greenhouse has a minimum winter temperature of 10°C (50°F), ideal for starting begonias and dahlias and, at 13°C (55°F) minimum, for growing cool-house orchids. A warm greenhouse with a minimum winter temperature of 15.5°C (60°F) is the most expensive to run and is suitable for tropical plants.

To choose a heater suitable for maintaining the required minimum winter temperature in your greenhouse, be guided by the manufacturer's recommendations for their models. Remember, it is always best to choose a heater with a slightly higher output than needed so that it does not run flat out all the time.

Remove moss and algae growing between panes of glass with a plastic plant label and also remove debris that has accumulated in gutters.

For optimum light transmission clean the glass, inside and out, by brushing with a detergent solution. Cover plants in the greenhouse to prevent damage from splashes. Note the position of leaks, as these can lead to distinct waterlogging of areas, causing 'damping-off' of seedlings and grey mould. Seal leaks with a flexible, transparent, silicone polymer applied with a mastic gun.

Check that electrical heaters are free from corrosion and that electrical connections are sound. If you are concerned about the safety of supply and connections, have a qualified electrician check the equipment. Check that thermostats are working correctly.

Doors and vents are sources of drips and draughts, as well as letting in frost and allowing heat to escape. Check and replace sealing strips, and oil the mechanisms. Use sticky-backed draught excluder, sold for draught proofing in the home, around ventilators, panes and doors for good, long-lasting seals.

Wash down the staging and floor with hot water and a garden disinfectant. This will reduce growth of mosses and algae and the number of disease spores. The resting stages of pests, especially the non-feeding adult females of red spider mites, can also be hit hard by washing down.

ESSENTIAL GREENHOUSE MAINTENANCE

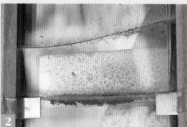

[1] Remove rubbish and weeds growing between panes with a stick or plastic plant label. [2] Repair and re-insulate cracked panes of glass. Use the manufacturer's glazing clips or flexible, transparent silicone polymer to hold the panes in place. [3] Ensure that all heating is in a good state of repair and working properly, especially any thermostats. [4] Give the entire greenhouse a thorough clean with hot water and garden disinfectant before a new season of use.

See also Moss and algae control, p.196

HOW TO AVOID OVERHEATING

How to avoid overheating

Greenhouses and conservatories can become too warm between spring and early autumn, so use a combination of ventilation and shading to keep temperatures below levels that cause damage to plants

Greenhouses often overheat in summer, and even winter sunshine can result in a rapid build-up of heat. Plant damage, in the form of pale growth, wilting and scorched or brown foliage, usually occurs at temperatures between 25–35°C (77–95°F) depending on the type of plant. Tomato growers, for example, take care not to let their houses exceed 30°C (86°F). To keep temperatures below these levels, provide ventilation to release hot air from the greenhouse, as well as some shading to exclude the heat of the sun.

Ventilation

Ventilation is most important as it does not cut down light, which is needed by plants for growth. Ventilating the greenhouse allows entry of fresh air containing carbon dioxide. When greenhouses are closed for long periods, plants can deplete the carbon dioxide supply and growth can be restricted.

A well-designed greenhouse or conservatory has ventilators in the roof. The 'chimney' effect means hot air rises and escapes through the vents. If such roof vents are the only means of ventilation, their area should be at least one-fifth of the floor area.

Air flow through a greenhouse is improved by providing side ventilators in the walls. Where these are fitted, an overall roof vent area of about one-sixth of the floor area should be sufficient.

Side and roof vents can be fitted with automatic openers. When the temperature falls at night, closing the vents in the evening helps to maintain the temperature. Adequate night temperatures are important for good growth and development. Tomatoes, for example, suffer from poor fruit set below 14°C (57°F).

In windy weather vents can be damaged if they are opened too wide or are in the face of the wind. However, opening them in the opposite direction (downwind) creates a slight suction, enhancing air flow. Fans are helpful, but are best only used as a supplement to vents.

Damping down

If the weather is hot the air in a greenhouse will dry out rapidly. Damping down – watering the ground and the foliage of plants – reduces temperatures because evaporating water absorbs heat. Damp down once or twice a day to help maintain good growing conditions, provided ventilation is adequate. When damping down in strong sunlight, wet the floor and staging but not the foliage, for fear of scorch. A house full of well-watered plants is more likely to stay cool. Red spider mite is often more troublesome in excessively hot, dry conditions.

Shading

When ventilation alone cannot prevent over-high temperatures, usually from mid-spring until early autumn, provide shading for the greenhouse. The most effective shading is provided by roller blinds on the outside of the greenhouse, which check solar heat before it enters. They are rolled down when the sun is shining and then up when there is no sun. Internal blinds are less effective. Automatic blind controls are ideal but expensive.

Cheaper solutions include the use of shade netting, attached either inside or out, but it is not easy to remove or put back. Left in place in dull weather it will reduce light and, as plant growth is directly proportional to light, performance may be reduced.

KEEPING A GREENHOUSE AT THE OPTIMUM TEMPERATURE

Applying shade paint to glass
Shade paint is messy to apply, but cheap. Some formulations are designed to become almost transparent when wet, improving their efficacy.

Side louvre vents
Used in conjunction with roof vents, side vents ensure excellent circulation, allowing fresh air to flow around the greenhouse.

See also How to control glasshouse red spider mite, p.197

PRACTICAL ADVICE

Alternatives to glass

Nothing beats glass, but some materials are almost as good

A plastic-covered tunnel is a good alternative

Glass has the quality of excellent light transmission, allowing solar energy to pass through, and is highly effective at trapping and retaining warmth in the greenhouse. However, it is also an expensive, brittle and, in some cases, even dangerous material to use. Safety glass can be used instead, but this is both heavy and expensive. As a compromise, safety glass is often used for doors and panels where limbs could come into sudden contact with the glass. Plastic materials can offer an alternative solution.

Double-layered polycarbonate is costly, transmits slightly less light and does not trap much warmth. It breaks down in sunlight over the years and is more prone to scratches, but makes a rigid, well insulated, safe and vandal-proof covering that gives almost as good results as glass.

Single-layered sheets of polycarbonate or acrylic sheets may flex, loosen and blow away in gales. They are poor insulators, although relatively inexpensive.

Robust, smart, plastic-covered tunnels are sold for garden use, and they can be covered with films treated in ways that make them nearly as efficient as glass. Tunnels offer an economical alternative to unheated greenhouses.

PLANTING IDEAS

Choosing conservatory plants

A heated conservatory provides a home for many decorative plants – the more warmth available, the more exotic the choice

If you go in for a heated conservatory – or indeed a heated greenhouse – you will be able to considerably increase the range of plants that you are able to grow. You will find they open up a whole new and exciting world. The most popular heated structures are the cool conservatory and the intermediate conservatory (or greenhouses). These are most often a realistic possibility for home gardeners as they are not too expensive to heat, and so plants for these conditions are considered here. ▷

PLANTS FOR THE COOL CONSERVATORY

The cool conservatory or greenhouse is suitable for growing a very wide range of plants and is probably the most popular with amateur gardeners as it is one of the least expensive to heat. You should maintain a minimum winter night temperature of 7°C (45°F). Some of the plants mentioned here are hardy but are also suitable for conservatory cultivation.

Climbers

Aristolochia macrophylla
Bomarea caldasii ♀
Cobaea scandens ♀
Eccremocarpus scaber
Hoya carnosa ♀ [1]
Jasminum polyanthum ♀
Lapageria rosea ♀
Mandevilla laxa ♀
Pandorea jasminoides
Passiflora 'Amethyst' ♀
Plumbago auriculata ♀ [2]
Sollya heterophylla ♀
Thunbergia alata
Tropaeolum tuberosum

Shrubs

Abutilon
Acacia dealbata ♀
Bouvardia longiflora
Brugmansia suaveolens ♀
Caesalpinia gilliesii
Callistemon citrinus 'Splendens' ♀
Chamaerops humilis ♀

Citrus
Clianthus puniceus ♀
Cordyline australis ♀ [3]
Dicksonia antarctica ♀
Dodonaea viscosa
Erica canaliculata ♀
Erythrina crista-galli ♀
Eucalyptus globulus
Genista canariensis
Grevillea robusta ♀
Lantana camara
Leptospermum
Nerium oleander
Pittosporum eugenioides 'Variegatum' ♀
Senna corymbosa
Tibouchina urvilleana ♀
Tweedia caerulea ♀

Perennials and bulbs

Agapanthus
Agave
Alstroemeria
Anigozanthos manglesii ♀
Aspidistra elatior ♀

Begonia grandis subsp. evansiana ♀
Billbergia nutans
Cacti
Calceolaria integrifolia ♀
Campanula isophylla ♀
Canna
Crinum moorei
Cyrtanthus elatus ♀
Freesia
Geranium maderense ♀
Gerbera
Hedychium coccineum ♀
Lachenalia
Nerine sarniensis ♀
Pelargonium
Salvia confertiflora
Salvia elegans 'Scarlet Pineapple'
Schizanthus
Strelitzia reginae ♀
Veltheimia capensis ♀
Watsonia
Zantedeschia aethiopica 'Green Goddess' ♀ [4]

See also Bougainvilleas, p.194; Cacti and succulents, p.195; Chinese hibiscus, p.196

CHOOSING CONSERVATORY PLANTS

THE INTERMEDIATE CONSERVATORY

With more warmth, provided by an intermediate conservatory, a different range of plants can be grown compared to a cool conservatory. You will need to maintain a minimum winter night temperature of 10–13°C (50–55°F).

Climbers

Clerodendrum thomsoniae ❀
Epipremnum aureum ❀
Ficus pumila ❀
Mandevilla splendens ❀
Monstera deliciosa ❀ [1]
Passiflora quadrangularis ❀ [2]
Philodendron scandens ❀
Rhodochiton atrosanguineus ❀

Shrubs and shrubby perennials

Aphelandra squarrosa 'Louisae' ❀
Brunsfelsia pauciflora ❀
X Citrofortunella microcarpa ❀
Gardenia jasminoides ❀
Justicia brandegeeana ❀
Pachystachys lutea ❀ [3]
Pilea cadierei ❀

Perennials and bulbs

Aechmea fasciata ❀
Asplenium nidus ❀ [4]
Ensete ventricosum ❀
Hymenocallis 'Sulphur Queen' ❀
Musa acuminata 'Dwarf Cavendish' ❀
Platycerium bifurcatum ❀
Ruellia makoyana ❀

See also Growing Chinese hibiscus, p.196

How to grow bougainvilleas

These climbers, native to tropical and sub-tropical South America, are grown in conservatories for their colourful, petal-like bracts

Two species and one hybrid are grown, but there are many cultivars of bougainvilleas. They are *Bougainvillea glabra*, *B. spectabilis* and the hybrid *B.* x *buttiana*.

In a well-prepared border *B. spectabilis* may reach 10m (33ft). In similar conditions, *B. glabra* can grow to around 7m (22ft). Bougainvilleas tolerate some restriction and grow to around 1.5–2.5m (5–8ft) in tubs.

Position and temperature

A bright sunny position is needed, although with some protection against the strongest summer sun. Bougainvilleas are suitable for cool and intermediate conservatories or greenhouses with a minimum winter night temperature of 7°C (45°F) and 10°C (50°F) respectively (*see p.190*).

Watering and feeding

Water freely during summer, but from mid-autumn allow compost to become drier between waterings. From late autumn keep on the dry side, watering occasionally, but thoroughly. Resume normal watering in late winter or early spring and pot on if necessary. In bright periods maintain a good level of humidity to encourage buds to break.

Around mid-spring, when plants are growing vigorously, begin feeding at weekly intervals with a high-nitrogen liquid feed. When the petal-like bracts show colour, change this regime to a balanced liquid feed.

When the bracts have dropped, resume feeding with a high-nitrogen

Bougainvillea 'Miss Manila'

fertilizer. Most bougainvilleas produce a second crop of bracts and when these begin to show colour, change to a high-potash feed. When flowering has finished, usually during early autumn, reduce the humidity and do not feed again until the following spring.

Pruning and training

Early in the growing season bend over and tie in young strong-growing side shoots to check sap flow and vigour, and to encourage bracts to form. When bracts have been shed, cut long growths back by half.

When flowering ends in autumn, cut the current year's growth back to 2.5cm (1in) spurs. This means to within 2.5cm (1in) of the old woody growth.

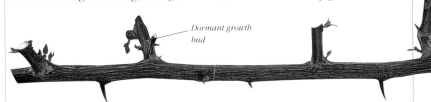

Dormant growth bud

Pruning: in autumn, cut back current year's sideshoots to 2.5cm (1in)

See also How to heat a greenhouse, pp.190–191

TECHNIQUES

Success with cacti and succulents

Cacti and succulents are easy to grow, and many will reward you by flowering freely each year, as long as conditions mimic their natural habitats

In the wild, cacti and succulents grow in deserts and rainforests. Desert species grow in conditions of low moisture, dry air, bright sunshine, good drainage and high temperature. Rainforest cacti generally grow as epiphytes, attached to tree branches. These types need high humidity and semi-shade. Most forest cacti can be distinguished by their flattened, leaf-like stems.

Compost

For desert cacti and succulents use a compost that is open and free draining, such as a mixture of 1 or 2 parts loam (preferably sterilized), 1 part leafmould (or peat, or peat substitute), 1 part sharp, horticultural-grade sand, plus a light sprinkling of a slow-release fertilizer. Alternatively, use a proprietary soil-based potting or cactus compost with extra grit or fine gravel added to the former. Grow forest cacti in soilless potting compost.

Position

Place desert cacti and succulents on a sunny windowsill at all times of the year, although full sun is not essential. Grow forest cacti, such as *Rhipsalis*, in semi-shade.

In winter provide a cool position with a minimum night temperature of 8–10°C (46–50°F), so they have a period of rest.

Watering and feeding

From mid-spring through summer water most cacti and succulents freely, allowing excess water to drain away. Allow the compost to dry out slightly between waterings, rather than keeping it constantly moist.

FLOWERING

A period of rest is needed to encourage many cacti and succulents to flower. Some plants flower in spring and must rest in winter, and a few succulents, mainly from South Africa, flower in late autumn after the rainy season, so should have a period of rest in summer. Check with a specialist reference book if in doubt.

From early autumn and through winter reduce watering to a minimum so that there is a period of reduced or non-growth. Allow the compost to virtually dry out before watering. Many desert cacti can be left unwatered from late autumn to mid-winter. Some cacti, such as *Schlumbergera* (Christmas cactus) grow and flower in winter and need more warmth and regular watering then, with a rest period in summer. If possible use tepid rainwater rather than tap water.

When well established, feed occasionally during the growing season with a general-purpose liquid fertilizer that includes trace elements such as iron and magnesium.

HANDLING CACTI

Some species of cacti have ferocious spines, which can be extremely painful when handling these plants. Use a cardboard strip to avoid getting pricked and also to prevent the spines from becoming damaged.

POTTING ON A CACTUS

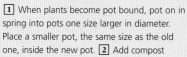

1 When plants become pot bound, pot on in spring into pots one size larger in diameter. Place a smaller pot, the same size as the old one, inside the new pot. **2** Add compost around the outside of the smaller pot and firm in. **3** Moisten the compost before removing the cactus from its old pot by gently sliding it out. **4** Remove the smaller pot from within its new home and carefully re-plant the cactus to the same depth as before. Fill in around the root ball with more compost if needed, firm well, then top with a layer of gravel.

See also Choosing conservatory plants, pp.193–194

GROWING CHINESE HIBISCUS

Growing Chinese hibiscus

The Chinese hibiscus, with its many cultivars in various colours, is grown in the home or greenhouse for its flamboyant flowers

The shrub *Hibiscus rosa-sinensis* (Chinese hibiscus) becomes tree like in the tropics, growing up to 5m (15ft) in height. It is not frost hardy, so in Britain it is grown as a pot plant, or as a specimen plant in a border, intermediate conservatory or greenhouse where it may grow to 1.8m (6ft) or more.

Growing conditions

Hibiscus are usually more successful in the humidity of a heated greenhouse than in drier, centrally heated indoor conditions where for much of the year there may be considerable fluctuations between day and night temperatures. Provide a minimum winter night temperature of 10°C (50°F).

When growing the plant indoors keep it in a sunny, well-lit situation, but avoid direct hot summer sun. In winter a bright, sunny, south-facing window is ideal. In the more humid atmosphere of a greenhouse, grow in bright light but shade from strong sun, and ventilate freely above 21°C (70°F).

In a greenhouse the plant may continue to grow and flower into the winter, but indoors with low night temperatures and low light levels it will usually cease to flower and developing flower buds will drop. During spring and summer water freely but in winter water sparingly. In cool conditions plants will winter in a semi-dormant condition and may lose some of their leaves.

Pruning and potting

Prune annually in late winter or early spring by shortening the previous years' longer growths. Cut back the growths of strong-growing plants to within 5–8cm (2–3in) of their base. This will leave the plant with a basic framework on which new flower-bearing shoots will develop. If necessary, remove weak, unproductive, or straggly shoots, or thin out excessive growth to prevent overcrowding. Prune back the shoots by no more than one-third if you want a larger plant. Remove the shoot tips of young plants to encourage bushiness.

Before pruning, pot on or re-pot if necessary, teasing out any restricted roots and removing a little of the old compost. Use the same type of compost – soil-based or soilless. When well established, usually six to eight weeks after potting, feed weekly with a general-purpose liquid fertilizer.

Chinese hibiscus
The *Hibiscus rosa-sinensis* (Chinese hibiscus) flowers freely, often when small, and comes in a range of bright colours, including white.

Moss and algae control

Unsightly moss and algae can affect the growth of seedlings

Moss, algae and similar growths on the compost surface of pot plants and seedlings may be encouraged by dirty water. Try to overcome the problem by keeping gutters, downpipes and water storage tanks clean, and keep stored rainwater in covered tanks.

You may gain some control of moss and algae with a proprietary water butt purifying material, available in good garden centres, added to fresh water, in a thoroughly cleaned water tank.

If you experience recurring problems with moss and algae on internal greenhouse surfaces, try increasing ventilation.

Algae, moss and liverwort growth can also occur if pots and seed trays are not thoroughly cleaned and sterilized before use, or if unsterilized seed and potting compost is used. Moss and algae growth are also encouraged where plants are potted too firmly, especially with soilless composts which need minimal firming, so that the surface tends to remain damp.

Where plants are to remain in their pots for some time, apply a layer of grit to the compost surface to check unwanted growth. This is particularly helpful with pots of slow-germinating tree and shrub seeds, or with seeds of bulbous plants, such as lilies, which may remain in pots or trays for one or two years before reaching a suitable size for transplanting.

Thoroughly clean the greenhouse and equipment at least once a year in winter, before the spring rush starts. Wash the greenhouse – inside and out – including staging, and used pots and seed trays with a solution of outdoor disinfectant, carefully following the manufacturer's instructions.

See also How to heat a greenhouse, p.190; Choosing conservatory plants, p.193

See also Greenhouse preparation, p.191

How to control glasshouse red spider mite

This sap-feeding pest attacks many greenhouse plants, with high temperatures causing massive population explosions

The spherical eggs, nymphs and adults of the glasshouse red spider mite (*Tetranychus urticae*) are found mainly on the undersides of plant leaves. The adult mites are less than 1mm (⅟₁₆in) long and are yellowish-green with darker markings towards the head or sometimes they are entirely black. In autumn and winter overwintering mites become orange-red.

Hot, dry conditions favour the red spider mite, when it can complete its life cycle in as little as seven days. In unheated greenhouses it overwinters as non-feeding adults and can be a problem from early spring onwards, but in warm situations it may be active throughout the year.

Symptoms

A fine, pale mottled discolouration develops on the upper leaf surface. In heavy attacks, leaves may dry up and fall prematurely. A fine silk webbing is produced between the leaves when mite numbers are high.

Control

You can use insecticides such as bifenthrin, but red spider mite is sometimes resistant to this pesticide. Resistance is less likely to occur if you use organic sprays such as vegetable

oils or fatty acids, but these will need more frequent application to break the red spider mite's life cycle.

An effective alternative treatment is biological control with the predatory mite *Phytoseiulus persimilis*, which is available from mail-order suppliers. It can be used from mid-spring to mid-autumn; in order to establish effectively it needs needs a daytime temperature of 21°C (70°F) or more. Introduce the predator before a heavy infestation has developed. The predator is susceptible to pesticides, so avoid applying them if you intend to control red spider mite with biological methods.

> ## USING WATER
>
> Some insecticides can remain harmful to predators for up to 10 weeks, so avoid these if you are using biological control. In warm conditions, damp down the greenhouse and spray water on to the underside of leaves to create a less favourable environment for spider mite and reduce its breeding rate.

Algae and moss form a green film on the glass

Algae grow readily on terracotta pots

> ## TIPS FOR CONTROL
>
> • Buy well-grown plants in the first instance, avoiding any where the compost surface is covered by moss or algae
> • Good hygiene is essential. Get into the habit of cleaning seed trays and pots rather than abandoning them
> • Ensure the greenhouse is properly ventilated

Fine, pale mottling

Red spider mite damage
Glasshouse red spider mite feeds on the undersides of leaves, which causes a fine, pale mottling to appear on the upper surface. The leaves may eventually fall off.

See also Using biological controls, pp.40–41

CONTROLLING MEALYBUGS

Controlling mealybugs

These sap-sucking pests can reduce the vigour of plants

Several mealybugs (*Pseudococcus* and *Planococcus* species) attack a wide range of greenhouse and house plants. They are soft bodied, greyish-white, oval insects up to 3–4mm (about ⅛in) long.

Symptoms

Mealybugs suck sap and, although sometimes found on leaves of plants, they generally prefer more sheltered situations, such as leaf axils or between twining stems. A fluffy, white waxy material often covers the bodies of the insects and this can be mistaken for a fungal disease. Heavily infested plants lack vigour and are further disfigured by a sooty mould, which grows on the honeydew excreted by mealybugs.

Control

Biological control, in the form of a predatory ladybird (*Cryptolaemus montrouzieri*), is available from mail-order suppliers. The ladybirds need high temperatures and good light, and so are suitable only for summer use. They will not work if chemical sprays have been used on the plants. At other times spray thoroughly with imidacloprid (not on edible fruits), fatty acids or vegetable oils.

Biological control or insecticides reduce infestations of mealybugs feeding above soil level, but have little effect against species that attack the roots. Defeat root mealybug (*Rhizoecus* species) by taking cuttings where possible to produce new, clean plants. Apply a compost-drench formulation of imidacloprid to reduce infestations. Plants that like dry compost, such as cacti, succulents and pelargoniums, are most at risk from root mealybugs.

See also Using biological controls, pp.40–41

Scale insects

Scale insects are more vulnerable to insecticides when young

Scale insects are sap-feeding pests that attack the leaves and stems of many greenhouse and house plants. They are immobile insects, hidden under waxy shells or scales, although newly hatched scales (nymphs) crawl around looking for suitable places to feed.

Several species of scale insect are found on greenhouse and house plants. Soft scale (*Coccus hesperidum*) has a yellow-brown, flat, oval scale, 3–4mm long. Oleander scale (*Aspidiotus nerii*), is a flat, roundish, whitish-brown insect up to 2mm across, and it does not produce honeydew. Hemispherical scale (*Saissetia coffeae*) has a deep brown, hemispherical, convex shell up to 4mm across.

Symptoms

Some scale insects excrete a sugary liquid called honeydew, which makes the foliage sticky and permits the growth of black sooty mould. Heavy infestations cause loss of vigour in plants and sometimes dieback.

Control

The stage in the lifecycle most vulnerable to an insecticide such as imidacloprid, or fatty acids or vegetable oils for edible plants, is that of the newly hatched nymphs. You may need to spray plants several times at seven-day intervals.

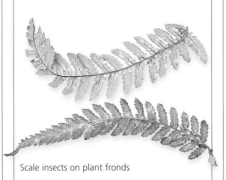

Scale insects on plant fronds

See also Systemic chemicals, pp.37–38

Glasshouse whitefly

This greenhouse pest is best controlled by biological means

Glasshouse whitefly: a common pest

Glasshouse whitefly (*Trialeurodes vaporariorum*) is a sap-feeding insect that breeds throughout the year on indoor plants. The adult is 2mm (¹⁄₁₆in) long, with white wings, and readily flies up when an infested plant is disturbed. Adults and the immobile, whitish green, oval, scale-like nymphs suck sap from the undersides of leaves.

Symptoms

Their sugary excrement (honeydew) makes foliage sticky and encourages the growth of black sooty mould. Heavy infestations will weaken plants.

Control

Spray ornamental and specified-edible plants with imidacloprid, bifenthrin, pyrethrum, fatty acids or vegetable oils to control established infestations. Biological control gives better results between mid-spring and mid-autumn, particularly where whitefly has become resistant to pesticides. This involves introducing a tiny parasitic wasp, *Encarsia formosa*, which kills the whitefly nymphs.

See also Using biological controls, pp.40–41

FRUIT &
VEGETABLES

GROWING VEGETABLES WITHOUT CHEMICALS

Growing vegetables without chemicals

Chemical preparations are widely used to control pests and diseases, kill weeds and maintain fertility, but alternative methods can be employed with excellent results

It is possible to grow a wide range of vegetables to high standards without synthetic chemicals, using gardening methods that are also useful in the ornamental garden (*see p.36*). A non-chemical plot can be remarkably healthy, although intervention may be needed to overcome the worst problems; some pests and diseases are difficult to control even with chemicals.

Cultivating the soil
Crops need open soil and a continual supply of foods, so look after soil fertility. Double digging (*see p.258*) loosens the soil so roots can explore a greater area for foods and moisture. Digging each winter buries weeds and mixes organic material into the soil.

During winter digging, incorporate garden compost or farmyard manure where brassicas, runner beans, onions, leeks, potatoes, celery or celeriac will be grown. If crops are rotated, the whole garden will be manured regularly; add at a rate of up to 6kg per sq m (a barrowful per 50sq ft). Some foods are lost in winter rain, so mulch with compost in spring.

Vegetables growing under netting
Good soil cultivation, scrupulous maintenance of the growing crops, and the use of nets against insect pests minimize the need for chemical solutions in this plot.

Digging in manure improves soil quality

Soil high in organic matter easily forms a crumbly tilth for sowing and planting. Use balanced fish-based fertilizers before sowing or planting. Give hungry crops, like potatoes, greens, celery, and runner beans, 130g per sq m (4oz per sq yd) and other crops 65g per sq m (2oz per sq yd). Peas and broad beans do not need feeding. Potatoes can be planted shallowly and covered with a thick layer of compost to retain moisture, provide foods and avoid earthing up.

These reserves of organic matter mean extra fertilizer during the growing season is not often needed; a seaweed-based feed can be used if necessary. When crops are cleared, spread compost and mix in well before sowing or planting. With this regime deficiency or starvation of plants will be rare. Lush growth is more often a problem, as the foods in organic manures and fertilizers are less soluble than inorganic types, so an overdose lasts longer.

RESISTANT CROPS

Calabrese 'Trixie' ♀, clubroot resistant

Chinese cabbage 'Harmony', clubroot resistant

Carrot 'Flyaway' ♀, carrot fly resistant

Potato 'Sante' ♀, eelworm resistant

Lettuce 'Little Gem' ♀, lettuce root aphid resistant

Lettuce 'Derby', lettuce root aphid resistant

Lettuce 'Musette', lettuce root aphid resistant

Runner bean 'Red Rum' ♀, halo blight resistant

Parsnip 'Lancer', canker resistant

Parsnip 'Gladiator' ♀, canker resistant

Pea 'Cavalier' ♀, mildew resistant

See also Organic Gardening, pp.254–255; Choosing and using fertilizer, p.267; Making a compost heap, p.271

Rotating crops

A traditional three-year rotation of crops (*see p.210*) ensures that different crops are grown on each piece of ground every year, with a two-year break between each type. Rotation is often said to be unimportant and impractical in small gardens; it is likely, however, that rotation delays the onset and reduces the severity of soil-borne diseases. Even on a small plot, many different vegetables can be grown using rotation.

Controlling weeds and diseases

A chemical-free version of the "stale seedbed" technique reduces weeding of growing crops. Prepare beds well before planting and hoe off any weeds that appear. By the time the crops are planted, most of the weed seeds will have germinated and been hoed off.

Vigorous cultivars outgrow diseases, and their roots search a large volume of soil for foods. F1 hybrids best meet these demands, particularly for carrots, parsnips, and brassicas. If the soil is infested with problems such as brassica clubroot disease, try resistant cultivars.

High levels of organic matter support many organisms that hinder pests and diseases. This effect is most marked where chemicals are not used, as these can harm helpful organisms. Sadly this beneficial effect is not very significant, but the improved water-holding capacity and structure of the soil and its fertility also result in strong, healthy plants.

Controlling pests

Barriers such as fleece and net are useful against pests. Fleece is a finely woven material that is draped over plants with the edges fixed into the soil, mainly to protect them from cold and wind (*see p.202*). Insects cannot get through the fibres, so plants beneath remain free of pests such as carrot fly, cabbage root fly and aphids, but weeds and slugs still thrive. The temperatures under fleece can be damaging in hot weather, so it is most useful in the cooler spring months.

Insect-proof nets are also used to keep pests off crops. Heat is lost more rapidly

Hoeing helps prevent weeds becoming established

through nets than through fleece, and overheating is less of a problem, but nets are heavier and need to be supported. Weeding beneath nets is also difficult.

Fleece or nets protect carrots against carrot fly, but barriers are better for this (*see p.205*); resistant cultivars are an alternative. Cabbage root fly can be controlled by net or fleece over closely spaced vegetables such as radishes or Chinese cabbage; cardboard discs placed

around the stem are more efficient for widely spaced and taller greens, like cauliflowers and Brussels sprouts. They stop the cabbage root fly from laying eggs at the stem base and can protect more effectively than pesticides.

Slugs thrive on plots high in organic matter, favourable conditions that will outweigh any benefit from the greater number of predators encouraged by the absence of chemical pesticides. Good plant vigour and scrupulous removal of rubbish reduce losses, but replanting or sowing is sometimes needed. Some potato cultivars show slug resistance, but not enough to be relied on. If slugs are numerous, grow second-early types such as 'Kestrel' or 'Kondor', which are harvested before slug numbers peak in the moist autumn weather.

Biological control of pests through introduction of predators and parasites is also possible (*see pp.40–41*). Occasional applications of naturally derived insecticides are needed when outbreaks of aphids or whitefly occur, but these can also harm beneficial insects. Serious outbreaks may be reduced where chemicals are not used, as predators and parasites are often sufficient to keep pests in check.

A waxed cardboard barrier protects a crop of carrots against carrot fly

Using fleece on early crops

Fleece laid over plants can bring earlier crops and other benefits

Fleece is a finely woven material that protects crops from wind and cold, and raises soil and air temperatures slightly, all helping plants to advance faster than unprotected crops. If it is anchored into the soil properly it also protects against flying pests, such as carrot root fly.

Because fleece allows water and air to penetrate, it reduces watering requirements and increases airflow around the plants. This encourages hardier growth and discourages disease build-up. If used carefully, fleece can last for many seasons.

Being porous, fleece does not warm the soil as well as plastic cloches or black plastic sheeting. It can also lay flat in wet conditions, making germination difficult, and it can easily tear on windy sites.

Fleece over an early crop of lettuces

OTHER USES OF FLEECE

- To extend the growing season, making maximum use of the garden
- To improve the performance of half-hardy crops, such as peppers
- To produce softer, more palatable growth in vegetables that become tough with winter exposure, such as spinach and chicory

Cut-and-come-again crops

Leafy greens and salad vegetables such as spinach and lettuce can yield several flushes of young, tender leaves

Leafy crops usually grown to produce mature heads or hearts can also be harvested as cut-and-come-again crops. Several crops can be taken from one sowing, as the foliage often regrows from the base. These crops take little space and are suitable for the smallest garden. Individual packets of seed can be expensive, so cut-and-come-again seed mixtures are often better value.

Well-drained, moist soil is essential. Raised beds of soil improved with organic matter to give a moderate level of fertility are ideal. Use containers or grow bags in a greenhouse or on a bright windowsill for autumn and winter crops, or where space is short.

Before sowing, water dry soils and allow to drain. As plants are harvested young, they can be closely spaced, 1cm (½in) apart in rows 10–15cm (4–6in) apart. Weeding can be tricky if seeds are sown broadcast, and it may be best not to mix some seeds, as the plants grow at different rates. After sowing, cover with fleece. The crop is usually cut before slugs can accumulate, and watering is all that is needed. When the leaves are of a worthwhile size, cut 2.5cm (1in) above the ground with scissors, ideally in the morning, before the heat of the day.

LEAFY CROPS TO TRY

Amaranth	Leaf celery
Beetroot leaves	Lettuces
Chard	Mizuna [1]
Chicory	Mustard [2]
Chinese cabbage	Pak choi [3]
Coriander	Radish leaves
Corn salad	Sorrel
Endive	Spinach
Kale, including red kale	Spinach beet
	Tatsoi
Land cress	

See also Baby-leaf salads, pp.218–219

Watering vegetables

Watering is essential for crops, especially at critical times such as when sowing and transplanting

Use a spray-gun attachment on a rigid lance fitted to the end of a hose to water between rows

When sowing, first soak the soil and allow to drain, or dribble water into the drill at about 1 litre per 30cm (1¾ pints per 12in) before sowing. Sow on the moist soil and cover with dry soil. Avoid watering after sowing, as this can pack the soil down. When transplanting young plants, water before and after planting and again a few days later. If they are not watered before planting out, make a hole big enough for the roots, set the plant in it, and saturate the surrounding soil; this takes 1–3 litres (1¾–5¼ pints).

After planting, water every 7–10 days in dry weather, at 20 litres per sq m (36 pints per sq yd), to wet the soil to about 25cm (10in) down. Closely planted beds usually need more water than vegetables grown in rows.

Efficient watering
Courgettes, cucumbers, and runner beans have a long flowering period and need repeated watering to do well.

Leafy vegetables, such as spinach and celery, produce more and better quality leaves and are less likely to run to flower if kept constantly moist.

In other cases, watering is most important at certain growth stages. Cabbages, cauliflower, and lettuces give good results from a soak two to three weeks before harvest. Water Brussels sprouts when the buttons begin to form. Soak legumes and sweet corn when flowering begins and when produce begins to form. Watering at other times increases foliage, not yield.

Onions show little benefit from watering. Root vegetables need less water than other crops, but do still benefit from watering, especially if grown densely; erratic supplies can cause splitting (see p.207). Potatoes do best when water is plentiful, but if pressed, concentrate on late spring, to boost tuber numbers, and late summer, when fluctuations in soil moisture lead to splitting and secondary tubers.

See also The benefits of mulching, pp.269–270

Perennial vegetables

Both ornamental and useful, these crops have specific needs

Crops that remain in the ground, such as asparagus, rhubarb, and globe artichokes, are a long-term investment in the vegetable garden. For this reason it is important to prepare the ground well before planting them. Remove all traces of perennial weeds from the proposed beds, as once the crops are established it becomes difficult to weed without disturbing the roots. This is especially important for asparagus (see p.214), because the fleshy roots are easily damaged.

While annual vegetable crops can be rotated to prevent build-up of related pests and diseases in the soil (see p.210), this is obviously not possible for perennial crops. Good garden hygiene is therefore important; remove all crop debris each autumn to limit potential reinfection the following spring.

Growing vegetables in the same location year after year will also deplete plant foods in the soil. Regular top dressings of fertilizers (see p.267), in the form of either organic mulches, such as well-rotted farmyard manure, or inorganic general-purpose fertilizers, are needed to maintain good yields.

Mulching around the base of globe artichokes

See also Growing asparagus, p.214

Ten easy vegetables

Many of the reliable and popular vegetables suggested here can easily be harvested in three months from sowing to provide nourishing, home-grown produce

For an easy vegetable garden choose plants that can be sown directly where they are to be harvested with little or no thinning. Large seeds, such as beans, are easy to sow, and courgettes, pumpkins, and squashes can be sown singly in pots under glass. Station sow easy-to-handle seeds, such as beetroot or lettuce, at their final spacing, sowing two or more seeds and thinning to the strongest.

Pumpkins and squashes

Most of these form large, trailing plants that can be trained in circles, over strong supports or left to sprawl. Sow the large seeds in pots in mid- to late spring or *in situ* in early summer. They require a moist soil and plenty of sun.

Early potatoes

For a supply of new potatoes, grow early potatoes that are harvested before potato blight (*see p.222*) or drought become problems. Plant chitted tubers (*see p.220*) from early spring for first earlies, early to mid-spring for second earlies, and harvest in 13 weeks.

Courgettes and marrows

Marrows usually trail, and courgettes are mostly bushy and are harvested young. Sow *in situ* after all danger of frost has passed, from late spring, or individually in pots in mid-spring for planting out. Harvest 10–14 weeks from sowing.

Lettuce

Choose small lettuces such as 'Tom Thumb' or 'Little Gem' for low wastage, harvesting 8–14 weeks from sowing. Sow in fertile, moisture-retentive soil with lots of compost. Start sowing from early spring, thinning early.

Beans

French beans need rich, well-drained soil. To avoid staking, choose dwarf cultivars like 'Purple Queen'. Sow outdoors in late spring to early summer, once the soil has warmed up, for harvest in 8–12 weeks.

Runner beans are easy, atractive, and prolific, needing daily harvesting. Sow in a well-prepared, sheltered site when the soil is warm from late spring to early summer. Harvest after 12–14 weeks.

Runner beans on a simple wigwam support

Broad beans are the hardiest beans. Dwarf cultivars require less space or staking. Sow from early to late spring for harvest 14 weeks from sowing.

Beetroot

The seed of beetroot is easy to station sow, but can be tricky to germinate. Sow from early spring and thin early. Choose cultivars resistant to bolting, such as 'Boltardy'. Harvest round cultivars from 11 weeks after sowing.

Radishes

Sow radishes fortnightly from early spring for a continuous crop; sow thinly to avoid the need for thinning. They should be ready in 3–4 weeks

Garlic and shallots

Garlic needs a well-drained, sunny site. Plant in late autumn; in heavy soils grow in modules outside and plant in spring. Lift and store from midsummer when the foliage starts to yellow. Shallots from sets in late winter to early spring yield 8–12 shallots per set after 18 weeks.

Harvest round beetroot from 11 weeks after sowing

See also Cut-and-come-again crops, p.202–203; Vegetable garden time management, pp.208–209; Growing pumpkins and squash, p.224–225

PLANT PROBLEMS

Carrot fly

Protect your crops from this damaging pest

Dark marks on surface

Damage spreads well into flesh

Carrot fly damage

The larvae of the carrot fly (*Psila rosae*) are slender, creamy-yellow maggots up to 9mm (⅜in) long, which bore into the tap root and leave rusty brown tunnels. Parsnip, parsley, and celery can also be damaged, but less severely. There are two generations of carrot fly during summer, and often a third in warmer areas. No pesticides are currently available for garden use, so alternative methods of controlling carrot fly are required.

Control

No carrot cultivars are fully resistant but 'Sytan', 'Resistafly', and 'Flyaway' are less susceptible. Sowing after late spring avoids the egg-laying period of the first generation of carrot fly, while early-sown crops escape the second generation if lifted before late summer. Sow thinly to reduce the need for thinning, which attracts flies to the smell of bruised carrot foliage.

Covering your carrot rows with horticultural fleece or fly-proof net (*see p.202*) prevents egg laying; but grow carrots in a fresh site each year, otherwise adult flies emerging from the soil will be trapped under the covering. Alternatively, surround the carrots with vertical barriers of insect-proof material at least 60cm (24in) high to deter the low-flying adult flies.

PLANT PROBLEMS

Cabbage caterpillars

There are three important caterpillar pests that attack cabbages and related vegetables

The large and small cabbage white butterflies (*Pieris brassicae* and *P. rapae*) have two generations a year, with caterpillars active from late spring to mid-autumn. When fully fed, the caterpillars crawl away and pupate above ground level in sheltered places. The cabbage moth (*Mamestra brassicae*) has one generation, with caterpillars feeding from midsummer to early autumn. This species pupates in the soil. Small cabbage white and cabbage moth caterpillars bore into cabbage heads, while those of the large cabbage white remain on the outer leaves.

Symptoms

Holes appear in the foliage and caterpillars can be seen on the leaves or in the heads of cabbages. The edible parts of brassicas are soiled with excrement pellets. Caterpillars of the large cabbage white butterfly are up to 4.5cm (1¾in) long and hairy, with yellow and black markings. Those of the small cabbage white butterfly are up to 3cm (1¼in) long and have a velvety green appearance. Cabbage moth caterpillars are up to 3.5cm (1½in) long and are greenish-brown in colour, with relatively hairless bodies.

Control

Young caterpillars are easier to control than older ones, so regular inspections are worthwhile. Hand picking will eliminate small infestations. Otherwise spray with approved insecticides. The biological control *Bacillus thuringiensis* may be available by mail order from suppliers of garden predators and parasites. Caterpillars become infected when they eat the treated foliage and die within 24 hours. This is a selective control for caterpillars, and is safe to use on food plants. Once caterpillars have bored into cabbage heads they are unlikely to be controlled by either insecticides or the bacterium. Growing brassicas under horticultural fleece (*see p.202*) can prevent eggs being laid on the foliage by the moth and butterflies, and will also protect the plants against cabbage root fly and pigeons.

Caterpillars of the large cabbage white butterfly

See also Biological controls, pp.40–41; Vegetables without chemicals, pp.200–201

Cabbage whitefly

This pest, resembling glasshouse whitefly, attacks only brassicas

Whitefly on a cabbage leaf

The cabbage whitefly (*Aleyrodes proletella*) can be found throughout the year and overwinters as adult insects on host plants. Adults have white wings with a faint greyish spot. They are 1.5mm (⅙₆in) long and fly up in clouds from beneath leaves when disturbed. Eggs are laid on the lower leaf surface and hatch into flat, oval, whitish-green, scale-like nymphs. Adults and nymphs both suck sap and excrete a sugary honeydew onto the leaves, which encourages the growth of fungi called sooty moulds.

Control

Brassicas are tolerant of this pest; even heavy infestations have little impact. Sooty mould can be a problem, mainly on Brussels sprouts, although only the outer leaves are affected and these can be discarded in the kitchen. This is lucky, as cabbage whitefly is hard to control, and waxy brassica leaves are difficult to wet with a spray. If control is needed, spray with bifenthrin, pyrethrum, or rapeseed oil.

Plants affected

All leafy brassicas, including Brussels sprouts, broccoli, cabbage, calabrese, cauliflower, and kale, are susceptible to cabbage whitefly.

See also Avoiding pests, pp.36–37

Clubroot

This debilitating disease is also known as "finger and toe"

Clubroot is caused by the slime mould *Plasmodiophora brassicae*. The microscopic mould spores spread in soil or water or on plants, and remain viable in soil for years without a host. Often the first symptom is wilting in hot weather, followed by recovery at night. Digging up the plant reveals roots distorted into a club or a cluster of swellings. Eventually the plant dies.

Control

Clubroot is most severe on wet, acid soils, so draining and liming are very useful. Raise seedlings in pots of compost and before planting dip the roots in thiophanate-methyl. As the disease probably lives for 20 years or more, crop rotation (*see p.210*) is of limited use, but can still be beneficial, especially if combined with cultural methods. Control weeds, because some harbour the disease.

Plants affected

Clubroot is severe on cabbages and affects related crops, such as turnips, swedes, and radishes, and some ornamentals, such as wallflowers.

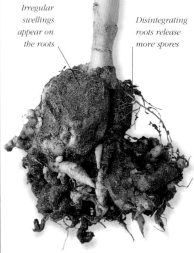

Irregular swellings appear on the roots

Disintegrating roots release more spores

Clubroot damage

See also Liming soils, p.265

Pea moth

This pest is an annoyance rather than the cause of serious losses

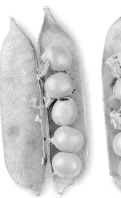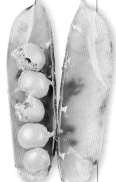

Pea moth damage in pods

Female pea moths (*Cydia nigricana*) lay eggs on pea plants in flower. On hatching, caterpillars bore into the pods and feed on the developing pea seeds. Often there is just one caterpillar in a pod so some seeds remain undamaged. Once fully fed, the caterpillars overwinter in silk cocoons in the soil.

Control

It pays to time the sowing of peas to avoid the moth's flight period. Sowings that are made in early and mid-spring, or even in late winter under cloches, will escape attack and so will late sowings, made towards midsummer. In both cases use early (quick-maturing) cultivars.

Pheromone traps for pea moth, similar to those used on apple trees against codling moth, are available. These capture male pea moths, and indicate numbers in the garden so that insecticide applications can be more accurately targeted. Should control measures seem necessary, peas can be sprayed with bifenthrin. Timing is important, as it is necessary to control the newly hatched larvae before they penetrate the pods. The best time is 7–10 days after the onset of flowering.

See also Avoiding pests, pp.36–37

Splitting root vegetables

Inadequate or erratic supplies of water can lead to this problem

Root vegetables such as carrots often split when dry soil suddenly receives excess water. Roots take up too much water and their skins, unable to cope with the swelling, split. Infections such as bacterial soft rot often follow.

Most vegetables that crop above ground can cope with more water when they near maturity, as flowering greatly increases their water demand. The water requirements of root crops, on the other hand, increase steadily as the season progresses, but continually over-watering them results in excess top growth and small roots, so careful watering is essential at all times, and especially near to harvest.

If roots are splitting, initially apply 4.5 litres (1 gallon) of water per metre (yard) of row every two weeks, gradually increasing to double this near harvesting, allowing for rainfall. Add organic matter to sandy soils and grit to clay soils to reduce fluctuations of moisture levels in the ground.

A carrot suffering from splitting

See also Watering vegetables, p.203

Green manures

Digging in fast-growing, leafy crops supplements fertilizers and improves the soil in vegetable and fruit gardens

While green manures contribute little organic matter, they do make the soil easier to work and reduce food loss and compaction by winter rains. They provide attractive, weed-suppressing cover and shelter for beneficial insects. *Tagetes minuta* is claimed to suppress eelworms and weeds; however, it does not replace other controls. Slug control may be needed after green manuring.

Green manure plants

There is usually a plant suitable for any situation. For overwintering, grazing rye (*Secale cereale*) or winter tares (*Vicia sativa*) are popular. For a quick spring or summer crop, mustard (*Sinapis alba*) or phacelia (*Phacelia tanacetifolia*) are used, although as a brassica, mustard can harbour clubroot and may affect rotation (*see p.210*). Lupin (*Lupinus angustifolius*) and clover (*Trifolium* species) fix nitrogen in the soil, while deep-rooting alfalfa (*Medicago sativa*) or buckwheat (*Fagopyrum esculentum*) draw up buried foods. Soil type influences choice. Alfalfa and trefoil (*Medicago lupulina*) prefer dry, alkaline soils, while lupins do best on dry, acid soils. Winter tares and winter field bean (*Vicia faba*) tolerate heavy soils while crimson clover (*Trifolium incarnatum*) is best on light soil.

Sowing and incorporating

Sow seeds broadcast and rake them in; green manures can be sown at many times of year. Autumn-sown manures prevent foods being washed away by rain. Hardy rye grows all winter and is dug in during spring. Fast-growing mustard can be dug in by mid-autumn, or its frosted remains left as mulch. Summer-grown manures, such as buckwheat, consume both space and moisture, but will smother weeds. Summer crops of lupins and clovers fix most nitrogen.

Dig in green manures when lush and leafy, before flowering and at least two weeks before planting or sowing crops. Older plants become woody and can "borrow" soil nitrogen while rotting, causing the soil to become depleted.

Digging in a green manure crop

See also Building soil fertility, p.259; What is organic gardening, pp.254–255

Vegetable garden time management

Producing home-grown fruit and vegetables need not mean hours of work, and people with busy lifestyles can still manage a productive vegetable plot in a reasonable time

Most vegetable gardeners only need to provide a little fresh food for family dinners. Stick to high-value crops that are much better fresh, such as lettuce, dwarf French beans, celeriac, calabrese, mangetout, curly kale, and early potatoes. Avoid main-crop potatoes, carrots, and onions, as those on sale in shops are cheap and tasty. One exception is later in the year, when potatoes can be planted to provide a delicious treat on Christmas Day. Raspberries and other low-maintenance fruit bear large, good-quality crops.

With some crops, like lettuce, sow a few seeds into the ground at a time, three weeks apart, to ensure a constant supply. To maximize the length of the productive season, grow small quantities of crops such as broccoli, endive, and raddichio. Sow carrots early in the year, some thickly to provide small "bunching" carrots,

Small successional sowings of crops such as lettuce use time and space efficiently

Gathering tasty young carrots

others in rows that are thinned to grow large crops for late summer and autumn.

Some crops, such as cut-and-come-again salad leaves (*see p.202*), are ideal for busy gardeners. Seeds of mixed lettuce cultivars are sold by some seed companies and these are among the easiest and most productive crops to grow, and much cheaper and fresher than pre-packed bags of mixed leaves from the supermarket. Sow sections of different leaves every month or so. This regime ensures a supply of fresh salad leaves all summer. Cabbages planted in autumn can be treated in a similar way if cut after producing six or seven leaves. Each plant should yield three or four harvests of tasty young leaves.

Spend a little money to save time

Some crops are sown direct, but for others you will need a greenhouse and a cold frame or other hardening-off area. Seed sowing and pricking out are very time consuming; timing and judging how many seeds you need are also tricky. Circumvent this by ordering plug plants.

Many mail-order companies now send these established seedlings ready to plant out, and these work well for vegetable gardeners with little spare time.

Plug plants are an example of where it is worth spending a bit of money to save a great deal of time and trouble. It will also provide you with just the right number of plants needed, at the most suitable time for planting out.

Use weed-free proprietary manures as mulches to suppress annual weeds and feed the soil. These do not add to the weed seed population as ordinary manures and composts do.

Minimize time-heavy tasks

In autumn, spread liberal amounts of well-rotted organic matter over the bare ground. This will have a positive effect on the structure of the soil and the beneficial organisms within it, resulting in a friable soil that is easy to work.

Organic gardeners know that pest, disease, and especially weed control can be time consuming. Synthetic chemicals can make a substantial impact on some

See also Raising plants from seed, pp.20–21; Avoiding pests and diseases, pp.36–37; Watering vegetables, p.203; Ten easy vegetables, p.204

jobs, but try to minimize their impact on the environment. Use glyphosate-based weedkiller, which does not persist in the soil, early in the year, because getting rid of weeds at this stage makes it easier to keep on top of them for the rest of the year. New plantings need protection against slugs, and cloches to keep off pigeons, which otherwise can cause great damage.

Timing can save watering. Soak peas and beans at flowering time and again when the first pods are forming. Lettuces and cabbages ideally need plentiful water all the time, but a thorough watering as hearts are beginning to grow is nearly as good. Grow thirsty plants such as cauliflowers, courgettes, and runner beans in shallow trenches and fill every week to ensure deep soaking.

Be realistic and discplined

Discipline is key to managing so much in such a short space of time. Many people go out to their garden with only

WISE WATERING

Use sprinklers to start plants off, then switch to drip irrigation once they are well-rooted. This reduces water use by 30 per cent, and also reduces the need for weeding.

the vaguest idea of what they are going to do. They can spend a good deal of time just looking around, seeing how things are doing, and making up their minds which job should come first. Always decide what you are going to do

the night before, and then stick to this rigidly when in the garden.

Half-an-hour in the garden every day is more useful than several hours at once, as you can observe closely how the plot is developing. A serious pest infestation takes time to build up, and constant monitoring forestalls major, time-consuming problems.

Even half of a traditional allotment or vegetable plot is a lot to handle, especially in the weeding, watering, and gathering period in summer. Winter digging can also be laborious, although a hired rotavator can make short work of this. A small plot, well tended, is usually more productive than larger, unkempt areas. Start on a small scale, covering spare ground with black plastic. When you know your needs, extend your cropped area or relinquish surplus ground. Alternatively, invest in relatively low-labour but delicious crops such as asparagus, rhubarb, and bush or cane fruits.

TIME-SAVING TIPS

Hoe weeds regularly
A rash of weeds does not appear overnight, so taking a "little-and-often" approach to weeding should prevent weeds reaching levels where they affect the yields from your crops.

Avoid making work
Keep a number of scaffolding planks around the plot to stand on when working. If the soil is not compacted by foot traffic, it will need less digging, saving time and effort.

Dispense slug pellets around plants
Scattering slug pellets around seedlings at the time of planting out will help see them through their most vulnerable stage. When they are established, the protection can be stopped.

Crop rotation

The principle of crop rotation is to grow specific groups of vegetables in a different place each year to help keep the soil healthy and productive

Rotation is a long-established practice that helps to maintain crop yields and quality. Crop groups are moved around in sequence so they do not return to the same spot for at least three years.

Why use crop rotation?

One benefit of rotation is pest and disease control. Plant families tend to be attacked by specific pests and diseases, so rotating crops breaks their life cycles and reduces their build-up. Some crops, such as potatoes and squashes, can also suppress weeds, minimizing problems for crops in following years.

Rotation also helps to maintain soil fertility and structure. Different crops have different soil requirements and benefits, and the groups reflect these. Changing crops each year minimizes deficiencies and helps to replenish the soil. It also provides opportunities to cultivate, weed, and manure at different times, preventing troubles accumulating.

The different plant groups

Different plant families have different needs, and these are the basis for grouping in a rotation scheme. Brassicas, such as radishes, cabbages, cauliflowers, and swedes, need nitrogen-rich soil and may need liming. Legumes – the peas and beans – need well-drained but moisture-retentive soil that is not rich in nitrogen, because they fix atmospheric nitrogen through their roots for future crops. Potatoes need

A large vegetable plot can be divided into blocks of different crops, rotated each year

soil high in organic matter and nitrogen, but no lime, and help to suppress weeds and break up soil structure. Onions, garlic, shallots, and leeks also need high levels of organic matter and may need liming. Root crops in the umbelliferous family, which includes carrots, parsnips, parsley, celery, and Florence fennel, need stone-free soil with a fine tilth that is not freshly manured; they will leave the soil with an open structure. Some crops, such as lettuces, can be placed in the rotation cycle as convenient.

Planning your rotation scheme

If you have the luxury of a large plot, you can plan to have a different section for each family each year. Divide the plot into four or more equal sections, depending on the range of crops you wish to grow. Group crops by plant family, and order them by needs and benefits. For example, potatoes leave a broken-up soil, ideal for later carrots or parsnips. Follow these with legumes. In the third year grow brassicas that use the nitrogen left by the legumes. Clear spent brassicas before mid-spring potato planting as the rotation starts again.

In a smaller garden, such a scheme may be impossible: you may want crops in differing proportions, or wish to concentrate on high-value crops, and seasons for different crops can overlap. This does not mean rotation has to be abandoned. A simpler three-bed system of brassicas, all the root vegetables and onions, and legumes and fruit vegetables may be more useful (*see box, left*). If the groups are rotated in this order, with the main aim of ensuring that there are two full cropping cycles without repeating a crop, many of the benefits of rotation can still be achieved.

A THREE-GROUP CROP ROTATION

	Bed one	Bed two	Bed three
Year one	Brassicas	Legumes, etc.	Root vegetables
Year two	Root vegetables	Brassicas	Legumes, etc.
Year three	Legumes, etc.	Root vegetables	Brassicas

See also Avoiding pests and diseases, pp.36–37; Vegetables without chemicals, pp.200–201

Vegetables running to seed

Vegetables are generally unusable if they develop flowers, or bolt, a problem that can occur with annual crops in the first year, while biennials may not bolt until the second year

Bolting is triggered by either a drop in temperature or changes in day length. Although it only happens when crops are fairly mature, it is triggered much earlier and once started, it cannot usually be stopped.

Bolting in annual crops

Crops sensitive to day length include lettuce, some radishes, and spinach. These initiate flowers when day length increases, and spring-sown annuals naturally run to seed in summer. An adequate crop should develop before this happens. Chinese cabbage bolts if sown too early: cold triggers flower formation, and longer days compound the effect. To prevent bolting, sow this crop from midsummer onwards.

Bolting in biennial crops

Onions, leeks, carrots, swedes, turnips, and beetroot are biennials grown for the large root produced in the first year before flowering the next. All produce flowers after a period of cold, normally winter, but unsettled weather early in the season can trigger flowers in the first year. This usually occurs after a prolonged cold spell; cold nights, hot days, and late frosts are less likely to cause problems. Biennial crops vary in sensitivity to cold. Turnips are sensitive as soon as germination begins, onions and some brassicas are only sensitive after they reach a certain growth stage, and celery and celeriac gradually increase in sensitivity as they develop.

Preventing bolting

Many horticultural practices help prevent this problem. Dry soil can encourage bolting, particularly with cauliflower, rocket, and spinach, so keep soil moisture levels constant.

Delay sowing cold-sensitive plants such as turnips, endive, and Swiss chard, until temperatures are more stable. Raise early crops of onions, beetroot, and kohlrabi in modules in a greenhouse and plant out when temperatures are warmer, or sow directly under cloches.

Crops that are only sensitive after a certain stage can also be manipulated. Sow onions bred for autumn planting in late summer: they should not reach their cold-sensitive stage before winter begins and will be less likely to bolt in spring.

A lack of nitrogen in early spring can also induce bolting in autumn-sown onions, so in midwinter top-dress with 70–100g per sq m (2–3oz per sq yd) of nitrochalk.

Spring cabbages are always quick to bolt. Sow around a month after the longest day (one week earlier in the north and one week later in the south). These crops will still bolt the following spring, but later than crops that were sown earlier.

Choose bolt-resistant plants

There are specially bred cultivars that are less liable to bolt, such as 'Boltardy' beetroot. These cultivars are particularly useful for early sowings of annuals such as spinach, and for biennials such as onions, carrots, and spring cabbages in autumn or early spring.

Bolting varies between cabbage cultivars, and red onions seem to be more prone to bolting than white or brown types, so try different types. If bolting in onions is a recurring problem, plant heat-treated sets in early spring; high temperatures suppress the flower-bud formation.

White flowers on bolted rocket

Pagoda-like bolted lettuces

Tall flowering stem on bolted beetroot

See also Growing onions from seeds and sets, p.220

Attractive climbing vegetables

Trailing tomatoes, climbing beans and hanging squashes all add interest anywhere in the garden, giving height and structure in what could otherwise be a two-dimensional space filled with low-growing planting

Few gardeners now have the space to devote large areas to vegetables. If you take advantage of the vertical surfaces around the garden, any plot can give room to dual-purpose planting. Many gardeners overlook the contribution that climbing or trailing vegetables, especially legumes and cucurbits, can make with their flowers, leaves, and often colourful crops, even before taking into account their productive value. Vegetables trained over supports such as tunnels, arbours, and arches can share space with ornamental climbers, complementing other plantings nearby.

Use and beauty

Vegetables grown over permanent garden structures and timed to follow on from ornamental climbers, such as roses, provide an extension of summer colour. Temporary supports, including canes or purpose-built wigwams, frames, and obelisks, can also be used to add height to beds and borders, and are ideal for peas, beans, smaller curcubits, and ridge (outdoor) cucumbers.

Vegetables can make living screens for partitioning the garden, or clothe fences with large, dramatic, and architectural leaves. Cucurbits, such as pumpkins, squashes, and marrows, are particularly useful for screening, and the densely packed foliage of climbing French and runner beans, both of which are rapid growers, can be used to great effect to cover a surface with a profusion of attractive flowers and pods.

For a less structured alternative, use tall sunflower cultivars as a support for peas and beans. Trail the legumes along the ground to begin with, then tie them into the sunflower stems until they start to cling by themselves. The plants will need encouragement through regular watering and feeding, and must be firmly staked to prevent wind damage.

When grown over greenhouses on a framework of canes, the foliage of marrows, squashes, pumpkins, or vigorous cultivars of beans provides shade from midsummer onwards. Choose cultivars with smaller fruits so they do not break through the glass.

The growth of climbers trained over an arch or tunnel is more open than that trained over traditional frameworks of canes, so the plants are less likely to become diseased. These are ideal supports for peas and beans, as the pods hang down through the centre and are easier to harvest.

Training cucurbits

All trailing cucurbits, including most winter squashes, certain summer squashes,

CHOOSING SUITABLE SUPPORTS

[1] Small pumpkins or squashes grown this way make a particularly attractive display, as the colourful fruits are highly visible. Strong, permanent structures such as pergolas and arbours with wood or wire trellis are advisable for large-fruited vegetables. [2] Rustic frameworks made from willow or hazel are sufficients for peas and beans, and their textured bark allows the tendrils to grip with greater ease than smooth bamboo canes. For easy wigwams, tunnels, and arches, plunge wands of willow or hazel into the ground to 30cm (1ft), then either weave them together or secure with twine at the top. [3] Fully clothed with leaves, a tunnel makes an attractive and productive garden feature.

See also Growing pumpkins and winter squashes, pp.224–225

pumpkins, and marrows, can be trained over suitably strong supports. Most seed packets state whether a cultivar is trailing – do not buy bush forms by mistake.

Pumpkin and winter squash cultivars vary considerably in size, shape, skin texture, and colour. There are squashes with ribbed or warty skins, or unusual shapes such as the flying-saucer-shaped 'Turk's Cap' squash, or elongated 'Crookneck PMR'.

Although the mature, often large fruits of cucurbits appear to be hanging precariously from their vines, in reality these stems are extremely strong. If they are planted to hang directly overhead, you may want to give some extra support with plastic netting as a safety measure. The plants dislike root disturbance, so are best sown where they are to grow, or grown in modules and planted out when the danger of frost has passed, as they are not frost-hardy. If grown in fertile soil, they will reward you with huge leaves and enormous fruits by early autumn.

Ornamental peas and beans

Runner beans were introduced to Britain in the 16th century as ornamental plants, grown for their profusion of delicate flowers produced over a long period. As well as the usual red flowers, there are cultivars such as 'Sunset' with pale pink flowers, the classic 'Painted Lady' in red and white, and 'White Lady' with white flowers that are yellow in bud and may be less attractive to birds.

Far too decorative to be hidden away are purple- or yellow-podded climbing French beans. These are often said to have the best flavour, as well as being self-pollinating. Purple-podded cultivars, which turn green on cooking, often have purple stems, leaves, and flowers, such as soft lilac 'Viola Cornetti'. As with all peas and beans, picking the pods continually prolongs the flowers.

In milder areas, the tropical lablab or hyacinth bean, with bronzed foliage, mauve flowers, and edible maroon pods, can be grown in the same way as climbing French beans.

Pumpkins make a striking display when their fruits are raised to eye level

With their striking mauve blooms and eye-catching pods, purple-podded peas associate well with sweet peas, particularly those that have purple in their flowers. Peas vary in height from 0.5–1.5m (1½–5ft) and benefit from being supported early on in their growth with pea sticks or wide-mesh wire netting.

Climbing cucumbers

Ridge cucumbers are shorter and have rougher skin than greenhouse cucumbers, and they are easier to grow. Tie trailing cultivars into a support such as trellis or wire netting until the tendrils take hold. They can be planted more closely this way than if they are grown along the ground, and it also helps prevent damage to the fruit. Pinch out the growing tips of all ridge cucumbers when they have reached the top of the support so that growth continues from the side shoots.

Some ridge cucumbers can be bitter, but 'Kyoto', a vigorous Japanese cultivar with narrow fruits up to 60cm (2ft) long, is less so. It can be quite ornamental trained on tripods of canes.

Growing asparagus

Asparagus is a perennial crop which has gained "luxury vegetable" status due to its long development period and a cropping season of just eight weeks

Asparagus can be grown from "crowns" (one-year-old plants) or seeds. Cultivars can be either non-hybrid or more vigorous and productive all-male F1 hybrids. Asparagus from crowns and F1 seed can be harvested two years after planting; plants from non-hybrid seed need an extra year. Non-hybrid seed is inexpensive, but produces male and female plants. Females have fewer spears and produce unwanted seedlings, so should be discarded.

The site for an asparagus bed must be well drained, as crowns can rot in waterlogged soils, and the soil ideally neutral to alkaline (see p.263). Avoid frost pockets and very exposed sites, and do not re-plant on an old asparagus bed that may harbour disease-causing fungi.

Clear all perennial weeds. Dig in plenty of organic matter the winter before planting, and double-dig or fork over in early spring.

Planting crowns

When planting one-year-old crowns, handle them carefully. Be prepared to plant the crowns as soon as they are delivered, as the delicate roots are prone to drying out. Dig a trench 25cm (10in) deep. Apply a general fertilizer and rake in well. For each row make a 10cm (4in) high ridge of soil and place the crowns on top, spreading the roots outwards. Cover with 5–7cm (2–3in) of fine soil and water in. Mound up with more soil periodically until the trench is full, keeping the plants well watered and the bed free of weeds.

Sowing seed

If using non-hybrid seed, sow in spring in a seedbed, 4cm (1½in) apart in drills 2.5cm (1in) deep and 45cm (18in) apart. Thin the seedlings to 15cm (6in) and keep well watered. Transplant the following spring to a prepared trench,

PLANTING AN ASPARAGUS BED

Traditional beds are three rows wide, with the plants 30cm (1ft) apart each way. **1** If space is limited, plant one row with crowns 30–45cm (12–18in) apart. This also yields thicker spears, but it is a less efficient use of space overall.

2 Once it is properly established, a healthy asparagus bed can continue to provide spears for up to 20 years, with each crown yielding 9–12 spears from mid-spring to early summer each year.

as for purchased crowns. For an all-male bed, delay transplanting for one year and discard the female plants, which will bear orange-red berries in autumn. Transplant the male plants the following spring and treat as one-year-old crowns.

More expensive F1 hybrid seed is usually sown in modules for reliable germination. The crop can also be harvested a year earlier. In early spring sow seeds individually into large modules and keep at 13–16°C (55–61°F). Harden off once plants are 10–15cm (4–6in) high and transplant in summer as for one-year-old crowns. Water plants in thoroughly, as in summer the roots are very prone to drying out.

Harvesting spears

The year after planting, topdress with a general fertilizer in late winter to early spring, and mound up the soil if necessary. There are a few hybrids that can be cropped lightly this year, but for most, do not harvest.

Two years after planting, spears can be cut from mid-spring for six weeks (in later years, harvest for eight weeks).

Cut spears with a sharp knife, roughly 2cm (¾in) below soil level. Harvest all spears, even poor ones, to promote new growth.

After harvesting, topdress the rows with a general-purpose fertilizer or a 5–7cm (2–3in) layer of well-rotted manure, which also suppresses weeds. Always allow the foliage to yellow in autumn before removing it, to avoid weakening the crowns. If the soil has subsided during the year, mound it up after removing the foliage.

WEEDING ASPARAGUS

- Asparagus beds must be weeded by hand to avoid damaging the roots
- Regular mounding up during the year should control weeds
- During the growing season, weed by hand or treat deep-rooted perennial weeds with glyphosate, taking care not to get any on the asparagus foliage
- During the dormant season, when no foliage or spears show above ground, a contact weedkiller can be used

See also Perennial vegetables, p.203

Asparagus beetle

This is the main asparagus pest, together with slugs and snails

Adult asparagus beetles (*Crioceris asparagi*) are 6–8mm (¼–⅜in) long with a black head, a reddish thorax, and black wing cases that have reddish edges and three pairs of yellow squares. The beetles overwinter in the soil, and in plant debris, emerging in late spring to lay rows of black, oval eggs on young shoots or the underside of the asparagus foliage.

The eggs hatch into creamy-greyish-black larvae that grow up to 10mm (½in) long with three pairs of legs towards the head end. These feed on the leaflets for about two weeks and then pupate in the soil. There can be three generations between late spring and early autumn.

Symptoms

Both adult beetles and larvae destroy leaves. They also gnaw bark from the stems. This disrupts the plant's uptake of water and if severe, causes the remaining top growth to dry up and become yellowish-white.

Heavy attacks of asparagus beetle are damaging because they weaken the plants and reduce the following year's crop.

Controls

Hand picking is an effective way of dealing with this pest in small asparagus beds. Pyrethrum can be used if this is not feasible, but avoid spraying while plants are flowering, because bees are frequent visitors to asparagus flowers. If spraying during this period cannot be avoided, make sure that you spray at dusk when bees are not flying.

Remove and burn all the dead plant material in winter to destroy some of the adult beetles.

See also Slugs and snails, p.46

Problems with beans

Legumes are generally easy crops, but they do suffer from some pests and diseases

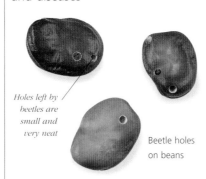

Holes left by beetles are small and very neat

Beetle holes on beans

Bean plants, particularly the leaves, may be attacked by pests and diseases. Bean rusts are common, particularly in warm and humid conditions. The beans themselves are not seriously attacked by pests or diseases.

Problem pests

A common pest of beans is the black bean aphid (*Aphis fabae*). Clusters of these black insects occur on shoots and under leaves where they suck sap. Treat them as for aphids in general (*see p.42*) or pinch out the succulent tips where they gather.

Gardeners who save their own seed might come across the bruchid beetle or bean seed beetle (*Bruchus rufimanus*). This particularly affects broad beans. Adult beetles are 4mm (⅛in) long and mottled black-brown and white. They lay eggs on the bean pods in early summer and the tiny grubs bore into the developing seed. They are so small that they go completely unnoticed in broad beans that are picked for eating, but they grow inside those beans that are allowed to develop and saved as seeds. Adult beetles emerge from the beans over winter, leaving tell-tale circular exit holes in the seed coats. There are no effective controls, but affected seeds will frequently still germinate anyway.

Problem diseases

Rusts affect mainly leaves but can also plague any part of the plant above ground level. Rust on French and dwarf beans is caused by the fungus *Uromyces appendiculatus*, while that on broad beans and field beans is caused by the fungus *Uromyces viciae-fiibae*, which also attacks some other legumes. Both fungi are dispersed by the wind or by contact, and spread quickly in warm and damp conditions during summer.

Early in the season the leaves of affected French and dwarf beans develop numerous pale, raised lesions on the upper surface, corresponding with white pustules on the underside, which release spores that re-infect the plant, causing brown pustules. These produce first ineffective "summer" spores and then black "resting" or overwintering spores. On broad beans and field beans, badly affected leaves simply turn brown and die.

Unfortunately, no fungicides are available to home gardeners to combat these problems. Remove the affected parts as soon as any symptoms appear; destroy badly affected plants.

Pustules release spores

Rust on a bean plant leaf

See also Avoiding pests and diseases, pp.36–37

Runner bean failure

Drought and heat can prevent bean flowers from setting

Watering in dry periods is essential for runner beans. Use 9 litres per sq m (2 gallons per sq yd) twice a week when flowers appear, as long as the dry spell lasts. Water the base of the plants; sprinkling the flowers does not seem to help. White-flowered cultivars of runner bean are claimed to crop more readily in hot, dry weather, but there is no real evidence for this.

Some bumble bees bite holes in the base of the flowers and gather nectar without any pollination. Fortunately new flowers in the morning are pollinated by other bees before these "robber" bees are on the wing. When the flowers are tattered and petal fragments litter the ground, suspect birds. Sparrows, especially, will peck at flowers, and netting is the only sure solution.

Bean crop
Beans should crop continuously until frosts arrive as long as they are continually picked; if seeds are allowed to ripen cropping will cease immediately. Pick and compost any surplus.

Growing chicory and endives

These are robust, hardy vegetables, valuable as winter salad plants, which are made less bitter by forcing and blanching

Witloof or Belgian chicory is forced in the dark in winter to produce tight conical buds of young, white leaves called "chicons". The tightly packed inner leaves of sugar-loaf chicory are naturally blanched and sweetened. Red chicory (radicchio) has red or variegated leaves, naturally blanched in the heart. Newer cultivars have the most tightly packed heads; some can be forced as for witloof chicory. Both sugar-loaf and red chicory can be sown as seedling salad crops (*see p.218*).

Flat and spreading frisée endives are ideal summer crops for blanching. Escarole endives are generally larger, with large, flat, sometimes coarse leaves. They are hardier, so can be used for winter and spring crops.

Radicchio 'Palla Rossa'

Site and cultivation

All types grow reasonably well on most soils except gravel and very heavy clay. Plant after a crop that was manured, and do not add organic matter during soil preparation. If this is not possible or in poor soil, use general-purpose fertilizer sparingly 10–14 days before sowing.

Sow chicory in modules for planting out later, or direct in rows 30cm (12in) apart, thinning to 20cm (8in) apart.

Sow witloof chicory in early summer for lifting in the autumn, sugar-loaf chicory in early to midsummer for an autumn crop, and in late summer for a protected winter crop. Sow red chicory in mid- to late spring for a summer crop, early to midsummer for an autumn crop, and late summer for a protected winter crop. Choose hardy cultivars for winter crops, bolt-resistant ones for spring crops.

In summer keep weed-free, and water during dry periods. Protect with cloches or straw in late autumn to prolong the season. If plants rot in wet weather, cut them down to a stump, which should re-sprout. Stumps left after harvest may give a second, often hardier crop of leaves.

BLANCHING ENDIVES AND CHICORY

1 Covering the centre of frisée endives with a plate allows light to reach outer leaves, giving an attractive gradation from green to white. To blanch the whole plant, cover with a bucket. Blanching takes about 10 days. Only blanch as many plants as you need, and use immediately. **2** Escarole endive and sugar-loaf chicory both form a heart and are self blanching. Tie up the leaves to blanch the entire heart. **3** Blanching chicory and endive hearts reduces bitterness.

Forcing for chicons

The forcing method for witloof chicory is to lift roots in late autumn and trim leaves off 2.5cm (1in) above the neck. Plant in a moist mix of equal parts soil and sand in a pot. Cover with another pot with blocked drainage holes to keep out the light. Kept at 18°C (64°F), heads should be ready in 3 weeks, when they should be 10–13cm (4–5in) high. Older cultivars may need a covering of soil to produce a tight head; plant in the soil under greenhouse staging, or in a cold frame, covering with 20cm (8in) of soil and sand mix. Water the soil if it becomes dry.

In light, sandy soils, forcing can be done outside. Cut plants in mid- to late autumn and earth up the stumps with 15–18cm (6–7in) of soil. Cover with straw or cloches. Heads will be ready from late winter to early spring.

SOME CULTIVARS TO TRY

Witloof chicory

'Witloof Belgian'

'Witloof Zoom' F1

Sugar-loaf chicory

'Biondissima di Trieste'

'Pain de Sucre' ('Sugar Loaf')

'Pan di Zucchero' ♀

'Snowflake'

'Zuckerhut' ♀

Raddichio

'Cesare' F1

'Indigo' ♀

'Leonardo' ♀

'Palla Rossa' ♀

'Rossa di Treviso'

Endives

'Frisée Glory' ♀ (Frisée)

'Jeti' ♀ (Escarole)

'Lassie' ♀ (Frisée)

'Pancalieri' ♀ (Frisée)

'Wallone' ♀ (Frisée)

Chillies and peppers

Ideal crops for containers, under glass or outdoors in warm areas

An indoor crop of chilli 'Hot Mexican'

Chillies and peppers will tolerate night temperatures of 12°C (54°F), but crop better if kept above 15°C (59°F); avoid temperatures above 30°C (86°F) under glass.

Sow seed for outdoor plants under glass in mid-spring, at 20°C (68°F). Harden off from late spring and plant out in well-drained, fertile, moisture-retentive soil, 38–45cm (15–18in) apart, 30cm (12in) for dwarf cultivars. Cover with fleece or cloches for wind protection and the extra warmth needed for good crops. Sow indoor plants in early to mid-sprng for final planting or potting on at flowering size in 8 weeks. Plant two or three in a grow bag or singly in 20–25cm (8–10in) pots.

Water peppers and chillies little and often to keep them evenly moist, and indoors maintain humidity by damping down twice a day in hot weather. Feed weekly with a balanced liquid fertilizer. Stake plants with three canes to avoid bending the brittle stems.

Pick early fruits when green to encourage more fruits. Later fruits will be sweeter (or hotter) if left to ripen on the plant, but yields will be lower.

See also Alternatives to glass, p.193

Courgette failure

Flowering problems can lower yields of courgettes

Female flowers have a swelling at the base

Sometimes, courgette plants will produce male flowers early in their flowering period when day length is short. Later, as day length increases and temperatures rise, plants will switch to produce mainly female flowers, which can be identified by a swelling (the immature fruit) at the base of the flower. Excessively close planting, low temperatures, and too much shade also encourage the production of male flowers.

An absence of fruits when there are both male and female flowers present suggests pollination may be at fault. Try hand pollinating, rubbing the male flower against the female. Fruits that are swelling only at the top, often with shrivelling and rotting, are also an indication of incomplete pollination, which is usually due to cold temperatures. This problem should naturally decrease as the season progresses.

Too many fruits on the plant can also cause rotting of small "fruitlets". This is the plant's way of balancing its resources, and the problem can be alleviated by promptly harvesting all the usable fruits.

See also Ten easy vegetables, p.204

Baby-leaf salads

Baby leaf salad crops may look exotic on the plate or the supermarket shelf, yet they are quick and easy to grow in the smallest of gardens

Bags of "speciality", ready-prepared, fresh salad leaves in supermarkets are usually sold at a premium price, which may give the impression that they are difficult to grow. In fact, the reverse is true – salad crops that can be harvested young are quick to grow, and these leaves are often easier to cultivate than traditional salad crops.

They are normally offered as "baby-leaf salads", which simply means that the leaves are harvested at the seedling-leaf stage. This is when they are at their most tender, succulent, and nutritious, and the combination of different textures and colours of leaves looks appetising on the plate.

This principle can be applied to almost any leafy salad crop including beet, rocket, mustard, cress, kales, Oriental vegetables such as pak choi, loose-leaf lettuces, and many herbs.

Keep the foliage dry when watering, to prevent mildew, by using a seep hose

Ornamental value

The varied leaves of these crops bring colour and texture to the vegetable plot. Strong contrasts can be achieved. Combine the scarlet leaves of red orach (*Atriplex hortensis*) with green crops, such as rocket; finely dissected leaves like those of cress 'Cressida' bring textural interest; and leaves with coloured stems or midribs (the central vein) such as Siberian kale 'Russian Red' provide a splash of colour.

Seedling salads undoubtedly warrant inclusion as temporary additions at the front of ornamental borders, provided you give careful consideration to the scale of other plantings nearby, and make ideal gap fillers. They can also be grown in pots on a patio or, if space is very limited, in seed trays or multicells.

Mix and match

Many seed companies offer seed mixtures that will produce salads with flavour characteristics such as bitter or

mild. These combinations have been pre-selected to combine similar growth rates and cultural needs (such as the same sowing time), and are designed to look good as a mixture on the plate. Such mixtures simplify selection and make an ideal starting point.

The huge array of individual crops available from seed catalogues also gives scope for experimentation, creating your own mixes for flavour, texture, or strength, whether spicy or mild. The wide range of strengths and flavours will provide something to suit all tastes.

Growing and harvesting

Choose a sunny site and incorporate well-rotted manure, garden compost, or other organic matter to improve the soil (*see p.259*). If it is really impoverished, rake in a general fertiliser, but do not overdo it as this may result in soft, lush, less tasty growth. Sow from early spring to late summer depending on the crop,

or year round with protection – excellent guidelines on the individual crops are available from specialist seed companies. Most Oriental greens and some other crops do not grow well in midsummer, running quickly to seed, so try to use more responsive alternatives, such as rocket, during hot spells.

First rake the soil to a fine tilth, then sow in drills approximately 30cm (12in) apart to allow room for hoeing out weeds between rows. Leave a 60cm (24in) path every four rows.

PREVENTING PROBLEMS

- Water from underneath with seep hoses or a similar device to prevent mildew forming on wet foliage
- In dry weather flea beetle can be a serious problem on young crops. Cover with horticultural fleece at initial growth stages for protection

See also Tips on seed germination, pp.20–21; Growing vegetables without chemicals, pp.200–201; Cut-and-come-again crops, p.202

SALAD MIXES TO TRY

Spring mix	Summer mix	Spicy mix	Italian mix	French mix	All green mix
Greek cress	Pak choi	Salad rocket	Rocket	Chervil 'Brussels Winter' [5]	Mizuna greens
Leaf radish	Mizuna	Mustards 'Red Giant' and 'Green Wave'	Sweet basil	Rocket	Komatsuma (spinach mustard) [6]
Pak choi	Mustard 'Tai Ping Po'	Mizuna 'Kyoto'	Radicchio [3]	Corn salad (lamb's lettuce)	Tatsai
Mizuna	Salad rocket [2]		Italian dandelion 'Red Rib'	Lettuce 'Red Batavia'	Kale 'Nero di Toscana'
Tatsai (rosette pak choi)	Misome		Oak-leaf lettuce	Sugar loaf chicory	
Mustard 'Suehlihung' [1]	Italian dandelion 'Red Rib'		Parsley 'Italian Giant' [4]		

Alternatively, take advantage of the small size of these salads to fill any gaps in vegetable or ornamental borders and beds. Sow fairly thickly at a rate of about 12g per sq m (⅜oz per sq yd) in shallow drills, lightly covered with soil. Thinning is not normally required, as the crops are intended to be harvested quickly, before they outgrow their space.

Because of their diminutive size, these seedling-leaf plants are the perfect crop for a highly productive containerized kitchen garden. A seed mixture could be broadcast sown thinly in pots with a minimum diameter of 25cm (10in), or in seed trays of potting compost. Similarly they could be grown on a sunny windowsill indoors throughout the year, in pots no smaller than 13cm (5in) in diameter. It is vital to keep any container well watered and apply a liquid fertilizer after the first leaves are harvested if repeat cropping is required.
Sow successively, every four weeks or so, to ensure a continuous supply of fresh new leaves. Keep the crops adequately watered to prevent bolting and running to seed.

Harvesting

Most baby-leaf salads are ready to harvest three weeks from sowing and should be cut when approximately 7.5cm (5in) high. Cutting above the seed leaves, leaving about 2.5cm (1in) of stem, or above the crown of the plant at this early stage will stimulate new growth, and should result in further harvests, a technique that is known as "cut-and-come-again" (*see p.202*).

GROWING ONIONS FROM SEEDS AND SETS

Growing onions from seeds and sets

Onions are a biennial crop, producing foliage in their first season and over-wintering as a bulb before flowering in their second year

Onions can be grown either from seeds or from "sets" (small bulbs). Seeds are cheaper and there are more cultivars to choose from, but sets have a shorter growing season and omit the difficult seedling stage.

The soil should be neutral to alkaline, well drained, and fertile. Dig over well in advance, and do not apply manure just before planting, as this can result in soft, disease-prone growth.

The main problem with onions is bolting (*see p.211*). Winter cold triggers flowering, and fluctuating temperatures trick the plant into thinking that it has experienced a full winter. Onions only become sensitive to cold at a certain size, so manipulation of sowing and planting dates lessens bolting.

Spring sowing

For large bulbs, early seed sowing is important because the size of bulb the onion produces is related to the amount of foliage it grows, and as soon as days become long enough bulbing-up begins. If very large bulbs are not required, sowing can be delayed until almost mid-spring. Small onions ripen better and generally last longer.

Early sowings also increase the risk of bolting, as the seedlings will become large enough to be sensitive to chilling at an earlier date. Prevent this by growing the onions in a heated greenhouse until late spring, and covering later direct-sown crops with fleece or glass cloches.

Onion sets have already completed one growing season and so are more sensitive to bolting. Heat-treated sets, where the flowering stalk has been destroyed by exposure to high temperatures, are available; otherwise plant no earlier than mid-spring.

Autumn sowings

Sowing in the preceding year will give a crop early the following year. Bolting can be more problematic, as there is more risk of the bulbs being exposed to variable temperatures, but autumn cultivars are bred to be less susceptible to bolting than spring types. Use them by early winter, as they do not keep.

Sowing in late summer or planting sets in mid- to late autumn should give plants that are large enough to survive winter cold, but small enough to be insensitive to chilling.

SOWING SEED IN LATE WINTER

1 Sow in late winter under cover, either in large modules of six seeds per block or singly in small modules. 2 Protect seeds sown

direct or planted-out seedlings with fleece or a tunnel cloche to protect them against cold temperatures that could trigger flowering.

See also Raising plants from seed, pp.20–21; Vegetables running to seed, p.211

Chitting potatoes

Potato "chitting" or sprouting encourages early growth

Rub off weak, pale shoots

Most shoots will be at one end

Chitting potatoes

Chitting extends the growing period and gives a heavier yield. Start chitting for early potatoes as soon as seed potatoes (small tubers) are available, and maincrop potatoes in late winter or early spring.

Healthy tubers are essential for a good yield. Home-saved tubers can carry virus diseases, so make sure that you buy certified seed potatoes at least every other year. Tubers the size of hen's eggs are the most economical to use, but larger tubers can be cut in half at planting.

Place the tubers in a shallow tray, the end with the most dormant shoots or "eyes" uppermost. Keep in a light, dry, frost-free place, out of direct sunlight for about 6 weeks, until sprouts about 2.5cm (1in) long have been produced. Shade and high temperatures both encourage unsatisfactory leggy shoots.

For early potatoes, rub off weak shoots to leave a few strong ones; otherwise you can leave them on. Plant out in a drill with 6cm (2½in) of soil to cover the potatoes. Plant with the shoots uppermost, aiming for 10–13 shoots per m (9–12 per yd) in rows 30–38cm (12–15in) apart.

See also Potato problems, pp.221–222

Potato tuber problems

Potatoes can suffer tuber damage from pests and diseases, which can lower the yield or cause problems with both the eating and storage quality of the crop

Most potato problems are caused by pests or infections for which there are few effective controls. Rotation (*see p.210*) and other cultivation methods can minimize them.

Problems on the skin

Scab or scurf diseases can affect skins. Common scab, caused by a bacterium-like organism (*Streptomyces scabies*), is found especially in light, sandy soil low in organic matter, or in heavily limed soil. Infection is usually superficial, causing raised, scabby patches with rough edges, and the potatoes are fit to eat. Powdery scab is caused by a fungus (*Spongospora subterranea*) and is worse in wet conditions. The scabby areas may have pustules with dusty brown spores, and severe attacks can render the tubers too distorted to eat. Silver scurf and black scurf are minor skin blemishes caused by other fungi.

There are no fungicide treatments for these problems. Plant clean seed with no skin blemishes and practice rotation. Adding organic matter and watering in dry weather will control common scab.

Problems in the flesh

Black leg is rot caused by a bacterium (*Erwinia carotovora* pv. *erythroseptica*) that spreads from infected seed tubers to stems. It starts as a black lesion at

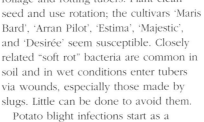

Lift potatoes as soon as they are ready

the stem base, leading to collapse of the foliage and rotting tubers. Plant clean seed and use rotation; the cultivars 'Maris Bard', 'Arran Pilot', 'Estima', 'Majestic', and 'Desirée' seem susceptible. Closely related "soft rot" bacteria are common in soil and in wet conditions enter tubers via wounds, especially those made by slugs. Little can be done to avoid them.

Potato blight infections start as a foliage problem (*see p.222*), but can

progress into the tuber. Sunken brown patches on the surface and brown staining in the flesh below rapidly become a foul-smelling, slimy mess. A soil-borne blight species (*Phytophthora erythroseptica*) sometimes causes rot, but it is not so serious.

Potato spraing, rusty brown rings in the flesh, is caused by a virus carried by soil-borne nematodes and harboured in many weeds. Use rotation, keep the site weed-free, and plant certified seed.

Holes in tubers

Holes are most often caused by keeled slugs (*Milax* species) living below the soil surface. Damage takes place in late summer to autumn, with round holes in the skin and much larger cavities inside. Limit damage by lifting potatoes promptly. The cultivars 'Sante', 'Wilja', 'Charlotte', 'Golden Wonder', 'Pentland Dell', 'Estima', and 'Pentland Ivory' are less susceptible, but they are not fully resistant. The pathogenic nematode *Phasmarhabditis hermaphrodita*, available by mail order from suppliers of garden predators and parasites, can be applied to moist soil once the potatoes are growing but before the top growth is too dense. Slug pellets used according to the manufacturer's directions are effective. Do not store slug-damaged tubers with sound tubers.

Potato powdery scab

Roughly circular scabby areas with raised edges

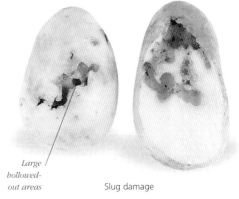

Large hollowed-out areas

Slug damage

See also Avoiding pests and diseases, pp.36–37; Crop rotation, p.210; Potato foliage problems, p.222

Potato foliage problems

Problems affecting the leaves of potatoes can devastate crop yield; buying certified seed potatoes and choosing resistant cultivars play an important role in avoiding them

The yellowing of potato foliage is a common symptom, but this is not always cause for concern. It is most often caused by the natural aging of the leaves, or the end-of-season dieback of foliage. With well-chitted tubers, especially of early or second-early cultivars, this may occur from midsummer. Yellowing of younger leaves often occurs in summer and can be caused by a number of deficiencies, and also by pests, such as red spider mite in hot weather, or diseases, such as blackleg (*see p.221*).

Magnesium deficiency
Magnesium is an important constituent of the green pigment chlorophyll. Potatoes grown on sandy soils are susceptible to magnesium deficiency, which causes yellowing between the main veins, giving a marbled effect. This appears on the older leaves first, as the magnesium is transported mainly to the developing young tips. End-of-season leaf yellowing mimics magnesium deficiency, so check plants regularly.

Drought or poor soil structure can both inhibit magnesium uptake by the plants. Add plenty of organic matter before planting and water well during growth. Too much potassium can exacerbate the problem, "locking up" magnesium in the soil. Use balanced fertilizers, rather than sulphate of potash. Foliar sprays of Epsom salts at 200g to 11 litres of water (about 3oz per gallon), with the addition of a few drops of soft soap or detergent to make the solution wet the foliage more effectively, will help to alleviate the symptoms quickly.

Potato blight
Spores of the fungus *Phytophthora infestans* are carried by air currents or rain splash. Warm, humid weather is needed for infection to occur. Brown patches develop, mainly on the leaf edges and tips. As they spread, the leaves wither and die. White fungal growth can develop on the underside of the leaf, particularly in wet weather or humid conditions. The infection can progress down the stems to the tubers (*see p.221*). Leaf infections late in the season may not reach the tubers, and so have little effect on yield, but early infections can be disastrous.

This is the most common and serious foliage disease of potatoes. It can be controlled by regular applications of copper-based fungicides or mancozeb. Some potato varieties, including 'Cara', 'Estima', 'Kondor', 'Maris Peer', 'Pentland Crown', 'Valor', and 'Remarka' show some resistance. Tomatoes and some ornamental plants can also become infected, and cross-infection occurs, especially to outdoor tomatoes late in the growing season.

Potato leaf viruses
There are three main leaf viruses of potatoes. Potato leaf roll virus causes leaf edges to roll up and the leaves to become stiff and brittle. Potato virus Y causes black streaks and reduced tuber yields. Potato virus X produces rather faint leaf mottling symptoms, best seen on overcast or dull days, and reduces yield significantly.

Viruses need carriers, or "vectors", to move from one host to another. They can then infect the host's cells and reproduce. Many viruses, including potato leaf roll virus and virus Y, are spread by aphids; virus X is mainly spread on tools used to cut seed tubers.

There are no chemical treatments for viruses, and it is not practical to control aphids outdoors by spraying. The only safeguard is to plant certified seed to ensure plants are initially virus free.

Yellowing between main veins

Rust-coloured areas may appear

Magnesium deficiency

Potato blight on leaves and shoots

See also Avoiding pests and diseases, pp.36–37; Using fungicides, pp.38–39; Chitting potatoes, p.220; Potato tuber problems, p.221

PRACTICAL ADVICE

Sweet corn pollination

Wind-pollinated sweet corn has some specific planting needs

Traditional sweet corn has half the starch content of maize. Supersweet cultivars have high sugar levels and low sugar-to-starch conversion rates, so although less creamy, they stay sweet for longer after picking. Sugar-enhanced cultivars have higher sugar levels and a creamy texture, but do not stay sweet for long after picking.

To retain their differing qualities, these types must be isolated from each other to avoid cross pollination. Pollen can carry at least 30m (100ft) on the wind, so isolating by distance is impractical. A two-week difference in flowering times can also be difficult to achieve. Consequently it is easier to grow just one type.

Each sweet corn plant produces only one male "flower" at its tip, but potentially two or three female cobs. A lack of pollen from the male flower can result in cobs that are empty towards the tip. For effective pollination, plant sweet corn in blocks rather than rows, with a minimum of 16 plants spaced 35cm (14in) or more apart in a block.

Poor "tip fill" due to a lack of pollen

See also Maximizing space, p.230

TECHNIQUES

Growing a giant pumpkin

Home-grown giant pumpkins make a Halloween treat

'Atlantic Giant' pumpkin

Begin by choosing one of the larger American pumpkin cultivars. 'Atlantic Giant', the biggest available to home gardeners, can grow up to 3m (10ft) in circumference. 'Big Max' makes a good alternative.

Start early, sowing seed under glass in mid-spring, potting up the best seedlings and hardening off in late spring. Plant out in good soil and mulch after planting. Do not feed at this stage, or the plant will produce lots of green growth and no fruit. (For full details on general growing requirements *see pp.224–225*).

Once the plant has set three or four fruits, choose the largest and take all the smaller ones off. Pinch out the shoots two leaves beyond the remaining fruits, and the tips of all other shoots and sideshoots.

Start feeding weekly with a high-potash fertilizer (such as a tomato feed), which will swell the fruit. Water regularly and generously throughout summer and trim back foliage if it starts to "run". On autumn nights, wrap the fruit in fleece to keep it in active growth for as long as possible before harvesting.

See also Growing pumpkins, pp.224–225

PRACTICAL ADVICE

Pumpkin and squash storage

Some squashes can be stored for several months

Use secateurs or loppers to sever the stems cleanly when fruits are ripe (*see pp.224–225*). Leave an 8–13cm (3–5in) stalk, but do not use this as a carrying handle, which can damage the fruit.

A wipe with disinfectant solution may help against moulds and bacteria. After drying outside or in a frost-free, sunny place under cover, "cure" the skins at about 27–30°C (81–86°F) in a humid place. A closed, warm shed with the floor damped down is ideal.

After a couple of weeks, move the fruits to drier conditions, aiming for 10–13°C (50–55°F). Fruits that are kept too warm will shrivel and lose flavour, while those kept too cold will rot. Letting the fruits touch encourages rotting. Semi-ripe fruits cured this way are almost as good as vine-ripened ones. Unripe, green fruits are edible but less tasty, and will not store.

Immediately remove stored fruits that show signs of rot. If you put them on the compost heap, remove any seedlings that appear when the compost is spread, as they are likely to be useless hybrids.

After harvesting, dry and cure the crop

See also Growing pumpkins, pp.224–225

GROWING PUMPKINS AND WINTER SQUASHES

Growing pumpkins and winter squashes

With their colourful, sometimes patterned skins and dense, sweet flesh, pumpkins and squashes have much to offer in the garden and kitchen alike

Pumpkins and winter squashes are perhaps the finest of all the winter storage crops. To ripen fully and store well, they need warm temperatures and full sun. Fruits often fail to ripen in cool climates, which have a shorter growing season; reduce the risk of this by sowing seeds early indoors and choosing early-maturing cultivars. Another problem is the amount of growing space these crops demand. Bush types are the most compact, but have low yields. The most commonly grown rambling "vine" types take the most space.

Pumpkin cultivars

Pumpkins usually have less flavour than squashes, but may grow larger. Pumpkins are more widely grown for decoration, including lantern carving at Halloween. 'Jack of all Trades' and 'Rocket' both make classic lanterns with deep orange skins. The fast growth of cultivars 'Racer' and 'Sunny' makes them good alternatives for gardeners faced with a shorter growing season.

Winter and spaghetti squash cultivars

Winter squashes have more flavour than pumpkins, and also store particularly well. The dense, sweet "butternut" types are widely grown. 'Sprinter' is high-yielding, but needs a good summer; the smaller 'Cobnut' has been bred to perform well in cooler summers. Other cultivars worth growing include 'Onion Squash', which has a beautiful orange-red, onion-shaped fruit, and 'Crown Prince', which has fruits with dark grey-blue skin that conceals sweet, bright orange flesh.

The flesh of spaghetti squashes forms long, thin strands with a mellow flavour when cooked. Boil spaghetti squashes whole in water for 45 minutes or until a skewer can be stuck into the flesh, then halve them and fork out the contents. They must be fully ripened before harvesting, or the flesh will be stodgy and not form strands when cooked.

Starting seedlings

Squashes and pumpkins are frost-tender annuals, and they should only be planted out after all danger from frost has passed. In cooler areas, sow the seeds direct at the end of spring, after the last frost, or in modules indoors in mid-spring before planting out after the risk of frost has passed – this is recommended if a longer growing season is needed. In warm areas, sow in modules under glass in mid-spring for planting out in late spring, depending on weather forecasts.

Do not overwater the seedlings. When two or three leaves have emerged, plant out as soon as possible, because seedlings are sensitive to root disturbance. Harden off gradually in a cold frame or similar protected area, and warm the soil in the intended planting position by covering with a cloche. Fleece (*see p.202*) or cloches insulate plants from late cold spells, and a plastic bottle cut through the middle and placed over the top of a plant will both keep it snug and protect it from slugs and snails.

Maximizing the crop

Choose a site that receives as much sun as possible. Pumpkins and squashes are hungry plants, but if they are over-indulged they will produce yards of huge leaves and few fruits. Plant in normal garden soil and mulch with a layer of compost or other organic matter. Each plant needs about 3sq m (30sq ft).

A selection of pumpkins and squashes
Although pumpkins and squashes vary so much in appearance (*left*) and use, they share growing requirements. 'Onion Squash' (*top right*) and 'Crown Prince' (*bottom right*) are good culinary cultivars.

See also Maximizing space, p.230; Growing a giant pumpkin p.223; Pumpkin and squash storage p.223

RECOMMENDED CULTIVARS

'Rouge vif d'Etampes' is a large, flat, heavily ribbed pumpkin with shiny, orange skin. Fruits are 30–60cm (12–24in) in diameter and more than 10kg (22lb) in weight, with excellent keeping qualities and flavour.

'Cream of the Crop' is an acorn squash with cream-coloured skin and flesh. It produces high yields of fruits weighing 1kg (2.2lb) or more on a semi-bush plant. **1**

'Jack-be-Little' is a tiny but extremely decorative orange pumpkin. **2**

'Sweet Dumpling' has ribbed fruits with cream skin flecked with green. The flesh is flavoursome and nutty.

'Pyjamas' is a high-yielding spaghetti squash. It is a new green-and-white-striped cultivar with sweeter flesh than some. **3**

'Long Island Cheese' is a winter squash that produces round, flat, beige fruits weighing 3–5kg (6.6–11lb), which store well. The orange flesh is moderately sweet. **4**

Place a stake next to each seedling at planting time to help locate its centre for watering later.

Where space is limited, exploit the scrambling habit of these plants by growing them over large, stable structures – such as a tunnel or bamboo wigwam (*see pp.212–213*) – or hedges. Plant them on the southern side of a structure or hedge for maximum light, mulch well around the roots, and tie in the stems regularly.

In bad summers or cool areas, grow plants through black plastic, which keeps the soil warm, conserves moisture, and reduces weeds. In cool weather, cover them with fleece to keep them growing actively. Once the plant has set enough fruits, trim the end of the vine to concentrate energy into the fruits.

Pumpkins and squashes need plenty of water, particularly at flowering time and fruit set, which also helps to prevent the problem of powdery mildew. Towards the end of summer, powdery mildew can cover the upper surfaces of the leaves with a white, powdery fungal growth. Do not ignore this, thinking that most of the growing has by now been completed; this period is crucial for the ripening and the subsequent storing qualities of the fruits. Try to prevent any periods of drought, as uneven growth puts the plant under stress.

Mildew may be controlled with fungicides based on sulphur. Spray or dust the plants at the first sign of disease, and if hot, dry conditions arise in late summer, it can be worth applying a preventative spray.

Ready for harvest

Squashes will only store well if they are ripened and cured properly. Towards the end of summer it can be tempting to cut the leaves from around the fruit to aid maturing, but the leaves are essential. The fruits are ripe when the stems dry and the skins harden, usually in mid-autumn.

If the fruits are gathered before they are fully ripe they may shrivel in storage, while delaying the harvest puts fruits at risk from frosts, although a light frost will do them no harm. Damp is another hazard; raising fruits on wooden blocks or tiles minimizes the risk of damage from this. Gently turn and move the fruits occasionally while they are ripening to reduce the pale, flattened patches that develop where the fruit rests. For the best flavour, leave the fruits on the vine to ripen as long as there is no risk of frost, then cure them for storage (*see p.223*).

Growing tomatoes

The classic summer crop, versatile tomatoes can be grown inside or out, in the ground or in containers, providing fruits for many weeks

There are tomatoes with fruits of all shapes and sizes from tiny, round cherry tomatoes through plum shapes to huge beefsteak types, with red, yellow, green, purple, or striped skins.

The other important consideration is how the plant grows. Vine or cordon tomatoes are grown as one stem on a support, which uses space efficiently in a greenhouse. Bush types have plenty of side branches, crop early, and are better for growing outdoors, but there is less variety available. Common cultivars of both types are widely available as young plants, but a greater variety is available as seed.

Starting your plants

Sow in seed compost in an 8cm (3in) pot, spacing seeds at least 1.5cm (½in) apart on the surface, to deter damping off (see p.20). Cover with a 5mm (¼in) layer of vermiculite or perlite and keep at 21°C (70°F). Seedlings should emerge after five days.

When the seedlings are large enough, two weeks after sowing, move them to a greenhouse at about 15–18°C (60–65°F). Fill 8cm (3in) pots with multipurpose or similar compost, water them well, and place with the plants to warm up. After two days prick out the seedlings, one per pot, and water them in lightly. As plants grow, space them out so that their leaves do not touch.

After a month, the seedlings will be ready to transplant. The rootball should hold together when taken out of the pot. If using grow bags or pots indoors, move them to their final position and water well a day before transplanting to allow the compost to warm up. Transplant carefully – water first and avoid holding the stem where possible – and water the plants in. Cordon tomatoes require 1.5–2.1m (5–7ft) supports of canes or string; bush cultivars can be loosely tied to a

GROWING FROM SEED

Sow tomato seed in spring – it germinates well. To avoid pricking out, start with two seeds per pot and discard the weaker seedling.

Helping tomato plants to fruit
Male and female parts are within the same flower. Shaking plants gently or damping down helps to transfer pollen to produce well-formed fruits.

1m (3ft) cane. Ties may need adjusting as the stems thicken, but string twisted around the stem in a spiral does not.

Continuing care

As the plants grow, continue twisting or tying in. Remove side shoots from cordon tomatoes by hand as soon as possible to produce optimum yields. Cut off any that are thicker than a pencil, as they often do not snap cleanly. Work from the top of the plant downwards in case the leader is accidentally broken off. If this happens, use a side shoot as a replacement leader. Remove the leader of outdoor cordons when plants have produced four or five fruit trusses; any later trusses are unlikely to ripen.

The water demands of young plants are quite low, but in the height of summer one plant can require 0.7 litres (1½ pints) a day. Plants in containers need more frequent watering than those in garden soil. Keep the plants well watered at all times, adding high-potash liquid tomato feed according to the manufacturer's directions.

Pollination, fruit set and harvesting

Tomatoes require high humidity to set good amounts of fruit. Humidity is adequate outdoors, but in greenhouses "damp down" periodically using a hose; ventilate to maintain adequate air-flow and deter disease.

Tomatoes are best when ripened fully on the vine. You can remove the foliage around ripening trusses on indoor tomatoes to improve airflow and make picking easier. At the end of the season, pick green fruits and ripen them indoors; bush tomatoes can be covered with a cloche to finish ripening; lay cordon tomatoes and cover with tunnel cloches. When harvesting, break off individual fruits at the stalk.

See also Tips on seed germination, pp.20–21; Tomato problems, p.227

Tomato problems

Several of the more common tomato problems are caused by fluctuating growing conditions, and can be avoided without any use of chemicals, simply by giving the plant what it needs

Tomatoes are often grown in grow bags or containers and so are free of soil pests and diseases. They are prone to potato blight (*see p.222*) and indoors can suffer from greenhouse pests (*see pp.197–198*), but erratic water levels or temperatures cause many problems.

Blossom end rot

More common at the beginning of the season, this is caused by poor calcium flow to the fruits, due to insufficient or irregular watering. Plants in containers and grow bags are most prone to it, as are plum and beefsteak tomatoes, because their larger fruits place greater demands on the plant. Too little water impairs the uptake of foods; excess tomato fertilizer, which inhibits calcium uptake, also contributes. A brown spot appears at the fruit's flower end, and eventually becomes a hard, sunken ring that gives the fruit a flattened look.

Keep the growing medium constantly moist, maintain humidity and water regularly at dusk (calcium transport is highest at night). Ventilation to avoid high temperatures helps. Foliar feeds of calcium do not, and can scorch leaves.

Discoloured and malformed fruits

Dicolouration can take the form of: greenback – distinct hard, green areas on the fruit shoulder, visible before

Tomato split

Tomato whitewall

ripening; or blotchy ripening – irregular yellow patches with no clear margin appearing during ripening. Together with whitewall (hard white tissue within the fruit) these result from excessive heat, light damage, or both. Control by ventilating adequately and providing shading where necessary.

In "catfacing", blossom sticks to the developing fruits, leading to puckering, scarring, and large corky lesions on fruits. This is caused by adverse weather during fruit set, and is less common as the season progresses. Cover plants with horticultural fleece on cold nights.

"Boxy" fruits appear normal outside, but when cut open have hollow compartments with no seeds. This is caused by extreme temperatures during fruit development. Aim to maintain a consistent growing environment.

Cracking and splitting

Cracking appears as concentric corky rings at the fruit's stem end. Splitting actually splits the skin to the pulp inside, often leading to secondary infections such as grey mould (*Botrytis*). Both are caused by a sudden burst in growth due to fluctuating moisture and temperature levels. Control by watering regularly and ventilating adequately.

Foliage problems

Tomato leaves curl up in cool night temperatures. This is not a problem, but can indicate that night temperatures are too low, with a risk of malformed fruits.

Twisted or distorted young foliage on outdoor plants is often caused by weedkillers. Keep a separate watering can for weedkillers; avoid spraying on windy days; do not compost the first mowings after using lawn weedkiller.

Magnesium deficiency causes yellow areas between leaf veins, particularly on the lower leaves. It is most likely to occur in tomatoes grown on sandy or acid soils, or where high-potash feeds have been over-applied. In severe cases the leaves drop, but mild cases are unlikely to affect yield or quality. If necessary, control with fortnightly foliar sprays of Epsom salts at 54g in 4.5 litres (2oz in 1 gallon) of water.

Sunken, leathery patch

Rest of fruit appears normal

Blossom end rot

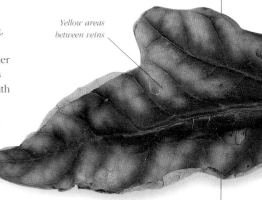

Yellow areas between veins

Tomato leaf with magnesium deficiency

See also Avoiding pests and diseases, pp.36–37; Overheating greenhouses, p.192

Everyday and exotic root crops

Root crops are perhaps not the most glamorous of vegetables, but they are an essential part of the kitchen garden and there are some unusual ones to try

For new flavours, colours and textures, less commonly grown root vegetables take some beating. Their freedom from pests and diseases and tolerance of poor soils make them easy to grow and suitable for organic gardeners. They also keep longer than leafy or fruiting vegetables so there is little waste.

Getting the best from root crops

Aim for a loose textured soil as free of stones as possible. Although manure and compost are sometimes blamed for fanged or forked roots, adding well-rotted material will not affect the root quality. Fresh manure is best left to rot before adding to the soil. Poor soils will benefit from a modest dressing of general-purpose fertilizer such as Growmore or blood, fish and bone.

As these crops compete poorly with weeds, try to create a "sterile" seedbed. Prepare the seedbed and allow weeds to germinate. Once they are just visible, remove the weeds by shallow hoeing and then sow the crop, taking care to disturb the soil as little as possible.

Carrots

It is easy to buy good cheap carrots, so go for less usual types, such as those with purple and white roots. To avoid running to seed, sow in late spring or early summer, into a sterile seedbed.

Leaves are also used in Asian cuisines

Well-drained soil yields plump roots

Colours range from orange to brown

Sweet potato

Bunches of young, fresh carrots sown in early spring are especially tasty. Carrot seed is slow to germinate, so try sowing a dozen seeds of round or short-rooted cultivars into small pots, germinate them on the windowsill or in the greenhouse and plant out as soon as the seedlings can be seen. Alternatively, raise crops in the greenhouse, in "spent" grow bags that have previously held tomatoes.

Sow 1–2cm (1in) deep, in rows 25cm (10in) apart and thin to 5cm (2in). Water only in prolonged dry spells. Harvest as soon as the roots are usable. It is not worth storing carrots for winter use; leave them in the ground covered with straw or cardboard beneath a plastic sheet. Protect from carrot fly (*see p.205*).

Parsnips

These hardy plants need a long growing season and are best sown as early as possible in spring. Pre-warming the soil with a clear plastic covering for at least six weeks before sowing will help the slow-germinating seed to grow. The vigorous F1 hybrid 'Gladiator' gives good results even in adverse conditions.

Sow 1–2cm (1in) deep, in rows 30cm (12in) apart and thin to 15cm (6in).

Watering is not needed. Harvest and store as for carrots (*above*).

Sweet potato

These sweet roots originate from tropical South America and need warm, moist fertile soil. Buy rooted cuttings or slips and plant immediately into small pots. Keep in warm, bright conditions until fully rooted, then plant in greenhouse borders or outside, ideally beneath cloches or fleece, allowing 50cm (20in) between plants to accommodate their trailing stems. Water freely in dry spells. Use the roots when developed. Store in a dry, warm place in winter, after "curing" the harvested roots for a week at 10–15°C (50–59°F). 'Beauregard' is the usual cultivar.

Scorzonera and salsify

These long-rooted European plants have distinctive earthy flavours when cooked in the same way as parsnips.

Scorzonera has most attractive black roots up to 90cm (36in) long. Salsify has slightly shorter brown roots. Both have pale flesh, and salsify is considered to have a stronger flavour than the more delicately flavoured scorzonera.

Grow as recommended for parsnips, sowing mid- to late spring. Gather the roots from autumn onwards. They can be left in the ground through the winter.

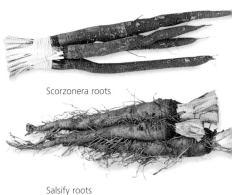

Scorzonera roots

Salsify roots

HARVESTING ROOT CROPS

Mooli radish
Lift mooli radishes as soon as they are large enough to use, because they quickly become "woolly" and unappetizing. Winter radishes need to be lifted before the first frost.

Chinese artichoke
Harvest these small but plentiful tubers in small batches as they are required, because unlike most other root vegetables they do not store at all well once they are lifted.

Hamburg parsley
The roots can be lifted from late summer and stored in a cool place in boxes filled with sand. Alternatively, they can be left in the ground until they are needed.

Hamburg parsley

Grow as for carrots from a mid- to late spring sowing, allowing 15cm (6in) between plants and 30cm (12in) between rows to get large roots. The roots have a mild flavour not unlike celery and are good cooked as you would carrots or parsnips. If you are short of parsley, the foliage can be used as a substitute, but it dies back in winter like a carrot top. Protect from carrot fly (*see p.205*).

Oca

This South America tuber is a member of the oxalis family and is exceptionally easy to grow. The tubers look like unshelled peanuts and can be cooked as you would potatoes, having a sharp, crunchy texture and foliage. Plant tubers, sometimes offered in catalogues, in early summer into moist, fertile soil, 5cm (2in) deep, in rows 45cm (18in) apart with 30cm (12in) between the tubers. Water freely in prolonged dry spells. The foliage smothers weeds, but the tubers do not form until early autumn. Protect the foliage from frost in autumn with a double layer of fleece. Gather the tubers when the foliage is cut back by frost. Store in cool, dry, frost-free conditions.

Chinese artichoke

Plant the tubers of this Eastern vegetable 5cm (2in) deep in mid-spring, in rows 45cm (18in) apart, and allowing 30cm (12in) between plants. Tubers are sometimes offered in catalogues and supermarkets and resemble little spiral maggots. They are very tasty boiled or stir fried, when their fresh, delicate flavour can be best enjoyed.

Moist soils are essential for good tuber formation. Gather the tubers from early autumn for immediate use.

Winter and mooli radishes

Winter radishes have large turnip-like roots with a hot, peppery, cabbage-like taste. They can be used in stews, soups and salads, but be aware that they can overpower other ingredients. Sliced, grated or cut into sticks, they can be added to winter salads or eaten, with drinks, as a snack. Good cultivars include 'Round Black Spanish' and 'Green Goddess'.

Sow direct in late summer in rows 30cm (12in) apart, 1cm (½in) deep, thinning to 15cm (6in), and harvest as required in autumn. Protect from hard frost, as suggested for carrots, to gather roots in mid- to late winter. Protect from cabbage root fly with fleece.

Leave some winter radishes to run to seed next summer – their immature seedpods are a tasty addition to salads and stir fries. The cultivar 'München Bier' is sold for this purpose.

Mooli radishes are a summer crop, sown in midsummer for pulling as needed in late summer and early autumn. These oriental vegetables can be used for stews, salads and stir frying. 'Minowase' is a reliable, commonly grown cultivar.

Maximizing space

Where space in the vegetable garden is at a premium, growing methods that use it to its full potential by combining crops can often prove invaluable

To use space efficiently, vegetable growers try to keep ground occupied as much as possible. One way of doing this is by double cropping, when three crops are grown in two years. An example might be following early potatoes with a crop of leeks to be harvested during the next winter, which leaves the ground free for a summer crop, such as maincrop carrots. Growing four crops in two years on the same piece of ground is more difficult!

Vegetable growers can also grow two or more crops in the same place at the same time, a method known as intercropping. The "three sisters" system of growing crops of sweet corn, beans and squash together (*see box*) is

an example of this from South America. Vegetable growers in China also practise this on a large scale. But in northern countries, there is much less light and the growing seasons are shorter, so opportunities to inter- and catch crop are greatly reduced.

A much used system is to plant quick-growing plants such as radish and lettuce between slower-growing ones such as Brussels sprouts. The latter are given a very wide spacing when they are planted in early summer, since they will take all summer to grow to their full size. In the meantime, lettuces or perhaps beetroot, calabrese, summer cabbage or turnips can be planted in between them for gathering in midsummer. By late summer

the Brussels sprouts cast too much shade for intercropping to be possible.

Cabbages for autumn and winter use are also planted in early summer with a wide spacing. Although there is less room than with Brussels sprouts, small plants such as radish and spinach can be grown in between them.

Although these intercrops can be started as seeds, they are often easier to arrange if they are raised as transplants in pots and modules to get them off to an early start.

Ample fertilizer and moisture must be supplied; otherwise the intercrops could easily act as "weeds" causing neither the main nor the intercrop to perform well.

Beginners can easily overreach themselves here and it is best to play safe and scrap the intercrop rather than let the main crop suffer. Although intercropping rows of peas, beans and potatoes looks like an attractive idea, in practice the rows have to be quite wide in order to achieve good results. Peas in rows 1.2m (48ins) apart can accept a row of winter brassicas or purple sprouting broccoli down the middle in midsummer, however. The brassicas and broccoli will then grow successfully when the peas are removed.

You can use catch cropping where an early-maturing crop such as shallots, over-wintered onions or early peas can be followed by a quick-growing crop of baby carrots, calabrese, endive, kohl rabi, lettuces, leafy salads, spinach or turnips for autumn use. Similarly, in spring, crops not planted out until after the risk of frost has passed can be preceded by fast-growing root and salad crops. In fact, late sown crops such as sweet corn or tomatoes can be planted among the catch crop leaving them free to exploit the space as soon as the catch crop is gathered.

THE "THREE SISTERS"

Traditionally, the three sisters crops were not only grown together but also eaten together. Corn supplies all but two of the essential amino acids, and these are available in the beans. Squash is high in carbohydrate and Vitamin A, and also in vegetable fats, which corn and beans lack. Together, they provide a fairly balanced diet of carbohydrates, proteins, and vegetable fats.

Growing fruit trees in a small garden

Compact trees, adjusted to the confines of a small garden but without sacrificing size or quality of crop, enable fruit to be grown in any garden

Compact trees for small gardens are produced by using several techniques; choose carefully the rootstock and cultivar, the tree form and pruning, and adopt the proper feeding regime.

Choice of cultivar and rootstock

Some cultivars are inherently vigorous, others more compact. Apples to avoid are 'Blenheim Orange', 'Gravenstein', 'Bramley's Seedling', 'Crispin', and the pears 'Doyenné Boussoch', 'Pitmaston Duchess', and 'Merton Pride'. These are also demanding in their pollination.

The rootstock determines the size of the tree. New rootstocks are sometimes introduced, so buy from good nurseries with detailed catalogues. Details of apple and pear rootstocks are given on p.233. For plums, Pixy is useful, and St. Julien A will produce a medium-sized tree on less fertile soil. Sweet cherries are hard to accommodate in a small garden. It is possible to grow

Cordon apples lining a path are both productive and decorative

wall-trained sweet or acid cherries on the rootstock Colt, and Malling F 12/1 can be used for sweet cherries on larger walls. Summer pruning helps to contain a wall-trained sweet cherry. In the open it is better to grow the culinary Morello cherry, which is inherently dwarf.

Choice of tree form

Apples and pears are best grown as a dwarf open-centred bush, or a restricted tree form such as a cordon, espalier, fan, or dwarf pyramid. A dwarf open-centred

bush is the most productive and the simplest to maintain, but requires most space. Cordons are planted closely in a row, and need a fence support system. Espaliers and fans can be grown on a wall, or wires, and are very attractive. The dwarf pyramid can get out of hand if summer pruning is neglected.

Peaches, nectarines, and apricots are best grown as a fan on a warm wall. Grow plums and gages as pyramids or fans; a summer-pruned plum pyramid makes a medium tree with a strong framework and regular cropping.

Annual maintenance

Fruit trees need careful pruning in small gardens. Prune most forms in summer, as winter pruning stimulates growth. Prune an open-centred bush in winter, and any excess growth in summer.

The feeding regime is important for trees in small spaces. Do not exceed recommended doses of nitrogen, as more than 30g per sq m (1oz per sq yd) can lead to soft, disease-prone growth, at the expense of fruits.

FRUIT TREES TO TRY

Apples
'Fiesta' ♀, dessert
'Kidd's Orange Red' ♀, dessert
'Lane's Prince Albert' ♀, culinary
'Pixie' ♀, dessert
'Sunset' ♀, dessert

Pears
'Beth' ♀
'Concorde' ♀

Plums
'Opal' ♀, dessert
'Oullins Gage' ♀, culinary and dessert
'Victoria' ♀, culinary and dessert

BUYING FRUIT TREES

- For most forms, choose one- or two-year-old trees, which establish better than older trees
- For fans and espaliers, partially trained three-year-old trees are best
- The widest selection of trees is available bare root, delivered between late autumn and spring for immediate planting
  - Plant container-grown trees at any time; check for strong roots, but ensure they are not pot-bound

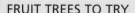

See also Growing fruit trees in pots pp.234–235; Pruning apple and pear trees, pp.236–237; Planting trees, pp.60–61; Feeding fruit trees, p.232

Storing fruit

Only store the best fruit, as poor pieces may spoil healthy ones

Storing apples in a plastic bag

Store fruit at an even temperature, above 3°C (37°F) but ideally below 7°C (45°F), in a well-ventilated, dark, and moist (but not damp) atmosphere. A cellar, garden shed, or garage can meet these requirements.

Containers should allow air to circulate. Stacking crates are ideal, but slatted wooden shelves, wooden orchard boxes, or polystyrene trays are also suitable.

Preparing fruit

Quince have a pungent aroma, so store them away from other fruits. Fruits can be stored unwrapped, but wrapping each one in tissue paper or newspaper gives better results. Leave pears and larger apples unwrapped. You can use plastic bags provided the temperature is kept even to prevent condensation. Pierce one hole per 500g (1lb) of fruit (two holes for apples), placing fruit in a single layer and folding over the end.

Poor ventilation or damaged fruit will cause rotting. Shrivelling indicates that the storage area is either too warm or too dry. Damp down the floor occasionally if you can, or store fruit in plastic bags.

See also Apple fruit problems, p.238

Feeding and mulching fruit trees

Like all crop plants, fruit trees need plenty of nutrients if they are to grow and fruit well

Fruit trees cannot benefit from regular cultivation of the soil. Instead, their needs can be met by mulches and granular or liquid fertilizers, and removing competition from weeds.

Mulches and watering

An annual mulch of bulky organic matter, such as manure, mushroom compost, spent hops, leafmould, or garden compost, will provide some food, suppress weeds, and reduce water loss. Even with mulches you may need to water in dry spells.

Pears, plums, gages, and damsons especially benefit from mulching and need watering in summer. Mulch newly planted fruit trees and cane fruits and water regularly. Red currants, white currants, gooseberries, and raspberries also benefit from mulching, especially on light soils.

Distributing mulch around a young fruit tree

Do not apply mushroom compost often to fruits except on very acid soils, as it often contains chalk, and most fruits prefer acid conditions. Never use it on raspberries. Straw can be used as a mulch, but if it is incorporated into the soil it must be well rotted first or extra nitrogen must be applied.

Applying fertilizers

Compound or general-purpose fertilizers provide all three major elements and sometimes some of the minor elements. They can be used as a general feed following the manufacturer's guidelines, adding nitrogen or potassium where necessary.

Nitrogen promotes growth and increases fruit size. Use dried poultry manure pellets or ammonium sulphate applied at a rate of 35g per sq m (1oz per sq yd) in spring each year. Culinary apples, pears, plums, gages, damsons, and blackcurrants appreciate more nitrogen, as do dessert apples when growth is poor; apply at a rate of up to 50–70g per sq m (1½–2oz per sq yd).

Phosphorus is essential for healthy root development and general growth. Apply 35g per sq m (1oz per sq yd) of superphosphate before planting and in winter every third or fourth year.

Potassium helps ripen wood for winter hardiness. Too much may lead to magnesium deficiency. Apply 15g per sq m (½oz per sq yd) of sulphate of potash every year in spring. Organic fertilizers are low in potassium.

Magnesium deficiency, indicated by yellowing between leaf veins, is mostly seen in apples, vines, raspberries, and blackcurrants. Treat with Epsom salts as a foliar spray 2 or 3 times at fortnightly intervals. For repeated deficiency, apply Epsom salts to the soil in winter at 70g per sq m (2oz per sq yd).

See also The benefits of mulching, pp.269–270; Choosing and using fertilizers, p.267

PLANT PROBLEMS

Poor fruit pollination

Poor pollination can produce irregular or misshapen fruit

Puckered areas were not fertilized

Poorly pollinated strawberries

Pollination is not usually a problem for fruit crops grown in the open with suitable pollinating partners nearby (*see pp.234–235*), although cold weather can prevent full fertilization of early-flowering fruits.

It may be seen in strawberries, where each ovule has to be pollinated and develop into a seed for the flesh around that seed to swell. The fruit will not mature fully around ovules that have not been pollinated, causing the strawberry to become distorted. Strawberries grown under cover must be ventilated daily to allow insects in.

Poor pollination can also cause "dry set" in tomatoes. The marble-sized fruits fail to swell to normal size and are hollow and seedless. To assist good fruit set, gently tap the open flowers daily to transfer pollen.

AVOIDING POOR FRUIT

- Ensure plants are either self-fertile or have suitable pollinators nearby
- Encourage insects by planting fruit crops in a warm, sunny site with shelter from winds and growing other nectar-rich plants
- Avoid using insecticides that harm pollinating insects

See also Tomato problems, p.227

PRACTICAL ADVICE

Choosing an apple or pear tree for the garden

When choosing apple or pear cultivars consider height, flowering time, continuity of supply, and disease resistance

Perhaps the first consideration is to grow a fruit you like. Some cultivars sold in supermarkets are grown in warmer countries, and growing these at home proves disappointing. Some are not seen in supermarkets because their flavour and texture, though wonderful fresh from the tree, rapidly deteriorate. Other cultivars will store for many months. Autumn apple-tasting events are becoming widespread, and these are a useful way of finding favourites. The majority of apple and pear cultivars are either dessert or culinary, although some are dual purpose, and many cooking apples become sweeter during storage.

Finding a tree to fit your garden

The size of a fruit tree is controlled by grafting the cultivar (variety) on to a rootstock. The most popular apple rootstocks are M27, M9, and M106, producing trees 1.5–1.8m (5–6ft), 2.2–3m (7–10ft), and 4–5.5m (12–18ft) tall respectively. For pears, Quince A is most common and gives a 3–6m (10–20ft) tree; trees grown on Quince C are 1.8–2.7m (6–9ft) tall. Soil type also influences growth rate, with light, sandy, or chalky soils limiting growth more than clay-based ones. Trees can also be grown in pots (*see pp. 234–235*).

Flowering and pollination

Although some apples and pears are classed as self-fertile, the majority require pollen from a different cultivar of the same crop to set fruit. Different cultivars flower at different times and so flowering groups have been identified. For proper pollination, both cultivars must be in the same or an adjacent flowering group. However, certain cultivars, called triploids, are ineffective pollinators, and this must be taken into account. Additionally there are some incompatibility groups with both apples and pears. Fruit in these groups are unable to set a crop either with their own pollen or with the pollen of any other cultivar within the same group. There are a great number of cultivars available, and a good supplier will be able to recommend a selection of compatible plants.

Healthy trees

Disease resistance is another important characteristic that varies between cultivars, with modern types often having higher levels of resistance than traditional ones. Disease prevalence can vary with the climate, so finding what grows well locally can be useful.

GRAFTED ROOTSTOCK

The join between the rootstock and the scion or top-growth should be visible above the ground. If it is buried, the scion may root and become a large, over-vigorous tree.

See also Growing fruit trees in a small garden, p.231; Growing fruit trees in pots, pp.234–235

Growing fruit trees in pots

With the correct pruning methods, growing fruit trees in containers is a flexible and practical solution that gives attractive and bountiful results

A lack of space, or indeed a lack of garden, need not stop you from growing fruit trees. Fruit trees in pots can be grown wherever desired, in the best aspect. Many fruit trees are also ornamental, especially when in blossom. Pot-grown trees will yield less fruit than those grown in the ground, and require more care and attention, but they can be grown on paved areas and courtyards in the smallest gardens. Container growing allows less hardy fruit, such as peaches and nectarines, to be easily sheltered in winter. Protect their flowers from frost in a cold greenhouse, and move them outside again when fruits have set.

Even in a large garden, pots can be useful for fruit trees that are best moved under glass in winter

Potting

Any well-drained outdoor container with a hole in its base and at least as deep as it is wide is suitable. Start with a pot about 30cm (12in) in diameter – slightly larger than the rootball of the young tree. Pot trees on to a larger size before the roots become pot-bound.

A maximum pot size of 45cm (18in) diameter is recommended – even this will need two people to lift it. Large terracotta pots can be extremely heavy and more brittle, so plastic might be preferred for practicality. Pot new trees at any time during the dormant winter months, making sure the graft union is visible above the compost surface (*see p.233*). Pot on or repot in late winter.

General cultivation

Place trees in a sunny, sheltered spot, avoiding places prone to wind eddying. Turn the pots regularly, especially if they are in a corner, to ensure even growth and ripening of wood and fruits. During the growing season, you may need to water as often as twice a day. Water copiously when the surface of the compost is dry, filling up to the rim. Water less often in winter, but never allow the compost to dry out completely.

For good fruiting, apply potassium-rich tomato liquid fertilizer weekly from mid-spring until late summer. Replace this once a month with general-purpose fertilizer to provide sufficient nitrogen. Alternatively, place controlled-release fertilizer tablets in the compost.

POTTING UP A FRUIT TREE

Use a soil-based compost, such as John Innes No.2 or No.3, to provide stability and nutrient retention. **1** Fill the pot to a level where the graft union of the fruit tree will be above the surface of the compost once it is planted.

2 Hold the tree upright in the pot and fill around the roots, firming the compost gently.
3 Add controlled-release fertilizer and then fill the pot to 2.5–5cm (1–2in) below the rim, leaving room to apply adequate water.

See also Growing fruit trees in a small garden, p.231; Feeding and mulching fruit trees, p.232; Choosing an apple or pear tree, p.233

SUITABLE FRUITS AND CONTAINERS

Decorative and productive pears
All pears provide a generous display of blossom, here on 'Doyenné du Comice'. The cultivars 'Beurré Hardy', 'Louise Bonne of Jersey', and 'Glou Morceau' also have good fruit colour.

Delicate peaches and nectarines
Compact cultivars, such as the peaches 'Garden Anny' and 'Garden Lady' and the nectarine 'Nectarella' are the easiest, but others can also be grown. Pots can be put under cover in winter.

Generous plums and cherries
Self-fertile dessert plums, such as 'Blue Tit', 'Opal', and 'Victoria', are the best for containers. Self-fertile sweet cherries, such as 'Sunburst' and 'Stella', can be kept small by container growing.

Topdress annually in spring with a layer of fresh compost, first scraping away about 5cm (2in) of the old growing medium. Repot trees every two to three years. Remove loose material from the pot and cut back any thick, thong-like roots if the tree is becoming pot-bound.

Ready-trained fruit trees are available, but if you want to train your own, obtain one-year-old feathered or unfeathered maidens. Different fruit types have their own pruning needs once the trained form is established.

Apples and pears
Almost all apples and pears need to be pollinated by a different cultivar that flowers at about the same time. Check when buying, and grow several together. Popular cultivars that are suitable and compatible include 'Greensleeves' and 'Sunset', both with attractive blossom, 'Kidd's Orange Red', 'Falstaff', and 'Fiesta'.

Grow apples in pots trained as pyramid or bush trees. M26 or M9 rootstocks (*see p.233*) are good choices,

but M27 is too dwarfing. Pears are best grown as pyramid or bush trees on Quince C rootstock.

Prune trained apples and pears annually. Shorten young leading shoots on branches of bush trees by one-third in winter. Prune sideshoots to four buds. Remove inward-growing branches from the centre. Prune pyramid trees in late summer, starting in the second summer. Prune sideshoots from an existing spur to a single leaf of the basal cluster and side shoots from a main branch to three leaves. Cut back young leading shoots on branches to five leaves, just above a downward-facing bud. Pot-grown fruit trees can over-produce, so thin to single fruits in early summer. Thin dessert apples and pears to 10–15cm (4–6in), culinary apples to 15–22cm (6–9in).

Peaches and nectarines
Peaches and nectarines are self-fertile so single trees can be grown. The easiest cultivars to grow in pots are compact or "patio" cultivars, standard trees on high

stems with a ball-like head. No pruning is needed, only the removal of any die-back. Conventional cultivars can also be grown as pyramid or bush trees.

Keep trees under glass at flowering time to protect them from frost. This also protects plants from the fungal disease peach leaf curl by keeping off the rain. Hand pollinate flowers with an artists brush. Remove fallen petals from among the branches to prevent the spread of disease, and thin fruits to 10cm (4in). On conventional cultivars, cut fruited wood back to young replacement shoots in late summer.

Plums and cherries
Most plums and some cherries are self-fertile, allowing you to grow single trees. Grow as pyramid trees, cherries on 'Colt' rootstock and plums on 'Pixy' rootstock. Summer prune from midsummer, cutting back young sideshoots to 10cm (4in) and new leading shoots of branches to 15cm (6in), both to downward-facing buds.

Finding apple fruit buds

Before pruning apples, identify the fruit buds and fruiting habit

Apple cultivars fall into three broad groups according to where the fruit bud is produced and the fruit carried. There are spur bearers, tip bearers, and a few partial tip bearers.

Growth bud

Compact bud held close to the stem

Large bud containing flower

Fruit bud

Spur bearers, the largest group, produce fruit buds on two-year-old wood, as spurs (short, branched shoots) on the older wood. This gives spur bearers a tidy, compact appearance. Tip bearers produce fruit buds at the tips of long shoots produced the previous year, and very few spurs. The overall appearance of the tree is more untidy than a spur bearer and the branches look sparse without spurs. Some cultivars are partial tip bearers, producing fruit on the tips of the previous year's shoots and also on some spurs.

Before pruning, it is essential to know the habit of the tree and prune accordingly. Fruit buds are larger and more rounded than growth buds, so the two are easily distinguished.

BEARING HABITS OF APPLES

Spur	Tip
'Cox's Orange Pippin'	'Irish Peach'
'Early Victoria'	'Cornish Gilliflower'
'Greensleeves' ♀	**Partial tip**
'James Grieve' ♀	'Bramley's Seedling' ♀
'Lane's Prince Albert' ♀	'Discovery' ♀
'Sunset' ♀	'Worcester Pearmain' ♀

Pruning apple and pear trees

Pruning your trees correctly on an annual basis ensures that they remain healthy and produce good quality crops

Prune fruit trees, such as standard and half standard trees, in winter to remove old growth and encourage new, more productive shoots. Avoid pruning in frosty periods, when the cut wood may be damaged. Trained forms are mainly summer pruned to restrict growth and promote the formation of fruit buds.

PRUNING AN APPLE TREE

1 All unrestricted pears and spur-bearing apples need winter pruning. Cut out crossing and overcrowded branches. Remove dead and diseased wood. **2** Shorten sideshoots (spur pruning). Thin out spurs and reduce any overlong or complicated spur systems. **3** Do not prune vigorous branch leaders.

Winter pruning

Apples can be spur- or tip-bearers, which have different pruning requirements, or partial tip-bearers that need a combination of methods (for how to identify these, *see left*). Treat pears as spur bearers. Be cautious when pruning: hard-pruned trees grow well but are unfruitful, whereas under-pruned trees crop heavily but bear small fruit and have weak and badly shaped growth.

Winter pruning is carried out on larger trees including standard, half-standard and bush trees. Cut out crossing and overcrowded branches. Remove any dead or diseased wood, back to the point of origin. Shorten the laterals to stimulate fruiting side shoots. Thin the spurs so they are regularly spaced, about 20cm (8in) apart. Reduce overlong, overlapping or complicated spur systems to two or three buds. Remove weak shoots and those on the underside or shaded parts of branches. Pruning vigorous shoots can lead to excessive growth; it is better to remove whole branches. When cutting out branches always choose old, congested and unproductive wood, but do not reduce the total volume of the tree by more than one-third in a single year.

For large and vigorous trees where pruning of individual shoots is impractical, remove sections of branches, or even whole limbs, to achieve an open habit while maintaining a strong framework.

On tip-bearers, cut back stronger laterals to about six buds to promote branching and therefore more fruiting tips. Removing some stems each year will maintain the tree's vigour. The weaker laterals that are left unpruned will carry fruit for the current season. As with spur bearers, completely remove overcrowded and misplaced shoots.

See also Growing fruit trees in pots, pp.234–235

Trained forms
Spur-bearing apples can be grown as espaliers. They need special pruning to establish the framework, but then annual pruning is as for all other spur bearers.

Winter pruning of cordons, fans, and espaliers is confined to occasional thinning out of old wood, removal of dead and diseased growth and ensuring that spur systems are well placed. The main pruning of these restricted forms is carried out annually in summer.

Summer pruning

Apples and pears trained as cordons, fans, espaliers, or other restricted forms grow vigorously in spring and summer. Remove the resulting, unproductive, growth when the bottom third of the new shoots has become woody, usually in late summer. Avoid early pruning as this encourages more growth.

First, shorten the laterals growing directly from the main trunk to three leaves above the basal cluster of leaves. Then prune back the sideshoots on existing laterals to within one bud of the basal cluster of leaves. Leave shoots less than 22cm (9in) long unpruned.

Cut back any regrowth to one bud in early autumn or during winter. Leave a few shoots unpruned to discourage secondary growth; nutrients travelling up from the roots will be drawn into these shoots instead of encouraging new buds on pruned sections.

Apple leaf problems

Apples can suffer from a range of diseases and disorders, but some cultivars have good resistance

In spring, apple problems can be easily recognised, and if they are treated early they can cause less serious damage.

APPLE POWDERY MILDEW

This fungus (*Podosphaera leucotricha*) overwinters in buds, so young foliage emerges in the spring already infected. More airborne spores are produced from these primary infections to infect leaves, shoots, and sometimes young fruits in summer. The most important hosts are apples, but pears, quinces, and medlars can be infected.

A white powdery coating of fungus appears on emerging leaves and blossoms in spring. Infected tissues soon wither, and affected buds may not even emerge. Later, white or buff patches of mildew appear on leaves. Young shoots can also be attacked, and young fruit may be russetted by the disease. The infections weaken the tissues and may cause early leaf fall.

Control

Keep apples well watered; dry soil encourages infection. Prune out primary infections immediately in spring. Spray with an approved fungicide, according to instructions. Resistant cultivars include 'Edward VII', 'Blenheim Orange', 'Ellison's Orange', and 'Worcester Pearmain'.

APPLE SCAB

The apple scab fungus (*Venturia inaequalis*) overwinters in fallen leaves and pustules on young stems. In spring, wind-borne spores are released and infect young leaves and stems. Later, more spores are released and infect young fruit. The spores need water to germinate; the warmer the weather, the smaller the amount of water required.

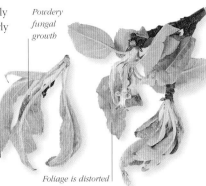

Powdery fungal growth

Foliage is distorted

Apple powdery mildew on leaves

Professional growers receive alerts when infection is likely. Apples and pears are affected, as well as the ornamental plants sorbus, pyracantha and cotoneaster.

Dark, sometimes velvety patches appear on the leaves, which may be distorted and fall early. Fruits develop dark, "scabby" patches, and the skin distorts and cracks as the fruit ripens.

Control

Rake up and compost fallen leaves and prune out scabby shoots. Prune trees to encourage air circulation. Spray with an approved fungicide. Resistant cultivars include 'Discovery', 'Laxton's Fortune' and 'Edward VII'.

Apple scab on leaves

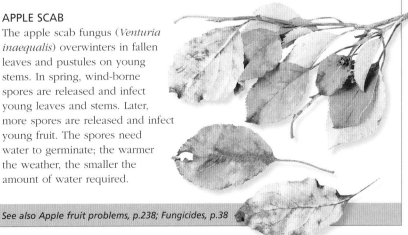

See also Apple fruit problems, p.238; Fungicides, p.38

Apple fruit problems

Growing conditions and pest attacks can damage your apple crop

Some general apple diseases that affect the whole tree can reduce yields or spoil the crops, but some problems affect only the fruit itself.

CODLING MOTH

Apples are the main hosts of the codling moth (*Cydia pomonella*), but pears and other fruits are occasionally affected. Adult females lay eggs on or near the developing fruitlets in early summer. The caterpillars bore into the fruits and feed in the core, leaving in late summer to overwinter under loose bark before pupating in the spring. The caterpillar may leave the fruit through the eye end or make a visible emergence hole in the skin.

Control

Spray with bifenthrin in early summer with a second application three weeks later. Calculate accurate timing of the sprays to kill the newly hatched larvae by placing a pheromone codling moth

Corky layer at flower end

Frost-damaged apples

trap in the trees in late spring. This captures male codling moths, both reducing populations and giving a good indication when the females will be laying eggs. The use of insecticides is only feasible on trees small enough to be sprayed thoroughly.

FROST DAMAGE

Early in the season, when fruits are still only marble sized, a late frost can damage the skin. This causes a corky layer to form, usually at the flower end of the fruit. In severe cases the fruit splits and the corkiness extends to most of the fruit. As the fruit expands, the area of damaged tissue increases, but the flesh remains perfectly sound and edible. Pears can also be damaged by frost; fruitlets tend to drop off, but any remaining on the tree will have a scarred, russetted, blackened, or cracked appearance. Frost-damaged fruits are often confined to one side or part of a tree, depending on the severity of the frost and the exposure.

Control

Avoid growing 'Bramley's Seedling', which is very susceptible, 'Lord Derby', and 'Ellison's Orange'. If late frosts are a constant problem, consider growing trees in pots (*see pp.234–235*), which can be protected.

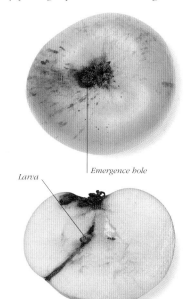

Larva |*Emergence hole*

Codling moth caterpillar in an apple

Renovating fruit trees

Overgrown or stunted trees need pruning, feeding, and extra care

A tree with a sound, healthy trunk and main branches, and signs of having made good growth and cropping in the past can be worth saving, but there are many factors to consider.

How poor is the condition of the tree? Neglect of feeding and spraying may weaken a tree and lead to damage by pests and diseases, and incorrect pruning results in unproductive growth. Damage by wind swaying or chafing due to poor staking can weaken a tree permanently. Is the tree in a good position? Competition from plants growing beneath can starve a tree. Shade from overcrowded trees can be lightened, shade from buildings cannot. If poor growth is due to shallow soil or bad drainage, consider replanting elsewhere. Finally, will the renovated plant be as good as a new tree? Many trees are now available on dwarfing rootstocks, cropping at an early age and taking up less space than trees on older, more vigorous rootstocks.

If you decide that rejuvenation is worth attempting, prune between late autumn and early spring, avoiding frosty weather.

Over-large and overcrowded trees

Aim to improve spacing of the limbs, allowing light and air into the tree and making spraying and picking easier. Remove branches that are dead, broken, badly placed, and crossing, and any that are low enough to obstruct passage, or too tall.

Cut branches back to the point of origin or to a side limb large enough to cope with increased vigour, not less than one-third the diameter of the main branch removed. Do not leave a stub; this might result in dieback. Always undercut first and complete the cut from above. Where branches are too

See also Apple leaf problems p.237; Storing fruit, p.232; Systemic chemicals, pp.37–38

See also Feeding, p.232; Pruning, pp.236–237

close in a very large tree with many branches, remove or shorten one so that they are at least 60cm (24in) apart if side by side or 1m (36in) apart if one is above another. In a smaller tree with fewer branches, prune more moderately.

If a lot of wood must be removed, spread the renovation over several years to lessen the shock to the tree. After such drastic pruning, the tree may produce many shoots in summer. Remove or thin any that are badly placed or overcrowded before the growth hardens.

Overpruned trees

After very hard winter pruning, most of the buds will grow out as shoots rather than fruit buds. Growth is strong, but the crop is small.

If the tree is growing vigorously or has been over-pruned, prune it lightly to discourage further extension growth. Thin where necessary, as described above, but avoid excessive use of secateurs. Use them only for dealing with crossing sideshoots and unwanted leaders, or the entire removal of clusters of strong, unproductive sideshoots that are overshadowing other spurs.

Stunted and starved trees

On a weak tree bearing a mass of dense, complex spur systems but making no new growth, remove worn-out and overshading spurs and reduce the others. More light reaching the remaining spurs results in bigger and better-quality fruit and encourages vigour. Use new shoots as leaders and sideshoots in the gradual replacement of a worn-out framework.

Waiting for results

Do not expect immediate improvement from a newly pruned tree. The effect will not be noticed for at least two or three years, and pruning is only one factor in the process of rejuvenation. Weak fruit buds, thin growth, small leaves, and early defoliation can all indicate starvation and sometimes a lack of soil moisture.

The tree should be fed, watered, and, if necessary, sprayed. Apply a general fertilizer annually in late winter until the tree recovers. Reduce weed competition by clearing at least 1m (36in) around the base, and mulch with organic matter to conserve moisture and keep the ground weed free.

Pruning blackcurrants

Blackcurrant fruit is mainly carried on one-year-old shoots

Blackcurrant pruning is carried out to promote heavy-cropping one-year-old wood; two-year-old wood bears less fruit, and older wood very little.

On planting new bushes in autumn or winter, cut all shoots down to one bud above soil level. This may seem drastic, but it will encourage strong regrowth in spring. The next winter prune out only weaker shoots. Plants will crop in the second summer.

Prune established bushes from leaf fall until late winter, or after harvest, cutting back to ground level all weak, damaged, or diseased growth and up to one in three of the woody older shoots, which have darker bark. This renewal pruning results in a regular supply of one-year-old shoots. It is not suitable for red or white currants.

BLACKCURRANT PRUNING

[1] Before pruning the bush is crowded, and poor air circulation can encourage disease.
[2] Removing some of the oldest shoots and thinning growth relieves overcrowding.

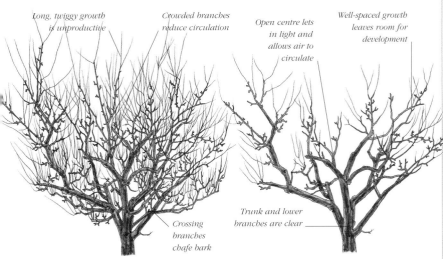

Long, twiggy growth is unproductive

Crowded branches reduce circulation

Open centre lets in light and allows air to circulate

Well-spaced growth leaves room for development

Crossing branches chafe bark

Trunk and lower branches are clear

Renovation over two years
Start pruning an overcrowded tree (*above left*) by removing all dead, diseased, and damaged wood and all crossing or misplaced braches. The following year, prune to improve fruiting, shortening unproductive extension growth, thinning regrowth from last year's pruning, and reducing congested spur systems. After pruning (*above right*), the tree should have an open framework of strong, well-placed branches with plenty of room for fruiting growth. Long shoots can be shortened to start fresh spur systems.

See also Currant problems, p.241

TECHNIQUES

Hybrid berry training

After harvest, cut out old fruited canes and tie in replacements

Fruits such as blackberries, tayberries, and loganberries are very vigorous. They need strict pruning and training and a sturdy support. Train plants on four wires (10-gauge), 30cm (12in) apart, the lowest 1m (3ft) from soil level, the highest 1.8m (6ft). Fruit is borne on one-year-old wood.

Training systems

A popular and simple method is the "fan" system. Fan canes out evenly and tie in. Loop long branches back down the wires. In late summer, these canes will flower and fruit while new ones grow up from the base. Support these new stems using bamboo canes or tie them onto the top wire.

You can also use the "rope" system. Twist fruiting canes together and tie, evenly spaced, along the lower wires. Tie new, non-fruiting canes to the top wire or to bamboo canes.

Pruning

Cut fruited canes to ground level after harvest, tying in new canes to replace them. Remove frost-damaged growth in spring. If too few new canes are produced, keep some old ones, although these will be less fruitful.

Train new canes out to replace fruited ones

PRACTICAL ADVICE

Autumn raspberries

These cultivars can give one large crop or two smaller ones

Good crop of autumn raspberries

The season of cropping from autumn raspberries can be lengthened by careful management. Unlike summer cultivars, autumn raspberries fruit on the current season's canes. If planted in a sunny position, the fruits ripen in late summer ready for picking in autumn, usually from early autumn through to the first frosts. To maximize this yield it is necessary to cut all fruited canes to the ground in late winter.

For an extra crop in early summer, consider only cutting half the fruited canes down to ground level in late winter. "Tip back" the remainder, removing the top section that has fruited. Fruiting spurs that develop lower down on these canes will produce raspberries in early to midsummer. New canes appearing in the spring will still have enough space to grow up through the old canes and crop in the autumn.

PLANT PROBLEMS

Gooseberry sawflies

These troublesome pests also attack red and white currants

The common gooseberry sawfly (*Nematus ribesii*) often develops three generations each year, and is active in late spring. Rows of whitish-green eggs, just over 1mm (1⁄16in) long, are laid on the undersides of leaves low down or in the centre of the bush. Larvae have black heads, pale green bodies with many black spots, and when fully fed are about 2cm (3⁄4in) long. The larval stage lasts about three weeks. After stripping the centre of the bush, young larvae eat their way upwards and outwards, quickly devouring the outer leaves before going into the soil to pupate.

There are other sawflies that defoliate gooseberries. Larvae of the lesser gooseberry sawfly (*Nematus leucotrochus*) are smaller with pale green heads; there is only one generation in early summer. The pale gooseberry sawfly (*Pristiphora pallipes*) has up to four generations of pale green larvae from late spring. Severe defoliation weakens gooseberry bushes and results in a poor crop the next year. Either remove the larvae by hand, or spray with an approved insecticide.

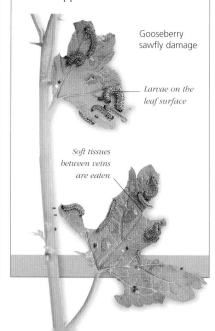

Gooseberry sawfly damage

Larvae on the leaf surface

Soft tissues between veins are eaten

Currant problems

The cropping potential, vigour, and general health of red, white, and blackcurrants can be seriously affected by pests and diseases

Some problems with currants are also common to other fruit. All currants can suffer leaf spot (*Drepanopezizsa ribis*); this can be controlled (on blackcurrants only) by spraying with an approved insecticide. Blackcurrants may be affected by American gooseberry mildew (*Sphaerotheca mors-uvae*). Plant resistant cultivars, such as 'Ben More'. Currants are also sometimes affected by rust (*Cronartium ribicola*), which can be controlled with copper-containing fungicides. The leaves of red and white currants can be eaten by gooseberry sawfly larvae (*see opposite*).

CURRANT BLISTER APHID

This aphid (*Cryptomyzus ribis*) overwinters on all types of currant as eggs. These hatch at bud burst, and the aphids suck sap from the lower leaf surface. In midsummer they develop wings and migrate to a wild flower, hedge woundwort, returning in autumn to lay overwintering eggs near buds.

Symptoms

During spring, leaves at the shoot tips develop raised, puckered areas, which may be yellowish-green or pinkish-red. Pale yellow aphids are visible on the underside of the affected leaves.

Control

This pest is disfiguring rather than seriously damaging. Spray the underside of leaves with an approved insecticide, fatty acids, or vegetable oils after bud burst (but not during flowering), to kill the aphids.

BIG BUD MITE

Enlarged blackcurrant buds are caused by microscopic mites (*Cecidophyopsis ribis*). These live inside infested buds, sucking sap from the embryonic leaves. In late spring, the mites leave the enlarged buds to infest new buds.

Heavy attacks reduce the plant's vigour and ability to fruit, and the mites can also infect the plant with reversion disease (*see below*).

Symptoms

During winter some buds become abnormally enlarged, being spherical instead of longer than they are broad. Such buds dry up and will fail to produce leaves in spring.

Control

No chemical controls are currently available to amateur gardeners. Pick off and dispose of big buds during winter on lightly infested bushes. Remove any badly infested, poorly cropping bushes after the fruit has been harvested and replace them with new stock in the autumn. The cultivars 'Farleigh' and 'Foxendown' are resistant to the big bud mite.

REVERSION OF BLACKCURRANTS

Blackcurrants are very commonly affected by this virus, which is spread by big bud mite. This pest helps to transmit the virus by feeding on a virus-infected plant, and then feeding on a healthy blackcurrant. The virus may also be passed on through cuttings.

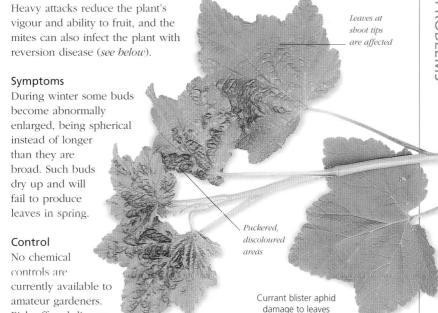

Leaves at shoot tips are affected

Puckered, discoloured areas

Currant blister aphid damage to leaves

Symptoms

The disease reduces vigour and yield but is often unnoticed. The leaves are slightly smaller than usual, with fewer veins, and flowering is also reduced.

Control

Buy certified virus-free plants and replace when vigour or yield declines. There are no chemical controls for the mites available to amateur gardeners, nor are there chemical controls for viruses. Remove infected plants, which act as a source of infection for healthy bushes. If you are taking cuttings, disinfect the knife between cuts.

Each bud contains hundreds of mites

Buds swell up during winter

Undamaged bud

Big bud mite on blackcurrant

See also Avoiding pests and diseases, pp.36–37; Systemic chemicals, pp.37–38; Using fungicides, pp.38–39

GROWING FIGS IN CONTAINERS

Growing figs in containers

Figs grown in containers will crop reliably and can be moved under cover for protection in winter

Containers provide the root restriction necessary to achieve a balance of healthy and productive growth in figs. In the open ground this is achieved by lining the planting hole with paving slabs. Container-grown plants have the added advantage that they can be placed where they are protected from frost in winter and then moved outside for the summer.

Pot plants in early spring using a rich, loam-based compost and ensure adequate drainage. Aim for a final container diameter of 30–38cm (12–15in). Established plants may need repotting every second or third year. Remove loose compost and trim thicker roots before repotting in the same or slightly larger container.

Choose a warm, sunny location for plants in summer. Water plants freely during the growing season and feed weekly, alternating a high-potassium liquid plant food with a balanced feed.

In winter, bring plants into a frost-free greenhouse, conservatory, garage, or shed. If this is not available, wrap

Ripening figs

the pot in bubble plastic and place against a sheltered house wall. Pack around the branches with straw and cover with hessian or fleece. Remove after danger of frost is past but before bud burst. Pay careful attention to watering, as dry conditions will result in poor fruit development.

Formative pruning and cropping

Container-grown figs are best grown as a bush on a short stem. Purchase plants with three or four branches coming from the stem around 38cm (15in) from the ground, or cut back single-stem plants to encourage branching. In late winter, cut back these branches by half to develop a compact framework. Once this is established, prune trees in spring (*see opposite*).

Outdoors, expect a single crop in summer from figs formed the previous summer, if protected from frost over winter. Under glass, especially in a heated greenhouse, the longer growing season means a further crop of figs formed in the spring may ripen in autumn. Figs are ready for picking when they turn soft and hang down and splits appear near the stalk end.

Remove suckers that appear in containers

See also Fruit trees in pots, pp.234–235; Maintaining and renovating fig trees, p.243

Getting figs to crop

Figs produce both an early and a late flush of fruit

The early crop is formed from the overwintering "embryo" figs, while the late crop develops in one growing season. Only figs grown in a heated greenhouse will ripen for the later crop. On figs grown in a cold glasshouse or outdoors the unripened fruits simply fall off in autumn.

An embryo fig

To encourage production of these overwintering embryo figs, both bush and fan-trained trees are pruned in summer. The embryos develop in late summer in the leaf axils of the current season's growth. To overwinter successfully, they need protection from frost, and should be roughly pea-sized by late summer – fruits that are too large or too small are less able to resist cold and usually drop off.

Prune figs in spring. From early summer, regularly pinch out the growing point of the current season's sideshoots in order to encourage the production of embryo figs on the resulting sideshoots. On figs in a heated greenhouse, this will also allow more light to reach the fruit that is currently ripening.

See also Maintaining fig trees, p.243

Maintaining and renovating fig trees

Figs are pruned in mid-spring, after the danger of frost has passed, to regulate their shape

With an established bush, remove crowded and crossing branches and frost-damaged growth. Keep the centre open by taking out upright shoots and pruning to buds on the lower sides of branches. Aim for a balanced, open crown that allows light into the centre of the bush.

For wall-trained figs, remove badly placed shoots that are growing into or away from the wall or crossing other branches, and remove some of the fruited wood. Cut back a few younger shoots to one bud to encourage fresh growth close to the main branches. Tie in the remaining new shoots so that they are evenly spaced.

Neglected trees

If a fig tree has been neglected for a number of years, most of the fruit will be borne on young shoots around the edge of the tree, with bare branches in the centre. Cut some of the older, bare branches back to a stub of about 5cm (2in) in mid-spring. If there are several older branches, spread the pruning over two or three years. As new shoots grow, keep the strongest and best placed and remove the others.

Neglected fan-trained trees are also pruned in mid-spring. First remove branches growing directly out from the wall, cutting back to their point of origin. Thin crowded branches by cutting back to a stub of about 5cm (2in). Again, if there are a large number of branches to remove, spread the pruning over two or three years.

With both forms, remove suckers arising from the base. These spoil the shape of the tree, taking strength from the other shoots.

Very overgrown specimens that are cut back to ground level usually make strong new growth. This is sometimes done where figs are being grown for their foliage rather than for fruiting.

A fan-trained fig tree tied in to a fence with soft twine

See also Getting figs to crop, p.242

Growing kiwi fruit

A sunny, sheltered site and correct pruning give good yields

Shorten sideshoots to six leaves beyond fruits

Kiwi fruit has male and female flowers on separate plants, so both are needed for cropping. New growth is tender. The vigorous vines need sturdy supports: train on a sunny wall or a pergola. Plant young vines in early spring, cutting back to 30cm (12in).

Pruning and training

Plants flower at the base of the current year's growth. To create a permanent framework, train two "rods" from the main stem, and from them grow "arms" 1m (3ft) long and 50cm (20in) apart.

Let three fruiting sideshoots develop from each arm. Pinch other shoots to a 2.5cm (1in) spur. Cut the fruiting sideshoots at five leaves and any other sideshoots to one leaf. Flowering shoots will develop from these sideshoots; prune any non-flowering shoots to five leaves.

Once fruit has set, pinch out six leaves beyond the last fruit (or blossom on male plants). In late autumn to early winter prune fruited shoots to four buds; these will produce new flowering shoots.

When an old sideshoot becomes congested, cut back in winter to a dormant bud at the base. Allow just one resulting shoot to develop; pinch to five leaves to reform a fruiting spur.

Problems with grapevines

Grapes can crop with great success in southern parts of the country, but are susceptible to several problems if growing conditions are not ideal

Gardeners should keep a lookout for several important diseases and disorders of grapes (*Vitis* species and cultivars) that can cause considerable damage unless controlled.

GRAPE POWDERY MILDEW

This fungus (*Uncinula necator*) affects grapevines and other *Vitis* species. It overwinters in the vine bud scales, which surround and protect the soon-to-emerge flowers or leaves. It spreads by airborne spores produced in large numbers from the powdery surfaces. The disease is encouraged by high humidity in the air surrounding the top-growth of the plant when grown under glass, and also by lack of water at the roots, which stresses the plants and makes them more vulnerable.

Symptoms

Early season infections occur on the young shoots, which show distortion, and the white, mealy appearance is typical of powdery mildews. Leaves may be affected through the season.

Grape powdery mildew

The most serious symptoms are on the fruits, which show brown discoloration and may split as they swell unevenly.

Control

The only fungicide available to amateur gardeners is sulphur dust (not flowers of sulphur), which should be applied as soon as symptoms appear. Improve air circulation under glass to reduce humidity, and water roots regularly to avoid water stress. Some cultivars, such as 'Seyval Blanc', have good resistance.

GREY MOULD OF GRAPES

Grey mould (*Botrytis cinerea*) infects a wide range of plants through wounds. In grapes the main point of entry is cracks in the fruit caused by powdery mildew, which damages the skin and causes them to swell unevenly. If conditions are right, this infection may lead to "noble rot", in which grapes develop a low volume of highly concentrated sugar and are used to make small quantities of very expensive sweet wines. Unfortunately this is not likely to happen.

Symptoms

This common fungal infection can affect both outdoor and indoor grapes, with the most important infections occurring on the fruits. The grapes crack and shrivel and may become covered with dense, grey, fluffy mould.

Control

The problem is controlled primarily by preventing powdery mildew (*see above*). Practise good hygiene, and remove dead material as soon as possible. There are no fungicides to control grey mould in grapes approved for amateur gardeners.

GRAPE SHANKING

Shanking, in which fruit fails to ripen and shrivels, occurs on indoor grapes. It can be caused by several factors, and

Grape shanking

is best prevented by good cultivation. Do not crop young vines in the first two years, and grow only one bunch per sideshoot on established vines. Stop sideshoots and shoots from them regularly, not in a single pruning at the end of the season. Water regularly to avoid root damage from drought or waterlogging, and prevent pests and diseases from damaging the plant.

Symptoms

This begins as a brown area around the fruit stalk, causing the affected grape or cluster to discolour and shrivel. Those of black cultivars turn dark red, while white cultivars go pale brown. The grapes then shrivel, resembling raisins. If eaten, they are watery and sour.

Control

Cut out affected grapes and reduce the number of remaining bunches by half. If done early, this may save the rest of the crop. If roots have been reduced or damaged, shorten sideshoots to help reduce the strain on the root system.

See also Avoiding pests and diseases, pp.36–37, Using fungicides, pp.38–39

Pruning and training vines

For successful cropping and healthy plants, prune grapevines before midwinter, and throughout summer

Vines are very adaptable to training on strong wires. Two useful methods are the widely used cordon and the more commercial Guyot system. In both the vines begin cropping in the third year.

Guyot system

This system for outoor vines of horizontal arms and annual vertical cropping shoots is helpful where summers are cooler. On planting, cut the leader back to three buds. In summer treat it as you would a cordon (*see below*). Next winter cut the leader back to three strong buds, and tie in the resulting shoots in summer.

In winter, pull down two shoots, cutting the third to three strong buds. In summer, stop vertical shoots from the horizontal arms at the desired height; allow only three sideshoots to develop from the central shoot.

In subsequent winters entirely remove the horizontal arms. Train two of the new sideshoots to replace them, and cut the third shoot back to three buds as a new central shoot, tying in summer.

Summer pruning all vines

In summer, pinch, de-shoot, and tie in all vines regularly. This reduces winter pruning. Pinch out shoots two leaves beyond the flowers, and non-flowering shoots at five leaves. Pinch out other sideshoots at one leaf. Generally allow one bunch of grapes every 30cm (12in) of stem; more are acceptable on grapes with small clusters, such as 'Brant'.

CORDON TRAINING

Use this flexible system for vines on walls and pergolas and under glass. **1** A permanent leader is trained vertically or horizontally, with fruit-bearing sideshoots growing from it.

Plant the vine in winter, cutting the leader back to a strong bud on ripe wood, and shortening any sideshoots to two buds. In summer, tie in the leader and prune the flowering sideshoots to five leaves and other sideshoots to two leaves. Remove any flowers. Repeat this pruning regime the following year.

2 The following winter, cut back the leader into ripened wood and prune the sideshoots. **3** Leave two buds on each pruned sideshoot. In this year you can begin harvesting from the vine. Summer-prune non-fruiting sideshoots to five leaves, and fruiting sideshoots to two leaves beyond the fruit cluster.

In all subsequent winters, shorten sideshoots to two buds. If a fruiting spur becomes too congested, prune it out in winter and allow a new sideshoot further back to replace it.

See also Pergolas and arbours, pp.28–29; Problems with grapevines p.244

Container-grown olives

Olives in pots can be brought indoors for winter protection

Olives need mild winters to fruit well

Mature olives will survive freezing conditions, but to flower and fruit well they need winters between 7.5°C (46°F) and 10°C (50°F). Container-grown olives can be brought into a cold greenhouse or conservatory in winter. Olives are mainly wind pollinated, and growing more than one cultivar improves pollination.

Start off with smaller pots, gradually repotting until you reach around 45cm (18in). Use loam-based compost with added grit. Put plenty of crocks in the bottom, and raise pots on feet for free drainage. Water freely and apply a balanced liquid fertilizer monthly during the growing season. Reduce watering in winter, without allowing the compost to dry out.

Prune in spring or early summer. To encourage a branching habit, select three or four shoots to form a framework, and shorten these. Thin new shoots each year and cut back when necessary to produce a compact plant. Keep pruning to a minimum on mature plants, thinning overcrowded or crossing branches and removing old and unproductive wood.

See also Growing trees in containers, p.59

GROWING STRAWBERRIES IN CONTAINERS

Growing strawberries in containers

Strawberries are the essence of summer and delicious when eaten freshly picked; a handful of plants grown in containers can yield a bumper crop of fruit

Strawberries are short-lived perennial plants. They grow well in the ground, but can suffer from soil-borne pests and diseases if grown on the same patch for several years. Where space is at a premium, strawberries also fare well for a year or two in grow bags, troughs, pots, and hanging baskets, and this approach has several advantages over growing plants in the ground.

Strawberries in containers can be given a prime position in a sunny and sheltered spot. Containers also raise plants off the ground, which helps to produce a more stable microclimate. They can be brought under protection in a greenhouse or porch to promote fruiting and removed once fruiting is over (*see p.248*). Container-grown plants also suffer less from soil-borne pests and diseases, and are at a more convenient height for picking. All gardeners can enjoy freshly picked strawberries, whatever the size of their plot.

A tiered plant stand accommodates large crops

STRAWBERRY CONTAINERS

- Window boxes can be used, taking no garden space at all
- Hanging baskets suit most cultivars, and pink-flowered 'Viva Rosa' is particularly attractive for this purpose
- Terracotta strawberry pots with planting pockets are compact, but can be heavy and provide uneven growing conditions
- Sectional tower pots are compact, can be made up to a range of heights, and provide more even conditions

Buying and propagating strawberries

Different cultivars will fruit at different times, so you can choose a range to provide fruits over a long period.

Garden centres supply pot-grown plants all year. Bare-root plants are usually better quality. Plant these in spring, or ideally in autumn, when they will crop heavily the following year. Cold stored ones are sometimes offered in spring and are a good buy, cropping in 60 days if you can keep them well watered in dry spells. Always choose certified, virus-free stock.

The majority of strawberries produce plantlets on creeping, rooting stems called runners. Most of these should be removed in summer but strong, healthy ones can be kept for propagation. Peg the runners into 8cm (3in) pots and once they have rooted, sever from the mother plant. Keep them outdoors, potting them on into 13cm (5in) pots as they develop. Plant out into their final positions in late summer and autumn for a good crop the following year.

Choosing containers

Pots are the easiest containers to manage. Aim for three plants in a 25cm (10in) pot – more plants are hard to keep sufficiently moist in summer. Soilless compost is light, but susceptible to under- or overwatering. Loam-based composts are heavy, but easy to manage.

Grow bags, including ones that have already been used once for tomatoes or

See also Avoiding pests and diseases, pp.36–37; Poor fruit pollination, p.233; Growing early strawberries p.248

other crops, can be used, containing five to ten plants, but they need very careful watering if they are not to be damaged by drying out in summer.

To help provide a stable environment with good air circulation, place grow bags on to upturned crates or boxes, or wooden planks laid on plastic crates or concrete blocks. For a more permanent structure, you could raise a plank about 1m (3ft) above the ground, supporting it on sturdy treated posts driven 45cm (18in) into the ground, or on a free-standing timber support; raised planters like this are available through some catalogues. A rail at each end of the support with a 15cm (6in) wide strip of rigid, small-mesh net stretched along each side of the bag will hold the fruit out in the sun, which helps to improve the sugar content. Yields of around 0.5kg (1lb) of fruit per plant can be achieved.

Continuing care

Water by hand or through drip lines. Strawberry plants in containers should remain moist but not waterlogged, and may require watering more than once a day in the hottest conditions.

As soon as growth begins in spring give a balanced liquid feed each week. During flowering and fruiting use a high-potassium feed such as a tomato fertilizer, then revert to a balanced feed

Terracotta strawberry pots are attractive but need careful watering to avoid uneven soil moisture

RECOMMENDED CULTIVARS

Perpetual

These fruit in early summer and again in late summer

'Aromel' ♀ 1

'Mara des Bois' (alpine)

'Viva Rosa'

Early

These fruit in early summer

'Honeoye' ♀

'Rosie'

Mid-season

These fruit from early to midsummer

'Elsanta' 2

'Elvira' 3

'Hapil' ♀

'Maraline'

Late season

These fruit in midsummer

'Rhapsody' ♀

'Symphony' ♀

if the plants are to be kept for a second year. Strawberry plants that are overfed will produce lush leaf growth at the expense of the fruit.

A winter chilling is vital for good flowering. Keep containers at ground level in a sheltered situation; if severe frosts are forecast, provide strawberries with protection, such as a covering of horticultural fleece or straw, which should be removed during the day.

Pests and diseases

Container-grown strawberries suffer from fewer diseases than those in the ground, but can attract pests, especially under glass. Aphids (see p.42) may infest spring growth, transmitting viruses. Spray at the first sign of damage with an approved insecticide suitable for strawberries.

Spider mite (see p.197) can be a problem, particularly in warmer situations, and is best controlled with the predatory mite *Phytoseiulus persimilis*, provided no pesticides are being used.

Vine weevil larvae (see p.48) are unlikely to be a problem in the first year in pots, but may affect plants grown on for a second year. In late summer water in pathogenic nematodes, which parasitize the larvae.

Place barriers around the containers or supports, or use slug pellets to protect the fruit from slugs. To keep birds away outdoors, place nets over baskets and pots, and over wire hoops around grow bags and troughs.

If certified stock is used, viruses should not be a problem in the first year. Symptoms include stunted growth and mottled foliage; destroy any affected plants. Grey mould can cause fruit to rot in wet conditions. Pick off affected fruits.

GROWING EARLY STRAWBERRIES

Growing early strawberries

Strawberries grown in a heated greenhouse can produce fruit in mid-spring, but for high-quality and well-coloured fruit it is better to aim for harvest in late spring

Whether you grow your strawberries in containers (*see pp.246–247*) or in the ground, it is worth bringing a few runners in for an early harvest. Choose healthy runners in early summer and peg them down singly into 9cm (3½in) pots, plunged in the bed if strawberries are grown in the open ground. Soilless compost is a suitable medium. Pinch off the runner beyond the young plant.

Three or four weeks later the runners should be well rooted and can be removed. Do not allow the new plants to become pot bound or suffer any check at this stage. Keep them well watered and in mid- to late summer transfer them into 15cm (6in) pots, using soil-based compost. Place the pots on an ash bed, or in an open cold frame in full sun and expose to the air until the end of autumn, by which time the plants will be fully dormant. Lay the pots on their sides against a wall for a month and cover with straw as a protection against frost. Provide as much air as possible if the pots are in cold frames, and cover only during severe frosts or heavy rainfall.

A greenhouse allows for early growth

'Cambridge Favourite'

'Tamella' fruits kept clean on a mulch of straw

Mid-spring harvests

Bring the pots into the greenhouse in midwinter, but give no heat and do not water until the first new leaves appear. Keep the atmosphere moist and restrict ventilation to sunny days when it is necessary to avoid overheating. Increase watering as the foliage develops and start to give gentle heat; keep night temperatures at about 7–10°C (45–50°F). Too much heat results in the growth of excessive foliage at the expense of flower trusses.

When the flowers open, increase the temperature to 15°C (60°F) and ventilate during the day, although maintaining a moist atmosphere except at pollination time. Hand pollinate the flowers daily with a soft brush to ensure good setting and fruit shape.

When the fruit has set, increase the temperature to 18°C (65°F). For the highest-quality fruit, thin immediately after the petals have fallen, leaving 8–10 fruits to mature. Reduce ventilation and keep the atmosphere thoroughly moist at all times until ripening begins. Water copiously, especially in sunny weather, to promote large fruits and discourage mildew. As the fruit ripens, increase ventilation, reduce watering, and keep the leaves and the fruits themselves dry to reduce the risk of fruit rot.

SUITABLE CULTIVARS

Varieties suitable for forcing under glass

'Cambridge Favourite' ♀

'Honeoye' ♀

'Royal Sovereign'

'Tamella'

Give the plants a half-strength liquid feed every 10–14 days until the fruit begins to colour. Too much feeding will result in soft, tasteless fruit and increase the risk of rotting.

Late spring harvests

Bring the pots into the greenhouse from early to midwinter. Start gentle heat about three weeks later, but at all times keep temperatures lower than for earlier forcing. Maintain night temperatures of 4–8°C (40–46°F) until flower trusses begin to appear, then raise the temperature to 10°C (50°F). Hand pollinate, water, and feed as for mid-spring harvests. After petal fall, increase the temperature to 13°C (55°F). A lower temperature once ripening begins improves colour and slows down the ripening process, resulting in well-flavoured fruits ready for picking in late spring.

See also How to heat a greenhouse, p.190; Alternatives to glass, p.193; Poor fruit pollination, p.233; Strawberries in containers, pp.246–247

ATTRACTING
WILDLIFE

Encouraging wildlife into the garden

A wide variety of insects, birds, mammals and amphibians will come to your garden if they are provided with a suitable environment, considerably enhancing the garden's interest and enjoyment

Your garden is more than a collection of plants. It also provides food, shelter and breeding sites for a wide range of wildlife. You can go further by planting and managing your garden in a way that is sympathetic to wildlife needs.

A garden pond

Installing a pond is the biggest single contribution you can make to encourage wildlife. Without water there is no breeding place for frogs, toads, newts, dragonflies and all the other aquatic creatures. A shallow pond margin provides a drinking and bathing area for birds and various animals.

Site the pond in a sunny place away from trees. Ensure at least one side slopes, so amphibians can reach land, and preferably include a muddy border for bog plants. This is more easily achieved using a butyl-rubber pool liner rather than a pre-formed structure.

When choosing oxygenating plants or 'water weeds' avoid rampant, non-native kinds such as Canadian pond weed (*Elodea canadensis*), floating pennywort (*Hydrocotyle ranunculoides*), parrot's feather (*Myriophyllum aquaticum*) and New Zealand pygmy weed (*Crassula helmsii*, sometimes sold as *Tillaea recurva*), and do not include rapidly spreading floating plants such as duckweeds (*Lemna* spp.) and water fern (*Azolla filiculoides*). Suitable oxygenators include rigid hornwort (*Ceratophyllum demersum*), spiked water milfoil (*Myriophyllum spicatum*) and common water crowfoot (*Ranunculus aquatilis*).

Plants at the pond margins are necessary for emerging dragonfly and damselfly nymphs, so plant yellow flag iris (*Iris pseudacorus*), greater spearwort (*Ranunculus lingua*), sedges (*Carex* spp.), rushes (*Juncus* spp.), purple loosestrife (*Lythrum salicaria*), water plantain (*Alisma plantago-aquatica*) and arrowhead (*Sagittaria sagittifolia*). Plants with leaves floating on the surface help to shade and cool the water. You could include frogbit (*Hydrocharis morsus-ranae*) and waterlilies (*Nymphaea* spp.).

Lawns

A bowling-green standard lawn is of little benefit for attracting wildlife, but if you allow the grass to remain uncut long enough for the plants to flower you will provide a better feeding area for birds, bees and other insects. If you add other flowering plants you will increase the wildlife value of your lawn.

For short turf, apart from the usual lawn 'weeds', attractive additions are bird's-foot trefoil (*Lotus corniculatus*), wild thyme (*Thymus polytrichus*), self heal (*Prunella vulgaris*), eyebright (*Euphrasia* spp.) and violets (*Viola* spp.).

If you are able to leave the grass uncut for most of the summer, taller plants will provide a source of food for bees and seed-eating birds. Choose from hemp agrimony (*Eupatorium cannabinum*), knapweeds (*Centaurea* spp.), wild marjoram (*Origanum vulgare*), field scabious (*Knautia arvensis*), devil's-bit scabious (*Succisa pratensis*), teasel (*Dipsacus fullonum*) and mallow (*Malva sylvestris*).

WILDLIFE HABITATS IN THE GARDEN

Rotten logs
Undisturbed piles of old, decaying logs help create the cool, dark and often damp environment that frogs, newts and beetles enjoy.

Dry-stone walls
Gaps and crevices found in sunny, dry-stone walls may attract toads and wood mice, and also make excellent winter shelters for insects.

Garden ponds
Marshy areas and ponds will encourage a wide range of creatures to visit your garden, including frogs, newts, aquatic insects and all kinds of birds.

See also Choosing plants for bees, p.252; Best plants for butterflies, p.253; How to encourage birds, p.256

large for most gardens but there are many smaller trees and shrubs that provide food for birds, bees and other insects, including mountain ash (*Sorbus aucuparia*), holly, silver birch (*Betula pendula*), hazel (*Corylus avellana*), goat willow (*Salix caprea*), spindle (*Euonymus europaeus*), crab apples (*Malus sylvestris*), wild or bird cherry (*Prunus avium*), *Buddleja davidii*, *Cotoneaster*, *Pyracantha*, wild roses and hawthorns (*Crataegus* spp.)

Use large trees as supports for climbing plants such as clematis, roses and ivy (*Hedera helix*).

Flower borders

Many annual and herbaceous plants in flower borders are of exotic origin but are extremely important as sources of nectar and pollen for bees, butterflies and other flower visitors. Avoid double-flowered forms as these often lack pollen and are shunned by bees. Later in the season seed-eating birds will be attracted to the seedheads. Useful garden flowers you could grow are sedums, scabious (*Scabiosa* spp.), sunflower (*Helianthus annuus*), Michaelmas daisies (*Aster*), wallflowers (*Erysimum cheiri*), aubrieta and golden rod (*Solidago*). You could also include native plants in your borders, such as foxglove (*Digitalis purpurea*), meadow cranesbill (*Geranium pratense*), primrose (*Primula vulgaris*), cowslip (*Primula elatior*), hemp agrimony (*Eupatorium cannabinum*), knapweeds (*Centaurea* spp.), teasel (*Dipsacus fullonum*) and red campion (*Silene dioica*).

Ways to attract wildlife
Top: Providing water, such as this stream, is one of the main ways of attracting wildlife into gardens.
Above: These *Digitalis purpurea* hybrids (foxgloves) will encourage insects such as bumble bees.

Hedges, walls and fences

Living boundaries, such as hedges, are of great value to wildlife but fencing and walls with climbing plants or shrubs are also useful. As well as providing nesting sites for birds, they also shelter the garden from strong winds. Informal hedges are better than those that are regularly clipped. Hedging plants such as hawthorn (*Crataegus monogyna*), holly (*Ilex aquifolium*) and privet (*Ligustrum ovalifolium*) will produce few or no flowers and berries if kept trim. To create the ideal wildlife hedge plant a mixture of plants such as hawthorn, field maple (*Acer campestre*), blackthorn (*Prunus spinosa*), beech (*Fagus sylvatica*), hornbeam (*Carpinus betulus*) and holly, with rambling plants such as wild rose (*Rosa canina*), bramble (*Rubus fruticosa*) and honeysuckle (*Lonicera periclymenum*) growing through them.

Trees and shrubs

Your garden's size will determine which trees you can grow. Forest trees are too

TIPS TO ATTRACT WILDLIFE

- Minimize the use of weedkillers, fungicides and insecticides
- Avoid excessive tidiness. For example, allow plants to set seed
- Provide nest boxes for birds and bees
- Leave a pile of logs lying around in a sheltered spot
- Maintain a compost heap

Choosing plants for bees

Plants whose flowers are rich in pollen and nectar are best for encouraging these beneficial insects into your garden; avoid choosing plants with double flowers as these are not attractive to bees

Bees visit flowers to collect nectar and pollen. Some of the plants listed here will provide pollen only, but they are, nevertheless, valuable to bees. However, some of these plants may not always prove attractive to bees. This is particularly true of certain trees and shrubs which, in some years, might not produce nectar in sufficient quantity to attract these insects. The extent to which nectar is produced is influenced by temperature, humidity and soil moisture.

Plants growing in sunny, sheltered places are more likely to be visited by bees than those growing in shaded or windswept situations. Low-growing plants such as annuals and herbaceous perennials are more attractive to bees if they are grown in large clumps or patches, rather than being scattered and mixed up with other plants.

Bee-friendly foxgloves
As well as adding a dramatic vertical dimension to the garden, foxgloves (*Digitalis purpurea*) are a favourite with bumble bees and ideal plants for naturalizing in a woodland garden.

PLANTS THAT ATTRACT BEES

Annuals

Borago officinalis, Callistephus chinensis, Centaurea cyanus, Centaurea moschata, Clarkia, Cosmos bipinnatus, Eschscholzia californica ✿, Gilia capitata, Helianthus annuus, Heliotropium, Iberis, Limnanthes douglasii ✿, Myosotis, Nemophila menziesii, Nigella damascena, Phacelia, Zinnia elegans

Biennials

Alcea rosea, Erysimum, Hedysarum coronarium, Lunaria annua

Perennials

Agastache foeniculum, Alyssum, Anchusa azurea, Anemone x hybrida, Arabis, Armeria maritima, Aster, Aubrieta, Campanula, Cynara cardunculus ✿, Dahlia, Doronicum, Echinops ritro ✿, Erigeron, Eryngium, Geranium, Geum, Gypsophila paniculata, Helleborus, Liatris spicata, Marrubium vulgare, Monarda punctata, Nepeta, Papaver orientale, Persicaria amplexicaulis, Polemonium caeruleum,
Rudbeckia, Salvia x superba ✿, Scabiosa, Sedum spectabile ✿, Sidalcea malviflora, Solidago, Stachys byzantina, Veronica longifolia

Bulbs, corms and tubers

Allium, Chionodoxa luciliae ✿, Colchicum, Crocus, Eranthis hyemalis ✿, Fritillaria, Galanthus, Hyacinthus orientalis, Leucojum, Muscari, Scilla siberica ✿

Trees and shrubs

Acer, Aesculus, Arbutus unedo ✿, Berberis, Buddleja globosa ✿, Buxus sempervirens ✿, Calluna vulgaris, Caryopteris, Catalpa bignonioides ✿, Ceanothus, Cercis siliquastrum ✿, Chaenomeles, Cornus alba, Corylus avellana, Cotoneaster, Crataegus, Cytisus, Daphne mezereum, Enkianthus campanulatus ✿, Erica, Escallonia, Fuchsia, Gaultheria shallon, Hebe, Hedera helix, Helianthemum, Hypericum, Ilex aquifolium ✿, Koelreuteria paniculata ✿, Laurus nobilis ✿, Lavandula, Lonicera x purpusii, Mahonia aquifolium, Malus, Olearia x haastii, Parthenocissus
quinquefolia, Parthenocissus tricuspidata ✿, Perovskia atriplicifolia, Potentilla fruticosa, Prunus avium ✿, Prunus dulcis, Prunus laurocerasus ✿, Prunus spinosa, Pyracantha, Pyrus, Ribes, Robinia pseudoacacia, Rosa, Rubus, Salix caprea, Sarcococca, Sorbus aucuparia, Symphoricarpos, Tetradium daniellii, Weigela florida, Ulex

Wild flowers

Arctium lappa, Bryonia dioica, Caltha palustris ✿, Centaurea, Chamerion angustifolium, Cirsium, Clematis vitalba, Convolvulus arvensis, Dipsacus fullonum, Echium vulgare, Eupatorium cannabinum, Filipendula ulmaria, Hippocrepis comosa, Knautia arvensis, Lamium purpureum, Linaria vulgaris, Lotus corniculatus, Lythrum salicaria, Malva, Melilotus alba, Melilotus officinalis, Papaver, Persicaria, Ranunculus ficaria, Salvia pratensis, Scrophularia, Sinapis arvensis, Stellaria media, Succisa pratensis, Taraxacum officinale, Trifolium, Tussilago farfara, Valeriana officinalis

See also Encouraging wildlife into the garden, pp.250–251; How to encourage birds, p.256

The best plants for butterflies

Grow a combination of suitable wild and cultivated plants, including annuals, herbaceous perennials and shrubs, and you will encourage various butterflies to feed and even breed in your garden

Butterflies visit flowers to obtain nectar, which they suck up with their long tongues. For best results grow the plants listed in the box below in sunny, sheltered places and in clumps, rather than single plants scattered around.

Food plants for caterpillars

The flowers listed in the box will attract the more common and mobile species of butterfly, but most are unsuitable as food plants for their caterpillars. The caterpillars eat leaves and often have a narrow range of food plants. With the exception of cabbage white butterflies, caterpillars often feed on wild plants, including:

• STINGING NETTLE (*Urtica dioica*): Used by peacock, red admiral, comma and small tortoiseshell. Grow in a sunny position to encourage egg laying. Prevent seeding by cutting plants down in midsummer after the first brood of the small tortoiseshell has developed.

• THISTLES (*Cirsium* and *Carduus* spp.): Painted lady lays eggs on plants such as welted thistle (*Carduus crispus*) and creeping thistle (*Cirsium arvense*).

• CABBAGES, OTHER BRASSICAS AND NASTURTIUMS: Large cabbage white and small cabbage white.

• GARLIC MUSTARD (*Alliaria petiolata*)

Buddleja davidii (butterfly bush) attracts various species of butterfly, such as the small tortoiseshell

and LADY'S SMOCK (*Cardamine pratensis*): Orange tip and green-veined white.

• MIXED GRASSES: Various grasses are used by speckled wood, wall brown, meadow brown, gatekeeper, marbled white, ringlet, small heath, large skipper, small skipper and Essex skipper. The habitat needs vary, particularly regarding grass type, height and whether it is dry or damp grassland. Leave the grass uncut during the growing season and mow it

in the spring, leaving a good basal growth on the tussocks.

• HOLLY (*Ilex aquifolium*) and IVY (*Hedera helix*): Holly blue lays eggs on holly flowers in spring and on ivy flowers in late summer.

• ALDER BUCKTHORN (*Rhamnus frangula*) and COMMON BUCKTHORN (*Rhamnus cathartica*): Brimstone butterfly.

• BIRD'S FOOT TREFOIL (*Lotus corniculatus*): Common blue.

PLANTS THAT ATTRACT BUTTERFLIES

Annuals and biennials

Ageratum houstonianum, Calendula officinalis, Callistephus chinensis, Centaurea cyanus, Dianthus barbatus, Erysimum cheiri, Heliotropium, Iberis amara, Lobularia maritima, Lunaria annua, Matthiola incana, Reseda odorata, Tagetes, Verbena rigida ♥

Perennials

Agastache foeniculum, Arabis alpina subsp. *caucasica, Armeria, Asperula hexaphylla, Aster, Astrantia major, Aubrieta, Aurinia saxatilis ♥,*
Centaurea, Centranthus ruber, Cynara cardunculus ♥, Dahlia, Echinops, Eryngium, Gaillardia, Hesperis matronalis, Hyssopus officinalis, Iberis sempervirens ♥, Liatris spicata, Mentha spicata, Nepeta x faassenii ♥, Phlox paniculata, Polemonium caeruleum, Scabiosa, Sedum spectabile ♥, Solidago

Shrubs

Buddleja davidii, Buddleja globosa ♥, Calluna vulgaris, Caryopteris x clandonensis, Crataegus monogyna, Daboecia, Erica, Escallonia, Hebe,
Hedera helix, Lavandula, Ligustrum, Mahonia aquifolium, Prunus laurocerasus ♥, Pyracantha, Rubus fruticosus, Thymus

Wild plants

Angelica sylvestris, Cardamine pratensis, Carduus, Centaurea, Cirsium, Dipsacus fullonum, Eupatorium cannabinum, Hieracium, Knautia arvensis, Lythrum salicaria, Origanum vulgare, Pulicaria dysenterica, Ranunculus, Salix caprea, Sedum acre, Succisa pratensis, Taraxacum officinale, Trifolium, Valeriana officinalis

See also Encouraging wildlife into the garden, pp.250–251; How to encourage birds, p.256

What is organic gardening?

Organic gardening methods avoid the use of manufactured fertilizers and other synthetic chemicals; many of these techniques are simply good practice and compatible with other forms of gardening

The term organic gardening is commonly used to describe cultivation systems that make minimal use of manufactured chemical substances. It relies on manures and fertilizers derived only from animal or plant remains. Conserving natural resources and avoiding pollution and health hazards are further important aspects of organic gardening.

Soil fertility

Improve and maintain the fertility of your soil (see p.259), except in special instances such as areas for wild flowers. Make sure the soil contains sufficient lime to supply calcium and provide the optimum soil pH for the uptake of other essential plant foods (see also p.263).

Ensure your soil has plenty of humus by adding well-rotted organic matter during digging. Well-rotted animal manures are ideal, as are plant residues such as seaweed, leafmould or compost made from garden and kitchen waste (for details on making garden compost see p.271).

If the soil is heavy, dig in autumn or early winter; if it is light soil, dig it in spring. Add organic matter whatever the soil, as evenly as possible, to the top 20cm (8in). Carry out annual digging and manuring of the vegetable plot to help maintain soil fertility. Occasionally carry out deeper digging.

ORGANIC PEST CONTROL

- Construct traps, such as an inverted flower pot filled with dried grass over a cane to attract earwigs
- Companion planting can reduce pest attack. Strong smelling herbs such as mint or garlic may repel pests
- A tidy garden will help keep pests under control

Leafmould: bulky but low in plant foods

You may find green manuring useful to maintain the soil structure and fertility on the vegetable plot, although it may be difficult to fit into crop rotation if you have a small garden. Grazing rye (*Secale cereale*) is a good green-manure crop for overwintering. Legumes, such as winter field beans (*Vicia faba*), clovers (*Trifolium* spp.) and bitter lupin (*Lupinus angustifolia*) have the added advantage of fixing nitrogen from the air in their root nodules. White mustard (*Sinapis alba*), fodder radish (*Raphanus sativus*), and *Phacelia tanacetifolia* are suitable annual plants for occupying vacant ground and digging in before the plants set seed.

Bulky organic manures provide only limited foods for demanding fruits and vegetables, and some types, such as leafmould, provide very little food indeed. Therefore, you will need to apply fertilizer. Processed organic materials such as hoof and horn and bonemeal provide nitrogen and phosphate respectively over an extended period, and dried blood is a quicker acting source of nitrogen.

Liquid fertilizers of organic origin, either proprietary or home prepared (for example, infusions of comfrey or animal manures), are also useful, especially for container-grown plants.

The case for no digging often features in organic gardening. Undisturbed soil provides a more amenable environment for many beneficial soil organisms. In some instances, this preserves the soil structure and reduces moisture loss through evaporation. Conversely, digging provides an opportunity for adding bulky organic matter; it is a means of improving drainage and root penetration by breaking up compaction; it aerates the soil; weeds can be destroyed; and soil pests are exposed to winter cold and predators. No digging is an option if your soil structure is naturally very good and you can skilfully manage the plot for crop establishment and weed control.

Pest and disease control

There are many alternatives to consider before you reach for the sprayer and synthetic chemicals.

Growth stressed or otherwise unthrifty plants generally succumb more readily to pests and diseases. Therefore, carry out careful husbandry. Ensure good soil fertility and timely watering. Bear in mind that clubroot disease of brassicas (*Plasmodiophora brassicae*) thrives on acid soil, and scab disease of potatoes (*Streptomyces scabies*) on limy ones. Powdery mildews are worse where soils are dry.

Raise ornamental plants and vegetables in cell trays or pots so that you can plant them out in optimum conditions for rapid establishment. Time your sowings to avoid a crop being vulnerable at a critical stage of insect activity. For example, sow swedes and turnips after late spring to miss the main

See also *Using biological controls, pp.40–41; Green manures, p.207; Mulching, p.269; Composting, p.271; Leafmould, p.272*

egg-laying period of the cabbage root fly (*Delia radicum*).

Practice crop hygiene, such as cutting out fruit tree wood infected with canker. Use physical barriers to exclude or deter pests, such as low-level screens around blocks of carrots to protect them from egg-laying carrot fly (*Psila rosae*). Grow brassicas under horticultural fleece to exclude insect pests. Put grease bands around the trunks of fruit trees in autumn to intercept female winter moths (*Operophtera brumata*). Use beer traps for slugs, and handpick pests such as caterpillars on brassicas.

Pheromone traps placed among apple trees can catch enough male codling moths (*Cydia pomonella*) to reduce the mating success of females and so may reduce the number of maggoty apples.

Try companion planting to foil pests, such as alternating rows of brassicas with other crops to reduce the incidence of mealy cabbage aphid (*Brevicoryne brassicae*) and cabbage root fly (*Delia radicum*). Practice crop rotation, particularly with vegetables, and do not replant roses on the same site.

If plants are congested through lack

Hang pheromone traps in apple trees to catch male codling moths, for fewer maggoty fruits

of thinning or too close planting, air flow is reduced and diseases may be encouraged. The same can be true where plants are given too much nitrogenous fertilizer. In both situations the ubiquitous grey mould (*Botrytis cinerea*) is likely to thrive.

Natural pest and disease control

Biological control, or the use of predators and parasites to combat pests, is well worth considering (for more details *see pp.40–41*).

Other biological controls include pathogenic nematodes for dealing with slugs, leatherjackets and chafer grubs outdoors, and a bacterium, *Bacillus thuringiensis*, for controlling caterpillars of pest moths and butterflies.

Plants vary in their susceptibility to pest and disease attack, so where possible grow the most resistant kinds. For example, hollyhocks (*Alcea*) that are relatively resistant to rust disease (*Puccinia malvacearum*) are available; the rose 'Elina' is less susceptible to black spot (*Diplocarpon rosae*), and the apples 'Sunset' and 'Ashmead's Kernel' are less affected by scab (*Venturia inaequalis*). Carrots 'Flyaway' and 'Resistafly' are less susceptible, but not immune, to carrot fly (*Psila rosae*).

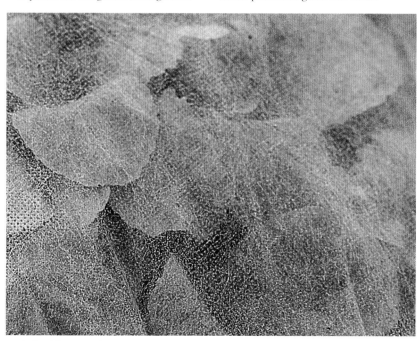

Horticultural fleece may be used to cover brassicas, protecting them from various insect pests

HOW TO ENCOURAGE BIRDS

How to encourage birds

Most birds will provide a great deal of enjoyment and interest in your garden, and many are decidedly beneficial, but they may need encouraging with suitable food supplies, water and shelter

Birds such as pigeons and bullfinches may damage plants, but most birds are welcome for the added interest they give to gardens. Some help to control insect pests, and seed-eating birds can reduce the spread of weeds.

You can make your garden more attractive to birds by planting and maintaining it to suit their needs.

Make a water supply
Birds need water throughout the year for drinking and bathing. A pond with a gently sloping side can meet this need, but in the winter it is likely to freeze over, so try to provide a non-frozen source of water. Ornate bird baths are expensive and no more effective than a shallow-sided container placed on the ground. Choose one that is at least 30cm (12in) in diameter with a capacity of up to 5cm (2in) of water.

Improve natural food supplies
During the summer nesting season most birds, including seed-eaters, collect insects and other tiny creatures to feed to their young, so try to create habitats for wildlife in your garden.

There are many garden plants that will provide food in the form of berries and seeds. Much of this becomes available in late summer and autumn,

Birds, including nuthatches, will appreciate seed scattered on bird tables all year round

when birds need to build up their fat reserves to survive the winter months.

You can cater for seed-eating birds by delaying cutting back annual and herbaceous plants until late winter.

Bird tables and seed feeders
Studies have shown that birds benefit from being fed throughout the year, rather than just in winter, since natural food sources are in short supply. A variety of foods, such as peanuts, seed mixtures and balls of fat, are available

from garden centres and pet shops, as are bird tables and other containers for dispensing food.

Provide shelter and nest sites
While some birds roost in trees, many smaller species prefer the shelter of shrubs and hedges, especially with dense branches. Conifers and evergreen shrubs give protection against cold winds in the winter. These plants will also provide nest sites for many birds, as will dense climbing plants.

FOOD PLANTS FOR BIRDS

Native plants
Alnus glutinosa (seeds), *Betula pendula* (seeds), *Carduus nutans* (seeds), *Centaurea scabiosa* (seeds), *Crataegus monogyna* (berries), *Dipsacus fullonum* (seeds), *Hedera helix* (berries), *Ilex aquifolium* (berries), *Knautia arvensis* (seeds), *Rhamnus frangula* (berries), *Rosa canina* (hips), *Rubus fruticosus* (berries), *Sambucus nigra* (berries), *Sorbus aria* (berries), *Sorbus aucuparia* (berries), *Succisa pratensis* (seeds), *Taxus baccata* (berries), *Viburnum lantana* (berries)

Cultivated plants
Berberis (berries), *Cotoneaster* (berries), *Crataegus* (berries), *Daphne mezereum* (berries), *Helianthus annuus* (seeds), *Ilex* (berries), *Ligustrum* (berries), *Lonicera* (berries), *Mahonia* (berries), *Malus* (fruits), *Photinia davidiana* (berries), *Prunus avium* (fruits), *Prunus cerasus* (fruits), *Pyracantha* (berries), *Rosa moyesii* (hips), *Rosa rugosa* (hips), *Sorbus* (berries), *Viburnum betulifolium* (berries)

NESTING BOXES

Birds need sheltered places where they can roost at night or shelter from bad weather. Homemade or bought nesting boxes can provide ideal nest sites for birds.

See also Autumn colour p.62; Bullfinches p.72; Encouraging wildlife into the garden pp.250–251

SOILS, COMPOSTS & FERTILIZERS

Why cultivate soil?

Create the right conditions for seedlings and plants to establish successfully by burying weeds and incorporating organic materials such as well-rotted manure

Cultivation is mainly undertaken to improve soil structure, bury weeds, cure compaction, and to incorporate fertilizers, bulky organic matter, sand, grit or lime. There is no need to do more than the minimum amount of work to achieve these objectives as over-cultivating damages soil structure.

Single or double digging

Digging, where the soil is inverted, is best done in autumn for clay soils, while early spring cultivation suits lighter, sandier soils. Turning over a spade's depth is called single digging. Double digging involves taking out a trench to a spade's depth to invert a second layer of soil. This is sometimes helpful where drainage needs to be improved or before planting deep-rooted, long-term crops. Digging may

not always be necessary, and forking the soil may suffice.

Fork organic matter such as garden compost or well-rotted manure into the bottom of the trench when digging.

Because digging leads to moisture loss, make sure you finish before warm mid-spring weather arrives. Consider hiring a rotary cultivator if time runs short. Easily worked ground can be handled by a light 2–5hp model, but harder soil needs a heavier machine. Rotary cultivating wet soil is extremely damaging, so wait for drier conditions.

Treat acid soils with lime (unless growing lime-hating plants), using the amounts specified by a soil test. Over-liming is damaging, so avoid guesswork. Lime takes many months to be fully effective. Alkaline soils can be made acid by adding sulphur. In practice this is too

SOIL COMPACTION

In compacted soil, the pores between the soil particles have been compressed over time. This means that there is no room for air, water or foods to circulate through it. The result is slow drainage and poor aeration, and plants will not thrive. Improve compacted soil by digging in grit and organic matter.

slow and expensive to be worthwhile. It is better to grow acid-loving plants in containers of ericaceous compost, if your soil is alkaline.

Improving the soil's surface

Digging is called primary cultivation. It is followed by secondary cultivation, which produces a fine, crumbly, moist, but firm surface layer called a 'tilth'. Work back and forth with a three-pointed cultivator, followed by raking. Treading crushes lumps, but it damages soil structure unless the soil is fairly dry. Avoid treading on wet soil by working from boards or paths.

For seedbeds aim for fine, friable soil deep enough to cover seeds and fine enough for moist soil to be in contact with the seeds. Soil should be firm, but neither compact or 'fluffy'; to be safe, lightly press the soil by patting with the back of a spade or rake head. Ideally the surface should be firm, with the underlying soil relatively loose. Avoid working wet soil as this can lead to soil slumping in rain, suffocating the seeds.

Sometimes a really fine tilth is impossible in wet weather. Here, you have to be reasonable and accept that you can only generate a coarse tilth, and raise your plants in pots or cell trays. Transplants are less demanding than seeds and can establish well even in the sort of lumpy soil that would make a poor seedbed.

HOW TO CULTIVATE THE SOIL FOR SEEDBEDS

1 Dig or fork over dry soil, breaking up clumps and removing any large stones and weeds. **2** If the ground is very compacted, a rotary cultivator may be the best answer and save any additional backache. **3** Once the soil is well and truly broken up, rake over the surface and remove any large stones, unbroken clods of compacted soil and weeds. **4** Firm the ground by treading gently in straight lines over the surface of the seedbed. **5** Finally, rake over the surface again to provide the fine tilth that is suitable for seed germination.

See also Improving drainage, p.260; Getting to know your soil's pH, p.263; Why lime soils?, p.265

PRACTICAL ADVICE

Soil fertility

A fertile soil is needed for good plant growth

It is often said that the key to a fertile soil lies with the addition of bulky organic matter, which rots down into humus. Two commonly recommended materials are farmyard manure and garden compost. The addition of fresh manure before it has rotted, can cause ammonia to be released, which may scorch plants, so make sure that you use composted or well-rotted manure. Garden compost has many of the same benefits, plus it is free if you make it yourself and recycles plant foods.

Both of these materials improve the moisture- and food-holding capacity of sandy soils. They also improve the structure of heavy soils by creating a more crumbly soil that is easier to work. It is difficult to apply too much organic matter, particularly on impoverished soils.

Garden compost improves the fertility of soil

GARDEN COMPOST

- Garden compost is an excellent soil improver. It can be dug into the ground even if it still contains a little semi-rotted material
- Although it seldom breaks down to the crumbly material produced by commercial composting, it is still very effective

See Successful garden composting, p.271

PRACTICAL ADVICE

Building your soil's fertility

You need to know your soil in order to improve its fertility

One benefit of mulching is a more fertile soil

Use a pH test kit to find out if lime is needed to counter excessive acidity (*see p.265*). Add lime in the winter to give it time to take effect before the growing season.

Fertile soils contain numerous air spaces. Large ones allow water to drain and air to reach the roots, while smaller spaces hold moisture that can be extracted by plants roots.

Digging, forking and other soil cultivation, especially the addition of organic matter such as well-rotted garden compost or manure, all promote good texture with adequate formation of air spaces (*see p.258*). Organic mulches around established plants have a similar effect, as organic matter binds soil into particles, thus creating air spaces.

In addition, clay soils need adequate calcium to coalesce. Apply calcium to acid clays as lime or to neutral clays as gypsum. Alkaline clays already have sufficient calcium. Add pea-sized grit to the top 15cm (6in) of clay soils to help open up air spaces for better drainage.

See Getting to know your soil pH, p.263

PLANT PROBLEMS

Alien flatworms

These foreign pests are causing problems in some areas

Australian flatworm

New Zealand flatworm

Flatworm invaders
These flatworms from Australia and New Zealand feed on beneficial earthworms, which may lead to soil problems. They have been introduced to Britain, where they have no natural enemies.

The New Zealand flatworm (*Arthurdendyus triangulatus*) and Australian flatworm (*Australoplana sanguinea*) are two alien flatworms that are causing concern in Britain. New Zealand flatworm is reddish brown with paler margins and may grow up to 17cm (7in) long. Australian flatworm is orange-brown and slightly smaller, growing up to 10cm (4in) long. Neither of them have segmented bodies.

Symptoms
Flatworms are easily spread by the movement of soil from infested gardens or nurseries. They feed on earthworms, in some areas virtually eliminating them. This may lead to soil problems, and can also have an impact on animals such as foxes, badgers, moles and birds because earthworms form a significant part of their diets.

Control
Flatworms have no effective natural enemies in Britain, and no control measures are available. If flatworms are present in your garden do not enable them to spread further by moving soil, compost or plants to other gardens that may be free of these pests.

GARDENING ON WET SOILS

Gardening on wet soils

Options include growing bog and water plants, improving drainage of the soil, or even constructing raised beds for plants

Poorly drained soil presents serious problems. Where there is impeded drainage, root systems tend to be shallow because lower down, waterlogging causes oxygen starvation. Lack of oxygen prevents growth and eventually kills roots. If the soil dries out temporarily during warm spells, a plant with a shallow root system is more susceptible to drought.

To find out if your soil is badly drained, wait until it is thoroughly moist, for instance after heavy rain, and then make a hole about 60cm (24in) deep and wide. Fill with water and wait to see how long it takes to drain. If it disappears within a couple of days there is no problem, but when water remains for longer than this, you have a drainage problem. If the hole acts as a sump, with water draining in from the surrounding soil, drainage is particularly poor and there is cause for concern.

If you have an area of poorly drained soil you could create a bog garden or a pond (*see pp.274–281*). However, if this is not practical, or you want to grow a wider range of plants, you will need to improve the soil.

Where there is a slight problem caused by slow-draining, heavy clay topsoil, carry out deep digging and add plenty of well-rotted organic matter, coarse sand, and grit.

If your soil remains waterlogged as a result of deep, impeded drainage, you will need an artificial drainage system (*see box, facing page*).

An alternative to artificial drainage is to construct a raised bed. This is especially useful if a high water table is the problem, where artificial drains would be unsuitable. A raised bed creates a freely drained rooting zone above the water table.

Retain the bed with a low wall constructed from bricks, stone or timber. Place a 15cm (6in) layer of gravel or hardcore in the base and fill the bed with a mix of the existing topsoil, organic matter and grit. Make sure there are holes at the base of the bed above the natural ground level to allow excess water to escape.

Many plants grow poorly in waterlogged soil, which is starved of oxygen

See also Raised beds, p.27; How to create a bog garden, p.274

Improving drainage

If digging won't cure bad drainage, install artificial drains

Poor drainage may be indicated by surface puddling after rain. This may be due to a high water table, compacted layers beneath the surface, or surface compaction. A particular problem on modern housing developments is that subsoil is compacted by building activity then covered by a cosmetic layer of loose topsoil.

Where poor drainage is due to factors other than surface compaction (which can be reduced by digging in organic matter and grit), you may have to install a drainage system. This can be as simple as digging a ditch about 90cm (3ft) deep with sloping sides across the lower end of a slope to take excess surface water. Where this is unsuitable, make French ditches by filling the ditch with coarse gravel topped with upturned turf and topsoil.

A more elaborate drainage system involves laying perforated plastic drainage pipes on a firmed 5cm (2in) bed of coarse gravel in a trench, and covering with 10cm (4in) of gravel (*see box, right*). You may want to hire a mini-digger or employ a specialist contractor for this.

Lay the system below the level of cultivation, usually 40–60cm (15–24in) deep and 3–6m (10–20ft) apart. The trenches must follow a natural slope, or a constructed one, with a fall of 1:40. Make a herringbone layout with the side drains meeting the main drain at an angle of 45 degrees. When using perforated plastic drainage pipe make sure the perforations face sideways to prevent excessive silting.

Do not install a drainage system unless there is somewhere for the excess water to go. This may be an existing ditch, authorized outlet, or a soakaway pit at least 1.8cu m (6cu ft) in capacity, and filled with rubble.

See also Why cultivate soil?, p.258

TECHNIQUES

INSTALLING DRAINAGE PIPES

[1] Hiring a mini-digger to excavate the trenches is the easiest method, as the trenches need to be 40–60cm (15–24in) deep. [2] Lay the perforated plastic drainage pipes on a firmed bed of coarse gravel 5cm (2in) deep. [3] Backfill the trenches first with a layer of gravel 10cm (4in) deep to assist drainage, before backfilling with soil.

How to improve clay soil

The secret of making clay soil better for plants is to add the right materials and to dig at the right time

Clay particles are extremely small, with 1,000 times the surface area in a given volume of soil compared with larger sandy soil particles. Clay packs closely and holds water tightly, therefore preventing water from draining away.

Sticky wet soils are likely where the clay content is greater than 30 per cent. Fortunately clay soils naturally break into small lumps when they dry, and they shrink in summer, allowing roots access to water and air. Adding bulky organic matter, especially composted bark, either as a mulch or dug in, helps to promote this texture, without which clay soils would support very little plant growth.

Where an open texture is needed, dig in abundant coarse material, such as well-rotted compost, to counter the clay's stickiness. First experiment on a small scale, mixing an 8cm (3in) layer of grit into the top 15cm (6in) of the soil, adding more if, after a month, the soil still seems too stiff. Too little can be worse than none at all.

Wet clay swells, preventing winter rain from escaping. In spring the water slowly evaporates, delaying planting, sowing and growth in relation to better-drained soils. Drainage (see left) or, on a smaller scale, raised beds can counter this. Walking on wet clay damages its structure when it is compressed or smeared. Instead, construct paths or stepping stones.

There are only brief periods in mid-autumn and mid- to late spring when clay soil can be easily dug and seedbeds made. In winter, freezing and thawing of ground dug in mid-autumn aids the preparation of seedbeds in spring. If you cannot cultivate soil in these periods, consider 'no-digging' beds, and set seeds and perennial and woody plants that are suited to clay into undug soil. Hoe, pull and spray weeds, and add a thick mulch.

Plant foods are held in a readily available way within clays, making these moist soils potentially very fertile. Although seedbeds on clay soils are tricky to prepare, trees, shrubs and perennials usually grow very well when their roots are able to penetrate the surrounding soil.

TIPS TO IMPROVE CLAY SOILS

- Dig in organic material like well-rotted manure, compost, or lime, to improve soil structure by breaking up soil clumps
- Earthworms improve clay soil by burrowing, which increases aeration and improves drainage
- Do not work the soil when the ground is wet

CHANGING SOIL MAKE-UP

Improving the structure and fertility of your soil will not happen over night. For an open texture, dig abundant amounts of coarse material, such as grit, into the topsoil.

See also Raised beds, p.27; Choosing plants for clay soils, p.262

Choosing plants for clay soils

It is hard work cultivating clay soil, but there will not be much work to do if you choose to grow permanent plants which are ideally suited to these conditions

SUITABLE PLANTS FOR CLAY SOILS

Provided the soil is well prepared before planting, and drainage has been improved if necessary, a wide range of plants can be grown on clay soil, from trees and shrubs to hardy perennials. Indeed, clay soil is extremely fertile so growth should be good, and as it is also a moist soil it is suitable for a wide range of moisture-loving plants.

Trees

Alnus cordata ♀ ‡ 25m (80ft) ↔ 6m (20ft) ▢ ◊ ✱✱✱

Amelanchier lamarckii ♀ ‡ 10m (30ft) ↔ 12m (40ft) ▢–▢ ◊ ☼ ✱✱✱

Betula ermanii ‡ 20m (70ft) ↔ 12m (40ft) ▢–▢ ◊ ✱✱✱

Laburnum x *watereri* 'Vossii' ♀ ‡↔ 8m (25ft) ▢ ◊ ✱✱✱

Malus floribunda ♀ ‡↔ 10m (30ft) ▢ ◊ ✱✱✱ [1]

Prunus avium 'Plena' ♀ ‡↔ 12m (40ft) ▢ ◊ ✱✱✱

Pyrus salicifolia 'Pendula' ♀ ‡ 5m (15ft) ↔ 4m (12ft) ▢ ◊ ✱✱✱

Conifers

Chamaecyparis lawsoniana ‡ 15–40m (50–130ft) ↔ 2–5m (6–15ft) E ▢ ◊ ✱✱✱

Ginkgo biloba ♀ ‡ 30m (100ft) ↔ 8m (25ft) ▢ ◊ ✱✱✱

Taxodium distichum ♀ ‡ 20–40m (70–130ft) ↔ 6–9m (20–28ft) ▢–▢ ◊ ☼ ✱✱✱

Taxus baccata ♀ ‡ 10–20m (30–70ft) ↔ 8–10m (25–30ft) E ▢–▢ ◊ ✱✱✱

Thuja plicata ‡ 20–35m (70–120ft) ↔ 6–10m (20–30ft) E ▢ ◊ ✱✱✱

Shrubs

Aucuba japonica ‡↔ 3m (10ft) E ▢–▢ ◊ ✱✱✱

Berberis darwinii ♀ ‡↔ 3m (10ft) E ▢–▢ ◊ ✱✱✱

Chaenomeles speciosa ‡ 2.4m (8ft) ↔ 5m (15ft) ▢–▢ ◊ ✱✱✱

Choisya ternata ♀ ‡↔ 2.4m (8ft) E ▢ ◊ ✱✱✱

Cornus alba ‡↔ 3m (10ft) ▢ ◊ ✱✱✱

Cotoneaster horizontalis ♀ ‡ 90cm (36in) ↔ 1.5m (5ft) ▢ ◊ ✱✱✱ [2]

Euonymus alatus ♀ ‡ 1.8m (6ft) ↔ 3m (10ft) ▢–▢ ◊ ✱✱✱

Forsythia x *intermedia* 'Lynwood' ♀ ‡↔ 3m (10ft) ▢–▢ ◊ ✱✱✱

Hypericum forrestii ♀ ‡ 1.2m (4ft) ↔ 1.5m (5ft) ▢–▢ ◊ ✱✱✱

Kerria japonica 'Pleniflora' ♀ ‡↔ 3m (10ft) ▢–▢ ◊ ✱✱✱

Philadelphus coronarius 'Aureus' ♀ ‡ 2.4m (8ft) ↔ 1.5m (5ft) ▢ ◊ ✱✱✱

Prunus laurocerasus ♀ ‡ 8m (25ft) ↔ 10m (30ft) E ▢–▢ ◊ ✱✱✱

Pyracantha rogersiana ♀ ‡↔ 4m (12ft) E ▢–▢ ◊ ✱✱

Ribes speciosum ♀ ‡↔ 1.8m (6ft) ▢ ◊ ✱✱

Viburnum tinus ‡↔ 3m (10ft) E ▢–▢ ◊ ✱✱✱

Hardy perennials

Anemone hupehensis var. *japonica* ‡ 60–120cm (24–48in) ↔ 45cm (18in) ▢–▢ ◊ ✱✱✱

Aster novae-angliae ‡ 1.5m (5ft) ↔ 60cm (24in) ▢–▢ ◊ ✱✱✱

Astilbe x *arendsii* ‡↔ 60–90cm (24–36in) ▢–▢ ◊ ✱✱✱

Helenium autumnale ‡ 1.5m (5ft) ↔ 45cm (18in) ▢ ◊ ✱✱✱

Helleborus x *hybridus* ‡↔ 45cm (18in) E ▢ ◊ ✱✱✱

Heuchera sanguinea ‡↔ 30cm (12in) ▢–▢ ◊ ✱✱✱

Hosta fortunei ‡ 55cm (22in) ↔ 80cm (32in) ▢–▢ ◊ ✱✱✱

Rudbeckia fulgida var. *deamii* ♀ ‡ 60cm (24in) ↔ 45cm (18in) ▢–▢ ◊ ✱✱✱ [3]

See also Why cultivate soil?, p.258; How to improve clay soil, p.261

Getting to know your soil's pH

You need to know the pH (acidity or alkalinity) of your soil so that you can choose the right plants and fertilizers: tests can be sophisticated or simple, according to your needs

Measuring the pH of your soil enables you to find out if it is acid or alkaline, or neutral. The pH scale ranges from 1 to 14. A low pH indicates acid conditions, a high reading denotes alkaline conditions, and pH7 is the neutral point. Under normal garden conditions it is rare to find pH levels outside the range of 4 to 8.

You can measure pH using one of two methods, depending on the accuracy and speed of analysis required. Laboratories use a pH electrode and meter, which is the most accurate method, but the equipment is expensive. You may prefer to buy a cheaper hand-held pH meter for home use but this will be less accurate.

The other main method is to use indicator dyes. Dried soil is mixed with the dyes and distilled water, and a colour change occurs depending on the pH of the solution. This method is not as accurate as a laboratory test, but is quick to perform, and if done properly, provides a perfectly adequate method on which to base fertilizer choice and plant selection.

Benefits of knowing pH

It is important to know the pH of your soil for several reasons:

Rhododendrons are acid-loving shrubs

Taxus baccata (yew) prefers alkaline soil

• The availability of plant foods in the soil varies with pH. For example, the trace elements iron and manganese become less available for plants in alkaline soils, which can lead to nutrient deficiency symptoms.
• Many soil organisms responsible for the recycling of organic foods cannot tolerate extremely acid conditions.
• Some plants have specific needs with regard to pH, the most notable of these being the ericaceous group, including rhododendrons, which, with a few exceptions, will not thrive under neutral or alkaline conditions. They prefer acid soils with a pH range of 4.5–5.5 (*see also p.266*).

Most garden plants will tolerate a range of pH conditions but for optimum growth a pH of 6.5 is generally recommended. If soil is too acid, liming with ground limestone or chalk will increase the alkalinity (*see also p.265*).

If soil is too alkaline, several courses of action are available:
• Do not apply lime or lime-containing materials.
• Use acidifying fertilizers such as sulphate of ammonia or a compound ericaceous feed.

• Incorporate an acidifying material, such as flowers of sulphur or sulphur powder, into the soil.

The last method is slow acting. It can be safely applied without harm to established plantings, and also provides sulphur, an element needed by plants. You will need to make repeated applications of sulphur to keep alkalinity in check.

Soils with a pH above 7.5 can be very difficult to treat successfully, especially if they contain a high percentage of clay or organic matter. It is therefore better to accept the soil's alkaline character and make a selection of the most tolerant plants accordingly (*see p.264*).

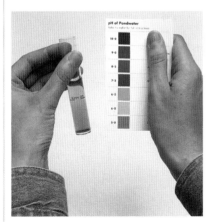

A tester kit will show you the pH of your soil

SOIL TESTING KITS

Home soil-testing kits use a chemical solution that changes colour when it is mixed with a sample of soil in a small test tube. You then match the colour against a chart, which will indicate the pH level. A yellow or orange colour indicates acid soil; green indicates neutral; and blue/dark green indicates alkaline soil.

See also Choosing plants for alkaline soils, p.264; Why lime soils?, p.265; Choosing plants for acid soils, p.266

Choosing plants for alkaline soils

There are instances where superb gardens have been created in old chalk pits, admirably demonstrating what can be achieved if the soil is alkaline or chalky – there is certainly no shortage of suitable plants

PLANTS THAT GROW WELL IN ALKALINE CONDITIONS

If you have an alkaline (limy or chalky) soil, it is best not to try and change it, but rather grow plants that really flourish in these conditions. In fact, there is a wide range of permanent hardy plants, from trees and shrubs to perennials, that you can choose from.

Trees and shrubs

Acer negundo ‡ 15m (50ft) ↔ 10m (30ft) ▢–▧ ◊ ✳✳✳

Berberis thunbergii ♀ ‡ 1.2m (4ft) ↔ 1.8m (6ft) ▢–▧ ◊ ✳✳✳

Buddleja davidii ‡ 3m (10ft) ↔ 5m (15ft) ▢ ◊ ✳✳✳

Buxus sempervirens ♀ ‡↔ 5m (15ft) E ▢–▧ ◊ ✳✳✳ 1

Carpinus betulus ♀ ‡ 25m (80ft) ↔ 20m (70ft) ▢–▧ ◊ ✳✳✳

Ceanothus impressus ‡ 1.5m (5ft) ↔ 2.4m (8ft) E ▢ ◊ ✳✳

Cistus ladanifer ♀ ‡ 1.8m (6ft) ↔ 1.5m (5ft) E ◊ ◊ ✳✳

Colutea arborescens ‡↔ 3m (10ft) ▢ ◊ ✳✳✳

Cornus alba ‡↔ 3m (10ft) ▢ ◊ ✳✳✳

Corylus avellana cultivars ‡↔ 5m (15ft) ▢–▧ ◊ ✳✳✳

Cotoneaster frigidus ‘Cornubia’ ♀ ‡↔ 6m (20ft) E ▢–▧ ◊ ✳✳✳

Crataegus x *lavalleei* ‘Carrierei’ ♀ ‡ 7m (22ft) ↔ 10m (30ft) ▢–▧ ◊ ✳✳✳

Euonymus europaeus ‘Red Cascade’ ♀ ‡ 3m (10ft) ↔ 2.4m (8ft) ▢–▧ ◊ ✳✳✳

Fagus sylvatica ♀ ‡ 25m (80ft) ↔ 15m (50ft) ▢–▧ ◊ ✳✳✳

Magnolia stellata ♀ ‡ 3m (10ft) ↔ 4m (12ft) ▢–▧ ◊ ✳✳✳

Paeonia delavayi ♀ ‡ 1.8m (6ft) ↔ 1.2m (4ft) ▢–▧ ◊ ✳✳✳

Philadelphus coronarius ‘Aureus’ ♀ ‡ 2.4m (8ft) ↔ 1.5m (5ft) ▧ ◊ ✳✳✳

Rhamnus alaternus ‘Argenteovariegata’ ♀ ‡ 5m (15ft) ↔ 4m (12ft) ▢ ◊ ✳✳

Sambucus nigra f. *laciniata* ♀ ‡↔ 6m (20ft) ▢–▧ ◊ ✳✳✳

Sorbus aria ‘Lutescens’ ♀ ‡ 10m (30ft) ↔ 8m (25ft) ▢–▧ ◊ ✳✳✳

Syringa vulgaris ‡↔ 7m (22ft) ▢ ◊ ✳✳✳

Viburnum x *bodnantense* ‡ 3m (10ft) ↔ 1.8m (6ft) ▢–▧ ◊ ✳✳✳

Conifers

Chamaecyparis lawsoniana ‡ 15–40m (50–130ft) ↔ 1.8–5m (6–15ft) E ▢ ◊ ✳✳✳

Cupressus macrocarpa ‘Goldcrest’ ‡ 5m (15ft) ↔ 2.4m (8ft) E ▢ ◊ ✳✳✳

Juniperus communis ‡ 0.5–6m (1½–20ft) ↔ 1–6m (3–20ft) E ▢–▧ ◊ ✳✳✳

Taxus baccata ‘Fastigiata’ ♀ ‡ 10–20m (30–70ft) ↔ 8–10m (25–30ft) E ▢–▧ ◊ ✳✳✳ 2

Thuja plicata ‡ 20–35m (70–120ft) ↔ 6–9m (20–30ft) E ▢ ◊ ✳✳✳

Hardy perennials

Acanthus spinosus ♀ ‡ 1.5m (5ft) ↔ 60–90cm (24–36in) ▢–▧ ◊ ✳✳✳

Achillea millefolium cultivars ‡ 60cm (24in) ↔ 60cm (24in) ▢ ◊ ✳✳✳

Anthemis punctata subsp. *cupaniana* ♀ ‡ 30cm (12in) ↔ 90cm (36in) E ▢ ◊ ✳✳ 3

Aquilegia vulgaris ‡ 90cm (36in) ↔ 45cm (18in) ▢–▧ ◊ ✳✳✳

Campanula lactiflora ‡ 1.2–1.5m (4–5ft) ↔ 60cm (24in) ▢–▧ ◊ ✳✳✳

Doronicum orientale ‡ 60cm (24in) ↔ 90cm (36in) ▧ ◊ ✳✳✳

Eremurus stenophyllus ♀ ‡ 90cm (36in) ↔ 60cm (24in) ▢ ◊ ✳✳✳

Erigeron karvinskianus ♀ ‡ 15–30cm (6–12in) ↔ 90cm (36in) ▢–▧ ◊ ✳✳✳

Eryngium alpinum ♀ ‡ 70cm (28in) ↔ 45cm (18in) ▢ ◊ ✳✳✳

Iris unguicularis ♀ ‡ 30cm (12in) ↔ 60cm (24in) E ▢ ◊ ✳✳✳

Kniphofia caulescens ♀ ‡ 1.2m (4ft) ↔ 60cm (24in) E ▢ ◊ ✳✳✳

Scabiosa caucasica ‡↔ 60cm (24in) ▢ ◊ ✳✳✳

Verbascum (Cotswold Group) ‘Cotswold Beauty’ ♀ ‡ 1.2m (4ft) ↔ 30cm (12in) ▢ ◊ ✳✳✳

See also Gettiing to know your soil's pH, p.263; Why lime soils?, p.265

Why lime soils?

Regular liming of soils, generally in the autumn prior to digging, is a long-standing gardening practice, especially in the vegetable garden, but the rationale behind it is often overlooked by home gardeners

Liming helps to maintain a balance between the soil's acidity and alkalinity. The degree of acidity or alkalinity is measured on the pH scale, ranging from 1 (highly acid) to 14 (highly alkaline). An increase in pH from 6 to 7, for example, records a 10-fold increase in alkalinity. A pH of 7 is neutral, with conditions neither acid nor alkaline.

The optimum pH for most garden plants and vegetables is 6.5 (slightly acid). If the pH varies significantly from this, plants may show signs of nutrient deficiency. High pH levels cause a reduction in the availability of phosphate and trace elements, while low pH levels reduce the availability of nitrogen, potassium and magnesium, and also discourage earthworm activity.

Lime provides calcium and raises the pH. It is used to counter acidity brought about by the effects of acidic fertilizers, the rotting of organic matter and the action of rainwater, which is a weak acid.

Soil structure, particularly of clay soils, may be improved by applying lime. Reducing the acidity of soil by liming improves crop growth, encourages root development, and increases the number of micro-organisms, which improve the crumb structure and levels of organic matter in the soil. Lime discourages serious diseases including club root of brassicas (*Plasmodiophora brassicae*).

How to carry out liming

Carry out a pH test to determine whether liming is necessary (*see p.263*). If your soil is already slightly acid or neutral, liming will be of no benefit and may be detrimental.

Autumn is the best season for liming, just prior to digging. The lime can then take effect over winter and will not damage young growth. Do not apply

Applying lime: autumn is the best time, just before digging, so that it takes effect over winter

lime at the same time as organic matter or fertilizers or it may cause the release of ammonia, which wastes nitrogen and may damage tender growth.

There are two types of lime you can use: hydrated lime (calcium hydroxide) and ground limestone or chalk (calcium carbonate). Hydrated lime is soluble in water and has a stronger liming action

APPLYING LIME

Although ordinary lime (calcium carbonate) is relatively safe to use, it is wise to take a few precautions when spreading or sprinkling lime. Choose a day without wind to stop the powder going over you or areas in the garden you do not want to lime, and always wear protective goggles to avoid damaging your eyes.

than ground limestone or chalk, but is less pleasant to handle and easier to over-apply. Ground limestone or chalk is now the most widely available and preferred liming material, and is sold under various names such as carbonate lime, garden lime, ground limestone or ground chalk. Application rates vary with the type of soil and degree of pH change needed.

As a general rule, a loam soil will need an application of 270g per sq m (8oz per sq yd) to raise the pH by half a unit. A clay soil will need slightly more, 420g per sq m (12oz per sq yd), and a sandy soil slightly less, 140g per sq m (4oz per sq yd).

If you need to make a greater change in pH, spread applications over several seasons rather than apply the whole amount in one go.

See also Clubroot, p.206; Why cultivate soil?, p.258; Getting to know your soil's pH, p.263; Adding wood ash to soil, p.268

Choosing plants for acid soils

Some of the most beautiful plants, including rhododendrons, heathers, magnolias and pieris, have adapted to grow well only in soils where the soil is acid: many also benefit from partial shade

ACID LOVING PLANTS

Trees

Acer palmatum ‡ 8m (25ft) ↔ 10m (30ft) ☐–☒ ◊ ✳✳✳

Amelanchier laevis ‡↔ 8m (25ft) ☐–☒ ◊ ✳✳✳

Amelanchier lamarckii ♀ ‡ 10m (30ft) ↔ 12m (40ft) ☐–☒ ◊ ✳✳✳

Arbutus menziesii ♀ ‡↔ 15m (50ft) E ☐ ◊ ✳✳✳ ☐1☐

Cercidiphyllum japonicum ♀ ‡ 20m (70ft) ↔ 15m (50ft) ☐–☒ ◊ ✳✳✳

Cornus kousa ‡ 7m (22ft) ↔ 5m (15ft) ☐–☒ ◊ ✳✳✳

Embothrium coccineum ‡ 10m (30ft) ↔ 5m (15ft) E ☐–☒ ◊ ✳✳✳

Eucryphia glutinosa ♀ ‡ 10m (30ft) ↔ 6m (20ft) ☐ ◊ ✳✳✳

Halesia carolina ‡ 8m (25ft) ↔ 10m (30ft) ☐–☒ ◊ ✳✳✳

Liquidambar styraciflua ‡ 25m (80ft) ↔ 12m (40ft) ☐ ◊ ✳✳✳

Magnolia campbellii ‡ 15m (50ft) ↔ 10m (30ft) ☐–☒ ◊ ✳✳✳

Nyssa sylvatica ♀ ‡ 20m (70ft) ↔ 10m (30ft) ☐–☒ ◊ ✳✳✳

Stewartia pseudocamellia ♀ ‡ 20m (70ft) ↔ 8m (25ft) ☐–☒ ◊ ✳✳✳

Shrubs

Berberidopsis corallina ‡ 5m (15ft) ↔ 2.4m (8ft) E ☒ ◊ ✳✳

Calluna vulgaris ‡ 10–60cm (4–24in) ↔ 75cm (30in) E ◊ ✳✳✳

Camellia ‡ 1.8–5m (6–15ft) ↔ 1–3m (3–10ft) E ☒ ◊ ✳✳✳

Daboecia cantabrica cultivars ‡ 25–40cm (10–16in) ↔ 65cm (26in) E ☒ ◊ ✳✳✳

Daphne tangutica ♀ ‡↔ 90cm (36in) E ☐–☒ ◊ ✳✳✳

Enkianthus campanulatus ♀ ‡↔ 4–5m (12–15ft) ☐–☒ ◊ ✳✳✳

Erica ‡ 20cm–6m (8in–20ft) ↔ 0.5–3m (1½–10ft) E ☒ ◊ ✳✳✳–✳✳

Gaultheria mucronata ‡↔ 1.2m (4ft) E ☒ ◊ ✳✳✳

Hamamelis ‡↔ 4m (12ft) ☐–☒ ◊ ✳✳✳

Kalmia latifolia ♀ ‡↔ 3m (10ft) E ☒ ◊ ✳✳✳

Magnolia x soulangeana ‡↔ 6m (20ft) ☐–☒ ◊ ✳✳✳ ☐2☐

Pieris ‡ 1.8–5m (6–15ft) ↔ 3–4m (10–12ft) E ☐–☒ ◊ ✳✳✳–✳✳

Rhododendron ‡ 30cm–4m (1–12ft) ↔ 0.5–4m (1½–12ft) E ☒ ◊ ✳✳✳–✳✳

Ulex europaeus 'Flore Pleno' ♀ ‡ 2.4m (8ft) ↔ 1.8m (6ft) E ☒ ◊ ✳✳✳

Hardy perennials

Gentiana sino-ornata ♀ ‡ 5–8cm (2–3in) ↔ 15–30cm (6–12in) ☐–☒ ◊ ✳✳✳

Iris innominata ‡ 15–25cm (6–10in) ↔ 25cm (10in) E ☐–☒ ◊ ✳✳✳

Kirengeshoma palmata ♀ ‡ 60–120cm (24–48in) ↔ 75cm (30in) ☒ ◊ ✳✳✳

Lupinus hybrids ‡ 90cm (36in) ↔ 75cm (30in) ☐–☒ ◊ ✳✳✳

Luzula sylvatica ‡ 70–80cm (28–32in) ↔ 45cm (18in) E ☐–☒–☒ ◊ ✳✳✳

Meconopsis betonicifolia ♀ ‡ 1.2m (4ft) ↔ 45cm (18in) ☒ ◊ ✳✳✳

Polypodium vulgare ‡ 30cm (12in) ↔ 45–60cm (18–24in) E ☐–☒ ◊ ✳✳✳

Primula bulleyana ♀ ‡↔ 60cm (24in) ☐–☒ ◊ ✳✳✳

Primula japonica ‡↔ 45cm (18in) ☐–☒ ◊ ✳✳✳

Primula pulverulenta ♀ ‡ 90cm (36in) ↔ 60cm (24in) ☐–☒ ◊ ✳✳✳ ☐3☐

Primula vialii ♀ ‡ 30–60cm (12–24in) ↔ 30cm (12in) ☐–☒ ◊ ✳✳✳

Tricyrtis formosana ♀ ‡ 80cm (32in) ↔ 45cm (18in) ☒–☒ ◊ ✳✳✳

Trillium ‡ 40cm (16in) ↔ 30cm (12in) ☒–☒ ◊ ✳✳✳

See also Getting to know your soil's pH, p.263

Choosing and using fertilizers

Plants trap light through their leaves to fuel the growing process and with the proper building blocks in place, optimum growth is achieved and encouraged through the correct choice of fertilizers

A plant's need for food

Bulky organic materials, such as garden compost and manure, are incorporated into the soil to help improve structure and supply some plant foods. However, food deficiencies may well remain but these can be corrected with fertilizers.

The major plant foods are nitrogen (N), which promotes leafy growth, phosphorus (P) for healthy root growth, and potassium or potash (K) for flower development and ripening wood. Other important foods that are sometimes needed less often include sulphur, magnesium and calcium. Boron and iron are examples of minor foods (or trace elements) that are only needed in much smaller amounts.

Types of fertilizer

Straight fertilizers such as sulphate of ammonia contain one major food (nitrogen in this instance), while compound fertilizers contain several (nitrogen, phosphorus and potassium).

A fertilizer's food content should be listed on the package and display the ratio of N:P:K.
• Concentrated organic fertilizers are of animal or plant origin, such as bone meal, chicken manure, fish, blood and bone, dried blood or seaweed. They tend to be slow-acting and become available to the plant slowly. Plant food can vary due to the natural fluctuations in the material being processed.
• Inorganic fertilizers are usually faster acting. They contain known concentrations of nitrogen, phosphorus and potassium, which will be constant as they are chemically manufactured. Some fertilizers contain organic and inorganic ingredients.

Specialized feeds

Some fertilizers are specifically blended to supply particular plants. These include ericaceous plants, tomatoes, citrus and lawns. There is often no need to buy fertilizers for every crop – for example, liquid tomato fertilizer can be used to

FOLIAR FEEDS

Foliar feeds are quick-acting and useful for supplying foods to plants where root function has been reduced following waterlogging or transplanting. Use also on plants showing nutrient deficiency symptoms.

feed hanging-basket plants, which also need plenty of potash.

Timing and application

Most fertilizers are applied in spring before growth begins. This allows the fertilizer to become active when the plant is most rapidly growing. Avoid applying nitrogen-rich fertilizers after midsummer as new growth may not ripen before winter. Instead use potassium-rich fertilizers such as autumn lawn feeds.
• Base dressings are incorporated into the soil before planting. There is a move away from using base dressings when planting trees and shrubs, as a better root system can develop by encouraging plants to search for foods already there in the surrounding soil.
• Topdressings are scattered over the soil surface around plants, avoiding the foliage. They are the most cost-effective way of feeding plants, especially when spread around the base.
• Liquid feeds are applied to the soil and tend to be rapidly absorbed by plants. They are especially useful for container-grown plants.

TOPDRESSINGS

Soluble fertilizers can be used as a surface application around established plants.
[1] Apply the fertilizer at the rate recommended by the manufacturer.

[2] Gently sprinkle it around the base of the plant, making sure that it is spread out evenly and not in piles. then lightly fork or hoe it into the soil surface.

See also Controlled-release fertilizers, p.174; Feeding and mulching fruit trees p 232; Soil fertility p.250

Adding wood ash to soil

Wood ash from your bonfire or fireplace is a useful soil improver

Ash from untreated wood has a slight liming action and can be used to raise soil pH. Be careful not to use ash around ericaceous or lime-hating plants such as heathers or rhododendrons. Freshly collected ash from young, sappy prunings contains useful quantities of potassium and traces of other elements. These are soluble and easily taken up by plants.

However, the plant-food content of wood ash varies, so precise application is difficult. Ideally, apply thin layers to your compost heap, where it will blend readily with other materials. Ash from older wood has little plant-food value, although there is still some liming action.

Consign coal ash to the dustbin because it has no benefit to the soil and may even contain harmful, heavy material.

ASH AS A SOIL IMPROVER

Ash from a fire that has been burning mainly from wood can be sprinkled on to the surface of the soil and then gently forked or raked in.

See also Why lime soils?, p.265

What are the alternatives to peat?

Although peat has served gardeners well for years, its harvesting can destroy lowland peat bogs, but there are other options

Peat consists of partially decomposed plant remains, mainly sedges, grasses, reeds and mosses. It forms as the natural processes of decay are arrested by waterlogging and the exclusion of air, and the remains of wetland plants become compacted.

Undisturbed lowland peat bogs support specialized plants and animals, so their existence is at risk when a peat bog is destroyed by peat harvesting for the horticultural industry. Peat has long been used in gardening, especially potting and seed composts, due to its unique characteristics of porosity, water-holding capacity, stability, sterility and low content of plant foods.

However, peat alternatives such as bark, wood waste, coir (ground-up coconut husks), bracken and green waste are being developed. The use of locally sourced, environmentally friendly peat alternatives can positively benefit local industry.

Comparative trials

The Royal Horticultural Society has undertaken comparative trials on peat and peat alternatives for gardening. The quality of peat alternatives is constantly being improved and they now produce comparable results to peat-based products.

Traditionally peat has been used for soil improvement and mulching, but it has been found that peat alternatives are superior. Soil is improved by adding well-rotted manure or compost and these materials also make better mulches, as do wood chips, wood shavings and bark.

A wide selection of alternative container composts, such as bark, wood waste, coir and green waste, has been assessed for the cultivation of ornamental plants and vegetables in

Coir, a peat substitute, here mixed with grit

different situations, including seed sowing and patio-style planters. Generally, the trials proved that most peat alternatives are able to support perfectly acceptable plants.

However, many peat alternatives seem to be very plant specific, so do not assume that because one plant has flourished another will similarly thrive. Some alternative composts are not yet completely satisfactory in sustaining containerized woody plants over more than one season.

Do not treat peat alternatives in the same way as peat. Read and closely follow any of the manufacturers' recommendations on the packaging.

PEAT SUBSTITUTES

There are several suitable alternatives to peat that are readily available. These include coconut fibre (coir), shredded bark, coarse bark, wood chippings, well-rotted animal manure, garden compost and leafmould. Some can be made easily in the garden, particularly leafmould and compost.

See also Successful garden composting, p.271; How to make leafmould, p.272

The benefits of mulching

Mulching is a traditional practice that helps to suppress weeds and retain soil moisture, but never before have there been so many materials available, both natural and artificial

Mulching the soil surface with an additional layer of organic or inorganic matter is good garden practice, but there is confusion over what, how and when it should be applied.

There are several benefits to the soil of mulching: moisture retention, weed suppression, temperature moderation during hot weather, protection of soil structure against damage from heavy rain or foot traffic, and in certain cases, release of plant foods.

What to use

A variety of mulches have been used by gardeners over the years. Readily available materials include garden compost, well-rotted farmyard or stable manure, leafmould and straw. Due to their organic origin, they slowly decompose and release plant foods and humus (decomposed plant remains) into the soil.

Other suitable organic materials for mulching include chipped bark, mushroom compost and cocoa shells. Cocoa shells are reputed to deter slugs,

Natural mulching
Above: Mulching helps to improve soil fertility, keeps the weeds down and prevents moisture loss.
Left: Proprietary sterilized manure contains no weed seeds.

but be aware that they contain chocolate residues that may harm dogs. Spent hops are sometimes used for mulching, but they are lightweight and may blow away when dry, and as they decompose quite rapidly, they require more frequent topping up.

Inorganic materials such as plastic sheeting and woven polypropylene can also be used. There are various proprietary mulching fabrics available. All of these are long lasting and very effective at suppressing weeds, but they do not decompose or release plant foods. ▷

See also Building your soil's fertility, p.259; Successful garden composting, p.271; How to make leafmould, p.272

THE BENEFITS OF MULCHING

Chipped bark is an attractive, long-lasting mulch that suppresses weeds...   ... but, compared with compost, it is expensive and releases few nutrients

Permanent mineral mulches are often used in ornamental situations, both for aesthetic reasons and the benefits of suppressing weeds and helping to retain soil moisture. Examples include pea shingle and other types of gravel, and slate and stone chippings. Pebbles of various sizes and colours are also used.

On a fertile garden soil the main benefits of mulching are improved water retention during dry weather and suppression of weed seed germination, particularly around newly established plantings, which take their food and water from the top level of soil.

Cocoa shells

Chipped bark   Organic mulching materials

Applying mulches

The best time to apply surface mulches, or to top up an existing organic mulch, is during mid- to late spring after the soil has had time to warm up but while it is still moist. Deep applications of organic mulch in autumn are not recommended since they can contribute to waterlogging and may also suppress soil temperatures early in the year, delaying the emergence of plants in spring.

Avoid laying a mulch on dry soil, because a mulch is often as effective at keeping moisture out as holding it in.

MULCHING WITH GRAVEL

Although it looks attractive, gravel is poor at retaining soil moisture, suppressing weeds and insulating the soil. It does, however, improve the surface drainage around susceptible plants.

If soil beneath a mulch is allowed to dry out, you will need to carry out slow and persistent artificial watering. Ideally, feed plants before mulching.

Suppressing weeds

The ability of mulches to suppress weed growth varies. The best weed suppression is achieved with artificial woven mulch fabrics and heavy plastic sheeting. These can be covered with an ornamental mulch. However, where this is cut for planting, weeds may still be a problem because shoots can grow through planting holes.

Organic mulches are not as effective as inorganic materials at suppressing weed growth, but provided they are applied to a depth of at least 5cm (2in), reasonable weed control is possible. Deeper applications can be more effective, but are more expensive and can smother small plants. Complete control of vigorous perennial weeds is impossible using an organic mulch, so kill any weeds like these before spreading the mulch.

Inevitably, choice of material will depend not only on the above factors but also on issues such as aesthetic value, availability and cost. The final decision remains with you.

See also Weeds and weed control, p.31; Successful tree and shrub planting, pp.60–61; What is organic gardening?, pp.254–255

TECHNIQUES

Successful garden composting

Composting can easily be achieved by building a compost heap, and provides an environmentally friendly way of converting plant waste into valuable organic matter, useful for improving soil fertility

For composting, use a mixture of dry, woody, carbon-rich materials such as shredded woody prunings and straw, and wet, soft, nitrogen-rich wastes such as vegetable scraps, grass clippings and manure. Ideally combine these in a ratio of about two parts' woody material to one part soft material. Woody material offers a source of carbon for micro-organisms and gives the heap an open structure, allowing air to permeate. The soft material provides nitrogen, other plant foods and moisture. You may not be able to select which wastes to use, but it will still result in satisfactory compost, although the process will take longer.

Making the heap

Choose a durable compost container that has easy access for loading and turning the compost, and good drainage so that water can drain out and soil organisms can enter.

For a rise in temperature to occur within the heap, you will need a sufficient volume of organic material, the minimum being about 1cu m (1.3cu yd). With less material, what little heat is generated is quickly lost through the sides of the heap. Insulated containers help to a degree, but the crucial factor is the initial volume of waste. The ideal situation is where the whole container is filled with fresh waste all in one go. A greater initial volume of fresh material stimulates more microbial activity leading to higher temperatures. In practice, small quantities of waste are added in layers over time.

When a container is filled, care is fairly straightforward. Do not allow it to dry out in summer or get too wet in winter. A good guide is to squeeze a handful of compost and see how much water comes out. Ideally, only a few droplets should ooze out. Use a lid or cover to prevent excessive evaporation and keep off the rain.

After about a week, turn the heap. This introduces air and enables thorough mixing so the cooler, outer material is exposed to the hotter, wetter conditions at the centre where decomposition is most rapid. If possible, turn it again 14 days later, after which you can leave the compost to mature for about six months. Recycle any material not fully composted by this time into the next compost batch.

If a heap has been built slowly, it will contain material at the bottom almost ready for use by the time the container is filled, so use the upper layers of undecomposed material to start a new heap and turn the older compost before leaving it for another two to four months. Use mature compost as a mulch or work into the ground before planting.

What to use for composting
Use a mix of woody material and soft waste, such as rubbish from the vegetable plot (*shown*). Soft waste is rich in nitrogen; woody material provides carbon.

ESTABLISHING A GARDEN COMPOST HEAP

A wooden compost bin is excellent for holding decomposing garden waste. Ideally you should aim to have at least two heaps on the go at the same time, shifting the upper layers of uncomposted material into a new heap when the lower layers of the first bin are nearly ready for use. A mixture of materials is best, rather than a concentration of, say, grass clippings.

See also Organic gardening, pp.254–255; Why cultivate soil?, p.258; The benefits of mulching, pp.269–270; How to make leafmould, p.272

PRACTICAL ADVICE

How to make leafmould

Produce a soil improver by stacking leaves in autumn

Leafmould is an excellent soil improver

Leafmould is formed from leaves rotting down to produce a humus-rich, friable soil conditioner. Fallen leaves are low in plant foods, although richer leafmoulds can be formed by adding small amounts of grass clippings. A quick way to achieve this is to spread the leaves out on a lawn and collect them with a lawnmower. This method not only adds grass, but it also shreds the leaves before composting.

Shredding is a good way to speed up the decomposition of tougher leaves such as sycamore, horse chestnut and sweet chestnut. Thicker, evergreen leaves like holly, *Aucuba* and cherry laurel are best shredded and added to the normal compost heap. Composting pine needles produces an acid organic medium, although their rate of breakdown is very slow and may take two or three years. For top-quality leafmould use leaves from oak, beech or hornbeam.

To ensure good decomposition, collect leaves after rain or wet them before stacking. Stack in large piles, wire-netting bins or black bin liners.

See also Alternatives to peat, p.268

TECHNIQUES

Helping plants through the wet winter months

In periods of excessive rain, plants may drown and disease can become more prevalent, but simple counter measures can reduce the damage

Most plants will survive short-term waterlogging, especially when dormant, but few tolerate saturated soils for long periods. In such conditions roots are deprived of the oxygen their cells need to function, leading to death and decay of the whole root system and ultimately the rest of the plant.

If your garden is wet and regularly waterlogged, choose plants that are more tolerant of such conditions; avoid grey- or silver-leaved perennials and those from drier natural environments. Incorporate grit, gravel or pea shingle to help keep the base of plants drier. Add it as a mulch 10cm (4in) thick and fork it into the soil. Avoid planting too deeply and plant on a slight mound; plant hedges into a raised ridge.

Keep off wet soils as compaction will damage the soil structure and reduce drainage still further.

Pot-grown plants

Improve drainage of container-grown plants by adding plenty of coarse grit or perlite to the compost.

Ensure good air circulation around plants. Protect the blooms of early flowering garden plants, such as *Helleborus niger* (Christmas rose), by bringing them under cover (*see below*).

IMPROVING SHORT-TERM WATER DAMAGE

1 To prevent the soil becoming compacted, use planks to walk over wet ground. **2** If water is lying on the ground, spike the affected area with a fork. **3** Place pots on their side to prevent rain from settling in the crown of the plant. **4** Plants sensitive to winter wet can be lifted, potted and taken under cover for the winter. Alternatively, protect them under open-ended cloches, or beneath panes of glass or clear rigid plastic supported on wire hoops.

See also Gardening on wet soils, p.260; The benefits of mulching, pp.269–270

WATER
GARDENING

HOW TO CREATE A BOG GARDEN

How to create a bog garden

The lush foliage and decorative flowers of many bog and moisture-loving plants make them interesting additions to any garden, especially when they come into bloom during spring and summer

You can build a bog garden from scratch, or convert a redundant pond or naturally waterlogged depression, either to give a pond a natural-looking edge or to create a separate area for bog and moisture-loving plants.

First mark out the area to be planted with sand or string, then dig out the soil to a depth of at least 45cm (18in). Line the hole with a plastic or butyl-rubber pond liner.

Bog plants do not like stagnant conditions or drying out, so lay a length of seep hose or porous pipe in the bottom of the hole and plug the underground end. Peg or weigh down hose and the liner edges before covering the hose with a 2cm (½in) layer of pea shingle to prevent soil from blocking the pipe. Pierce the liner with a fork every few feet to allow drainage of excess water and replace the soil. If your soil is a light, sandy type, incorporate some well-rotted leafmould or garden compost.

The best time to plant bog and moisture-loving plants is early spring. There are many ornamental, native and wildlife-friendly plants to choose from.

SUITABLE PERENNIALS FOR THE BOG GARDEN

Acorus gramineus ‡ 8–35cm (3–14in) ↔ 10–15cm (4–6in) ▫ ✳✳✳

Actaea racemosa ♀ ‡ 1.2–1.8m (4–6ft) ↔ 60cm (24in) ▫ ✳✳✳

Astilbe x arendsii ‡ 60–90cm (24–36in) ↔ 45–60cm (18–24in) ▫ ☙ ✳✳✳

Caltha palustris ‘Flore Pleno’ ♀ ‡↔ 25cm (10in) ▫ ✳✳✳

Darmera peltata ♀ ‡ 1.8m (6ft) ↔ 90cm (36in) ▫–▫ ✳✳✳

Eupatorium purpureum ‡ 1.8m (6ft) ↔ 90cm (36in) ▫–▫ ✳✳✳

Euphorbia sikkimensis ♀ ‡ 1.2m (4ft) ↔ 45cm (18in) ▫ ✳✳✳

Filipendula ulmaria ‡ 60–90cm (24–36in) ↔ 60cm (24in) ▫–▫ ✳✳✳

Gunnera manicata ♀ ‡ 2.4m (8ft) ↔ 3–4m (10–12ft) ▫–▫ ✳✳ ☐1

Hosta fortunei ‡ 55cm (22in) ↔ 80cm (32in) ▫ ✳✳✳

Iris ensata ♀ ‡ 90cm (36in) ↔ 45cm (18in) ▫ ☙ ✳✳✳

Iris laevigata ♀ ‡ 80cm (32in) ↔ 60cm (24in) ▫ ☙ ✳✳✳

Iris pseudacorus ♀ ‡ 1–1.5m (3–5ft) ↔ 90cm (36in) ▫ ☙ ✳✳✳ ☐2

Ligularia przewalskii ♀ ‡ 1.8m (6ft) ↔ 90cm (36in) ▫ ✳✳✳

Lobelia cardinalis ♀ ‡ 90cm (36in) ↔ 30cm (12in) ▫–▫ ✳✳✳

Lysichiton americanus ♀ ‡ 90cm (36in) ↔ 1.2m (4ft) ▫–▫ ✳✳✳ ☐3

Lysimachia punctata ‡ 90cm (36in) ↔ 60cm (24in) ▫–▫ ✳✳✳

Lythrum salicaria ‡ 1.2m (4ft) ↔ 45cm (18in) ▫ ✳✳✳

Mimulus cardinalis ♀ ‡ 90cm (36in) ↔ 60cm (24in) ▫–▫ ✳✳

Mimulus luteus ‡ 30cm (12in) ↔ 60cm (24in) ▫–▫ ✳✳✳

Parnassia palustris ‡ 20cm (8in) ↔ 10cm (4in) ▫ ✳✳✳

Primula bulleyana ♀ ‡↔ 60cm (24in) ▫–▫ ☙ ✳✳✳

Primula florindae ♀ ‡ 1.2m (4ft) ↔ 90cm (36in) ▫–▫ ☙ ✳✳✳

Primula japonica ‡↔ 45cm (18in) ▫–▫ ☙ ✳✳✳

Primula pulverulenta ♀ ‡ 90cm (36in) ↔ 60cm (24in) ▫–▫ ☙ ✳✳✳

Primula rosea ♀ ‡↔ 20cm (8in) ▫–▫ ☙ ✳✳✳

Rodgersia aesculifolia ♀ ‡ 1.8m (6ft) ↔ 90cm (36in) ▫–▫ ✳✳✳

Trollius x cultorum cultivars ‡ 90cm (36in) ↔ 45cm (18in) ▫–▫ ✳✳✳

Zantedeschia aethiopica ♀ ‡ 90cm (36in) ↔ 60cm (24in) ▫ ✳✳

See also Encouraging wildlife into the garden, pp.250–251; Gardening on wet soils, p.260

Installing a pond filter

A pond filter will help to eliminate decomposing fish waste and plant debris, which release toxins into ponds and reduce oxygen levels

You can fit a simple mechanical filter directly on to a submerged pump. The electric pump draws water in through decreasing grades of brush and foam to remove solids. They are suitable for small ponds with only a moderate fish population. To keep the filter working properly, clean it regularly (about once a week in the height of summer). Self-cleaning models are also available.

Combined filters

Combined filters that use mechanical, biological and even ultraviolet methods are more suitable for larger ponds with large fish populations. Most combined filters are pump-fed and have a gravity outlet, so position them higher than the water return point. Partially bury more complex pressure-fed models.

Biological filtration relies on naturally occurring bacteria that colonize a specially designed filter medium with a large surface area. The bacteria convert ammonia, which is toxic to fish, and other nitrogen-based compounds into nitrates. These are used by pond plants, thus removing nitrogen from the water. Biological systems are essential for ponds with large fish populations, especially koi. Unless bacterial supplements are used, the bacterial population takes six weeks to build up. If the filter is switched off for more than 24 hours the bacteria die and a further six weeks is needed to rebuild the population. Clean biological filters only at the end of the season.

Place an ultraviolet (UV) clarifier at the front of the biological filter system. It kills green algae and makes them clump together, easing mechanical filtration. However, it will not remove nutrients from the water. Pond water is exposed to radiation from a UV lamp held inside a quartz tube. There are lamps of different wattage for various pond sizes; most need to be replaced every six months or so.

Having chosen the correct filter type for a pond, calculate the size needed. Mechanical filter sizes are easy to relate to water volume, calculated by multiplying the pond's average length x width x depth. (In metres, multiply this final figure by 1,000 to get the volume in litres; in feet multiply by 6.25 for volume in gallons).

CHOOSING AND INSTALLING A FILTER

[1] A simple pond filter, which is attached to a pump, is sufficient for a smaller pond with a fairly small fish population. Clean regularly, about once a week, in the height of summer to keep the filter working properly.
[2] There are much more complex filters available, which would suit a larger pond with a substantial fish population. Combined filters use mechanical, biological and even ultraviolet means. Unless you have a pump that can handle small solids without clogging up, place the filter before the pump.

See also How to control pond algae, p.281

Repair of leaky ponds

There are ways of repairing holes and cracks in ponds

REPAIRING CRACKS

After cleaning with a stiff wire brush around the crack, fill it with mortar using a trowel, pressing well in. Allow the mortar to dry completely before applying a pool sealing compound around the repair.

Butyl-rubber pond liners are much easier to repair then plastic liners, which will always be prone to leaking, although the former can be difficult in any folded areas.

A kit consisting of a special glue and patch is available for each type of liner. Before applying the patch, thoroughly clean and dry the area to be repaired. Follow the instructions supplied with the kit and make sure the glue has set before filling the pond with water.

To repair cracks in concrete ponds, scrub clean and leave to dry. Enlarge the crack and roughen the edges to make it easier to fill. Mix 1 part cement to 2 parts sand and 4 parts gravel, add some waterproofing compound, and mix to a stiff but moist consistency. After filling the crack leave it for up to a week and then apply a sealing compound.

If the repair is not effective, consider lining the pool with a butyl-rubber liner.

CHOOSING WATER PLANTS

Choosing water plants

Stock your pond with water plants, including purely functional types – particularly submerged oxygenators – and decorative kinds grown for the beauty of their flowers and foliage, such as marginals and water lilies

All plants that grow rooted, floating or deeply submerged in water are broadly termed water or aquatic plants. They are classed as submerged, surface-floating or marginal according to the depth of water in which they grow.

Depth is measured from the surface of the soil around a plant's roots to the surface of the water.

As ponds should be created in sunny positions, all the plants recommended thrive in full sun.

OXYGENATORS/FLOATERS

Submerged oxygenators

Submerged oxygenating plants are vital to pool hygiene and balance, keeping the water clear. The following plants produce considerable volumes of oxygen during the day. Plant them in aquatic baskets unless otherwise stated.

Callitriche hermaphroditica also suitable for running water ↔ indefinite ✳✳✳

Ceratophyllum demersum suitable for deep water, free floating (no need to plant) ↔ indefinite ✳✳✳

Fontinalis antipyretica best planted attached to a stone, suitable for running water ↔ indefinite ✳✳✳

Hottonia palustris do not move or plant in summer ↔ indefinite ✳✳✳

Myriophyllum spicatum, M. verticillatum ↔ indefinite ✳✳✳

Potamogeton crispus ↔ indefinite ✳✳✳

Ranunculus aquatilis also suitable for running water ↔ indefinite ✳✳✳ [1]

Floating plants

Floating plants do not need anchorage in soil. To plant, simply drop them into the water. While floating on the surface of the water or just below, they reduce the amount of sunlight penetrating the pond and keep the water cooler, discouraging algae. Aim to keep around 50 per cent of the surface clear of vegetation, if necessary by thinning occasionally during the summer.

Hydrocharis morsus-ranae sinks to the bottom in winter ↔ indefinite ✳✳✳

Nymphoides peltata ↔ indefinite ✳✳✳ [2]

Stratiotes aloides floats just below surface, sinks in winter ↔ indefinite ✳✳✳

WATER LILIES

The leaves and flowers float on the water surface, helping to shade the pond. Plant in aquatic baskets and stand in the correct depth.

Water 75–120cm (30–48cm) deep

Nymphaea alba ↔ 1.7m (5½ft) ✳✳✳

N. 'Attraction' ↔ 1.2–1.5m (4–5ft) ✳✳✳ [3]

N. 'Gladstoneana' ♀ ↔ 1.5–2.4m (5–8ft) ✳✳✳

Water 45–60cm (18–24in) deep

Nymphaea 'James Brydon' ♀ ↔ 90–120cm (36–48in) ✳✳✳

N. 'Marliacea Chromatella' ♀ ↔ 1.2–1.5m (4–5ft) ✳✳✳

N. 'Rose Arey' ↔ 1.2–1.5m (4–5ft) ✳✳✳

N. 'Masaniello' ↔ 90cm (36in) ✳✳✳

Water 30–45cm (12–18in) deep

Nymphaea 'Caroliniana Nivea' ↔ 1.2–1.5m (4–5ft) ✳✳✳

N. 'Ellisiana' ↔ 90cm (36in) ✳✳✳

N. 'Froebelii' ↔ 90cm (36in) ✳✳✳

N. 'Laydekeri Fulgens' ↔ 1.2–1.5m (4–5ft) ✳✳✳

N. 'Laydekeri Liliacea' ↔ 60cm (24in) ✳✳✳

N. 'Lucida' ↔ 1.2–1.5m (4–5ft) ✳✳✳

N. 'Madame Wilfon Gonnère' ↔ 1.2m (4ft) ✳✳✳

Water 10–30cm (4–12in) deep

Nymphaea odorata var. minor ↔ 45cm (18in) ✳✳✳

N. 'Pygmaea Helvola' ♀ ↔ 25–40cm (10–16in) ✳✳

N. 'Pygmaea Rubra' ↔ 30cm (12in) ✳✳

N. tetragona ↔ 25–40cm (10–16in) ✳✳ [4]

See also How to create a bog garden, p.274; Avoiding alien pond weeds, p.280

MARGINAL PLANTS

These plants grow in the shallow water at the edges of the pond but are not essential to its balance. They have attractive flowers and foliage and soften the often harsh outlines of ponds. Marginal plants are also valuable for shading pond margins where algae may otherwise multiply in the warm, shallow water. For small ponds, plant separately in 15cm (6in) diameter aquatic baskets and divide and re-pot when overcrowded. Heights given indicate length of leaves or flowers above the water surface.

Water 30cm (12in) or more deep

Alisma plantago-aquatica ‡ 60–90cm (24–36in) ↔ 45cm (18in) ✳✳✳

Aponogeton distachyos ‡ 5cm (2in) ↔ 1.2m (4ft) ✳✳ ⑤

Water 15–30cm (6–12in) deep

Menyanthes trifoliata ‡ 15cm (6in) ↔ indefinite ✳✳✳

Zantedeschia aethiopica ♀ ‡ 75cm (30in) ↔ 60cm (24in) ✳✳

Zantedeschia aethiopica ‘Crowborough’ ♀ ‡ 75cm (30in) ↔ 60cm (24in) ✳✳ ⑥

Water 5–15cm (2–6in) deep

Acorus calamus ‘Argenteostriatus’ ‡ 60cm (24in) ↔ 60cm (24in) ✳✳✳

Butomus umbellatus ♀ ‡ 60–75cm (24–30in) ↔ 45cm (18in) ✳✳✳

Calla palustris ‡ 22cm (9in) ↔ 60cm (24in) ✳✳✳

Carex elata ‘Aurea’ ♀ ‡ 45cm (18in) ↔ 45cm (18in) ✳✳✳

Glyceria maxima var. *variegata* ‡ 60cm (24in) ↔ indefinite ✳✳✳

Iris laevigata ♀ ‡ 60–75cm (24–30in) ↔ 60cm (24in) 🕸 ✳✳✳ ⑦

Iris pseudacorus ♀ ‡ 90cm (36in) ↔ 60cm (24in) 🕸 ✳✳✳

Juncus effusus f. *spiralis* ‡ 45cm (18in) ↔ 60cm (24in) ✳✳✳

Lysichiton americanus ♀ ‡ 1m (39in) ↔ 1.2m (4ft) ✳✳✳

Lysichiton camtschatcensis ♀ ‡ 70cm (28in), ↔ 75cm (30in) ✳✳✳

Orontium aquaticum ‡ 10–12.5cm (4–5in) ↔ 60–75cm (24–30in) ✳✳✳

Pontederia cordata ♀ ‡ 1–1.5m (3–4½ft) ↔ 60–75cm (24–30in) ✳✳✳

Ranunculus lingua ‘Grandiflorus’ ‡ 1.2–1.5m (4–5ft) ↔ 1.2–1.5m (4–5ft) ✳✳✳

Sagittaria latifolia ‡ 30–90cm (12–36in) ↔ 90cm (36in) ✳✳✳

Sagittaria sagittifolia ‘Flore Pleno’ ‡ 75cm (30in) ↔ indefinite ✳✳✳

Schoenoplectus lacustris subsp. *tabernaemontani* ‘Albescens’ ‡ 1.2–1.5m (4–5ft) ↔ 60cm (24in) ✳✳✳

Schoenoplectus lacustris subsp. *tabernaemontani* ‘Zebrinus’ ‡ 45–120cm (18–48in) ↔ 60cm (24in) ✳✳✳

Typha angustifolia ‡ 1.2m (4ft) ↔ indefinite ✳✳✳

Typha laxmannii ‡ 90–120cm (36–48in) ↔ indefinite ✳✳✳

Typha minima ‡ 75cm (30in) ↔ 30–45cm (12–18in) ✳✳✳

Water less than 5cm (2in) deep

These plants are ideal for very shallow water and mud (list includes bog plants).

Acorus gramineus ‘Variegatus’ ‡ 20–30cm (8–12in) ↔ 15cm (6in) ✳✳✳

Acorus gramineus var. *pusillus* ‡ 8–10cm (3–4in) ↔ 10–15cm (4–6in) ✳✳

Caltha palustris ♀ ‡ 22–30cm (9–12in) ↔ 45cm (18in) ✳✳✳

Carex pendula ‡ 90–120cm (36–48in) ↔ 1.5m (5ft) ✳✳✳

Cotula coronopifolia ‡ 15cm (6in) ↔ 30cm (12in) ✳✳

Houttuynia cordata ‡ 60cm (24in) ↔ indefinite ✳✳✳

Houttuyna cordata ‘Chameleon’ ‡ 60cm (24in) ↔ indefinite ✳✳✳

Iris ensata ♀ ‡ 60–90cm (24–36in) ↔ 60cm (24in) 🕸 ✳✳✳

Mimulus cardinalis ♀ ‡ 30–45cm (12–18in) ↔ 60cm (24in) ✳✳✳ ⑧

Mimulus lewisii ♀ ‡ 30–60cm (12–24in) ↔ 45cm (18in) ✳✳

Mimulus luteus ‡ 30–45cm (12–18in) ↔ 60cm (24in) ✳✳✳

Mimulus ringens ‡ 45–60cm (18–24in) ↔ 30cm (12in) ✳✳✳

Myosotis scorpioides ‡ 23cm (9in) ↔ 30cm (12in) ✳✳✳

Saururus cernuus ‡ 30cm (12in) ↔ 30–45cm (12–18in) ✳✳✳

WINTER POND CARE

Winter pond care

Don't let ice destroy your pond, plants, or fish in winter

If ice forms over a pond it may cause concrete or pre-formed structures to crack. It can also trap methane gas released by decaying vegetation, which may kill fish.

Keep a small area of the pond free of ice to prevent these problems. Do not smash the ice, because this can shock and sometimes kill fish. Instead, float a medium-sized ball on the surface or stand a pan of boiling water on the ice to maintain a small area of open water.

Alternatively, use a floating electric pool heater, which will give out enough heat to maintain a small area of water in the pond.

A shallow water feature may freeze solid in extreme weather conditions, so move it under cover if possible or else empty it.

If not in use, remove, clean and store any pumps, filters and lights in a dry place. Run a pump weekly to keep it working if it is left in place over winter.

In cold areas remove more tender plants and place them in buckets of water in a frost-free place to overwinter. Alternatively, store them in moist sand in cool conditions when the foliage has died back. Cut off any ripe seed pods of invasive plants, which will prevent them setting seed over the winter months.

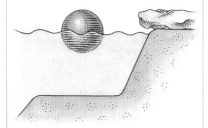

A floating ball will help to stop ice forming

See also Installing a pond filter, p.275

Why clean out ponds?

Complete cleaning out gives you the chance to remove all accumulated debris and to divide and re-pot plants, taking special care with wildlife

Small ponds may need complete cleaning out every four or five years, larger ponds after ten years or longer.
• Cleaning removes decaying debris at the bottom of the pond and provides opportunities for making necessary repairs (*see p.275*), for propagation, and for planting.
• The best time to clean out ponds that are mainly stocked with plants is late spring, and this is also a good time to split plants. Cleaning can be damaging for wildlife ponds, but less so in autumn or late winter.
• Plan the operation so that it can be completed in one day if possible, as this is less stressful to fish.

First, prepare a holding tank in a shady spot for fish and submerged water plants. Marginal plants will survive out of the pond provided they are kept moist and shaded. Use pond water to fill the holding tank; unless this is cloudy, it can also be used when refilling the pond, reducing the need to use tap water.

Drain the pond, using a pump, if possible. If the pond has a submersible pump, use the return pipe to empty the pond. Start to remove the fish as the water level falls and they become less active and more visible. You should also remove plants as the water level drops.

Remove decaying plant material when the water has been drained away and pile it beside the pool for disposal later. This will allow any hidden creatures to return to the pool. Move any remaining fish to the holding tank.

Remove the silt in the base of the pond, and spread it on to nearby borders. Make sure you keep back some of it for adding to the clean pond to re-establish microscopic life.

Clean and inspect the liner, taking care not to damage it. Make any necessary repairs (*see p.275*).

Return the saved silt and any removed pond water to the cleaned-out pond. Refill the pond, and replant in the different levels as the water rises. If necessary, divide and re-pot plants before returning them to the pond, finishing with those plants sited around the margins. Finally, examine fish for diseases before returning them to the pond, then completely refill with water.

OUTSIDE THE POND

Providing areas away from the pond for shelter is extremely important, particularly if you have a wildlife pond. Good places for amphibians to hide or escape to include piles of logs, rocks, compost heaps and under hedges. So, do not be over zealous in clearing these types of areas during your cleaning spree.

See also Encouraging wildlife into the garden, pp.250–251; Repair of leaky ponds, p.275

A healthy pond
Small ponds need cleaning out only every four to five years. It enables you to remove debris from the bottom, and divide and re-pot plants if necessary.

Wildlife ponds

Avoid cleaning out wildlife ponds in spring when frogs, toads and newts are breeding. Ideally remove one-third of the water and accumulated debris every few years rather than attempt a complete overhaul. Thin out over-vigorous plants in late summer.

On a fine day in autumn or winter when the pond is not frozen, cut back all the dead, tall vegetation and rake out the decaying leaves. Skim off all traces of duckweed.

In summer amphibians seek out damp, sheltered areas in the garden or further afield. Frogs overwinter on land, although some spend it under water.

PLANT PROBLEMS

Preventing blanketweed

Aim to stop this choking pond weed from building up

To remove blanketweed, wind it around a stick

This troublesome, thread-like alga is seen as floating, silky masses of slimy green filaments, often containing bubbles of air. It thrives in bright light and increasing temperatures, and where the water is rich in plant foods. If left unchecked it will choke other plants and restrict the free movement of fish. Here are some tips to deal with it.

• Allow about one-third to half of the surface area of the pond to be covered with water lily leaves to reduce light and keep the water temperature steady.
• Regularly remove organic debris to reduce levels of plant foods.
• Keep water changes and top-ups to a minimum as these disturb the sediment and add plant foods.
• Try submerging nets containing barley straw in the pond (*see p.281*), which can help suppress the growth of blanketweed.
• Remove blanketweed as necessary: use a rake to lift it out or wind it around a stick.
• A garden pond is a sensitive biological balance of micro-organisms, wildlife and plants. Use chemical control of blanketweed, such as an algicide, only as a last resort.

See also How to control pond algae, p.281

PRACTICAL ADVICE

Fallen leaves

Be alert for falling leaves – they foul pond water

Leaves that fall into ponds turn into black sludge that spoils the water when disturbed. As they decay the water turns brown and they produce a gas that is toxic to fish.

If there are trees near your pond, place a net over it before leaf fall in autumn. Secure the net under bricks around the edges or use a wooden frame to create a stronger fixture.

If your pond is too big to net, surround it with a low wire-netting fence supported by canes or stakes. Drifting leaves then bank up against the fence, making removal easy.

If there are no trees nearby and your pond is small, regularly skim the surface with a fish net or wire rake to stop leaves accumulating.

Don't let leaves foul the water

REMOVING DEBRIS

• Netting with a small mesh size will prevent leaves and other debris from getting into the pond
• Debris can easily be removed with a pond skimmer, pond pincers, an ordinary rake or a long-handled fishing net

See also Winter pond care, p.270

AVOIDING ALIEN POND WEEDS

Avoiding alien pond weeds

In recent years a growing problem has been posed by a number of introduced, rampant aquatic plants, which are widely available from garden centres, often incorrectly named and rarely labelled as invasive

Alien pond weeds include oxygenators such as *Crassula helmsii* (Australian swamp stonecrop or New Zealand pigmyweed), sometimes sold as *Tillaea recurva* or *T. helmsii*, and *Myriophyllum aquaticum* (syn. *M. brasiliense* or *M. proserpinacoides*) (parrot's feather). Surface-growing invasive plants include *Hydrocotyle ranunculoides* (floating pennywort), sometimes sold as marsh pennywort, which is also the common name of the British native *H. vulgaris*, and *Azolla filiculoides* (water or fairy fern).

These alien plants have no natural competitors. Where they escape into the wild they can quickly take over, smothering native plants and threatening survival of native fauna. They can reduce oxygen in the water and cause local flooding by choking drainage dykes and sluices. It is illegal to introduce these plants into the wild.

Other rampant aquatics, especially *Eichhornia crassipes* (water hyacinth),

Salvinia molesta (giant salvinia), *Pistia stratiotes* (water lettuce) and *Trapa natans* (water chestnut), have a serious environmental impact in warm countries.

Control of invasive pond weeds can be difficult. Chemicals, the only effective means of eradication, are expensive and may lead to serious habitat destruction. In Britain there is no weedkiller approved for aquatic use by gardeners. If you have a large pond or lake, employ a contractor with a license to buy and apply professional products.

If your pond is small, remove excess oxygenators by hand or with a rake to keep them in check, but take out as much cut weed as possible, because as this rots away it will deplete oxygen in the water. Remove floating plants with a rubber rake or hose them to the pond edge. If your pond is large, use a boom in the form of a thick rope to skim the surface. Stack weeds beside the pond overnight to allow any creatures to return to the water.

HOW TO AVOID POND WEED

- Keeping the water in the pond clean and well oxygenated is essential to the health of the fish and plants
- Once you notice a build up of weed, remove as much as you can with a rake before it gets out of control
- Destroy pond weeds by composting or burying them

Thoroughly compost, bury or burn invasive alien pond weeds as they can regenerate from fragments of stem. Never release into the wild any aquatic plant from your garden, for example by pouring pond water into a public drain.

There are many non-invasive British and exotic aquatic plants that are ornamental and encourage wildlife (*see pp.276–277*).

Duckweed

Common duckweed (*Lemna minor*), although small as individual plants, can completely cover extensive areas rapidly if the water is still or slow moving. Each plant consists of a single, rounded, leaf-like body floating on the surface, from which dangles a slender root. The plant usually overwinters on the pool bottom, to surface again the following spring.

Duckweed can be introduced to garden ponds unknowingly with newly bought water plants. It may also be brought in on the feet of birds moving from one pond to another.

Weed-eating water birds, such as ducks, moorhens and coots, provide some degree of control. If you only have a small pond, then simply remove duckweed with a fish net, but if it is fairly large use a floating boom to sweep the pond from end to end. Sweep at intervals from early in the season until winter dormancy.

Duckweed (*Lemna minor*) can completely cover the water if it is not controlled

See also How to create a bog garden, p.274; Choosing water plants, pp.276–277

TECHNIQUES

How to control pond algae

Algae in garden ponds are unsightly and can prevent a good 'balance' being obtained, with desirable crystal-clear water, so make every effort to control these primitive green plants

The most important pond algae are the single-celled, free-floating types that turn the water dark green, and the filamentous alga or blanketweed that smothers aquatic plants (*see p.279*). Small, shallow ponds in sunny positions are particularly susceptible. A minimum pond depth of 75cm (30in) will help prevent problems.

In established ponds, algae are kept in check because the natural balance of plant and animal life ties up the plant foods on which they feed. New ponds usually have an excess of foods and it can take some time for a balance to be achieved. Do not be tempted to change the water in a new pond when it turns green, as this will delay a long-term natural solution. Aquatic creatures such as tadpoles and daphnia feed on algae and can be introduced from established ponds.

A suitable range of water plants can also help to reduce problems with algae. Plants with floating leaves such as water lilies (*Nymphaea*) and *Aponogeton distachyos* (water hawthorn) reduce the surface area of water exposed to sun. Aim to cover

CLEARING BLANKETWEED AND ALGAE

1 The most effective method of reducing the spread of blanketweed is to remove it regularly with a rake or stick, preferably before it becomes too invasive and swamps the pond.

2 Submerge a bag of barley straw or lavender to control algae. Use fine-mesh vegetable bags, recycled from the greengrocer. Do not submerge the bags too deeply.

FISH IN PONDS

Most people with ponds enjoy seeing fish. However, larger fish, such as koi carp, can affect the roots of plants like water lilies, so ensure you choose fish and plants carefully.

between one-third and half of the pond. Rushes (such as *Typha*), *Iris pseudacorus* (flag iris) and other marginal plants will provide additional shade. Oxygenating plants are essential for achieving a balance in the pond.

Regularly remove floating debris, dead plants and leaves that take up oxygen and release plant foods as they decay. If you want to include fish in the pond, goldfish, orfe and shubunkin are the best ones to use in garden ponds. Large numbers of fish create high levels of plant foods; the only remedy is to reduce numbers or install a filtration system (*see p.275*).

Controlling algae

Chemical treatments are available for the management of algae. Some provide a reasonable degree of control for a limited period.

For more effective control, however, use barley straw. Lavender clippings are also effective but use more available oxygen and so are most appropriate for larger ponds or those with pumps that oxygenate the water.

If loose straw or lavender is available, roughly chop it and place it in net bags. Use several small bags rather than one large one, ballast them with bricks and lower them on string to just below the surface of the water. Application rates vary from between a few grams to 50g per sq m (about 1oz per sq yd) of surface area, depending on the severity of the problem.

Use the bags from early spring onwards, bearing in mind that it takes about two months before the straw starts to have an effect. Replace them when the straw or lavender has decayed and turned black.

See also Choosing water plants, pp.276–277; Preventing blanketweed, p.279

Camellas - 13. 78. 81

INDEX

INDEX

ACKNOWLEDGEMENTS

Dorling Kindersley would like to thank the following contributors for the original material adapted for this book:
Paul Alexander; Jim Arbury; Jon Ardle; Guy Barter; Helen Bostock; William Denne; Tony Dickerson; Sarah Durrant; Jim England; Caroline Gorton; Lucy Halsall; Andrew Halstead; Beatrice Henricot; David Hide; Ian Hodgson; David Jewell; Jackie Larner; Lia Leendertz; Andrea Loom; Alison Mundie; Chris Prior; Andrew Salisbury; Alan Toogood

The publishers also wish to thank:
At the Royal Horticultural Society: Simon Maughan, Susanne Mitchell and Barbara Haynes
Editorial assistance: Candida Frith-Macdonald, Jane Simmonds, Pamela Brown, Pamela Marmito, Letitia Luff
Design assistance: Ursula Dawson, Alison Donovan, Gillian Andrews
Index: Hilary Bird

Dorling Kindersley would also like to thank the following for their kind permission to reproduce their photographs:
(Key: t=top, b=bottom, r=right, l=left, c=centre)

8: Royal Horticultural Society, Wisley: Michael Crabtree/Troika Photos; **14:** DK Images: Jacqui Hurst (t); **37:** Royal Horticultural Society, Wisley (bc); **39:** Chris Prior, Royal Horticultural Society (br); **41:** Holt Studios International: Nigel Cattlin (tr), (bl); **44:** FLPA – Images of nature: David Dalton (t); **45:** Holt Studios International: Phil McLean (tc); **52:** A–Z Botanical Collection; **53:** A–Z Botanical Collection: Julia Hancock (b), (t); **60:** Holt Studios International: John Adams (bl), (bcl), (bcr), (br); **62:** Photos Horticultural (tr); **90:** Garden World Images (tr); **102:** Photos Horticultural (bl), (br); **112:** Royal Horticultural Society, Wisley (tl); **115:** Royal Horticultural Society, Wisley (bl); **140:** A–Z Botanical Collection: Elsa M. Megson (br); **148:** Holt

Studios International: Nigel Cattlin (c), (bl); **150:** Holt Studios International: Nigel Cattlin (bc); **153:** Royal Horticultural Society, Wisley (tl), (cl); **179:** Corbis: Tom Stewart; **181:** Alamy Images: Rex Argent; **194:** A–Z Botanical Collection: Steve Owens (tl); **197:** Photos Horticultural (b), (t); **199:** Corbis; **200:** DK Images: Steve Wooster (t); **222:** Garden World Images (bl); **223:** A–Z Botanical Collection: Malcolm Richards (t); **227:** Royal Horticultural Society, Wisley (bl); **234:** Holt Studios International: Rosie Mayer (bl), (bc), (bcl); **235:** Garden World Images (tc), (tr); **248:** A–Z Botanical Collection: Ailsa Allaby (bl); Garden World Images (tc), (tr); **256:** Alamy Images: NaturePicks (br); DK Images: Kim Taylor (t); **265:** Garden World Images; **273:** DK Images: Jacqui Hurst.

All other images © Dorling Kindersley or Tim Sandall, *The Garden*.
For further information see www.dkimages.com